I heartily recommend *Customer-Responsive* ... a competitive advantage in today's increasing ... ers (and those contemplating the journey to mass customization) should put down whatever else they are reading and study this book. I expect to refer to it again and again, especially the chapters on the customer-responsiveness model (with its informative discussion of scheduling versus dispatching), protocols, and customer-responsive economics. The last chapter, in particular, has already had a profound effect on my thinking. Davis and Manrodt have made a lasting contribution to the growing body of knowledge on mass customization, paving the way for companies to serve their customers efficiently and uniquely.

—*B. Joseph Pine, President, Strategic Horizons Incorporated*

Our company is a major provider of services to the Lotus Notes industry. This book accurately explains the market paradigm shift toward relationship management that is driving the current success of Notes and the Internet. Business survival in the twenty-first century will require information infrastructure and cultural change. This book addresses both of these issues and what is behind them.

—*Tom Sudman, President and Chief Executive Officer, Digital AV*

Other management books in recent years have underscored process-oriented management approaches to better meet customer needs, but Davis and Manrodt have synthesized streams of research from relationship marketing, logistics, total quality management, organization theory, and information technology to create a practical model to increase organizations' responsiveness to customers.

—*Kenneth D. Bopp*
Director, Health Services Management Group, University of Missouri

In my consulting work with many of the world's leading companies, I often notice that business leaders and their management teams confuse variety with customization. Bombarding the marketplace with more and more choices and selections is not the same as responding to specific customer needs. Companies that want to sustain a competitive advantage would do well to embrace the principles of customer responsiveness.

—*James H. Gilmore, CSC Fellow, CSC Consulting*

Customer-Responsive Management is a textbook that contains principles and ideas that will be extremely useful to students, managers, and entrepreneurs. It is easy to read and its "how to" element is something that progressive business people will want to review time and again. Having worked extensively overseas, I can attest to the broad appeal many of the principles discussed in this book have.

—*Bryant H. Wadsworth*
Former U.S. Agriculture Minister to Japan, Canada, and the European Union

CUSTOMER-RESPONSIVE MANAGEMENT:
The Flexible Advantage

Frank W. Davis, Jr.
The University of Tennessee, Knoxville

Karl B. Manrodt
The University of Tennessee, Knoxville

BLACKWELL
Business

First published 1996

Blackwell Publishers, Inc.
238 Main Street
Cambridge, Massachusetts 02142 USA

Blackwell Publishers Ltd.
108 Cowley Road
Oxford OX4 1JF UK

Library of Congress Cataloging-in-Publication Data

Davis, Frank W. (Frank White), 1939-
  Customer-responsive management : the flexible advantage / Frank W.
Davis, Karl B. Manrodt.
    p.   cm.
  Includes bibliographical references and index.
  ISBN 1-55786-505-1 (pbk.)
  1. Customer services – Management. 2. Consumer satisfaction.
I. Manrodt, Karl B., 1957-   . II. Title.
HF5415.5.D384   1996
658.8′12 – dc20   95-51325
                                                                           CIP

British Library Cataloguing in Publication Data

A CIP catalogue record for this book is available from the British Library.

Typeset by Cornerstone Composition Services.

Printed in the USA on acid-free paper.

This work is dedicated to our families
who endured and never lost faith
or ceased to be encouraging.

CONTENTS

1 AN INTRODUCTION TO CUSTOMER RESPONSIVENESS 1

How Are Customer-Responsive Activities Different? 4
Does Customer-Responsive Management Only Apply to Services? 5
How Are Customer-Responsive Activities Different from
    Mass-Marketing Efforts? 8
Is Customer Responsiveness a New Concept? 9
    Mass Production to Mass Customization 10
    More Flexible Organizational Structures 13
    The Simplification of Transactions between Groups 15
    The Development of Responsive Networks 16
    Customer Responsiveness Creates Customer Value 21
Customer Responsiveness Requires Flexibility 24
Summary 24
References 26

2 THE EVOLVING ECONOMIC FOCUS: FROM CONQUEST TO RELATIONSHIP 27

The First Era 28
The Second Era 29
The Third Era 29
Capitalism – The Roots of Modern Business 30
The Production Stage of the Mass-Production Era 34
    Standardized Interchangeable Parts 34
    Production Line 34
    Scientific Management 35
    Cost Accounting 35
The Mass-Marketing Stage of the Mass-Production Era 37
    Mass Merchandising 37
    The Marketing Concept 37
    Market Segments 38
The Supply-Chain Logistics Stage of the Mass-Production Era 39
The Total Quality Stage of the Mass-Production Era 39
The Fourth Era – Customer-Responsive Management 43
Summary 48
References 49

Contents

3 WHY SHOULD ORGANIZATIONS BE RESPONSIVE?   **51**

Responsiveness Improves the Fit between Customer Need
and Delivery   51
Responsiveness Increases Customer Retention and Profits   56
Responsiveness Decreases Costs   58
Responsiveness Makes Organizations More Responsive to
Competitive and Environmental Change   60
Summary   61
References   62

4 CUSTOMER RESPONSIVENESS IS ACTIVITY BASED   **63**

Four Components of Every Activity   63
An Event Triggers the Activity   64
The Definition of the Response   69
The Coordination of Activities   82
The Delivery of Desired Benefits   88
Summary   90
References   92

5 THE CUSTOMER-RESPONSIVE MODEL   **93**

The Establishment of a Customer-Responsive Strategy   97
Step 1: Establish a Relationship with the Customer   97
Step 2: Diagnose the Individual Customer's Needs   99
Step 3: Determine the Organization's Ability to Meet the
Individual Customer's Needs   100
Step 4: Commit to the Customer   101
Step 5: Enable Customer Response   101
Step 6: Develop Delivery Plan   101
Step 7: Dispatch Individual Needs   102
Step 8: Monitor the Delivery Process   102
Step 9: Mentor Partners   103
An Example of Response-Based Manufacturing   103
Responsiveness Can Be Increased by Separating the
Dispatching of Work from the Scheduling of Capacity   104
Responsiveness Is Limited by Work Quality   107
Responsiveness Is Limited by the Flexibility of the
Delivery Units   107
Responsiveness Is Limited by the Orientation of the
Support Organization   108
The Effect of Responsiveness on Business Philosophy   108

Summary 115
References 116

6 EXAMPLES OF CUSTOMER-RESPONSIVE ORGANIZATIONS 117

The Subway Example 118
The Pizza Hut Example 119
Coordination by Prioritized Dispatch List 120
Distribution Center Example 124
Military Campaigns 126
The Hospital Example 130
The Union Bank of Switzerland 133
Roadway Logistics Systems 136
Summary 141
References 142

7 THE CUSTOMER RELATIONSHIP MANAGEMENT TASK 143

Relationship Management 143
Interaction Management 149
Diagnosis Management 153
    Listening-Based Diagnosis 154
    Display-Based Diagnosis 155
    Question-Based Diagnosis 156
    Prototype-Based Diagnosis 158
    Screening-Based Diagnosis 159
Customer-Service Management 160
    "Can You . . . ?" 161
    "Will You . . . ?" 163
    "Did You . . . ?" 164
    "Why Did You . . . ?" 165
    "Why Should I . . . ?" 166
Summary 167
References 168

8 DELIVERY COORDINATION MANAGEMENT TASK 169

Best-Practice Guideline Management 169
Task Management 173
Capacity Management 175
    Improving the Forecasting of Capacity Needs in the Short Run 176
    Cross Training Employees 179

Contents

Developing Cooperative Networks for Immediate Run
    Flexibility 179
Resource Interface Management 187
Delivery Coordination Summary 189
Yield Management 190
Summary 193
References 194

9   CUSTOMER-RESPONSIVE DEMAND ECONOMICS   195

Benefits versus Capacity Orientation 195
Demand Curve Construction 196
    All Demands Are Derived from Individual Needs 197
    Solution Value = (Customer Value * Fit) – Hassle 198
    Customer Value 198
    The Factors that Affect Yield 202
    The Determinants of Customer Value 209
    How Benefit Value and Capacity Are Determined for
        Customer-Responsive Activities 211
    The Methods for Changing the Characteristics of Activities 212
Summary 214
References 215

10   CUSTOMER-RESPONSIVE COST ECONOMICS   217

Role of Inventory 217
What Is the Cost of Capacity? 219
Capacity Management Is Immediate-Run Management 220
Immediate-Run Decisions Determine the
    Revenue Generated from Scheduled Capacity 222
How Are Costs Used to Make Decisions? 224
Is There a Relationship Between Fixed and Variable Costs? 224
Customer-Responsive Relationships Between Fixed and
    Variable Costs 227
    Economy of Use 228
    Economy of Modularity 230
    Economy of Networking 233
The Capacity Inflexibility Dilemma 236
Summary 238
References 239

11 CUSTOMER-RESPONSIVE PRICING   241

Product-Based Pricing	241
Public Good Pricing	244
Responsive Activity Pricing	249
The Value of the Benefits to Customers	253
The Out-of-Pocket Cost of Providing Benefits	254
Pricing Implementation	258
Fit	258
Intensity of Response	259
Hassle	259
Posted Pricing	260
Experience Pricing	260
Negotiated Pricing	261
Package Pricing	261
Summary	261
References	262

12 THE CUSTOMER-RESPONSIVE ORGANIZATION   263

Planning the Responsive Planning Process	263
Process	264
Resources	264
Infrastructure	265
A Biological Analogy for Organizations	269
A Generalized Responsive Model	274
Individual Delivery Process	274
Infrastructure Development Plan	276
Logistics Is the Management of Responsive Activities	282
Summary	286
References	287

13 CUSTOMER-RESPONSIVE INFORMATION INFRASTRUCTURE   289

The Basis for Customer-Responsive Infrastructure Design	290
Customer Relationship Strategies	291
Resource Relationship Strategies	291
Knowledge-Based Development Strategies	292
Operating Strategies	292
Information Infrastructure Strategies	292
Consensus-Building Concept Room	295

Contents

Design Criteria for Responsive Information System 297
The Customer-Responsive Process 299
The Requirements of a Customer-Responsive Infrastructure 301
    The Capture, Storage, Retrieval, and Sharing
      of Customer Information 301
    The Storage, On-Demand Retrieval, and
      Evaluation of Processes 303
    The Identification of Resource Ability and the Capacity for
      Responding to Customer Needs 304
    The Ready Identification of Individuals Responsible for
      Coordinating the Relationship 306
    The Capture, Storage, and Retrieval of All the Information
      Necessary to Totally Define the Request 307
    The Capture, Storage, and Retrieval of All the Steps
      Necessary to Dispatch the Delivery 307
Developing Visualization Tools 307
    Context Diagrams 308
    Entity Relationship Diagrams 312
    Business-Event Diagrams 316
Implementation Strategy 319
    The Structure of the Information Required 319
    The Linking of the Processes 320
    The Structure of the Process 320
    The Importance of Authentication 321
    The Importance of Information Security 321
Summary 325
References 326

14 RESPONSIVE RELATIONSHIPS 327

Relationships Defined 329
    What Is a Relationship? 330
    Why Cultivate Relationships? 331
    What Makes Relationships Work? 334
    What Makes Relationships Fail? 337
Steps to Build a Strong Relationship 339
    Contracting Tends to Make Relationships
      Unresponsive 342
    Building Relationships 344
Summary 363
References 365

THE EVOLVING BUSINESS FOCUS: PRODUCTION TO CUSTOMER
15 RESPONSIVENESS   **367**

Rethinking the Mass-Production Approach to Productivity	367
The Rise and Restructuring of the Services Economy	371
The Evolution of Organizations	377
The Shifting View of Capitalism from Ownership to Resource	379
The Evolution of the Information Age	384
First Trend – Miniaturization and Microcomputers	385
Second Trend – Development of Interface Standards	385
Third Trend – Self-Identification	386
Fourth Trend – The Mobile Connection	387
Fifth Trend –Systems Development Shifts Toward Users	387
Structured Information Systems for Highly Routine Activities	391
The Information Modeling Approach to Analysis	391
Traditional Statistics	392
Information Theoretic Statistics	394
Customer-Responsive Health Care Providers	401
Summary	404
References	407

INDEX   **409**

TQM SERIES FOREWORD

In August of 1991, six US corporations with substantial global operations, American Express, Ford, IBM, Motorola, Procter & Gamble, and Xerox, sponsored The Total Quality Forum. The Forum was an annual gathering of academic leaders and corporate executives. Its purpose was to discuss the role of Total Quality Management in the United States and its role on US campuses, especially in business and engineering schools.

The chief executive officers of the six sponsoring companies summarized the importance of the topic in the November-December 1991 issue of the *Harvard Business Review*, "An Open Letter: TQM on Campus."

"We believe business and academia have a shared responsibility to learn, to teach, and to practice Total Quality Management. If the United States expects to improve its global competitive performance, business and academic leaders must close ranks behind an agenda that stresses the importance and value of TQM. Working together, companies and institutions of higher education *must* accelerate the application of Total Quality Management on our campuses if our education system and economy are to maintain and enhance their global positions." (94 – 95)

In 1989, 14 leading European corporations founded the European Foundation for Quality Management. By 1993 the membership had grown to nearly 300 European organizations (corporations and universities). The September 1993 Membership Information brochure included the following objective and vision.

"The European Foundation for Quality Management (EFQM) believes that, through Total Quality Management, Western Europe will become a leading force in the world market. Our objective is to create conditions to enhance the position of European industry by strengthening the role of management in quality strategies. EFQM's vision is to become the leading organization for promoting and facilitating Total Quality Management in Western Europe. This vision will be achieved when TQM has become an integrated value of the European society, and European management has achieved a global competitive advantage."

The commitment of the Japanese to quality management is legendary.

TQM Series Foreword

Herein lies the theme of this series of books on TQM. As a system of management, whether in the Americas, the Pacific Rim, or Europe, TQM has become important for global competitive positions. Therefore, learning about TQM models and practices is relevant in universities, in corporate training centers, and in individual development.

Michael Stahl
Series Editor

Notice to Internet Users

Businesses have made a major transition from the mass-produced style adhered to in the first half of the century to a more flexible (TQM, JIT, lean production, mass customization) approach in the latter half of the century. As these techniques increase production flexibility, firms can focus on being more responsive to individual customers. Much of this responsiveness is made possible by advances in technology.

These technological advances now permit authors to respond to individual readers. Instead of just being able to offer a book to the reader, the author can share questions and experiences over an Internet discussion board. We will provide such a discussion board to allow individuals to ask questions, provide case studies, present methodologies, or post any other entry they believe can be helpful. In this way, customer-responsive practitioners will be able to develop a network of users with similar needs and interests, thereby creating a common knowledge base.

To participate in the discussion board, go to the UT home page (HTTP://www.utk.edu/) and look for the section on individual home pages. Frank Davis and Karl Manrodt will have personal home pages that will request the information required to certify you for the discussion board. In providing this service, we hope to build a network of individuals who are interested in customer-responsive management and who will help one another with ongoing managerial issues.

ACKNOWLEDGMENTS

The authors wish to thank many colleagues who have contributed to this work. They have patiently reviewed drafts, offered comments, and helped with language. These include Tom Sudman, Chris Lovelock, Dennis Grim, B. Joseph Pine II, James H. Gilmore, Bob Woodruff, Bryant H. Wadsworth, Ken Bopp, Carl Evans, Bruce Burns, Tom Mentzer, John Grover, Hamparsum Bozdogan, Rosalie Risley, Greg Kellar, and Swanee Sexton. A special thank you to Joan Waldrop for her help and patience in securing the permissions for the book. We are especially indebted to Jo Lynn Cunningham who provided structure, direction, and editorial help. We were fortunate for the many ideas gleaned from the Services Marketing conferences sponsored by the American Marketing Association and the Research Committee, which directed the study "Logistics in the Services Industry" that was sponsored by the Council of Logistics Management. We especially want to acknowledge our students who have been very helpful in making suggestions and refining ideas. We, however, must assume responsibility for all errors and mistakes in this book.

Frank W. Davis, Jr., Ph.D.
Karl B. Manrodt, Ph.D.

In addition, Karl Manrodt would like to highlight the guiding work of Frank Davis. Davis's intellectual capability and creative genius directed the concepts you will find in the following pages. Many of us find Frank to be a true trailblazer, leading us forward to a new and exciting appreciation of logistics. It has been an honor to work with Frank on this project. I owe him much, and for all he has done, I am thankful.

Karl B. Manrodt, Ph.D.

CHAPTER 1

AN INTRODUCTION TO CUSTOMER RESPONSIVENESS

Two major philosophies of management developed during the 20th century. The first, a uniquely American innovation, was mass production. Eli Whitney's concept of interchangeable parts, Ford's development of the production line, Frederick W. Taylor's scientific management, and cost accounting methods developed by GM and Dupont form the foundation of mass production.

Mass-production management focused on large-scale production and mass marketing of standardized, low-cost products produced for homogenous markets. Product planning, process planning, production scheduling, and market planning were typically centralized and separated from daily operations. Customers were researched so the right product was offered to the market place. Customers with special needs that could not be met by standard products were ignored as simply being outside the organization's target market.

The second major philosophy of management began to develop about 1960. This philosophy evolved as new competitors, often foreign, began to offer products for market segments that the mass producers had ignored because they were too small. These new competitors evolved during turbulent times when markets were often saturated, energy prices and interest rates were rapidly changing, and technology was creating dramatic new changes. Thus these firms developed flexible management styles that enabled them to be more adaptable to changing conditions and responsive to smaller markets. [1]

This second management philosophy recognized that forecasting and planning were more difficult as the marketplace and environment became more turbulent. Therefore emphasis was on taking steps that minimized the time and cost required to recognize and respond to changes. Although mass production was based on defining a product and designing the most efficient means of producing large quantities of the product, the new management philosophy designed flexible processes

1

that could produce a wide range of products, making it easier to respond to changing conditions. The role of inventory changed in the process of making the firm more responsive. Under mass production, inventory allowed purchasing, production, distribution, and sales to function at their own optimal flow rate, without influencing the other. In responsive systems, however, inventory not only increased costs but reduced the ability of the organization to respond. These firms sought to minimize inventory. The ultimate goal, zero inventory, occurred when the firm learned to create the product on demand. Thus the ultimate goal of responsive production management is mass customization [1–5], where products for individual customers can be customized at a price that is competitive, if not lower, than the standardized mass-production item.

While production management has been moving toward mass customization, marketing has realized that it is not longer limited to mass markets. Marketers can communicate directly and, in many cases, interactively with individual customers. National magazines can insert ads for distribution to a state, city, zip code, or even an individual. *Reader's Digest* can even print 220 million sweepstakes announcements, each customized to the individual recipient. Membership clubs can now identify individual purchase patterns for every customer. Reverse 900 numbers, the Internet, and many other developments facilitate two-way communication and direction of payments. This enables the organization to interact with individual customers as easily as it could broadcast one-way promotions under the mass marketing approach to management. This has been called "1:1 marketing." [2]

With the ability to interact 1:1 with individual customers and the ability to produce in response to individual customer requests, an opportunity is created for firms to shift from a product to a truly customer focus. This is not the same as market research that samples customers to guide product design. In that case, the objective is to design the product, not to understand and respond to individual customer needs. Customer-responsive management is the subject of this book. It covers the basis for responsiveness, the organization of respective firms, the economics of responsive activities, and the basic management principles required of responsive firms.

Just as management paradigms had to be rethought in moving from mass production to flexible, mass customization, so paradigms will have to be rethought from the from the traditional product-offering orientation to a customer-responsive orientation. Central to this transition is that customers want solutions to their individual needs at a reasonable cost and with a minimum of hassle. They are not looking for more products or services. They are not looking for a wider range of choices. Customers simply want solutions to their individual needs – whether it be in preparing an afternoon snack, helping a teenage son or daughter become more interested in school, providing for the care of an elderly parent, or creating a feeling of security. The solution can take the form of a product, a service, or a combination of both. Regardless of how benefits are provided, customers want what they want – when, where, and how they want it. [6] They are not looking for another mass marketer trying to sell them something.

Customers often have a sense of product (or service) overload just as they sense data overload. "Data overload" refers to the torrent of non-beneficial data – whether from catalogs, promotions, newsletters, computer printouts, cents-off coupons or e-mail – that seems to engulf us daily. We all know how it feels to have mail boxes, in-boxes, and e-mail files stacked with data we ought to read because it might contain some important information. The reason we continue to endure this flood of data is the perpetual worry that somewhere in this mass of data are a few pieces of information that will sometimes help us make important decisions.

We dread more data. Data are unneeded, unwanted, and a hassle to handle. On the other hand, information has *value*. We hunger for it. It helps us make decisions. The eternal quest – the *raison d'etre* of a library, a personal file cabinet, or the Internet – is to have easy access to information that has value.

The terms "solution" and "offering" can be used to distinguish between solutions to our individual needs and the torrent of offerings in the marketplace. Just as they laboriously seek information, customers must search through the many different offerings available to find the ones that may provide beneficial solutions. We all have lists that we use to remind us of problems that need to be solved. To-do lists, for example, typically include needs that may require the customer to research possible solutions. Once we select an offering that we hope will provide an acceptable solution, we add it to our shopping list.

When offerings were few and demand was relatively stable, firms could focus on producing more new offerings and rely on the best of these to attract the customer's attention in the marketplace. This is an *offering-based* approach to meeting customer needs. As competition for customers' attention intensifies, it becomes easier to focus on meeting individual customer needs rather than on simply proliferating the number of offerings and hoping that they attract notice in the already crowded marketplace. This is a *customer-response-based* approach to meeting a customer's needs. Mass marketing focuses on producing and distributing offerings to mass markets. Customer-responsive management focuses on defining needs and coordinating deliveries to individual customers.

How Are Customer-Responsive Activities Different?

Customer-responsive management has two dimensions: interacting with individual customers to identify their specific needs and responding to these requests with customized solutions. This concept is illustrated in Figure 1.1.

Offering-based and customer-response-based activities are organized very differently. The fundamental difference between them is that the offering-based activities anticipate customer needs and define solutions before interacting with individual customers while customer-response-based activities involve developing a process which allows interaction with each individual customer one-to-one to define his or her need and then to customize the delivery in response to that need.

The word "activity" is used here instead of the word "firm" or "organization" for a very specific reason. It is an *activity* that is offering-based or customer-response-based, not a firm. Granted, some firms may focus on producing offerings for the marketplace and others may be almost totally customer responsive, but most mix these two activities. A clothing manufacturer, for example, may make ready-made suits that are offered for sale in the marketplace but depend upon the retail outlet to provide customized alterations. Likewise, a paint company produces and sells cans of base paint and allows the color to be customized on a can-by-can basis at the retail outlet. Even in the most offering-based organizations, logistics and customer service are typically responsive to individual customer requests.

Each type of activity requires a different type of organizational structure. One type of organization works well for researching market opportunities, planning the offering, and scheduling all of the steps required to produce and distribute the offering to the marketplace (where

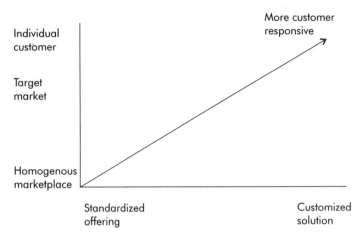

Figure 1.1.   Mass production to customer responsive continuum.

it is selected or rejected by the customer). It takes a very different type of organization to build long-term relationships with customers so that they call you first when they have a need because they trust that you will be able to respond with an effective solution. This is the subject of this work. This is customer-responsiveness management.

Does Customer-Responsive Management Apply Only to Services?

Many services are responsive, but many are not. The *Oxford English Dictionary* contains two general definitions of "service."

- The section of the economy that supplies needs of the consumer but produces no tangible good.
- To be of service to; to serve; conduct tending to the welfare or advantage of another; an act of helping or benefitting; at one's disposal; ready or available for one to use.*

---

* The Oxford English Dictionary, 2d edition, Oxford: Clarendon Press, 1989, pp. 37 and 39.

The first definition, described as the economic definition, emphasizes *intangibility*. According to this definition, services are intangible products that cannot be inventoried or stored for future use. The second

5

definition, the non-economic definition, emphasizes *responsiveness* to the customer or beneficiary. According to this definition, public utilities are a service, even though the output – water – is very tangible. The first definition is product-oriented; it provides a means of classifying products into tangible goods or intangible services. The second definition has a customer (beneficiary) rather than production orientation; it calls for a delivery that is responsive to the individual customer's desires.

When the terms "product" and "service" are used together, the definition of a service that stresses intangibility is implied. When the word "responsiveness" is used, the second definition is appropriate. A customer-responsive management approach begins with the interactive definition of the individual customer's problem, the development of a customized solution, and the delivery of that customized solution to the customer. The solution may consist of a tangible product, an intangible service, or some combination of both. It is not the mix of the solution (be it product or service) that is important, but that the organization interacts with each individual customer to define the specific need and then develops a solution to meet that need.

> The owner of a home health care appliance store noticed the reaction of customers when approached by sales clerks with the familiar "How can I help you?" opening. Many customers were hesitant, indicating that they were not sure or were only looking. He felt that many customers appeared to interpret the "How can I help you?" opening as "Tell me what you want so I can ring you up, take your money, and get you out of the store." He counseled his staff to use a different opening. "What problem can we help you with today?" Almost immediately customers began to respond by stating their need. "My mother had a stroke and is unable to. . . ." Once the customers shared the problem with the staff member they were relieved when the staff person understood and solutions were suggested. The ensuing dialog consisted of suggestions, questions, and responses. When the customer left he/she understood options, the reason a specific solution was suggested and knew how to use the equipment supplied. The business did not change, but in the first case salespersons were selling equipment. With a simple phrase, staff members began solving customer problems, not pushing products.

To a production-oriented organization, it is important that products be classified, because intangible products cannot be inventoried and resold and must be managed differently. Customers with a need are only concerned with finding a solution to their need; whether or not a product is part of that solution is irrelevant to them. If the firm is responsive, customers will be able to explain their need and expect a solution. If the firm is not responsive, the customer has to keep searching until an appropriate solution is found. Responsive firms assume the responsibility of finding such solutions. If the firm is not responsive, the hassle of finding the appropriate solution is incurred by the customer.

A man with a large family (ten cars in the family) was a very loyal customer of a large membership warehouse store. He had a flat that could not be fixed, so he simply went to his trusted supplier to buy a set of tires. The car had standard 205 65 × 15 tires. Unfortunately, the store only had one brand in that size, but it had a low treadwear ratio, and the store personnel said they were constantly rebalancing these tires. When asked if the customer could get a premium tire, the salesperson responded, "I am sorry, but we cannot sell you that tire because your size is not listed in the book." "But the 215 60 × 15 is shown as an option." "Only for the '93, and your car is a '92. "There is no difference in the two cars, and the 215 60 × 15 is about the same size as the 205 65 × 15." "I'm sorry, but I have asked for training to understand all of these sizes, but management will not give me any. All I am told is that I can only sell what is in the book. If you want to buy them, then it is up to you." The customer bought the tires and asked for them to be mounted on the car. Returning four hours later, he found that nothing had been done. His trusted store had not solved his problem. The weekend was over, and he still had a leaking tire. Five people from the store tried to explain why he couldn't buy the tires he wanted from the store. "We only go by the book." "These tires will work perfectly, but if I vary from the book I will lose my job." "The tires we have for your car will not stay in balance." "I have been here for three years, and even though we keep asking for it, management will not give us any training so we understand differences in tire sizes." "We are not a tire store. We are professionals who will only put the correct tires on a car."

The customer had a problem he wanted resolved. He did not argue about the price. Why couldn't the store check out the details? Why spend so much time telling a customer what you can't do rather than helping him solve his problem? Maybe the customer, believing his confidence betrayed, decided to find a store that will solve his tire problems not only this time but also in the future.

In mass marketing, the offering is the focus and the sales transaction is the goal. It is the offering (whether tangible product or intangible service), that must be defined, produced, and distributed. All measures of activity (e.g., cost, revenue, and profit) are based on the offering. In customer-responsive activities, the emphasis is on delivery effectiveness (how well individual problems are diagnosed and solved) and delivery efficiency (how few resources are required to solve the problem).

Organizations that depend on mass marketing emphasize deterministic planning (e.g., the best offering, the best way to produce and deliver the offering, and the best way to inform potential customers about the offering). Such firms view the term "best way" from an operational perspective. What is the best way to operationally serve the target market that has been selected? The "best" method is typically based on the anticipated need of a prototypical customer who represents the needs of the target market. Success depends on how many customers buy the offering. Customer-responsive activities are used to find the best way to solve the individual customer's need. They focus on flexibility – the flexibility to obtain the capacity and capability needed to respond to a wide variety of each customer's requests. "Capability" defines the range of customer needs to which such activities can respond. "Capacity" defines how many needs they can meet.

While mass marketing tries to "sell a single product to as many customers as possible," one-to-one marketing organizations try to "sell a single customer as many products as possible – over a long period of time, and across different product lines."[7] Such organizations do not limit activities to selling products. To such companies, success depends upon how many things they can do for each customer as well as how many customers the organization serves.

How Are Customer-Responsive Activities Different from Mass-Marketing Efforts?

Customer-responsive activities are based on a very different paradigm from that used in mass marketing. As stated earlier, customer-responsive activities are organized to interact with each individual customer and deliver solutions that effectively meet his or her needs. These activities are focused on relationships rather than transactions. The responsive model shown in Figure 1.2 illustrates this concept.

Figure 1.2. Context model for a customer-responsive activity.

Organizations that perform customer-responsive activities have three objectives:

- Building relationships (expectations) so that customers contact this organization first when they have a need.
- Building organizations that can provide effective diagnoses and respond when customers do call. This requires having a network of resources (both inventory and service capacity) on-line so they are available when needed.
- Creating processes and infrastructure that enable front-line employees to cultivate relationships with customers and cost-effectively coordinate each individual delivery of benefits.[8]

The purpose of the customer/organization relationship is to interactively define individual customer needs. The relationship with the customer is based on the organization's ability to continually solve the individual customer's needs at a reasonable cost and with a minimum of hassle when it is requested to do so. Hassle reduction is often the most important factor in this relationship.

The goal of a responsive organization is the cost-effective delivery of an interactively defined need. The relationship with the resource network used to make this delivery is based on the organization's ability to coordinate activities, make effective use of resource capacity, and minimize interactive hassle.

Is Customer Responsiveness a New Concept?

Before mass production and mass marketing, products and services were typically delivered by craftsmen (e.g., bakers, butchers, blacksmiths) to meet the need of the individual customer. It was the introduction of mass production and the dramatic economies that resulted from it that began

9

the emphasis on the centrally planned and coordinated production of standardized offerings using standardized methods.

Mass production is a relatively modern concept; the 20th century has been characterized by attempts to make mass production more responsive to customers. Two dramatic changes are occurring. First, marketing is shifting from an impersonal "arms-length" interaction in the marketplace to a personalized, long-term collaborative relationship. Second, mass production is shifting to more flexible, responsive, and just-in-time (JIT) manufacturing methods. These two trends require changes in organizational and management methods, including:

- A shift from mass production to mass customization;
- A move toward more flexible organizational structures;
- The simplification of transactions among groups;
- The development of responsive networks.

Mass Production to Mass Customization

Production is moving from mass production through continuous improvement to mass customization. Pine et al. traced this development.[2-5] Figures 1.3, 1.4, and 1.5 illustrate this transition.

Under the mass-production paradigm, firms invented and produced. Invention was the process for creating new products and new production processes. Mass production occurred when standardized products were produced in large quantities using a standardized process. Neither products nor processes changed, at least not substantially. Mass production was the focus of American businesses during the first half of this century. Then the Japanese, inspired by Ohno (Toyota) and Deming, introduced the concept of *continuous improvement*. Continuous improvement implies recognition that processes are dynamic (i.e., that they are continually changing and improving) even when the product design remains stable. In fact, continuous improvement allows the product to become even more standardized, enabling companies to brag about maintaining smaller tolerances (and thus greater consistency) at the 6 sigma level. This step is shown in Figure 1.4.

Mass customization, as illustrated in Figure 1.5, is based on the concept of a modular organization that is able to customize deliveries by snapping together components, Lego style. This can be done in many ways. Personal computers, for instance, have a standardized bus that

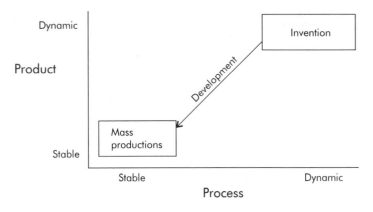

Figure 1.3. The mass-production paradigm. [4,5]

Source: Bart Victor, Andrew C. Boynton, and B. Joseph Pine II [Note 18]

allows a virtually unlimited number of controller boards to be inserted to provide customized units (the so-called "plug and play" feature). In another case, Motorola has developed the line of Bravo pagers, which offers 29 million possible combinations of hardware and software. Salespeople can enter customer preferences into a portable Apple computer and transmit the order to Motorola in Schaumburg, Illinois. The order is then transmitted to computers at Boynton Beach, Florida, where the order is put together by twenty-seven Seiko robots. Seventy-five minutes after the customer needs are defined, the pagers have been produced, packaged, and made ready for shipment to the customer.[9]

Mass customization is based on the concept of modularization. An example is NoteStation's touch-screen kiosk that allows customers to "see a piece of music, listen to their selection, change the key (to fit the individual customer's voice or instrument), and print it out, right on the spot."[10] Lutron Electronics integrates mass customization and invention: "(E)ngineers design a new product line that offers only a few options at first. Then, by working with individual customers to discover their needs, the engineers extend the line with product after product. Eventually, Lutron may have, say, 100 models available for purchase – too many to produce efficiently. At that stage, engineering and production sit down together and rationalize the product line down to a more workable number of models. They then create a set of standardized,

11

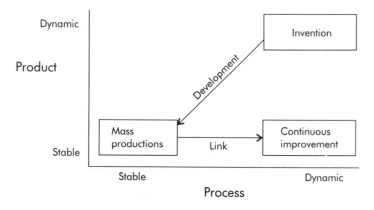

Figure 1.4. The continuous-improvement paradigm.[4,5]

Source: Bart Victor, Andrew C. Boynton, and B. Joseph Pine II [Note 18]

modular components that can be configured into the same 100 models customers want."[11]

The key to mass customization is that the firm achieves production flexibility by developing standardized processes for customizing solutions for individual customers. (Pine suggests that the process is continuous. The learning firm is continually reinventing new products and processes.) Next, standardized processes are developed and continuously improved. Then products can be customized through modularization. Once mass customization is in place, the process must again be renewed through reinvention.

Firms can select a mass-production, continuous-improvement, or mass-customization production strategy. The choice will depend upon the dynamics and diversity of the organization's environment.[12][1] As long as conditions are totally static and there is little variation among individual customers' needs, a mass-production strategy may be appropriate. This may be especially relevant for commodity-type products. If, on the other hand, competitors are continually improving the quality and consistency of their product and if such improvements are important to customers, a continuous-improvement strategy may be needed. If individual customers have widely varying needs or if competition and

---

1. Pine uses the word "turbulence."

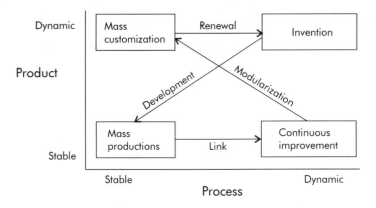

Figure 1.5. The mass-customization paradigm.[4,5]

Source: Bart Victor, Andrew C. Boynton, and B. Joseph Pine II [Note 18]

technology are rapidly changing, mass customization provides the flexibility to adopt to these changes.

Thus the production role of the firm can vary from mass production through continuous improvement to mass customization. Not only have production techniques been changing to allow greater customer responsiveness, but firms have been rapidly changing the way such activities are coordinated.

More Flexible Organizational Structures

Perhaps the most dramatic is the move to flexible organizations. Pine et al. have described the transitions that were necessary to allow the shift from mass production to continuous improvement and mass customization.[3] Work in the mass-production firm was organized and controlled by function (e.g., marketing, finance, production, or distribution). Each function was organized by subfunction (e.g., green machining, heat treating, grinding, or final assembly). Work typically required the involvement of multiple functions but was controlled functionally. The integration of work was accomplished through process design. Coordination was conducted on paper, over the telephone, and in group meetings. Documents accompanied work between functions. Telephones were used to expedite, track, and trace activity. Meetings were used for group communication. Continuous-improvement proponents showed

13

An Introduction to Customer Responsiveness

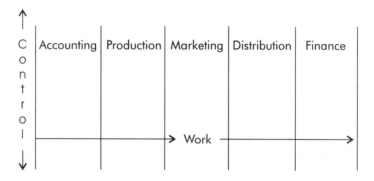

Figure 1.6. The *functional silos* of mass production.

their frustrations with this type of organization by calling these activities *functional silos*. (See Figure 1.6.)

The continuous-improvement movement recommended that work be organized by multifunctional teams that would meet in quality circles to continually improve the processes for which they were responsible. Because they were responsible for the work from beginning to end, the teams began to see their work from a holistic viewpoint. Although the workers' job was to continually improve the production process, it was not to "question the basic design of the product that they are assigned to build"; they (must) "assume it to be what customers want."[13] Functional integration is continually improved by multifunctional teams using visuals such as process flow charts, Pareto charts, and fishbone charts. Coordination is handled in group meetings. The multifunction team concept is illustrated in Figure 1.7.

Although the horizontal multifunctional teams work well for a single product or production line, they do not allow the flexibility needed for mass customization. For example, when Toyota attempted to use this organizational structure to implement mass customization, it failed.[13] Horizontal silos proved to be as rigid as vertical silos. The focus was on a single production process, not flexible processes for solving individual customer needs. Mass customization requires a different type of organization. It requires the use of networks.

Continuous improvement strives to *be the best*. It is "eternally striving to tighten the links between processes so that every team and individual worker knows how its function affects others and ultimately

14

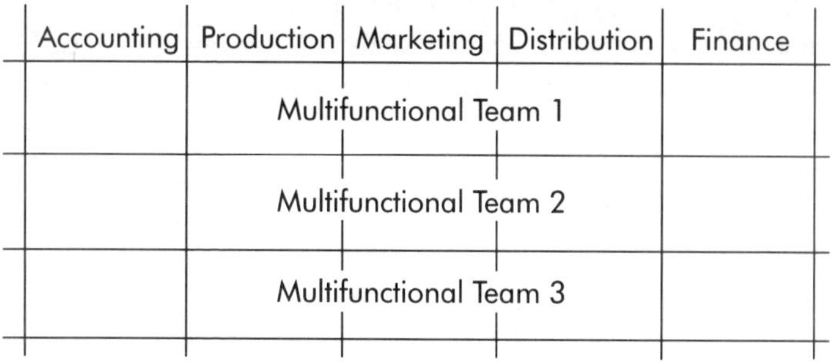

Accounting	Production	Marketing	Distribution	Finance
		Multifunctional Team 1		
		Multifunctional Team 2		
		Multifunctional Team 3		

Figure 1.7. The structure of a continuous-improvement organization using multifunctional teams.

the quality of the product or service. . . . Mass customization, on the other hand, requires a dynamic network" comprised of resource modules each with its own core competency. "The modules, which may include outside suppliers and vendors, typically do not interact or come together in the same sequence every time." The way they interact "is constantly changing in response to what each customer wants and needs. From continually trying to meet these demands, the responsive organization learns what new capabilities it requires. Its employees are on a quest to increase their own skills, as well as those of the unit and the network in a never-ending campaign to expand the number of ways the company can satisfy customers."[13] "Managers . . . are coordinators whose success depends on how well they perfect the links that make up the dynamic network." Their objective is to increase the range of skills in the network and to develop methods to link the network "instantly, costlessly, seamlessly, and frictionlessly."[14] A number of technological innovations are currently making networking possible. Voice mail, e-mail, the Internet, document sharing, and groupware all facilitate dynamic group interaction without the cost and time delays of meetings and travel.

The Simplification of Transactions between Groups

Oliver Williamson has written that many costs are incurred because of the methods a company uses to govern internal and external activities. This is referred to as *governance*.[16] Governance consist of the rules, policies, procedures, and other activities necessary to protect the organization from excessive costs, which Williamson calls *transaction costs*.

There are basically two types of transaction costs. The first is the cost incurred when groups interact. These interactions may be intrafirm (required when work moves between departments) or interfirm (e.g., orders, purchases, and receipts). The second type of transaction cost is the risk incurred when activities are disrupted or do not go according to plan (e.g., contracts and inspections). Many expenses, typically classified as overhead, are actually efforts to control transaction costs. Williamson equates these costs to friction.

"Transaction costs are the economic counterpart of friction. Do the parties involved in the exchange operate harmoniously, or are there frequent misunderstandings and conflicts that lead to delays, breakdowns, and other malfunctions? Transaction cost analysis supplants the usual preoccupation with technology and steady-state production (or distribution) expenses with an examination of the comparative costs of planning, adapting, and monitoring task completion under alternative governance structures."[16]

Traditionally, activities between departments, plants, divisions, partners, and customers were rigidly defined and carefully controlled. Variation in the process was minimized. Although this approach was effective in a precomputer, stable, mass-production environment, today's organizations are making major efforts to perform the same functions without losing the flexibility and responsiveness inherent in the traditional methods. These efforts may take advantage of new technologies or more flexible management practices. Some of these efforts are summarized in Table 1.1.

The Development of Responsive Networks

The Toyota experience of trying to use continuous-improvement teams to implement flexible customer responses illustrates a fundamental principle: *As organizations attempt to become more flexible, they become more modular and shift to a network orientation rather than a fixed systems orientation.*[2] There is a fundamental difference in the way

---

2. Systems purists would suggest that conceptual systems can be totally flexible. In practice, however, systems planning typically begins by defining boundaries and objectives for systems performance. Perhaps the best way of illustrating the concepts being contrasted here is to compare the difference between the traditional, programming-oriented approach to information systems design and the object-oriented approach. Under the for-

Table 1.1. Management Methods for Reducing Transaction Costs

Method	Purpose	Result
Paperless office	Reduces in-process communication costs	Reduces the cost of coordinating inter- and intragroup communication
Electronic data interchange	Reduces cost of communication between organizations	Allows the economic use of resources whether they are owned or not because the burden of interorganizational cost is minimized
Self-identification (scanning, truck transponders)	Reduces the cost of capturing data	Activities can be monitored on a real-time basis instead of relying on ex post facto reporting
Collaborative partnerships	Allows relationships based on long-term relationships rather than individual transactions	Suppliers can become actively involved in solving problems and modifying processes; firm can take advantage of suppliers' knowledge base as well as supplies they provide; reduces the need for protective measures
Cross training	Human resource flexibility	Employees can be used in many ways
Just-in-time	Temporal flexibility	Reduces risk of inventory obsolescence
Flexible manufacturing	Fixed-asset flexibility	Production lines can produce a variety of models and products
Virtual corporation [17]	Capital flexibility	Assets do not have to be owned to be used; this allows firm to focus on market need rather than finding use for existing assets

systems and networks are designed. Deterministic systems are designed to optimize a selected *process,* whereas networks are designed to provide effective *results* under widely varying conditions.

Consider, for example, the design of a land transportation network for an airport. In major markets, airports have several ways of enabling customers to arrive or depart from the airport. They may take a shuttle or a cab, use a mass-transit alternative (such as a bus or light rail), or drive their own cars. For the sake of simplicity, let's consider two of these alternatives: the shuttle, which uses a predefined systems approach, and a taxi company, which uses a responsive network approach.

Fixed systems are coordinated by deterministic planning. For the shuttle company, system design would begin by estimating demand patterns (arrival times, most popular hotels) and then identifying the optimal combination of routes and departure times to meet anticipated demand at the lowest cost (see Figure 1.8).

Thus, a deterministic systems approach would:

- Define the system boundaries (the hotels to be served and the expected ridership to each);
- Define the desired results (travel time, wait factors, and load factors);
- Plan the optimum process for achieving these results (design routes and schedules);
- Manage performance according to a plan (conformance to planned routes and schedules).

Systems performance, once implemented, can be extremely efficient, but the planning and implementation life cycle required to develop a new system or to modify an existing system can be very time consuming. Therefore, systems can be extremely effective and efficient at performing the tasks they were designed to perform. Problems arise, however, if unexpected demands are made on the system. It would be difficult, for

---

mer approach, the program leads the user through a fixed path of activities to process specific transactions. In the object-oriented approach, the user selects an object and the desired action. The next part of the program to be run depends upon the object and action the user has just requested. This form of system development is thus user responsive. Customer-responsive organizations are based on networks, flexibility, and enabling tools, not the design of highly structured, tightly defined processes.

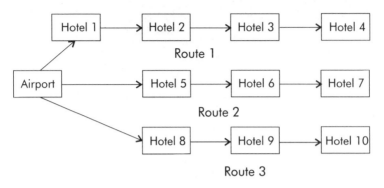

Figure 1.8.   A three-route, predefined airport shuttle system.

example, for the shuttle system to respond to a large conference being held at a hotel not on the route or outside of the provider's operating authority. Changing deterministic systems is very difficult and expensive in terms of time and money. If conditions and assumptions change, the entire planning process has to be repeated.

By contrast, networking companies, such as taxi companies, have an entirely different orientation from the shuttle operators. They design standardized interfaces so that a virtually unlimited combination of options can be used to respond to any given request at any given time. Consider the customer-response system shown in Figure 1.9.

The network is designed to respond to the individual customer request. The departure time and destination are specified by each individual customer, not by the provider. Routing is done after the driver determines where riders want to go.

Network management for the cab company consists of:

- Defining the range of expected requests (e.g., residence, hotels, industry, post office, local travelers, airline passengers, mail, packages, and baggage);
- Establishing a network of resources (e.g., cabs, drivers, and communications) that can respond to needs when they arise;
- Designing a process for effectively identifying individual passenger needs and efficiently dispatching resources to respond to these needs;
- Streamlining the taking of requests, dispatching, monitoring, and tracking of deliveries.

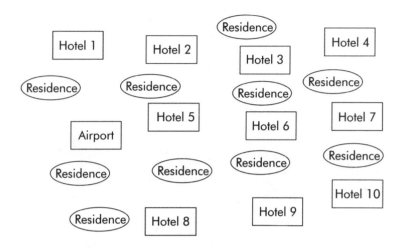

Figure 1.9. A responsive taxi network of potential service sites.

Deterministic systems are designed to optimize a predefined, static process where needs are predictable and relatively stable. Resources are organized and managed according to plan. Networks, on the other hand, are designed to optimize results for a wide variety of rapidly changing needs. Resources are organized to be managed dynamically. Resources are selected case by case, depending upon each resource's ability to effectively deliver the desired results. The networking process enables the dynamic selection of available resources depending upon the available capability (i.e., competency) and capacity. Lastly, resources can be a part of many networks. Carriers can deliver for many different customers. Distribution centers can inventory products from many different producers and pick up for and ship to different customers. Repair services can fix many different types of machines from a wide variety of vendors. Physicians can be a resource to many different hospitals and hospitals can serve many different physicians.

The ability to process information is critical to networking. *Networks are enabled by the ability to process information on a real-time basis. Networking, in turn, enables organizations to be flexible. When the organization is flexible, it can be responsive to individual customer needs.* Information, networking, and flexibility make customer-responsive management possible.

Customer Responsiveness Creates Customer Value

Customer-responsive activities create customer value by solving individual customer problems. This is a much different concept from the traditional, value-added focus of product-oriented firms in which the retailer purchases goods and resells them. The difference between selling price and purchase price is the value added by the retailer. Likewise, the manufacturer buys raw material and hires labor to produce a product. The difference between the selling price of the output and cost of the input is the value added by the production or retailing process. This concept is illustrated in Figure 1.10. Each step of this process strives to maximize the difference between the selling price of the output and the purchase price of the input. The goal of product-oriented firms is to maximize profit (i.e., sales less cost of goods sold) or value added.

Many business terms reflect the value-added orientation. Value-added resellers, mark-ups, margins, supply chains, value chains, and middlemen are just a few examples of this focus. There is always an input and an output. Profit is made by adding value to the input.

Customer-responsive management visualizes the firm from the customer's perspective rather than from a production prospective. Customer-responsive activities create value for the customer by solving the individual customer's need. It is irrelevant whether a product is part of the solution or not. In fact, when products are used, they are typically called supplies. Examples of supplies include sutures and anesthesia in the operating room, paint and caulk used to repaint a house, and paper and pencils used in the classroom. The painter, physician, and teacher do not focus on adding value to the supplies they use but on creating value for the customer by solving his or her need. (See Figure 1.11.) A product may or may not be involved. The focus is not on the input but rather on creating value for the customer.

If the organization is effective in meeting the customer's needs, the customer will have come to have a greater trust and reliance on the organization. The objective is not to add value to some input and find a market for the output but to:

- Build relationships with customers so they call you first when they have a need;
- Build organizations that can effectively respond when customers do call;

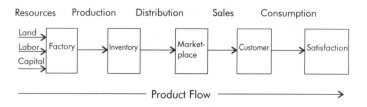

Figure 1.10. A value-added supply chain with each step adding value.

- Create processes and infrastructure that enable front line employees to interact with customers and coordinate benefit delivery.

The strength of the relationship is determined by the customers' expectations of the value the organization can create for them. Value creation from the customers' perspective is the difference between the value of the solution minus the economic cost and hassle of obtaining the solution. The greater the value created, the more delighted the customer. The more delighted the customer, the greater the bonding between customer and provider. Delighted customers regularly return to have their next need met and become annuities to the provider, rather than a simple, one-time transaction.

Value creation also takes a very different approach to measuring profitability. The value-added firm looks at the value added (the markup) less the cost of adding the value. The difference or profit is calculated as the value added less the cost of the process required to add value. The customer-responsive organization, on the other hand, focuses on yield (i.e., the value created and the capacity required to create the value). Another way of expressing value creation is delivery effectiveness – that is, the effectiveness in meeting the customer's need. Delivery efficiency is a measure of the capacity required to create the value. The term *cost effectiveness* is used to describe the combination of delivery effectiveness and delivery (cost) efficiency. Collectively, delivery effectiveness and cost efficiency define resource yield.

Delivery effectiveness enhances the value created by providing a better solution to the customer's need and minimizing the hassle of obtaining the solution. When delivery is effective, customers are willing to pay more and they return for additional deliveries. Revenue is increased by the higher charges and from subsequent requests.

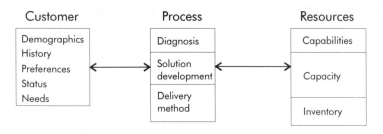

Figure 1.11. A value-creation view of an organization.

Delivery becomes more efficient when fewer resources are required to create the value. Because capacity cannot be inventoried, any capacity not used to provide benefits is wasted. Unused capacity cannot be saved and used later. That is why measures such as occupancy rate, load factors, percent bilabial hours, and percent deadheading are used to measure delivery efficiency. Delivery is efficient when work is assigned in a way that minimizes wasted capacity. By increasing both delivery effectiveness and efficiency, yield is increased.

Customer responsiveness increases yield by lowering the cost of delivery. The mass-production approach to delivery may be the least expensive method of producing a product under a given set of conditions. In fact, mass production and mass marketing are based on the concept of planning how best to produce a standardized product and distribute it to the marketplace at a relatively constant rate under specified conditions. This approach works well unless conditions change. Customer needs may change, as they did during the oil embargoes of the 1970s. Competition may change. The environment may change, as when interest rates soar, retaliatory tariffs are established, or large areas of the country are flooded. The more turbulent the changes, the greater the advantage of flexibility. The cost of restructuring highly structured activities can be very high. Network organizations, on the other hand, are designed to respond to changes. Consequently, by the time the highly structured system has had to be changed several times, the network is frequently the least expensive way of delivering benefits. Therefore, customer-responsive management lowers costs by making the delivery system more responsive to change.

Customer Responsiveness Requires Flexibility

Every organization wants to be more responsive to customers. Unfortunately, mass-production and mass-marketing organizations often perceive flexibility to be too costly. In some cases this may be true. But in many cases, the inflexibilities are self-inflicted and not real. The major cause of self-inflicted inflexibility is the way firms are organized to coordinate work. If a firm tries to adopt the traditional mass-production organizational structure used to define, plan, and control offerings, it will have difficulty being responsive. The customer-responsive approach, however, is designed for flexibility. Whereas the mass-production-based organization has difficulty being responsive, the more flexible responsive approach always has the ability to handle operations when less flexibility is required.

The objective of this book is to help the reader understand how flexible organizations operate and are managed so that their operating principles can be applied to a multitude of business operations. If there are some compelling reasons not to use flexible, responsive methods, then the deterministic methods based on planning and control can be used. However, when a firm has a viable option, it will always want to select the more flexible approach because it allows the company to be more (as well as less) responsive to individual customers and changing conditions. Customer responsiveness allows it to deliver benefits that more closely fit customer needs. This is what provides value to customers, revenue to providers, and profits to efficient providers.

Summary

Some businesses see their role as producing and presenting offerings to the marketplace. Customer-responsive organizations, on the other hand, view their role as solving individual customer needs at a reasonable cost and a minimum of hassle. Part of the hassle minimization process consists of helping customers avoid the hassle of searching through the proliferation of offerings in pursuit of a solution.

Customer responsiveness is not a new concept. Customer responsiveness is only new to individuals primarily trained and familiar with the mass-production approach to organizing work. Many service organizations such as consulting, health care, repair services, transportation, and counseling are required to interact with customers first before they decide on the solution they will deliver to the customer. Virtually all organizations can be either offering based or customer responsive. Mass transit, for example, provides a predefined, fixed solution to providing transportation. Taxicabs, on the other hand, are responsive to individual customer request. Many retail stores show you their offerings and make no effort to help you if your needs cannot be met by their offerings. Others attempt to identify your needs and find solutions for you even if it takes special orders or effort on their part.

Offering-based companies are organized to centrally plan what they will do, carefully supervise and control the implementation of their plans, and position the planned offerings to potential customers. Responsive organizations build relationships with customers so the customers call them first when they have a need, build organizations that can respond when the customer does call, and create the organizations and infrastructure necessary to facilitate relationship building and individual delivery coordination by front-line workers.

As customers have more options, competition and cost containment are forcing organizations to become more responsive. These organizations are doing this by developing more flexible, modular delivery organizations, reducing transaction costs both within and between organizations, and networking resources. Network management requires an information infrastructure that can process information on a real-time basis. The information systems enable organizations to be flexible. This flexibility, in turn, enables the organization to be responsive to customers.

Responsiveness creates value for the customer by delivering more effective solutions. Responsiveness reduces costs for the providers by reducing capital cost, increasing capacity utilization, and making planning activities more efficient and effective.

Chapter 2 traces the evolution of management concepts and shows how customer-responsive management was preeminent before the introduction of mass production and how during the mass-production era business firms continually strived to become more flexible and responsive to customers.

References

[1] Reprinted by permission of Harvard Business School Press from *Mass Customization: The New Frontier in Business Competition* by B. Joseph Pine II, Boston, 1993. Copyright © 1993 by the President and Fellows of Harvard College.

[2] Don Peppers and Martha Rogers, *The One to One Future: Building Relationships One Customer at a Time*, New York: Doubleday, 1993. p. 15.

[3] Reprinted by permission of *Harvard Business Review*. An excerpt from "Making Mass Customization Work" by B. Joseph Pine II, Bart Victor, and Andrew C. Boynton, Vol. 71, Issue 5 (September / October 1993), pp. 108–119. Copyright © 1993 by the President and Fellows of Harvard College; all rights reserved.

[4] James H. Gilmore and B. Joseph Pine II, "Driving Reengineering with New Business Strategies," presented at the Council of Logistics Management Annual Conference in Cincinnati, Ohio, October 17, 1994.

[5] Ann Drake and Stephan H. Haeckel, "Adaptive Enterprise: A Strategy for Survival in Turbulent Times," presented at the Council of Logistics Management Annual Conference in Cincinnati, Ohio, October 17, 1994.

[6] Reprinted by permission of *Harvard Business Review*. An excerpt from "Do You Want to Keep Your Customers Forever?" by B. Joseph Pine II, Don Peppers and Martha Rogers, Vol. 73, Issue 2 (March / April 1995), pp. 103–108. Copyright © by the President and the Fellows of Harvard College; all rights reserved.

[7] Peppers and Rogers, op. cit., p. 15.

[8] Taken from the Departmental Vision for the Department of Marketing, Logistics and Transportation, University of Tennessee, Knoxville, 1993.

[9] Pine, op. cit. (Mass Customization), pp. 147–148.

[10] Jon Monday and Tom Pomeroy, Letters to the Editor, *Harvard Business Review*, November-December 1993, p. 178.

[11] Joel S. Spira, Letters to the Editor, *Harvard Business Review*, November-December 1993, p. 180.

[12] Pine, op. cit. (*Mass Customization*), pp. 66–75.

[13] Pine, Victor, and Boynton, op. cit., p. 109.

[14] Pine, Victor, and Boynton, op. cit., p. 110.

[15] Pine, Victor, and Boynton, op. cit., p. 110.

[16] Oliver E. Williamson, *The Economic Institutions of Capitalism*, New York: The Free Press, 1985, p. 13.

[17] Ibid., p. 2.

[18] William H. Davidow and Michael S. Malone, *The Virtual Corporation: Structuring and Revitalizing the Corporation for the 21st Century*, New York: HarperCollins, 1992.

[19] The first version of this framework appeared in Andrew C. Boynton and Bart Victor, "Beyond Flexibility: Building and Managing the Dynamically Stable Organization," *California Management Review*, Vol. 34, No. 1, Fall 1991, pp. 53–66.

THE EVOLVING ECONOMIC FOCUS: FROM CONQUEST TO RELATIONSHIP

It is often difficult to comprehend how dramatically business and society change over time. Unless one understands these changes, it is easy to fall into several traps. Such traps include:

- Embracing current principles as eternal truisms rather than seeing them as relatively recent developments. Basic concepts such as capitalism, employment for a wage, discounted cash flow, and the quality movement are key examples.
- Embracing principles simply because they are currently general practices used by highly respected firms. But firms can rapidly blossom or decline. It does not take a historian to remember the dominance of firms such as A&P, W. T. Grants, IBM, and GM or to remember when Wal-Mart, Microsoft, and Dell were virtually unknown. Of the Fortune 500 companies of five years ago, 143 are not included in that list today. Of the 43 companies cited as being "excellent" in Tom Peters's *In Search of Excellence*, half no longer qualify. In fact, winning the prestigious Baldridge Award does not ensure a sound economic future.
- Grasping for the latest business "fad," Richard Tanner Pascale suggests that "an indicator of managerial panic is the consumption rate and shelf life of business fads."[1] He notes that in 1991 there had been over two dozen such fads since 1950 and that half of these occurred in the last five years of those four decades. The problem with fads is that "companies apply them in a piecemeal fashion and shift from one to another too frequently. What is lacking is a grasp of the broader context in which they must be embedded."[1]

---

1. Fads listed by Pascale include familiar concepts such as Theory Z, matrix, managerial grid, T-groups, intrapreneurship, demassing, one-minute managing, corporate culture, Management by Walking Around (MBWA), wellness, value chain, strategic business units, and Management by Objectives (MBO).

This chapter is presented to help the reader understand the contexts within which many managerial concepts were developed and how change is evolving.

Normally a historical chapter would provide a historical overview of the last five, ten, or fifty years. But because it is so easy for readers to believe that concepts such a capitalism, the marketplace, money, production, and mercantilism have always dominated the economy, this chapter will take a longer view. It will draw on Robert L. Heilbroner's popular work, *The Making of Economic Society*, to cite three economic eras that Heilbroner identified:

- Era 1 – Economic control by political, military, and religious leaders;
- Era 2 – Economic control by landowners or lords;
- Era 3 – Marketplace competition by producers and distributors of products.

Capitalism, the marketplace, money, production, and mercantilism did not dominate until the third era. Customer responsiveness may be seen as the beginning of a fourth economic era that is now rapidly evolving.

Heilbroner suggests that "societies tend to reward most highly the activities they value most highly."[2] During the first two eras, economic activities were largely performed by slaves or serfs, and resources were controlled not by the marketplace but by central authority. It was not the producer that society rewarded but the central authority. In the first era, control was by political, military, and religious leaders. In the second era, economies were controlled by landowners. It was not until the third era that economic wealth, power, and status went to the individuals who produced and distributed products in a competitive marketplace.

The First Era

During the first economic era, entrepreneurs – if we may use that word – became wealthy by obtaining gold and silver and by acquiring slaves. One method used to acquire wealth was to raise armies that could conquer foreign nations. Politicians recognized that nations could also benefit from this process by authorizing the army to conquer in the name of the state for a share of the wealth. Although the conquest era was typically associated with antiquity (e.g., ancient Greece, Rome, and Egypt), it continued into the Americas, where the conquistadors conquered the Incas and Aztecs and sent shiploads of gold back to Spain in return for royal sponsorship. The conquering armies left troops behind to maintain order and to keep the tribute flowing to sponsoring countries, where economic activity was conducted by slaves, not by the free citizenry. For as Aristotle wrote, "the citizens may not lead either the life of craftsmen or of traders, for such a life is devoid of nobility and hostile to perfection of character."[3]

The Second Era

The second economic era began with the decline of the Roman Empire and continues to the current day in some countries. Although there was some industrial production in the city guilds, life revolved around the manorial estates. The "lord of the manor was not only landlord, but protector, judge, police chief, administrator."[4] The serf was tied to the land and could not leave. In return for the right to live and work the land, the serf had to work for the landlord. Not only did the landowner control the use of resources, but political power (e.g., membership in England's House of Lords) was based on land ownership. Land could not be bought or sold; it could only be obtained through inheritance by the oldest son (primogeniture) or through marriage. This type of economic structure could be seen as late as 1940 in rural areas of the United States where sharecropping was common or today in some of the South American countries where land ownership and resources are controlled by a small portion of the population.

The Third Era

The third economic era was brought on by the industrial revolution. The development of machines that could spin and weave cloth allowed a few workers to produce enough material to meet the needs of many customers. This marked the end of the subsistence economy, in which each person only produced enough for him or herself. The surplus resulting from the industrial revolution required the development of marketplaces in which to sell the products, the creation of currency and a banking system to facilitate trade, and the creation of transportation companies to get products to market. Another result was the fencing of manorial lands by landlords to raise sheep. It was more profitable to raise sheep than to have large groups of serfs doing subsistence farming. As lords "rightsized" their manors, thousands of displaced serfs were forced to move to the cities, where for the most part they lived in abject poverty.

Just as the Magna Carta, signed by King John in 1215, formalized the rights of second-era landlords in England, the works of Adam Smith, published in that same country in 1776, formalized the mechanism for shifting economic control from the landlords to the manufacturers and merchants. Smith formalized the principles of capitalism.

Capitalism – The Root of Modern Business

Adam Smith did not create the industrial revolution, but he did formalize the concepts of capitalism and the economic mechanisms necessary for it to work. Before Adam Smith, land generally was not bought and sold. Laborers could not be hired but were attached to the land of the feudal lord. Money was not commonly used. Heilbroner described this economy:

> It was not at all "natural" and "normal" to have free, wage-earning, con-tractual labor or rentable, profit-producing land or fluid, investment-seeking capital. They were creations of the great transformation of a pre-market into a market society. Economics call these creations the factors of production, and much of economics is concerned with analyzing the manner in which these three basic constituents of the productive process are combined in the market mechanism.[5]

It was Adam Smith that showed how these factors of production worked together to form an economic system.

Adam Smith had been a student of François Quesnay, physician to Madame de Pompadour and Louis XV. Quesnay was an economist in an era when armies had become a burden, not a resource, and when the nobility had begun to resort to taxation to support their grandiose lifestyles. Because the clergy and nobility were exempt from taxation, the burden fell almost exclusively on the common landowner and the peasant.[6]

Quesnay was concerned about these taxes. He believed that agricultural production – not plunder or mercantilism – was the true source of wealth. As Heilbroner has written, "in contradiction to the ideas of the day which still held that wealth was the solid stuff of gold and silver, Quesnay insisted that wealth sprang from production and that it flowed through the nation, from hand to hand, replenishing the body social like the circulation of blood."

Terms such as "product flow" and "cash flow" probably trace their roots back to this analogy used by Quesnay to describe the functioning of an economy: "Since the primary industries, agriculture in particular, are the source of the net product upon which the prosperity of a nation rests, agriculture would be encouraged above all in an ideally functioning economy."[7]

Quesnay further suggested that there were three classes of people: the proprietor class (the nobility), the cultivator class (the tenant farmers), and the sterile class. Quesnay argued that only the cultivator class was productive. Thus taxes should be reduced on the tenant farmers because they were uniquely able to create a net product. Artisans, domestic servants, proprietors, merchants, financiers, and anyone else who was not a cultivator were considered to be sterile because they were not able to create a net product.[8] This was a dramatic change from the first era when Aristotle insisted that production was considered to be devoid of status and should only be conducted by slaves.

After returning to his native Scotland after studying with Quesnay, Adam Smith began work on his book, *An Inquiry into the Nature and Cause of the Wealth of Nations*. He was convinced that not only agriculture but also manufacturing and mercantilism created wealth. (This is reminiscent of a more recent time when many argued that manufacturing was the only basis of wealth and that consequently a service economy could never produce prosperity.) Consequently, the study of production economics was founded on the belief that manufacturing and merchants were also sources of value and that the study of economics, as we know it, thus had the production and distribution of products as its central focus. This point is emphasized in the *Encyclopaedia Britannica* entry describing microeconomics: "[Microeconomics] approaches the economy as if it were made up only of business firms and households (ignoring governments, banks, charities, trade unions, and all other economic institutions) interacting in two kinds of markets – product markets and markets for productive services, or factor markets."[9][2]

---

2. Productive services are those services that add value to a product, such as

Therefore, it is important to show that Adam Smith carefully defined economics to exclude what he defined as nonproductive activities and to understand why he so meticulously excluded activities that did not produce a tangible, marketable product.

Smith clearly delineated between what he defined as productive versus unproductive activity: "There is one sort of labour which adds to the value of the subject upon which it is bestowed: there is another which has no such effect. The former, as it produces a value, may be called *productive*; the latter, *unproductive* labour. Thus the labour of a manufacturer *adds*, generally, to the *value* of the material which he works upon. . . . The labour of a menial servant, on the contrary, adds to the value of nothing."[10]

Although many might agree that menial servants add little of value, it is important to understand the basis of Smith's beliefs. As Smith wrote, "His *services* generally perish in the very instant of their performance, and seldom leave any trace or value behind them for which an equal quantity of service could afterwards be procured."[11]

In other words, the menial servant did not add value to a vendible product that could be sold so the revenue could be used to produce more products. But, according to Smith, menial servants were not the only ones who did not produce products: "The labor of some of the most respectable orders in the society is, like that of menial servants, unproductive of any value, and *does not fix or realize itself in any permanent subject; or vendible commodity* [emphasis added], which endures after the labour is past, and for which an equal quantity of labour could afterwards be procured."[11]

Smith then identified the providers of the unproductive labor to include "the *sovereign*, with all the officers both of justice and war who serve under him, the whole army and navy. . . . In the same class must be ranked, some both of the gravest and most important, and some of the most frivolous professions: *churchmen, lawyers, physicians, men of letters* [emphasis added] of all kinds; players, buffoons, musicians,

---

the storage of corn or the transportation of rock records to the marketplace. The study of transportation economics has typically focused on the transportation of freight because freight transportation is productive in that it adds value to the product. Because people are no longer bought and sold, it is difficult to find an economic basis for passenger transportation.

opera-singers, opera-dancers, etc. . . . . Like the declamation of the actor, the harangue of the orator, or the tune of the musician, *the work of all of them perishes in the very instant of its production*" [emphasis added].[11]

We must assume that Smith did not mean to imply that the work of a physician is not beneficial but the labor of the carpenter is valuable. (Is the work of a carpenter who builds a casket more valuable than a doctor who saves the life of a patient?) However, it is clear that Adam Smith was interested only in the production of vendible products. The study of economics is about the production and distribution of products. Alfred Marshall confirmed 122 years later that "*services and other goods* [emphasis added], which pass out of existence in the same instant that they come into it, are, of course, *not part of the stock of wealth*" [emphasis added].[12]

Thus third-era economics are production economics. They revolve around the production of a tangible product that can be distributed and sold in the marketplace. These products are produced in a capitalist system where land, labor, capital, and other resources can be freely purchased. The primary exception has been the study of productive services (i.e., factors of production) such as labor or transportation that add value to products.

Today, when the press is heralding the growth of the service economy and the dawning of the information age, business students still take microeconomics courses that teach concepts that were never intended to apply to services or to the information age, where bits and bytes can be captured, copied, and transmitted at virtually no cost. Although microeconomics still retains its production orientation, business practice has dramatically evolved since the time that discipline was created. Today the product is no longer the central focus; emphasis is on customer value, industrial partnerships, and customer service. These concepts are the beginning of fourth-era concepts.

Fourth-era economic principles are as different from third-era principles as Quesnay's ideas were from those of Adam Smith. But before addressing the fourth era, we need to understand how the third era has evolved. The industrial revolution enabled the shift from subsistence to an exchange economy. It allowed individuals to specialize in the production of a single product that could be exchanged for money, which could be used to buy other items desired. The industrial revolution allowed economies of scale in production, the rise of banks to finance transactions, transportation companies to take products to market, and the creation of currency to facilitate transactions. Adam Smith provided the knowledge base for understanding how capitalism worked so that there was a rationale for changing laws, policies, and guild rules. He explained why institutional and societal change were necessary. This knowledge base created an explosion of productive activities using craft production management methods.

The Production Stage of the Mass-Production Era

When Adam Smith introduced capitalism, there was a severe shortage of virtually all products. Smith's economic theories provided the conceptual basis for the production of more products at lower costs so that their market was no longer limited to the wealthy. Thus attention was focused on methods for increasing production. Major increases in productivity again came from the discovery of mass production – the large-scale production of standardized products using standardized processes on a highly specialized production line.

Standardized Interchangeable Parts

Eli Whitney developed the concept of *standardized interchangeable parts* that allowed the cloning of products. Accordingly, organizations (or individuals) could specialize in the production of a single, standardized part. Multiple parts could then be assembled to form the final product. Broken products could be repaired by simply replacing a single part. This formed the basis of true mass production. Once components were standardized, the next step was to standardize the production process.

Production Line

Henry Ford developed the *assembly line* where interchangeable standardized parts were brought to workers at a controlled rate so that each could specialize in performing a single assembly task at a planned pace. The goal of the assembly line was to reduce the production process to a series of simple, repeatable tasks that could be learned in a matter of minutes. Therefore, production became very predictable because it synchronized the workers. Now work could be carefully planned and scheduled with precision.

Scientific Management

Once production could be broken into individual tasks and coordinated by the production line, attention could be focused on making individual tasks more efficient. Frederick Winslow Taylor was the founder of *scientific management*. Now that the process, tasks, and flows could be standardized, it became possible to plan or determine the best way to produce the product. This optimum method for performing each task could be quickly taught to unskilled workers who could become very productive within a short period of time.

Peter F. Drucker has suggested that this was the first application of knowledge to study the work process. He contends that it was this study and understanding of work that helped the United States to defeat Nazi Germany in World War II: "The United States did not have much of a merchant marine, and its destroyers were few and ludicrously obsolete. It also had almost no optical industry. But by applying Taylor's Scientific Management, U.S. industry trained totally unskilled workers, many of them former sharecroppers raised in a pre-industrial environment, and converted them in sixty to ninety days into first-rate welders and ship-builders. Equally, the United States trained the same kind of people within a few months to turn out precision optics of better quality than the Germans ever did – and on an assembly line to boot."[13]

There was also a need to develop a standardized method for measuring results so that the effectiveness of various strategies and tactics could be compared. This gave rise to cost accounting.

Cost Accounting

Although financial accounting was developed in the late 1400s by Fra Pacioli, a Venetian monk, cost accounting did not evolve until the evolution of large enterprises, such as the textile mills in the early 1800s, the railroad and the steel companies in the mid- to late-1800s, and the retail chains in the early 1900s. As H. Thomas Johnson and Robert S. Kaplan have explained, "These organizations really had to do only one activity well: convert raw materials into a single final product such as cloth or steel, move passengers or freight, or resell purchased goods."[14] Such enterprises developed a cost-accounting system that aggregated indirect cost and direct cost. The cost of the product was the sum of direct cost and indirect cost. Indirect cost was typically allocated by some direct measure such as labor hours, machine hours, or floor space required. This approach worked well as long as the firm had a single product or activity and indirect costs were relatively small in comparison to direct costs. No effort was made to keep cost accounting and financial accounting data consistent.[15]

A different problem evolved in the early 1900s. In 1903 a number of family-run and independent companies were combined as the Du Pont Powder Company. The vertically integrated firm presented a new problem: How should management allocate capital between each of these individual units? "F. Donaldson Brown, the chief financial officer of Du Pont, decomposed return on investment (ROI) into its component parts – the operating ratio (return on sales) and stock turn (sales to assets) – used by single-activity organizations."[16] Return on investment (ROI) allowed top management to focus on capital allocation based on "a forecast of cash flows . . . required to determine the maximum amount of new construction to which the firm could commit itself. Cash flows were forecast by multiplying the projected quantity of explosives to be sold each month (based on sales department estimates) by the estimated contribution margin per unit for each product (based on accounting department records)."[17]

In 1920 Du Pont invested in the floundering General Motors Corporation. Pierre Du Pont became president; he was assisted by Alfred P. Sloan, Jr. They turned to Du Pont's Donaldson Brown to develop an accounting system that would manage the evolving, multidivisional firm. Johnson and Kaplan have described this effort:

> GMs management accounting system performed three tasks to permit what Brown described as "centralized control with decentralized responsibility." First, it provided an annual operating forecast to compare each divisions ex ante annual operating goals with top management's financial goals. Top management used the operating forecast to coordinate each division's expected performance with company-wide financial policy. Second, the system provided sales reports and flexible budgets that indicated promptly if actual results were deviating from planned results. . . . Third, the management accounting system allowed top management to allocate both resources and managerial compensation among divisions on the basis of uniform performance criteria.[18]

The purpose of this accounting system was to allow management to plan and manage by the numbers. Plans were based on producing at "standard volume" (i.e., 80 percent of planned capacity). "GM managers attributed any discrepancy between the actual and desired rate of return to either unanticipated deviations from the projected selling price, unplanned changes in factory price, or unexpected alterations in operating efficiency."[19]

These innovations were successful. Production increased dramatically, in fact so much so that a new problem developed that required a fresh management focus and led to a new stage of the production era. Manufacturers found they could no longer depend on customers to come to them to buy all the products their factories could produce. As supply became greater than demand, firms realized they had to do something to make it easier for customers to become aware of and to obtain their product. Attention then turned to mass marketing.

The Mass-Marketing Stage of the Mass-Production Era

Just as there were pivotal paradigm changes in the mass-production stage, there were also pivotal concepts that drove the evolution of mass marketing. The first of these was mass merchandising.

Mass Merchandising

As supply began to outpace consumer demand, attention turned to distribution and promotion. The first step was to recruit and send *salespersons* out to the marketplace to sell the product. *Channels of distribution* were developed as salespersons recruited wholesalers and retailers to routinely handle their product lines. The obvious next question was how to extend the influence of the salesperson beyond the wholesaler and retailer to the customer. This led to the use of *advertising* and *promotion*. The purpose of promotion was to get the customer into the retailer's store to purchase the product. Although management began to pay attention to the marketplace in the late 1800s, the first marketing textbooks did not appear until around 1915.

The Marketing Concept

The early sales and promotion efforts were successful in selling what the factories could produce until the onset of the Depression, after which there was little money to buy anything. During World War II, military production demanded so much productive capacity that consumer goods were often rationed. After the war, "G.I. Joe" and "Rosie the Riveter" had many pent-up needs. Because goods had been rationed, they had not been able to spend the money they had earned during the war. But by the 1950s, companies again found that they could not sell all that they could produce and promote. Mass marketing turned its attention to market research and product planning. Wouldn't it be easier to produce what the customers want to buy instead of trying so hard to sell them what the firm had planned to produce? This was the *marketing concept*. *Market research* departments were developed to survey customers and design products based on market preferences.

Market Segments

Market researchers discovered that there was great diversity in individual customer preferences. Seldom did a single product meet the needs of all users. Most customers had to make do with what was available because it was the best solution they could find to their needs. Why not develop a method to determine when it was more profitable to make multiple products instead of only one? The concept of *market segmentation* was developed to answer this question. Segmentation methodology allowed market researchers to divide diverse customer needs into various categories or segments that could then be analyzed independently. The result of this research was different offerings targeted to each segment. For example, automobile makers began to produce different models, and soft-drink makers produced different flavors. When customers' needs were perceived as being too diverse, firms had to choose which markets they would pursue. The chosen markets became known as *target markets*. Market research would identify the preferences of each target market and design a product (or *market mix*) to appeal to them.

As marketers expanded their focus to include the full market mix of product, price, promotion, and place, they began to understand the interactions among the elements of the market mix. Not only were there product-price tradeoffs, but customers would willingly pay more for an inferior product if it was available when needed. Likewise, promotion and distribution had to be coordinated if promotion was to be effective. It did no good to promote a product that was not yet on the store shelves. Business turned to the field of logistics to integrate activities among organizations (e.g., transportation, warehousing, and wholesalers) and to coordinate individualized transactions and deliveries.

The Supply-Chain Logistics Stage of the Mass-Production Era

Attention was first focused on physical distribution. Physical distribution departments coordinated distribution activities to reduce stock outs, reduce distribution costs, and coordinate delivery time to support the general market strategy. ("Right product, in right quantities and the right condition at the right place at the right time for the right customer, at the right cost."[20]) When interest rates peaked in the 1970s, the focus shifted from physical distribution to the reduction of inventory. Techniques were developed to reduce stock-keeping units (SKUs) and the number of inventory locations; information systems were created to expedite order entry and to coordinate transportation options better.

Once the physical distribution functions demonstrated how effectively they could coordinate activities and integrate outside vendors (e.g., transportation companies and distribution centers) into the mass-market process, firms began to use these methods to supply their production lines. The name of the function was changed from physical distribution to logistics. Logistics then developed methods to coordinate flows among suppliers, production, marketing, and the marketplace. These functions acquired names such as *material requirements planning* (MRP) on the physical supply side and *distribution requirements planning* (DRP) on the distribution side. These were methods for integrating the plans of other groups (e.g., suppliers and channel members) with the production and marketing plans and for coordinating the flow among channel members.

Marketing segmentation and supply-chain management created a conflict. Marketing wanted to increase segmentation, but mass production and supply chain logistics sought to decrease the number of stock-keeping units. While firms struggled with these conflicts, customers began to discover firms that were more concerned with customers' needs than with production and distribution efficiencies. This ushered in the total quality stage of the production era.

The Total Quality Stage of the Mass-Production Era

The total quality movement was sparked by changes in competition rather than a change in demand levels. When customers had a choice, they began to buy products that met their needs. Customers didn't want tailfins and chrome as much as dependable transportation that did not require repeat visits to the repair shop. Customers began to value and choose products that worked over shiny "new" models. When customers began to buy from Japan instead of from domestic producers, management began to realize that customers wanted benefits, not just products. During this transition, terms such as *quality* and *customer value* began to be used to describe this preference for products that provide preferred benefits. Again there were pivotal paradigm changes that forced managers to extend their focus from producing and distributing products for the marketplace to producing and distributing products that provided benefits that were valued by customers.

Joseph M. Juran, who wrote his first book in 1964, defined quality as "fitness to use."[3][21] Customers buy a product because they want benefits. They want to be able to rely on it for the benefits they need. Juran defined five dimensions of fitness for use. *Quality of design* addresses product attributes such as those that might be contrasted by comparing a Rolls Royce with a Volkswagen beetle. *Quality of conformance* was a measure of how well the design prototype was cloned during production. (Cloning describes how well production variances were controlled.) *Availability* expresses concern about the customer's concern about lack of product availability because of breakdown. *Safety* was a concern about the potential of a customer's suffering an injury while using the product. *Field use* was a term used to express the concern that the product might not be the same by the time it reached the customer as it was when it left the factory. Field use concerns focused attention on packaging, storage, and transportation. To get his concepts across to management, Juran developed a cost-of-quality accounting system. This system included the:

- *Internal failure costs* caused by the need to scrap and rework defective parts;
- *External failure costs* incurred when defects are discovered in the field and must be corrected;
- *Appraisal costs* required to inspect and examine material to determine that it is not defective;

---

3.   Joseph M. Juran and Frank M. Gyrna, Jr., *Quality Planning and Analysis*, New York: McGraw-Hill Company, 1980. Reprinted with permission of the McGraw-Hill Companies.

- *Prevention costs* incurred to develop techniques and procedures to prevent the previous three costs from occurring.

Philip B. Crosby focused on convincing top management that "quality is free."[22] This notion ran counter to the traditional management belief that quality was determined by product design. Crosby emphasized that quality was determined not by design but by the process by which the product was produced. It cost less to manage the production process so that waste was eliminated than it did to inspect, rework, scrap, perform warranty work, and do all of the other actions required to correct a defect once it had been produced. Crosby estimated that defects in most organizations accounted for between 15 and 20 percent of total production costs.

W. Edwards Deming used statistical process control, a concept developed by Walter Shewart at Bell Labs in the 1930s, to show that many of the production errors were not caused by the workers but by the production process itself.[23] It was up to management to change the production process. Deming emphasized that workers wanted to do a good job but that management had not provided them with the appropriate tools and methods. In 1982 Deming wrote, "The basic cause of sickness in American industry and resulting unemployment is failure of top management to manage."[24]

Deming also emphasized that business success came from the constant and continual improvement of existing activities, not the quest for the ultimate new product design. Deming also recognized that the relationship between the manufacturer and the customer was not an arm's-length relationship. The provider must know and understand what kind of product the customer wants and how he or she wants to use it. Thus suppliers should not be selected on the basis of price alone but on the total cost of using what they have supplied. Deming encouraged the cultivation of long-term relationships with relatively few suppliers that could be trained to meet the exact needs of their customers. Instead of the traditional arm's-length, zero-sum game between buyer and seller, industrial partnerships should be developed to promote win-win relationships in which the provider wins a more stable market by providing benefits that have greater value to the customer.

Genichi Tuguchi expanded the integration of design, production, and consumption still further. He indicated that 80 percent of product cost was determined during the design stage, not during the production process.[25,26] Thus Tuguchi developed a methodology for listening to the "voice of the customer" to determine which product attributes were critical. Then he designed a product fully aware of how design considerations would influence the cost of materials and production. The result was a "robust" design that optimized production resources while producing attributes that were important to the customer.

Another major concept change was the integration of these concepts into a program of continuous improvements as opposed to a dramatic periodic introduction of a new and improved model.[4]

The total quality movement's emphasis on process created different demands for accounting departments. It was not sufficient to total expenses and divide by output to determine costs. It was not sufficient simply to compare ROI from various operating units. Data were needed to design and modify the process of performing the task.

Process cost modeling changed the focus from recording to planning and from past activity to future activity. Process cost modeling is used to "simulate the impact of cost drivers on activity networks (processes) back to organizational resources. From these simulations, managers can better understand how to deploy and align resources to accommodate anticipated activity demands."[27] "The nature and environment of today's organization requires overall cost effectiveness rather than departmental cost effectiveness, cost reduction rather than cost control, and cost as an ex ante design issue rather than cost as an ex post evaluation issue."[28]

The total quality management stage turned attention to customers needs and forced a rethinking of traditional management methods. Part of this rethinking included the unquestioned acceptance of the mass production approach to management. Taiichi Ohno, former Vice President, Toyota Motor Corp., in an effort to reduce costs at Toyota, discovered over several decades that the best way to reduce cost was not through mass production but through flexible manufacturing. He introduced concepts such as just-in-time production, small lot production, the interdispersement of a variety of models – and even makes – on the same production line, production to order, and methods for increasing the range of models that could be produced. These innovations provided an option for resolving the dilemma between marketing, which wanted

---

4. For an excellent discussion of this concept see Masaaki Imai, *Kaizen: The Key to Japan's Competitive Success*, New York: McGraw-Hill, 1986.

more options for more market segments, and production and logistics, which wanted to reduce the inventory of SKUs.

This led to efficient consumer response (ECR), epitomized by the industrial partnership between P&G and Wal-Mart. These cooperative, industrial partnerships enable more efficient merchandising and distribution. Sales are captured when products are scanned at the checkout counter. This information is automatically transmitted to vendors who keep the shelves full through automatic replenishment. Shipments are made directly from factories to retail outlets, thus bypassing distribution centers, break-bulk terminals, and many other stages that traditionally caused increased costs. Such systems not only reduce inventory but allow quick responses to rapidly changing markets. Quick-response systems enable inventory spins rather than mere turnovers, allowing inventory to become a capital source rather than a consumer of working capital.

Thus, the total quality management stage challenged the mass-production paradigm. New technology (especially electronic data interchange (EDI), scanning, and the downsizing of information systems) enables production to be much more responsive. Mass customization efforts allow products to be customized for each customer. One-to-one marketing techniques, augmented by database marketing, now allow the buyer-seller relationship to be based on something other than the traditional, impersonal transaction in a faceless marketplace. The authors now see the beginning of a new phase they call *the customer-responsiveness era.*

The Fourth Era – Customer-Responsive Management

Though it has been labeled by many as a new age (e.g., the third wave, the service age, the postcapitalism age, the information age, the globalization age, the customer value age, the postquality age), the customer-responsiveness era can also be seen as part of a continual evolution of business. The big distinction of this era is the focus of the organization.

The precapitalist era focused on land ownership and self-sufficient farms. The capitalist era emphasized land, labor, and other resources that could be purchased. Adam Smith's economics of capitalism was applied to the production and distribution of resellable products through the marketplace. Production, marketing, logistics, and quality efforts were all focused on the product. The customer-responsiveness era reflects a new emphasis – on meeting the needs of the individual customer. There are many new dimensions to this shift to customer responsiveness.

From Offering to Solution. Customers are not looking for more offerings or larger assortments. They simply want solutions to their problems at a reasonable cost and with a minimum of hassle. Most offerings have no value to a person or business unless they solve a specific need. (Think of all the seldom used items at garage sales.) When providers understand that customers want their needs met and not just have standardized offerings, they will change the way they do business. When organizations are offering based, it is the customer's responsibility to determine which product best solves his or her need. The customer must do sufficient market research to effectively select the offering preferred and to learn how to use (or consume) the product to deliver the desired benefit.

The customer-responsive firm adds greater value for the customer by eliminating the hassle required to research the product and to learn how to use it. An excellent example of this concept is currently being demonstrated by a hotly debated political issue. People want to be healthy. Employers want their employees to be healthy. Capitated payment programs have evolved to pay for health care benefits. Program members are willing to pay a per-person annual fee for these benefits. However, many health care practitioners still view themselves as selling services and prefer a *fee-for-service* (transaction) pricing mechanism. The health care providers that are able to make the adjustment to a benefit-based fee plan and keep people healthy can receive an annual payment even if no office visits are ever made. Prevention and early detection become even more important than office visits, surgery, and chemotherapy. Preventive medicine is benefit oriented, whereas remedial care is offering based and requires that the patient do extensive research about which specialist to see and when to seek advice.

From Marketplace to Relationship. The central focus of the production era has been the product. Products were produced on the farm or in the factory and taken to the marketplace, where buyers could examine the offerings and make a selection. The marketplace was based on impersonal, arm's-length transactions during which each person examined the offering, came to understand its benefits, and made a decision based on his or her individual needs. The marketplace – whether street bazaar, supermarket, hardware store, trade fair, or stock exchange – was based on this concept.

In the customer-responsive era, customers will seek providers that are consistently able to respond to their individual needs. Customers go to hardware stores not just for a product but also for advice on how to approach a do-it-yourself project. Instead of browsing through the large assortments of offerings in the library, they call the reference desk to solicit the specific information that provides value. Instead of shopping for specialists in the medical complex, they develop a relationship with a family practitioner, clinic, or health maintenance organization (HMO) that can provide them with a strategy for staying healthy. Customers will refer to *their* barber, *their* mechanic, or *their* physician. This language indicates a relationship in which the customers believe that *their* providers will consistently take care of them. Likewise, many businesses are currently establishing industrial partnerships with a few firms that they feel confident can meet their needs. Just as sales are a measure of marketplace activity, so customer retention rates and repeat purchase patterns are measures of the strength of a customer-responsive organization's relationship with customers.

From Cost Reduction to Hassle Reduction. When the focus was on the offering, the price of that offering was emphasized. Markets were cleared by lowering price. In the customer-responsive era, there will be recognition of two prices: the *economic price* (or purchase price) and the noneconomic cost commonly known as *hassle*. The quality movement demonstrated that people will pay more if they are more confident that the product will consume well (i.e., will effectively provide them with benefits). *Consumer Reports* has recognized this and highlights frequency-of-repair and cost-of-repair surveys when it rates automobiles and other products. Often, the customer believes that product reliability is more important than style. In the customer-responsive era, providers will not claim to be the cheapest producers, but they will compete to see how effortlessly and completely they can meet customers' needs.

From an Internal to an External Focus. When the emphasis is on defining, producing, and distributing an offering to the marketplace, there is no need for one-to-one involvement with individual customers. A firm can unilaterally take whatever steps it believes necessary to anticipate future customer needs, define the ideal offering for the market, set up production, produce, and distribute the offering. Once the offering is in the marketplace, the firm can try to sell the offering. Again, this is a unilateral activity. As with the airport shuttle, described in Chapter 1, the offering and all the systems necessary to make it available are internally planned before any interaction occurs with individual customers. Customer-responsive organizations, on the other hand, focus on the diversity of customer needs. They plan infrastructures that enable them to organize a network of services, communications, and processes so they can interact with customers, diagnose needs, develop customized delivery plans, and track results. The customer-responsive organization organizes resources so it has the ability to interact with the customer and bilaterally define the details of the delivery. Instead of selling, the emphasis is on identifying a need and responding to it.

From Optimization to Flexibility. The role of the offering-based organization is to anticipate, define, produce, and distribute the optimum product in the optimum way for the marketplace. There are two assumptions inherent in this type of organization. First, it is assumed that there will be a standardized offering to a generalizable marketplace or to a few target markets. Second, the role of the organization is to perform all activities optimally (i.e., in the best way).

The customer-responsive organization rejects these two assumptions. First, it is designed to give customized responses, not standardized ones. Second, it does not attempt to define the best delivery method. Instead, it attempts to blend customized tasks to operate at full capacity. Whereas an offering-based organization emphasizes planning and stability for a limited number of offerings, a customer-responsive organization emphasizes flexibility: the flexibility to be responsive to customers and the flexibility to minimize wasted capacity.

From Control to Monitored Empowerment. A different organizational structure is required for unilateral and bilateral activities. When the objective is unilateral, someone must identify the objective and plan for its realization so that the organization knows what to do. In the traditional production organization, there are managers who plan what needs to be done, workers who are responsible to do the work, and supervisors who are responsible for making sure that the work is done according to plan.

As the emphasis shifts to increasing customer responsiveness, building an organization that can interact and respond to individual customers on a one-to-one basis becomes more important. The primary work of the organization is not directed by centralized plan and direction but by customer request and the front-line planning of deliveries. In a responsive organization, the role of management is not to plan the details of the work but to create the vision and organize the infrastructure (e.g., the knowledge base, the tools, and the information and communication systems) that enable the front-line employees to interact with customers, define needs, and coordinate delivery. Instead of planning the details of the work, management monitors how effectively the employees are accomplishing these tasks. The more effective employees are then encouraged to mentor less efficient employees so that everyone can understand the best practices for improving deliveries.

The unilateral mission organization is basically a hierarchical one, with the person at the top defining the mission. The bilateral responsive organization is a network organization, where flexibility occurs because the organization is able to coordinate a number of different competencies and capacities as they are needed to make customized deliveries.

From Periodic Management to Continual Management. Offering-based management is long-term project management. Each offering is a new project. Thus, customer needs are anticipated to determine market opportunities. Then projects are defined. The role of the staff is to plan each project or offering and to anticipate the potential revenue and costs based upon the methods selected. Top management's role is to decide which projects to fund. Front-line management's task is to make sure that implementation conforms to plan. Workers perform the work. Accounting collects data on sales and cost and generates periodic (monthly) reports that are used to evaluate if the project is on plan. If it is, all the parties involved are satisfied. If not, corrective action may need to be planned. The key project measures are profit and ROI.

Customer-responsive organizations have a much different orientation. First, relationship building requires that each customer be a separate project. The objective is to maximize the value created for the customer. This is done by doing more things for each customer and by extending the duration of the relationship. Second, each delivery is a separate project and must be planned and costed accordingly. (Responsive services frequently give estimates of costs.) The project is defined and monitored by the front line. Each project will have its own unique characteristics and must be tracked and monitored individually. It is not sufficient for Federal Express to look at month-end reports to tell if a shipment was lost. It is not even sufficient to explain to the customer whose package is missing that FedEx delivers 99.999 percent of all packages by 10:30 a.m. the following business day. The customer is interested only in the answers to these two questions: "Where is my package? When can I expect it to be delivered?"

This difference in orientation also creates another major difference in orientation. Firms that produce a standardized offering for stable markets usually focus on economies of scale. This means a small increase in capital can make a major change in production costs. These firms frequently prefer to be asset based because they believe asset ownership provides control and capability. Customer-responsive firms, on the other hand, are concerned about flexibility: the flexibility to customize responses to individual customers, the flexibility to respond to different customers, the flexibility to respond to competitive changes, and the flexibility to respond to changes in the business environment. The more specialized the asset, the less the flexibility. When flexibility is important, organizations fear having their assets tied up in inflexible capacity. Therefore, an emphasis is placed on minimizing investment so that virtually all costs are variable instead of fixed. Emphasis is on yield, not ROI and assets.

Summary

In 1750, economists were convinced that agriculture and mining created wealth and that merchants and manufacturers were a sterile class that could not create prosperity for the state. Adam Smith sought to show that was not the case. His work formed the foundation for modern business thought for the last 200 years. During this time, production-oriented firms shifted from a craft approach to a mass approach to management. With this flexibility, organizations can now become customer responsive. Through each of these changes, the product or offering was the central focus. Now, as technological and information developments provide flexibility, organizations are becoming more customer responsive. The shift toward customer responsiveness will introduce many different changes in business practices that may be even more far-reaching than those brought about by the shift from the feudal to capitalist ages.

Customer responsiveness emphasizes customer need, not the product. It concentrates on building relationships, not on the marketplace. It emphasizes infrastructure, not capital. Emphasis is on empowerment and communication, not control. Management is continuous, not periodic.

Chapter 3 will explain the advantage of customer responsiveness. The remaining chapters will present the principles of customer-responsive management.

References

[1] Richard Tanner Pascale, "Worldly Observations," *Marketing Insights*, Summer 1991, pp. 8–9.

[2] Robert L. Heilbroner, *The Making of Economic Society*, 9th edition, Upper Saddle River, NJ: Prentice-Hall, © 1993, p. 23.

[3] Ibid., p. 24.

[4] Ibid., p. 28.

[5] Ibid., p. 57.

[6] I. M. Rima, *Development of Economic Analysis*, Homewood, IL: Richard D. Irwin, 1967, p. 43.

[7] Robert Heilbroner, *The Worldly Philosophers*, New York: Simon and Schuster, 1967, p. 44.

[8] Rima, op. cit., pp. 76–78.

[9] "Microeconomics," *Encyclopaedia Britannica*, Chicago: Encyclopaedia Britannica, Macropaedia, 1974, Vol. 6, p. 286.

[10] Adam Smith, *An Inquiry Into the Nature and Causes of Wealth of Nations*. Reprinted from *Great Books of the Western World*, Chicago: Encyclopaedia Britannica, © 1952, 1990, Vol. 39, p. 142.

[11] Smith, op cit., p. 43.

[12] Alfred Marshall, *Principles of Economics*, London: MacMillan and Co., 1898, p. 126.

[13] Peter F. Drucker, *Post Capitalist Society*, New York, HarperCollins, 1993, pp. 36–37.

[14] Thomas S. Johnson, and Robert S. Kaplan, *Relevance Lost: The Rise and Fall of Management Accounting*, Boston: Harvard Business School, 1987, p. 9.

[15] Johnson and Kaplan, op. cit., p. 10.

[16] Johnson and Kaplan, op. cit., p. 11.

[17] Johnson and Kaplan, op. cit., p. 69.

[18] Johnson and Kaplan, op. cit., pp. 101–102.

[19] Johnson and Kaplan, op. cit., p. 111.

[20] John J. Coyle, Edward J. Bardi, and C. John Langley, Jr., *The Management of Business Logistics*, 5th edition, St. Paul, MN: West Publishing Company, 1992, p. 6.

[21] Joseph M. Juran and Frank M. Gryna, Jr., *Quality Planning and Analysis*, New York: McGraw Hill Company, 1980. Reproduced with permission of The McGraw-Hill Companies.

[22] Philip B. Crosby, *Quality Is Free*, New York: McGraw Hill Company, 1979. Reproduced with permission of The McGraw-Hill Companies.

[23] Reprinted from *Quality, Productivity and Competitive Position* by W. Edwards Deming by permission of MIT and The W. Edwards Deming Institute. Published by MIT, Center for Advanced Engineering Study, Cambridge, MA 02139. Copyright 1982 by the W. Edwards Deming Institute.

[24] Ibid., p. i.

[25] Philip J. Ross, *Taguchi Techniques for Quality Engineering*, New York: McGraw-Hill, 1988.

[26] Raghu N. Kackar, "Taguchi's Quality Philosophy: Analysis and Commentary, Quality Progress," December 1986, pp. 21–28.

[27] Tom Greenwood and Jim Reeve, "Process Cost Modeling," working paper, The University of Tennessee, Department of Accounting, Knoxville, TN, 1992.

[28] A. Nanni, Jr., J. R. Dixon, and T. Vollmann, "Integrated Performance Measurement: Management Accounting to Support the New Manufacturing Realities," *Journal of Management Accounting Research*, 1992, p. 2.

WHY SHOULD
ORGANIZATIONS BE RESPONSIVE?

There are various benefits of customer-responsive management. These benefits can be considered within the following four main categories:

- Those that improve the fit between the customer's need and what the organization delivers;
- Those that increase profits through customer retention;
- Those that increase profits by reducing costs;
- Those that make the organization more robust to changes.

Responsiveness Improves the Fit between Customer Need and Delivery

Product design would be simple if all people had the same needs. However, individuals have broadly varying needs. We do not have the same physical proportions, tastes, talents, family situations, experiences, or job, and thus our needs differ.

When a firm designs a product for the marketplace, it must develop a strategy for serving the market. Should it attempt to serve the market with one, three, or fifteen different products? The answer depends upon the diversity of customers' needs, the sensitivity of customers to an exact fit, and the cost of producing and distributing the additional inventory units. In some cases customers are not very sensitive to fit. The length of a man's tie, for example, can be adjusted when it is put on, and the current fad is for everyone to wear extra-large sweatshirts. In other cases, such as running shoes, fit is critical.

The mass-production shoe manufacturer, being acutely aware of the cost of adding stock, may decide to create a shoe that fits the average foot. Data may be collected and the size of the average foot determined. This approach seems logical, given that the firm believes that it is too expensive to produce multiple offerings and so must target the average customer. However, averages are not a very good predictor of fit.

Why Should Organizations Be Responsive?

Secretary of Labor Robert Reich has been quoted as saying that "Shaquille O'Neal and I average about 6 feet tall, but that is not very descriptive." (O'Neal is 7 feet 1 inch tall; Reich measures 4 feet 10 inches.) A shoe made to fit the average foot would fit very few people well. Figure 3.1 presents a range of foot sizes. It also shows a single offering labeled "medium." The difference between what is desired by customer 1 and the offering provided is the *lack of fit.* Lack of fit creates market and/or customer dissatisfaction.

The shoe firm that decides to manufacture only one size of shoe may be able to do well if it has no competition. But if it does, customers will tend to buy from firms that provide a better fit. Customers know that the advertising slogan that "one size fits all" actually means that few are fit very well. Dissatisfaction may lead the customer to consider other options available in the market. If the firm perceives a need to increase customer satisfaction to improve its competitive position, it may attempt to segment the market and provide two different offerings. This segmentation, as shown in Figure 3.2, increases customer satisfaction by increasing the number of customers who experience a reasonable fit. However, there still are customers who are not well served by the choices available.

For instance, consider customers 1, 2, and 3 shown in the Figure 3.2. Customer 1 can select either the small or large offering but will probably select the large size and wear additional socks. The small size is the best offering for Customer 2, who will also probably have to wear additional socks. Customer 3, on the other hand, will find the large size too small but may "make do" by not wearing any socks, by having the shoes stretched, or by enduring a long break-in period.

Most shoe companies have developed a more targeted strategy in which they offer a range of sizes. The range may be small, medium, and large or from sizes 6 to 14 in half-size increments. The more sizes offered, the better the fit.

When fit is very critical, many aspects must be considered. Should each size be offered in one width; in narrow, medium, and wide; or in increments from AAAA to EEEE? Even this approach would not be sufficient, as it considers only two dimensions. How about the other 16 standard dimensions, such as arch height, heel width, toe length, and so forth? There are also individual considerations such as bunions or individuals with feet that are of different sizes. As long as the shoe

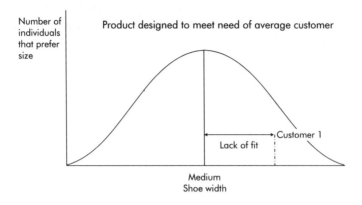

Figure 3.1. A single-offering model.

manufacturer adopts a mass-production philosophy to serving the market, it will be virtually impossible to identify all possible needs. Therefore the firm targets the markets it deems profitable and ignores trying to fit the rest. What is forgotten is that even the targeted markets are not fit perfectly. Even those customers who can adapt to standard sizes often need shoes to be stretched or broken in before they feel comfortable.

The customer-responsive approach recognizes that customers are not just looking for shoes but for shoes that fit. Instead of producing many different sizes, shoe manufacturers can develop a customer-responsive strategy in which they first interact with each customer to determine individual needs and then customize the delivery to that individual customer.

The paint industry has done this very effectively. Instead of trying to predict and produce all possible color options that customers could desire or only producing a limited selection of colors, they have devised a system whereby customers can select the color they want and have it mixed while they wait. The emphasis has been on helping diagnose customer needs. If the customer has a color he or she wants to match, there are spectrometers that will examine the color and calculate the pigment formula. There are charts showing which hues provide an attractive matching or contrasting effect. The benefit lies in helping the customers develop a desirable color scheme, not just in providing them

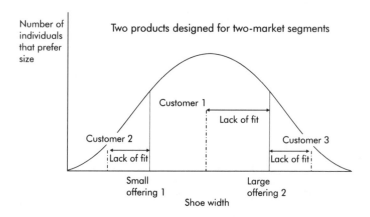

Figure 3.2.   A two-market-segment offering model.

with paint. Each paint store has the pigments necessary to provide a perfect fit for a wide range of colors. The hard part is not being able to produce the color the customer wants but helping the customer define what color he or she wants.

This same approach could be applied to shoes. Instead of focusing on the offering, attention could be directed to giving the customer better physical fit and more options (see Figure 3.3). One approach would be to allow individuals to go to a local store to have their feet measured. Their foot sizes could be captured in the form of a cast or as dimensions captured in a computer database. Instead of inventorying finished shoes, the manufacturer would store individual cast specifications or dimensions on the computer. When customers wanted a pair of new shoes, they would simply call the manufacturer, identify themselves, choose the desired style and material, and decide on the method of payment. The primary feature of this approach is that the shoe would be built using the customer's individual cast (last). The shoes could be sent directly to the customer, thus avoiding any distribution channel.

Consultants could likewise select either the offering approach or the customer-responsive approach. The mass-production model would have the consulting firm first complete studies and write reports for all types of corporate problems it would want to be able to address. When clients called, the firm could simply determine what report to give them. Alterna-

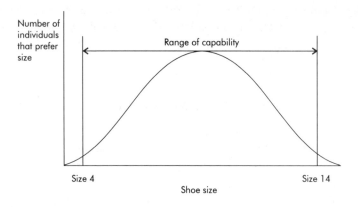

Figure 3.3. A responsive fit strategy.

tively, reports could be printed and distributed through bookstores and grocery stores. The customer-responsive approach, on the other hand, would have the consulting firm first diagnose the needs of each client and and then develop a solution specifically for each.

Both delivery strategies are valid. It does not matter whether the delivery is for a tangible product or an intangible service. It is simply a difference in the organization's orientation. The offering-oriented approach focuses on defining, producing, distributing, and promoting predefined offerings that it tries to sell in the marketplace. The customer-responsive approach focuses on individual customer needs. One creates value by producing products; the other accomplishes this by developing processes for responding to the needs of individual customers. The customers can go to the marketplace to compare offerings or call the firm they trust, explain their needs, and expect solutions. It is easier to provide a more effective solution when you understand such needs in advance. It is less of a hassle to call a firm you trust – one that already knows and understands your needs – than it is to do extensive comparison shopping.

When firms focus on offerings, each offering must be planned, produced, distributed, and promoted. Emphasis is on reducing the number of offerings to control cost. When emphasis is on designing flexible processes for responding to diverse needs, there is no need to restrict appeal to narrowly defined target markets. The firm can thus be more things to more people. Customer-responsive firms emphasize building relationships with customers. Relationships are built by providing better fit (delivery effectiveness) and reducing hassle. This introduces the second question: Why emphasize relationships?

Responsiveness Increases Customer Retention and Profits[1]

Customer loyalty has a profound effect on profitability. According to a study by Reichheid and Sasser, customer profitability increased every year for different types of businesses: credit cards, industrial laundry, industrial distribution, and auto service industries. For example, profitability from an average industrial customer was $45 the first year, $99 the second year, $121 the third year, $144 the fourth year, and $168 the fifth year.

This increase in profits is explained by several factors. There are no additional customer acquisition costs. (Once the customer has developed a rapport with and a trust in the provider, that customer begins to increase purchases and, in the case of credit cards, maintain higher balances.) The customer and the organization understand how to interact with each other, which reduces interaction costs. And a satisfied customer may make referrals to other potential customers. Finally, customers tend to continue to patronize organizations that they trust. For example, it costs a company offering credit cards approximately $51 to obtain a new customer, research his or her credit history, place the customer in its database, and issue a card.[1] New customers typically do not use a card as consistently as customers who have a well-established habit of using one. Or a customer who has confidence in an auto mechanic or physician probably will not go to the hassle of extensive price shopping but will instead continue with a provider that is known, understood, and trusted – even if there is a price premium for doing so.

The approximate value of a customer can be determined easily if the profitability of customers by year and the defection rate – the turnover of former customers being served by the busines – are known. The average life of a customer = $\frac{1}{\text{defection rate}}$. For example, if the average

---

1. This section is adapted from Frederick F. Reichheld and W. Earl Sasser, Jr., "Zero Defections: Quality Comes to Services," *Harvard Business Review*, September-October 1990, pp. 105–111.

annual customer defection rate is 50 percent, then the typical customer can be expected to have a two-year relationship with the business. If only 10 percent of the customers defect each year, then the typical relationship is ten years. The value of the customer will be the present value of the projected yearly profit rate over the expected length of the relationship. From such simple calculations, the value of a Domino's pizza customer in Montgomery, Maryland, can be estimated at more than $5,000 over the life of a ten-year franchise.[1]

Because customers become more profitable each year, the best determinant of profit is not sales but customer retention rate. For example, a 5 percent increase in customer retention would lead to a 40 percent increase in profits for an insurance brokerage, 30 percent increase for industrial laundry, and over 60 percent increase for credit card companies.

To grow, a firm needs to recruit new customers at a rate greater than its defection rate. By monitoring defection rates, new customer recruitment, and customer profitability by year, a firm has an excellent predictor of long-term profitability because the defection rate is an absolute measure. It is a composite of all attributes affecting customer satisfaction and loyalty. Customers that defect can be interviewed to determine the reasons for the defections. This is much easier than trying to determine the attributes of customer satisfaction, measuring those attributes, and using that information to project defections (or conquests). Also, existing customers are already defined and will probably be easier to interview than a general marketing sample.

To increase profits, a firm should place at least as much emphasis on decreasing customer defections as it does on making new sales. Terry Vavra has used the terms "relationship marketing" and "conquest marketing" to describe these two approaches.[2] Relationship marketing is focused on understanding and responding to current customers, whereas the emphasis in conquest marketing is on making first-time sales to new customers.

Few individuals would argue that firms should be less responsive or that responsiveness to individual customer needs increases customer retention and thus profits. The problem is that responsiveness is perceived by many as being desirable but too expensive. This belief is based on an almost blind faith in the ability of mass production to reduce costs. In reality, the opposite is true. Responsiveness may actually reduce costs if the organization is organized to be responsive.

Responsiveness Decreases Costs

In 1983, Taiichi Ohno, who rose from machining department manager to become the vice president of Toyota, was primarily responsible for the development of the Toyota production system. In the foreword to his book describing the Toyota production system, he summarized the essence of his 39 years of experience in the following words:

> We are now unable to sell our products unless we think ourselves into the very hearts of our customers, each of whom has different concepts and tastes. Today, the industrial world has been forced to master in earnest the *multi-kind, small-quantity production system.*
>
> The starting concept of the Toyota production system was, as I have emphasized several times, a thorough *elimination of waste.* In fact, the closer we came to this goal, the clearer became the picture of individual human beings with distinct personalities. There is no real substance to that abstract mass we call "the public." We discovered that industry has to accept orders from each customer and make products that differ according to *individual requirements.*
>
> All kinds of wastes occur when we try to produce the same product in large, homogenous quantities. In the end, costs rise. It is *much more economical to make each item one at a time.* The former method is the Ford production system and the latter is the Toyota production system. . . .
>
> Manufacturers and work places can no longer base production on desktop planning alone and then distribute, or push, them onto the market. It has become a matter of course for customers, or users, each with a different value system, to stand in the front line of the market-place and, so to speak, pull the goods they need, in the amount and at the time they need them.
>
> The Toyota production system, however, is not just a production system. I am confident it will reveal its strength as a management system adapted to today's era of global markets and high-level computerized information systems.[3] (Emphasis added.)

Responsive organizations follow Ohno's model; they interact with the customer, determine individual customer needs, and then produce the items needed by that individual customer. In fact, Toyota is now able to take custom orders and deliver the requested automobile in five days in Japan. Whereas Ohno used his definitions to define manufacturing management, customer-responsive management methods are not limited to manufacturing – they can be applied to all activities.

Ohno did not claim (nor is it claimed here) that responsiveness is always a lower cost alternative than the traditional Ford approach to mass production.[2] Mass production is carefully planned to be the least expensive way to mass produce, in cookie-cutter fashion, large quantities of a standardized product. What we are suggesting is that customer-responsive management is the most cost-effective way to solve customer needs. Thus an objective cost-effectiveness comparison must include questions such as:

1. Are customers willing to pay more for solutions that better fit their needs?

2. Are customers willing to pay to avoid the hassles of having to learn about alternative approaches to solving the problem, selecting from among the offerings available, and resolving conflicts among different parts of the solution? This is one advantage of having a provider who will take total responsibility for a total turn-key solution.

3. Is it more cost effective to first find out what your customers want and then deliver a solution for their specific need or to try to predict what the market will want and define an offering that may or may not be accepted in the marketplace?

4. Is it more cost-effective to produce and deliver solutions to the well-defined needs of known customers or to produce generalized offerings, locate retailers willing to stock them, stock the retailers' shelves, and do sufficient promotion to entice potential customers to go to the retailers and seek out your offering?

5. Is it more cost-effective to teach each salesperson in each retail outlet throughout your market area to answer sales, technical, and service questions for customers or to have customers contact your customer assistance centers (where you have their records on file) for whatever help they need?

---

2. There are multiple ways of calculating cost. One is to simply look at the cost of producing 10,000 units deliverable as soon as they are manufactured. Another is to look at the cost of supplying 10,000 units to the marketplace over a period of time. Inventory carrying cost, for example, would not be considered in the first case where time is not a factor.

6. Who will be most effective in positioning your company to customers: sales clerks in many different retail stores throughout your market area or your own customer assistance centers staffed by individuals who have already built a relationship with your customers?

7. Is it more cost-efficient to expand by communicating with your existing customers and responding to more of their needs or by developing new offerings, new distribution channels, and new markets?

The purpose of presenting Ohno's premise in this chapter was not to explain the Toyota production system or to give an overview of its principles; it is discussed here to show that responsive, small-lot deliveries not only meet customer needs better but also reduce costs – even in traditional mass-production industries such as automobile manufacture. If it applies in automaking, should it not also apply in fields less well known for mass-production successes?

Customer-responsive management promises to enhance revenue and reduce costs. Furthermore, an even more important benefit is the ability to increase a firm's ability to respond appropriately to change.

Responsiveness Makes Organizations More Responsive to Competitive and Environmental Change

Toyota is not the only firm that recognizes the need to be responsive. In fact, responsiveness – known in manufacturing as *flexible manufacturing* – is based on a belief that the competitor that can read the market more quickly, manufacture a greater diversity of products, switch between products faster, make smaller lots profitably, and introduce new products faster will win the competitive battle.

Nissan's flexibility strategy is based on the "5 any principle": to make anything in any volume anywhere at any time by anybody. Nissan recognizes that it would cost about 20 percent more to build flexible production lines, but this additional cost would be recovered with the first changeover. Additional flexibility for Toyota cost around 10 percent, but allowed a 60 percent reduction in changeover costs.[4]

Using flexible manufacturing techniques, Fuji reduced the time it took to fill an order from three days to one and reduced their work force and inventory by a third while increasing their assortment to 8,000 varieties – a 300 percent increase. This total quality management (TQM) move toward flexibility was described in a *Fortune* article that suggested that manufacturing "follows an inevitable progression from quality (doing it right), through reliability (always doing it right), and only then to flexibility – adding variety and speed." In short, quality was just a start; now flexibility needs to be addressed.

Flexibility is the operational requirement for organizations to be responsive. Flexibility involves the capability to do many different things. To achieve responsiveness requires that the flexibility is always oriented toward the customer. Flexibility allows an organization to interact with customers in many ways instead of restricting it to a limited number of offerings. Responsiveness also means that the flexible organization actually views itself as a service company able to respond to individual customer needs, whether they can be satisfied by an off-the-shelf product or a service.

Summary

Responsive organizations are able to provide higher levels of customer satisfaction and customer retention, decreased costs, and greater responsiveness to competitive and environmental change. Responsive organizations tend to be more profitable. To be responsive, organizations must have the flexibility to be able to respond to change.

References

[1] Reprinted by permission of *Harvard Business Review*. An excerpt from "Zero Defections: Quality Comes to Services" by Frederick F. Reichheld and W. Earl Sasser, Jr., Issue 5 (September / October 1990), pp. 105–111. Copyright © by the President and Fellows of Harvard College. All rights reserved.

[2] Terry G. Vavra, *Aftermarketing: How to Keep Customers for Life Through Relationship Marketing*, Homewood, IL: Business One Irwin, 1992, pp. 9–17.

[3] From *Toyota Production System: Beyond Large-Scale Production* by Taiichi Ohno. English translation copyright © 1988 by Productivity Press, Inc., P.O. Box 13390, Portland, OR 97213-0390. (800) 394-6868. pp. xiv–xv.

[4] "Brace for Japan's Hot New Strategy," *Fortune*, Vol. 126, No. 6., September 21, 1992, p. 74. © 1992 Time Inc.

CHAPTER 4

CUSTOMER RESPONSIVENESS IS ACTIVITY BASED

We have contrasted the centralized planning of standard offerings with the process used to enable customer-responsive deliveries. At this point a look at planning of standardized offerings would include a description of the planning power beginning with forecasting and ending up with a total delivery process, including product design, product production process, distribution channels, and promotion of sales efforts. In contrast, we will describe the components that must be in place so that a customized delivery plan can be developed on the spot for each customer when he or she calls.

Organizational success occurs when work, workers, and suppliers are coordinated to accomplish the mission of the organization. Coordination consists of defining the purpose of the work, assigning workers to tasks, and determining if the purpose was accomplished. Without effective coordination, the organization is inefficient and nonresponsive.

During the third era, the product was the central focus of activity coordination. Management's responsibility was to plan, implement, and control the design, production, distribution, and promotion of the offering to the marketplace. In reality, the role of management is much broader. A product is only one method of delivering benefits to customers. As firms enter the fourth era, customer-responsive managers must begin to see their role as managing and coordinating all the activities required to create value for the customers, not just managing product-related activities.

Four Components of Every Activity

Whether product-oriented or responsive, work or play, any activity involves four steps. These steps, as shown in Figure 4.1, are:

- The event that triggers the activity;

Figure 4.1. The components of activities.

- The definition of the action that needs to be taken in response to the triggering event;
- The coordination of the defined actions;
- The delivery of the desired benefits.

An Event Triggers the Activity

Every activity is triggered by an event. This may be something as dramatic as a fire in a skyscraper or as routine as a meeting to review the firm's annual strategic plan. It may be as formal as the passing of a congressional mandate or as informal as a single customer asking the airline why his or her bag did not come down the conveyer with the other luggage. It may be external, as when a parent asks the child to take out the trash. It may be internal, as when the same child recognizes that the trash needs to be taken out. The event may also be triggered by time, such as the filing of income tax returns by April 15th. Formal or informal, dramatic or routine, internal or external, each activity is triggered by an event. There are several conditions that surround the event provide the motivation for the action. The motivation may be survival, profitability, market expansion, customer convenience, or some other goal.

Delivery units are the basic building blocks for providing benefits to the customer. Each unit has a knowledge base, tools, and facilities to perform in its area of competence. The element may be in-house or organized and operated by an independent organization. Ownership and location are not important; the key is that the delivery unit has the ability and capacity to deliver the desired benefit as needed and that the organizational effort required to dispatch and coordinate the delivery is minimized.

Capability refers to the unit's ability. It describes what the organization can do. The unit may be inventory in a distribution center, an intensive care unit at a hospital, a hazardous materials consultant, or an electrician. Capability typically is determined by the knowledge base, tools, and facilities available for use by the delivery unit.

Capacity is a measure of how much the delivery unit is able to do. This is determined by staffing schedules. These schedules may be work schedules, flight schedules, production schedules, schedules of store hours, hospital wing schedules, or hotel room schedules. Because the availability of capacity is scheduled, there is a relatively long lead time. Some organizations (e.g., airlines) pay their workers (e.g., pilots) to be on call, meaning they can be available to work within two hours if additional capacity is needed.

Coordination is the process of defining what is to be done, when it should be done, where it should be done, how much should be done, and what is expected of all parties involved. Coordination provides the structure so that individual delivery tasks are synergistic rather than conflicting. Coordination can be by plan, schedule, and control or by best-practice guidelines, dispatch, and monitoring.

Effectiveness is a term used to describe how well the delivery has met the individual customer's needs. When the delivery is effective, the customer's needs are met and the customer is satisfied. No matter how well the organization performs, the delivery is not effective if the customer's needs are not met or if the customer is not satisfied. Effective delivery requires two types of quality. First, there is diagnostic quality, which means how effective the organization was in discovering and understanding the customer's needs. This is different from responding to a customer's request. Customers may not know what they want. They may or may not recognize what they want until after they see it. To be truly effective, the organization must be able to interact with customers and diagnose their real needs. The burden of proof is on the provider. The second type of quality is determined by how well the actual delivery met the diagnosed need.

Efficiency is a term used to describe the organization's ability to organize resources so that effective delivery is accomplished with a minimum of resources. Excess inventory, wasted capacity, having to make the delivery a second time to get it right, unnecessary organizational complexity, and other activities that do not provide benefit to the customers are inefficient.

Cost effectiveness is a term for the balance between internal efficiency and external effectiveness. Effectiveness is a measure of how well the customer's needs were met. There is little value in benefit delivery that is effective but too expensive or ineffective but inexpensive. The organization needs to find the balance that provides the greatest value or "bang per buck" to the customer.

Activities can be classified by when events occur. If activities are planned before contact with individual customers, the firm is unilaterally defining its offering to the customer. If, on the other hand, the firm interacts with the customer to determine individual needs and then plans the delivery, it is responsive. For example, if a performer sings a preplanned concert, this represents an offering that the singer has planned for the audience. If, on the other hand, the performer seeks requests from the audience and then sings the requested songs, he or she is being responsive. In the first case, the singer unilaterally plans the concert and offers it to the audience for their approval. In the second case, the singer bilaterally interacts with the audience to determine their interests. The first case is easier to implement because the singer knows exactly what to expect; there are no surprises unless the singer incorrectly predicts the audience's tastes. The second case requires a much more versatile performer, but the resulting concert may better match the audience's tastes.

Table 4.1 is organized to show the difference between offering-based activities and responsive activities. (Although there are those that may say that era 3 was offering based and era 4 is responsive, this is not correct. The offering-based orientation was a result of the inflexibilities required by the highly specialized production lines thought to be necessary for mass production to occur. It was much more common even during era 2 for the guilds to produce armor, bread, or many other products to request.)

There may be a reluctance to think about events triggering actions because the concept seems reactive rather than proactive. This misses the point. Every action, proactive or reactive, is triggered by an event. These events provide the organization with a reason to respond.

The term "proactive" takes on very different meaning when it is associated with offering or responsive activities. For an offering-based firm, reactive activities are the result of poor planning. That is, the organization did not correctly understand some environmental, competitive, customer-related, or operational issue, and a crisis has occurred that must be reacted to. Proactive activities occur because the organization unilaterally decided to trigger the action at its pleasure and was not forced to respond to a crisis. Success in an offering-based organization is measure by the consistency between performance and plan. Success can

Table 4.1. A Comparison of Triggering Events for Offering-Based and Responsive Activities

Organizational Step	Offering-Based Activities	Responsive Activities
Triggering Event	Internal Action Proactive • Strategic Plan • Reporting Period • Organizational Study • Organizational Meeting Reactive Market Crisis Operational Crisis Environmental Crisis	Request by Customers (internal or external) Proactive • Firm has responded to this type of request before and has a formal protocol for guiding response Reactive • First time this type of request has been received and new protocol must be developed for guiding response

be achieved by better planning or by restricting the activities to those whose performance is in the delivery plan. A singer, for example, may feel very comfortable performing ten songs and absolutely refuse to sing any other selection or even give an encore. In corporate lingo, this would be stated as "you can't be all things to all people," "you must decide what business you want to be in," or "if you do it for one person, you must do it for everyone."

The terms "proactive" and "reactive" are used differently with responsive activities. If an individual drives up to his or her house and notices flames coming from the roof, this will trigger a reaction. It is a reaction because it has never occurred before, so the individual does not have a knowledge base for responding to the event. If the same event occurred to members of the fire department, they would make a proactive response. The fire department has a protocol in place for responding to fires. Its employees know what information is required to diagnose the need. If a new need occurs, however, the fire department does not have the luxury of refusing to respond; it has a commitment to meet the needs of its customers (the community). The only response is to follow the protocol that most closely approximates the situation and respond reactively to what is not covered by the protocol. Although firefighters react to new needs, their reactions are influenced by their extensive and ever-growing knowledge base.

Organizations that perform primarily offering-based activities learn by deciding what they need to know and conducting studies to learn it. Responsive organizations learn by experiencing and doing. Each time firefighters or singers encounter a new request, their actions are based on experience, that is, their knowledge of the desired delivery. The knowledge base can be formal or informal. If it is informal, then each individual gains experience by encountering new situations or by swapping "war stories." John Seeley Brown, director of the Xerox Palo Alto Research Center, has indicated that the most effective method of training field-service personnel is to facilitate communication between individuals so that the personnel with more experience can share their knowledge base and thought processes with less experienced individuals or individuals who have not yet encountered the same experience. This is reminiscent of mature hunters sitting around the campfire and telling what they did in specific situations. Although it may sound like swapping war stories, in reality it is conveying the logic or thought process that the person went through to diagnose the problems and develop an approach for resolving them.

A more formal approach is to capture the knowledge base so it can be retrieved as needed. This can be done by having a group of experienced, front-line people convey their knowledge so that it can be incorporated into an expert system. Expert systems can be paper based or computer based. It does not matter how the knowledge base is captured and communicated, only that it receives the constant review and modification of the experts – the front-line workers who are the experts.

There are basically two parts of the knowledge base: knowing how to interact with customers to diagnose needs and knowing how to interact with resources to organize and coordinate the delivery of benefits.

Expert systems are used to diagnose customer needs. If a routine request is received, an existing work-coordinating protocol is presented to the front-line worker. If new situations occur, the system is used to present similar protocols and to capture the response modifications. Later, the more experienced workers review the approach used and suggest changes so that the next time the situation is encountered, a protocol is already in place to guide the response.

The need for a diagnostic knowledge base consists of different approaches used to help customers express their needs. It may consist of a series of questions in which the response to one question determines the follow-up question. Another option is to perform a number of diagnostic tests. This method is used by physicians, auto mechanics, and computer help groups. In still other cases, it may consist of visualization tools or prototypes. Storyboards, sketches, presentations, and architectural models are all examples. Some methodologies work best when firms interact with individuals. Others work best with groups. For example, the information systems area is realizing major productivity gains by using joint application development (JAD) and rapid application development (RAD) methodology. Whatever the process, for whatever size group, the objective is the same: interaction with the customer, defining the need, and building a consensus among all parties.

The work coordination knowledge base is the methodology for organizing resources to deliver the desired solution. This knowledge base generally consists of knowing how to divide work up into tasks, identifying individuals capable of performing it, assigning the work, and monitoring activities to ensure that they are completed as needed. The method used to maintain the organizational knowledge base will determine how the organization will respond to the request.

The Definition of the Response

Once the decision to act is triggered, the response must be defined. There are basically three types of action that can be defined. These actions may address three types of situations:

1. One-time projects, such as the construction of a highway or the managing of a conference;
2. Mass-production activities, typified by the repetitive performance of standardized activities, such as the production of consumer packaged goods, the staging of a concert tour, or washing cars at the local car wash;
3. Customer-responsive activities, where there is wide variation in each request, such as a 911 monitoring and dispatching, consulting, FedEx shipping, or hospital emergency room activity.

Customer Responsiveness Is Activity Based

There is a major difference in how each of these activities is performed.

One-Time Projects. One-time projects are carefully defined to make sure that the need is well understood. Highway planners, for example, have a very elaborate process for defining highway needs and community preferences. Engineers will develop sketch plans that will be presented to community leaders for their response. The reactions from the leaders are used to develop a few preferred options. The preferred options are then presented to community groups at public hearings to glean additional input. The objective is to make sure that every possible opportunity is available to identify potential problem areas that should be considered. This is important because the project is performed only once and mistakes can be irreversible – in the case of construction projects, often literally locked in concrete. Once the project is defined, the engineers and technical personnel organize the work by task and define who should perform each task. The work is then scheduled with time lines drawn. The time lines indicate beginning and ending dates for each task and the level of effort (i.e., the person-hours by skill level) required for each task. Many organizations will develop three time lines showing the most *optimistic* (everything going perfectly without complications), the *expected* time requirements and most *pessimistic* (everything being complicated with unforeseen difficulties)

Recognizing that some tasks can be performed simultaneously but that others are dependent upon certain tasks being completed, firms identify the critical paths – those tasks that must be completed on schedule to achieve the desired completion date. Closest attention is given to those tasks on the critical path to identify any slippage that could delay completion. Once the project is complete, the project manager goes to another project. The project manager (e.g., the architect) may not be an expert in performing any specific task but should be an expert at the process of defining needs and building consensus for the plan. The implementation manager (e.g., the construction foreman) is an expert at identifying tasks, locating resources to perform the tasks, and coordinating work between the various groups to ensure that the work is completed on schedule, within the budget, and to meet the requirements. Architects, engineers, and meeting planners are specialists at defining needs and building consensus for the plan. Construction forepersons and project managers are specialists at implementation.

Project management is the management of one-time activities. There is also management of continuous activities. Continuous activities can be standardized or diverse activities. Mass-production management focuses on the continuous production of standardized activities. Customer-responsive management, which will be discussed later, describes the continual performance of diverse activities.

Mass-Production Activities. The continuous performance of standardized activities is similar to the planning process used for one-time activities, but there are several major differences. First, mass production requires mass marketing. The word "mass" is used because the market is so large that the individual client (i.e., the customer) is not identified. A one-time activity is usually performed for a specific community, company, or department. Mass markets are addressed differently. Solutions are defined, produced, and distributed in advance before contact with the individual customer. Thus customers' needs must be predicted based upon statistical samples of potential customers. The statistical generalization allows the creation of a market stereotype. The groups can be large (i.e., mass markets) or small (i.e., target markets). Stereotypes are often given names descriptive of the attributes of the stereotype for that market segment. One well-known segmentation called VALS™, developed by SRI International in California, is focused on values and lifestyles. This system includes groups such as the following:

- *Fulfilleds* are mature, responsible, well educated, open to new ideas and social change, home centered, high income, and practical.
- *Believers* are individuals of modest income, principle oriented and conservative and have lives centered on family, church, community, and nation.
- *Achievers* are high-income, status-oriented individuals who are politically conservative and respect the status quo.
- *Strivers* are low-income achievers who attempt to emulate those they admire.[1]

Although the statistics provide a convenient method of visualizing the market, they often mask an understanding of individual customers. For example, if a photographer took a picture of a deer just before it jumped over a fence and another after it cleared the fence, on average there should be a picture of a deer right over the fence. The success of the products planned using this method are dependent upon the accuracy of the prediction.

Closure is also more difficult. When the individual customers and their specific needs are identified, it is easy to tell when benefit delivery is complete. Was the delivery what the customer wanted? Without the individual contact, the mass-marketing firm can only use a surrogate to determine success. This surrogate is the number of sales. Unfortunately, the sales level does not let the firm know if the product meets the customer's need or if the customer simply selected what was convenient. The firm does not know if the customer is a repeat customer or a new customer trying the product on a one-time basis. In fact, in many cases the firm does not know if the order is a legitimate sale or one being made to a channel member (e.g., wholesaler, retailer) who is ordering in anticipation of sales but will return the item if it is not sold.

The second major distinction of mass production is that it is a continuous process. Therefore, not only are the tasks planned and scheduled, but each task is analyzed in detail to make the delivery as efficient as possible. Consequently, firms may make extensive studies to reduce production cost by a few cents per unit. Once the process is optimized, it is carefully controlled to make sure that there are no deviations from the optimum. Once the product, production, and distribution methods have been planned – a one-time project – operations are carefully controlled. The only monitoring that needs to be done is periodic (monthly or quarterly) review to make sure everything is operating according to plan.

Customer-Responsive Activities. Customer-responsive activities are a combination of project management and mass-production management. They involve adaptation of methods from both areas. Like project management, customers are identified and their specific needs are defined. The emphasis is on identifying and satisfying individual customer needs, not on performing for a generalized marketplace. Secondly, like mass production, the activity is continuous – not a one-time project. Therefore, every effort must be made to make the diagnosis and the delivery process as efficient and effective as possible. By "efficient," we mean that the activity is performed with a minimum of resources. By "effective," we mean that the delivery fits each individual customer's need. In fact, customer-responsive organizations are like project management firms except that they may have hundreds of different requests (i.e., projects) each day. Many of the requests will be similar, but there can be a wide variation among them. Therefore, customer-responsive management is like project management except that protocols are developed to guide responses to the continual flow of requests.

Just as with the coordination of a one-time project, the role of customer-responsive management is to define the customer's need interactively and develop a customized delivery plan to meet it. There are, however, several major differences that make customer-responsive management different from project management.

1. *Projects are smaller.* An ambulance call or a second-day UPS pickup is a much smaller effort than building a bridge or civic coliseum. The smaller the project, the less time and money are available for detailed diagnosis and planning. Therefore, customer-responsive organizations must have processes in place to diagnose needs and develop customized delivery plans quickly and effectively.

2. *Customer requests are often more similar.* Project management often works with major, one-of-a-kind projects such as bridges and highways. Customer-responsive organizations, on the other hand, have many similar requests with varying levels of differences. A hospital emergency room, for example, can expect a large number of broken arms, cases of the croup, heart attacks, and major injuries each night. Many delivery plans are similar, but there will be unique characteristics of each one. It is the ability to respond to these unique features that makes the delivery effective. When projects are totally unique, each must be planned uniquely. When there is often similarity among many different projects, firms build protocols for addressing them while allowing front-line workers to respond to new encounters and make modifications as necessary.

3. *Lead time is typically shorter.* Major projects often have very long time lines between definition and delivery. Customer-responsive organizations, such as fire departments, software support firms, customer service organizations, and transportation services are expected to provide just-in-time responses each time a customer calls.

Customer Responsiveness Is Activity Based

Customer-responsive organizations, then, are knowledge based rather than plan based. Firms are expected to apply their knowledge to interactively diagnose individual needs and develop customized delivery plans on a just-in-time basis. If the organization has an informal knowledge base, it will respond to a customer request by assigning a knowledgeable person to the task. Where the knowledge base is informal (i.e., collected and retained in the minds of individuals), knowledge-based management is accomplished by assigning people to tasks based on their training. Some individuals, for example, may be more experienced with transmission repair, mainframe operating systems, tax questions, timber depletion, or allergies. Once the knowledgeable person is assigned, it is then up to that individual to apply his or her personal knowledge base and determine what needs to be done. When the knowledge base is informal, the organization's capacity to respond to each type of need is limited by the number of people trained in each area.

Where the knowledge base is more formalized, a different approach can be used. The purpose of a formalized knowledge base is to make itself available to all individuals within, and often outside, the organization. Unless the knowledge is captured, it will only be available to those who have personally experienced it or learned it. The captured knowledge base becomes a list of "best practices" to guide responses to requests. Fortunately, many requests are similar, but many have slight differences that can dramatically change the way the organization responds. For example, if there is a school fire, will the proactive response be different if the fire occurs at rush hour? On July 4? On the night of the championship basketball game at the school? The knowledge base must allow for situation specific conditions. It is the *conditional* nature of the knowledge base that enables the organization to be responsive to a diversity of needs. It is the conditional nature of the knowledge base that allows the fire department to always respond instead of responding with "we have not been trained in that type of fire" (the firefighting equivalent of "I am sorry, but we do not serve that market segment").

The knowledge base is a *guideline* because it is always modifiable by the front line when new conditions arise. It recognizes that in responsive organizations new conditions are encountered by the front line, and it is the front line that must learn and update the knowledge base. It is the ability to modify the guidelines to fit new conditions that allows the firm to be a learning organization. It is the ability to continue learning that allows the organization to be responsive to a variety of needs.

The phrase "best practice" is used to convey the notion that the knowledge base is proactive rather than reactive. These guidelines are not prototypes nor is their management casual. Although best-practice guidelines may be created initially in response to a new situation, they are evaluated continually to make sure that they always reflect the organization's most current understanding of the best way of responding to each request.

The word "guidelines" is plural here because the organization is there to serve customers, not to discipline customers to accept the organization's offerings. This is a major difference between customer-responsive organizations and production organization. The responsive organization builds a knowledge base to respond to diverse needs of customers. The focus is on each customer and his or her needs. The firm focused on mass production is in business to produce an offering. Even though production organizations research the customers, the purpose is to determine how to get them to buy an offering. Therefore, the responsive organization is expected to have the ability to make a variety of responses to a variety of customer requests. When a single offering is produced, workers can be trained to perform the task by rote. When a wider variety of responses is required, then there need to be guidelines or protocols to direct responses. A hospital, for example, will have best-practice guidelines or protocols for each type of diagnosis. We use the phrase "conditional best-practice guidelines" and the word "protocol" interchangeably. "Protocol" is shorter, but sometimes "conditional best-practice guidelines" is used to emphasize the concept.

There are two separate customer protocols. The first protocol is used to diagnose the need. The second protocol is used to define and coordinate the delivery plan. The primary purpose of the diagnostic protocol is to make sure that all key conditions are identified. It will consist of questions or tests to determine key conditions.

Once the key conditions have been identified, a customized individual delivery plan can be developed. Figure 4.2 illustrates a sample decision-tree protocol for an emergency room patient who has had an acute myocardial infarction (a heart attack). In this decision tree, there is a major first condition. Is the patient a candidate for an anticlotting drug? If the patient is a candidate for an anticlotting (thrombolytic) drug,

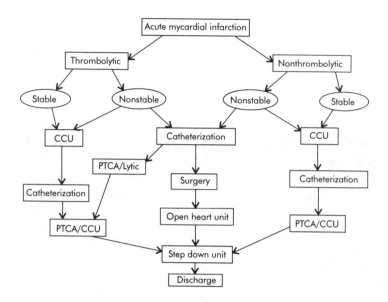

Figure 4.2. An acute myocardial infarction decision tree.

he or she may be given heparin until the physician arrives. Then the patient may be given t-PA or streptokinase, depending on the results of the EKG and his or her age. If this stabilizes the patient, he or she may be sent to a coronary care unit (CCU) or to the catheterization lab for a heart catheterization. The catheterization may indicate the need for a angioplasty (the use of a small balloon inside the artery) or heart bypass in the open heart unit (OHU). Afterwards the patient will be sent to a step-down area to receive less intensive care until he or she has stabilized and is ready to go home.

Once the conditions have been identified and the delivery plan selected, the individual tasks are identified. The individual tasks also have protocols. Table 4.2 shows a sample procedural protocol for an outpatient cardiac catheterization, including a description of support activities to prepare and follow through after the procedure. This procedural protocol is presented in a database format. At a minimum, a protocol must include the following six elements:

• A list of tasks necessary to perform a desired benefit delivery;

Table 4.2. An Outpatient Cardiac Catheterization Protocol.

Protocol ID	Task ID	Skill	Description	Prior Task	Next Task	Condition	Capacity Required (sec)	Lead Time (sec)
00125	1	family	NPO (nothing by mouth)		2		600	
00125	2	HCP	obtain consent	1	3			
00125	3	orderly	shave & prep R&L groin and R arm	2	14			
00125	4	lab tech	draw two blood samples	2	5			
00125	5	lab	complete blood count (CBC)	4	14			3,600
00125	6	lab	SMA-7 (blood profile)	4	14			3,600
00125	7	lab	PT	4	14			3,600
00125	8	lab	PTT	4	14			3,600
00125	9	lab	EKG	4	14			
00125	10	nurse	record height & weight	2	14		90	
00125	11	nurse	mark pulse with pen—L&R dorsalis pe	2	14		60	
00125	12	nurse	mark pulse with pen—posterior tibial	2	14		30	
00125	13	nurse	Void	2	14		30	
00125	14	RN	Valium—10 mg po	17-30 min.	18	<60 years old	120	
00125	15	RN	Valium—5 mg po	17-30 min.	17	>=60 years old	120	
00125	16	RN	500 cc D5W-IV@50 cc/hr in L arm catheterization	17-30 min.	17		300	
00125	17	nurse		upon reqst	18		3600	
00125	18	cath lab		17	19			14,400
00125	19	nurse		18+2 hrs.	33			
00125	20	nurse		18	23	if active and unable to lie flat		
00125	21	nurse		18+15 min (inc)	22		120	
00125	22	nurse		22+2 hrs.	23		120	
00125	23	nurse		22	32			
00125	24	nurse	check vital signs, BP, foot pulse, and cath.	23+QID	32		120	
00125	25	nurse	notify MD	18	32	if unusual bleeding, swelling, pain, absent pulse or cold extremity	120	
00125	26	RN	Empirin #3. 1 tab q 3-4 hrs. PRN	18	32	if pain and not allergic	60	
00125	27	RN	Darvon plain 65 mg. 1-2 caps q 4 hr. PR	18	32	if pain and allergic	120	
00125	28	card tech	routine EKG	18+4 hrs.	32		90	
00125	29	RN	insert straight catheter PRN	18=<4hrs.	32	if bladder distention	300	
00125	30	nurse	Compazine 10 mg. PO or IM PRN	18=<4hrs.	32	if nausea	60	
00125	31	MD or PA	be seen by MD or PA		33		300	
00125	32	MD	discharge patient	32				

HCP = Health care professional (MD, PA, RN); RN = Registered Nurse; Nurse = RN or Licensed Practical Nurse (LPN)

- The skill level (e.g., type of person, department, organization, or machine) required to perform the task;
- The event that triggers each task;
- The time window in which the task must be performed (i.e., the next dependent task or time after prior task);
- The conditions under which the task is required;
- The capacity requirements and lead time required to perform each task.

In the sample protocol shown in Table 4.2, steps 14 and 15 are age-based conditions, and steps 26 and 27 are pain-based conditions. Step 25 is based on complications such as infection, hemorrhage, or shock. There also are additional protocols that are appropriate if the patient has complications such as hemophilia, diabetes, or AIDS.

It is advantageous to know the approximate amount of time required to perform each task. The listing can give optimistic, expected, and pessimistic times required. This information can be used for scheduling capacity requirements. It is also helpful to note any lead times required to perform a procedure. For example, task 4 in Table 4.2 requires only a few minutes for the lab technician to draw the blood, but it may take an hour or more for the lab to return the results. This information is necessary for efficient scheduling of subsequent tasks.

Plans, Contingency Plans, and Conditional Best-Practice Guidelines. The following paragraphs will clarify the distinction between plans and protocols.

A *plan* is a detailed list of actions that need to be taken to accomplish a desired goal. For example, if a person desires to go from Knoxville, Tennessee, to Seattle, Washington, he or she will develop a trip plan that includes the route; the departure date; the vehicle to be used; and methods for paying for fuel, lodging, and meals while en route.

A *contingency plan* is a detailed list of actions that need to be taken to accomplish a desired goal. For example, an individual may develop one travel plan that will be followed if he or she makes the trip in January and a contingency plan that will be followed if the trip is postponed until July.

A *protocol* is a *process* for creating a *plan*. A protocol is followed by the American Automobile Association (AAA) to develop travel plans for individual members. The diagnostic part of the protocol begins with asking key questions such as origin, destination, and desired stop-off points. Also important are questions about desires for the most direct route, the most scenic route, or the fastest route. There may also be a protocol for identifying threatening weather patterns or scheduled highway construction. Once the key conditions are defined, a customized plan can be developed. Again, there is a protocol for designing the detailed travel plan. If the scenic route is desired, does the member want natural, historic, scientific, or other sights? How far is the person willing to deviate from the route to see a sight? How important is highway grade? A traveler pulling a travel trailer, for example, may want to avoid the Rockies.

Protocol development can be a daunting experience. It must be evolutionary. As each new request is received, it either is covered by an existing protocol or not. If not, new tasks must be added for the new conditions. There is often no time to review the protocol when a need is encountered, but periodically each protocol will be reviewed to see if steps need to be changed to make it more effective. Protocol development must be incremental.

Conditional best-practice guidelines or protocols specify the processes required for diagnosing needs and developing customized delivery plans. When all conditions are defined, a conditional protocol becomes a plan. A plan is a conditional protocol in which all conditions are defined. Before a plan can be created, all conditions must be defined. If there is a limited number of undefinable conditions, a contingency plan can be developed for each undefined condition.

The key difference between mass marketing and customer responsiveness is how the conditions are identified. Mass marketers do not interact with individual customers but rather with survey groups of consumers to identify potential market segments. These market segments are statistically generalized. Plans are then made based on the conditions that are predicted to meet the needs of these generalized markets. Unless reality exactly matches predicted conditions, the goals will not be realized. The objective is to maximize profit from the production and distribution of offerings.

Customer-responsive management interacts with individual customers to determine conditions specific to a particular customer's need at a specific point in time and develops a customized delivery to solve that need. The objective is to maximize organizational yield by creating value for the customer. Customers value solutions that meet their individual needs.

When new situations are experienced in a responsive organization, the response developing a new protocol or modifying an existing one. There is no time for this task to be given to a planning committee. The front-line worker must develop (or modify) a protocol on the spot.

For example, in the heart-attack decision tree in Figure 4.2, there are two conditions: those where medication to dissolve the clot is called for and those where it is not. This assumes that all heart attacks are caused by clots. A particularly astute physician, however, might encounter the rare case where a young mother has a heart attack following childbirth. In a few rare cases, a mother with lupus (autoimmune syndrome) may have a heart attack when the immune system response is amplified as part of the uterine purging that occurs after delivery. In the case of lupus, the body's immune system attacks its own body tissue, destroying it just as if the blood supply had been obstructed by a clot. Hopefully, the physician will develop a new protocol on the spot based on his or her extensive experience handling other autoimmune patients.

When new protocols are added (or when a deviation from a protocol has been used), there should be a method for capturing not only the new protocol but its results. By capturing the results of the innovation, these can be analyzed and added to the best-practice guidelines if they were effective. It is the judicious use and measurement of best-practice guidelines that makes the organization a learning organization. It is the dynamic development of best-practice guidelines that keeps the organization flexible in responding to new needs and in making continual improvements to the process as new techniques and technologies develop. Any time a guideline is modified or developed, automatic monitoring begins.

Because the front-line worker is under the gun to resolve the need, it is not sufficient to provide access only to the formal, organizational knowledge base. The front-line worker must also have access, on an as-needed basis, to coworkers who can help him or her think through the response to the new situation. In responsive organizations, the knowledge base should allow the front-line worker to handle the vast majority of the requests, but when special situations arise there should always be someone this worker can turn to for technical support.

Table 4.3 summarizes the definition stage for offering-based and response-based activities.

Once the response has been defined, whether by plan or conditional

Table 4.3. A Comparison of Response Definitions for Offering-Based and Responsive Activities

Organizational Step	Offering-Based Activities	Responsive Activities
Defining response	Define needs of market groups by: • Surveying samples of customers to identify their needs • Developing stereotypes for each target market Develop plans based on stereotype condition to operationalize production, distribution, and promotion Operate according to plans: • Perform planned activities • Avoid unplanned activities • Knowledge base developed by need to know – planners define need, workers trained in what they need to know • Employees trained according to plan	Interact with individual customers to define needs Develop customized delivery plan for each delivery Use protocols to respond to familiar requests – develop new responses to new requests Knowledge generated as new problems encountered Capture knowledge as new responses are developed Constant review of protocols (peer review) Knowledge base dissemination by war stories and information systems Support front line as they develop responses to needs Front line active in experiential learning and creating knowledge base

best-practice guideline, it is time to assign the work to the various delivery units responsible for delivery. If the task is to be performed by one person, and if that person also received the request, coordination is not necessary. For example, if a customer asks a Home Depot clerk where to find rope or light bulbs and the clerk knows this information, there is no need to coordinate the response with other employees. But when the customer wants a customized home built, there are many different tasks to be performed by many different organizations. Just as a general contractor needs to coordinate all the tasks and groups involved in constructing a home, so customer-responsive activities must be integrated (i.e., all groups must work toward a common delivery plan) and each task must be coordinated (i.e., the work is scheduled and tracked).

The Coordination of Activities

Coordination consists of assigning work to workers; making sure they have the necessary materials, facilities, and tools to perform the work; and establishing time windows for accomplishing the work. Once the work has been assigned, it needs to be monitored to ensure that tasks are on schedule and performed as needed.

Coordination can be deterministic ("best way") or responsive. "Scheduling" typically is the term used to describe the deterministic method of coordination. "Dispatching" refers to the responsive approach to coordination. Dispatching can also be viewed as just-in-time (JIT) scheduling. These two methods of coordination are dramatically different as can be seen with two illustrations.

The Scheduling Model. *Scheduling* is the process used when all activities have long lead times. Scheduling is a method of coordinating lead-time conflicts. Scheduling begins with the master production schedule (MPS) that "details exactly what end products a company must manufacture or assemble, and when the customers need them."[2] Once the production plan is established, the materials requirement plan (MRP) is developed. An MRP is "a decision-making technique that is used to determine how much material to purchase and when to purchase it."[3]

The schedule determines when each task is to be performed, who does it, and how much is to be done. These schedules are used to coordinate purchasing of supplies and, ultimately, staffing. The lead time is dependent on the amount of time necessary to obtain the raw materials and to do the scheduling.

Scheduling provides certainty and predictability. Individuals can look at their schedules and know what they can expect to be doing in the future. Once the overall schedule is available, individuals know what is expected of them and they can develop their own personal schedules. Everyone knows when work will be done. Unfortunately, scheduling also has major disadvantages. Scheduling can inhibit responsiveness for the following reasons:

1. *Scheduling takes time.* When a number of interdependent tasks need to be performed, it takes time to consider all possible scheduling combinations necessary to avoid conflicts.

2. *Scheduling creates inflexibility and time delays.* Scheduling works well as long as all conditions are known in advance and are static. If something happens that necessitates changing one part of the schedule, every other part of the schedule must be changed.

3. *Scheduling makes it difficult to combine different work priorities.* Physicians, for example, have difficulty scheduling regular patients if they must also respond to emergency calls. How does an automobile-repair center combine emergency repairs and scheduled repairs?

4. *Scheduling makes an organization inflexible.* As long as conditions remain relatively static or change according to forecast, scheduling works well. But imagine a fire department that works by schedule. All subscribers must submit their requests to the scheduler at least ten days before the beginning of the month if the response is to be included on the monthly plan.

5. *Scheduling makes an organization unresponsive.* Consider a transit system that carefully defines all bus runs down to the fraction of a minute. All buses are coordinated so that they arrive at interchange points at exactly the right time. Schedules are published. Everything about the system can be scheduled and optimized, but riders complain that buses do not travel when and where they need to go. If a passenger has a special need, there is little flexibility to bend the schedule.

Customer Responsiveness Is Activity Based

But what is the alternative to scheduling? The answer is dispatching.

The Dispatching Model. The dispatching method is very different from scheduling. Dispatching is a JIT approach to the coordination of activities. Perhaps the best way of describing the difference between scheduling and dispatching is to contrast two familiar modes of transportation: transit systems and taxis.

Transit bus routes are planned very carefully. After extensive study of travel patterns and geography, buses are scheduled. Schedules that contain plans of the exact minute when the bus should be at each stop are published. Bus riders must become familiar with transit schedules if they want to know what the bus companies offer. Performance is measured by how well actual operations conform to the schedule.

Taxis, on the other hand, are dispatched. Cab availability is scheduled. That is, the cab company will schedule capacity (i.e., the number of vehicles and drivers that will be available to provide service). Cab availability is all that is known at the beginning of the day. Then customers begin to make requests. If the request is made by phone, the dispatcher has a protocol to follow for determining which cab to dispatch for the trip. Other requests may be made when a passenger hails a cab on the street or walks up to a cab waiting at a stand or hotel. In this case, the cab driver notifies the dispatcher that he or she is working and not available for dispatch. In still other cases, the company may have standing orders to pick up flight crews, school children, or mail every day at predetermined times. Standing orders are given to the dispatcher, who dispatches a cab when the work is to be done. Regardless of how the request is made, an available cab is dispatched to serve that customer. Once the cab is dispatched, it is totally responsive to the needs of that individual customer. Once that customer's needs are served, the cab driver notifies the dispatcher that he or she is again available for a dispatch.

Lead time is the time between resource commitment and delivery completion. Commitment can be in the form of a schedule or by dispatch. However it is done, commitment occurs when the organization decides to do something and assigns the resources to do it. Once the commitment is made, all other groups affected make their plans based upon the commitment.

The *flexibility* of the organization is limited during this lead time. To increase flexibility, the organization must reduce lead time between commitment and delivery. Because so many tasks are integrated, any change during lead time can require redoing the entire schedule.

Dispatching minimizes lead time. This occurs because resources are committed on a JIT basis.

Scheduling is necessary when lead times are long, as was the case when transportation was slow, coordination was by paper flow, and communication was difficult. In the era of overnight delivery, interactive information systems, and mass customization, the planning and scheduling process often is the major cause of long lead times. When this condition exists, the primary constraint to improved customer responsiveness is the management method used to define and coordinate work.

This does not mean that dispatched trips are not predictable or that dispatch patterns should not be studied. The distinction is that studies of dispatches are done to locate and schedule capacity, whereas scheduling studies are done to assign work and to commit resources to tasks. Rural Metro, an ambulance company, regularly studies the location of response sites by time of day and day of week. This information is incorporated into the best-practice guidelines. When an ambulance has completed a call, it needs to know where to wait for the next call. (This is the last item in their best-practice guidelines.) It may be assigned to locate at certain intersections during the morning and afternoon rush hours, near youth athletic sites after school, or near the night-life districts on weekend nights. The purpose for staging the ambulance in these locations is to reduce response time.

Table 4.4 summarizes the coordination stage for offering-based and response-based activities.

The Impact of Activity Coordination Method on Organizational Structure. There is a major difference between the ways in which scheduled and responsive activities are organized. The transit and cab examples provide familiar examples. Scheduled systems require extensive planning. First there are extensive studies to determine demand patterns, changes in land-use planning, building construction patterns, and any other factors that will affect ridership. Next, extensive public hearings are conducted to make sure that all possible community interests are identified. Then routes are designed based upon predicted travel patterns.

Table 4.4. A Comparison of Activity Coordination for Offering-Based and Responsive Activities

Organizational step	Offering-based activities	Responsive activities
Activity coordination	Work is defined	General level of activity is predicted
	Work is divided into steps or tasks	Capacity (people, facilities, tools) are scheduled
	Tasks are scheduled	
	Resources are scheduled to perform tasks	Work requests are queued according to priority and critical path
	Success is measured by conformance to plan and schedule	Work is dispatched to resources

Transfer locations are identified. Schedules are developed to minimize waits at transfer sites and to arrive at popular destinations at desired times. Make-up time is built into each schedule so that drivers can get back on schedule if they encounter unusual conditions such as congestion or construction. Drivers are then given the opportunity to bid on routes based on seniority. The route selections are typically valid for six months or more. Drivers operate in strict accordance with the route schedules. Supervisors check operations to make sure that buses arrive at each stop according to schedule. Schedules are published that list the time each bus will be at each stop during the day so that customers can obtain schedules and understand the service that the bus company offers. Theoretically, the extensive planning process ensures that the buses are operated on the routes that are optimum for the population as a whole.

Where travel needs are very stable and predictable, the scheduled system works well. For other than routine commuter trips, however, the bus is not responsive to the individual traveler. The reason most people give for not using mass transit is that it does not go "when and where I want to go." It is also a hassle to learn schedules and routes. The private automobile, on the other hand, is responsive to individual users' needs.

To many individuals, this responsiveness justifies the hassle of congestion and parking and the expense of operating a car. Like mass marketing, mass transit makes an offering that gives the customer only one option: acceptance or rejection of the offer.

Responsive transportation is dispatch based. Planning studies are used to forecast capacity requirements so that capacity can be scheduled and staged. Work on the other hand is dispatched. Work is assigned in response to individual customer requests. Dispatched activities are unpredictable and must be monitored continually to determine their effectiveness and efficiency. Dispatched activities are evaluated on the basis of effectiveness in meeting customer needs and operating efficiency. Dispatched activities are coordinated by the continual interaction among customer, worker, and dispatcher. Dispatched activities require the continual flow of information between each of these parties. Drivers must report when work is complete to notify the dispatcher when they are ready for additional work. Dispatchers must be aware of customer needs and the availability of cabs in order to assign tasks. Drivers must interact with customers to determine travel needs. Communication is continual. Dispatched activities are assigned task-by-task on a JIT basis.

Scheduled activities by definition cannot be responsive. Success of such activities is measured by conformance to plan and schedule, not by the responsiveness to customer request. Once the schedule is completed, commitments can be made. Changes cannot occur within the scheduled period without disrupting the schedule. Some organizations develop "work arounds" for situations in which reality does not match the schedule. Special groups are frequently organized to expedite or make other changes necessary to adapt the schedule to reality.

Even with such adjustments, however, scheduled activities cannot be fully responsive. The ability of any organization to respond can be determined by the time required to place an activity into the work schedule. When multiple tasks must be performed by multiple groups, responsiveness is limited by the time required to get the work on each group's work schedule plus the time required for the schedulers in each group to coordinate the schedules. Because dispatching is done on a task-by-task approach, a new task can be inserted into a dynamic dispatch list at any time. The dispatch list is continually prioritized and dispatched to the next available delivery unit.

Customer Responsiveness Is Activity Based

For a firm to be totally flexible in responding to individual customers, the firm must develop three things:

- A process for interacting with individual customers and defining their individual needs;
- Conditional best-practice guidelines for defining how the organization will respond to various types of requests. It is the conditional best-practice guidelines that allow the response to be customized to individual customers' situation-specific needs;
- A dynamic dispatching system that allows work to be assigned as needed by the customer. It is the dispatching of work that provides JIT assignment of work to resources.

The Delivery of Desired Benefits

Just as there are deterministic and responsive ways to define and coordinate deliveries, there are deterministic and responsive ways to make deliveries. The deterministic firm uses channels or highly structured systems, whereas the responsive firm uses networks.

The deterministic firm develops a plan. The plan includes not only the product design but also the channel that will be used to deliver the product to the customer. Figure 4.3 illustrates one possible distribution channel. Where there are multiple market segments, the firm may elect to have multiple distribution channels as shown in Figure 4.4.

The horizontal blocks are not named in Figure 4.4 because many different intermediaries (e.g., carriers, distribution centers, wholesalers, and retailers) are part of the channel. In this model, there are different channels for different markets (e.g., chain groceries, convenience stores, vending machines, cafeterias, and campus bookstores). It is not the number of channels that is important but rather the need to establish different organizations to respond to different needs. When organizations do not have the flexibility to respond to a wide variety of needs, a different system must be established to meet each type of need. This makes it very expensive to respond to new markets. Once the distribution system is designed, each channel member knows what to expect and begins to plan and schedule activities according to the monthly forecast, whether provided by the manufacturer or by the channel member.

The responsive firm tends to build networks of resources that it can call upon as needed. The 911 desk described earlier has a network

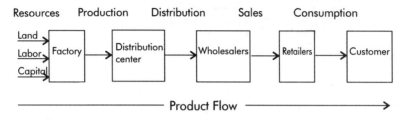

Figure 4.3. A deterministic, single-channel distribution system.

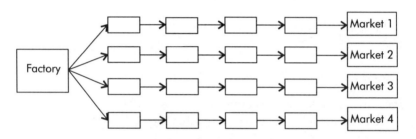

Figure 4.4. A deterministic, multichannel distribution system.

of resources that it can call upon as needed. Some calls may need animal control personnel or other hazardous materials experts, whereas others may need a SWAT team, wreckers, fire personnel, police, or an ambulance. The responsive network delivery system is illustrated in Figure 4.5.

The customer-responsive firm is able to put together a large combination of resources according to conditional best-practice guidelines to respond to a wide range of needs. In some cases, the delivery path may involve only one or two resources. In other cases, hundreds of resources may be used in the delivery. Resources become part of the network when a relationship is established, when capabilities are known, and when these capabilities become integrated into one or more best-practice guidelines. The relationship begins when there is a way to assign and monitor work. The key concept to remember is that there is an *infinite* number of paths and relationships in the network.

Table 4.5 summarizes the benefit delivery stage for offering-based and response-based activities.

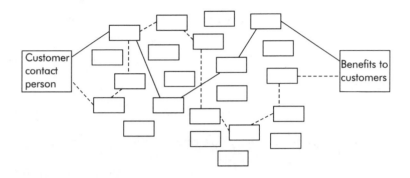

Figure 4.5. A responsive network delivery system.

Summary

Every activity consists of four parts. The first is an event that triggers the activity. Whether these events are internal or external, formal or informal, dramatic or routine, these events provide the motivation for the organization to respond. Second, there is a definition of the action or actions that should be taken in response to the event. The request may present a new problem never encountered before or may be for a predictable response. Frequent responses can be guided by conditional best-practice guidelines. New responses are captured to become part of the organizational knowledge base. Third, there is the coordination of the defined actions in response to the event. Coordination may be done by scheduling the activities prior to customer contact or by dispatching the resources once specific needs are identified. Finally, the desired benefits are delivered to the customer.

Predetermined activities are different from customer-responsive activities. Activities are predetermined if the detailed delivery plan is developed before contact with the individual customer, whereas customer-responsive activities are developed by interacting with the customer. For this reason, care must be taken not to confuse market research sampling with individual customer contact. For instance, a firm may survey samples of customers to learn buyer behavior and customer preferences so it knows what the firm must do to "sell" the customer. In contrast, a customer-responsive organization needs to interact with each individual

Table 4.5. A Comparison of Benefit Deliveries for Offering-Based and Responsive Activities

Organizational step	Offering-based activities	Responsive activities
Benefit Delivery	Emphasis is on operating according to plan. Diversity of needs or offerings addressed by building different systems and/or organizations to handle each need. For example, trucking companies may have separate TL, LTL, and courier divisions.	Emphasis is on identifying and organizing a network of resources that can be dynamically assigned a wide range of tasks on an as needed basis.

customer so delivery can be customized to fit the individual customer needs.[1] Flexibility permits customer responsiveness.

In some cases there are valid reasons for not customizing individual deliveries – especially when the product is a commodity or where there is a long lead time in producing the product. However, to the degree that inflexibilities are institutionally caused by organizational structure, the inflexibility is self-inflicted. When inflexibilities have natural causes, competitors will not be able to gain a responsive advantage. When inflexibilities are self-inflicted, competitors will develop the ability to be responsive and have a competitive advantage.

How then do organizations organize their interactions with customers to become more responsive? Specifically, what organizations demonstrate many of these qualities? By knowing how these organizations respond to meet the needs of their individual customer, it will be possible to further understand and apply these principles in other organizations.

---

1. For an outstanding reference on capturing data to customize relationships, see Terry G. Vavra, *Aftermarketing: How to Keep Customers for Life Through Relationship Marketing*, Homewood, IL: Business One Irwin, 1992.

References

[1] J. Paul Peter and Jerry C. Olson, *Consumer Behavior and Marketing Strategy*, Homewood, IL: Irwin, 1993, p. 560. This material originally appeared in Martha Farnesworth Richie, "Psychographics for the 1990s," *American Demographics Magazine*, Vol. 11, July 1989, pp. 24–26ff.

[2] John J. Coyle, Edward J. Bardi, and C. John Langley, Jr., *The Management of Business Logistics*, 5th edition, New York: West Publishing Company, 1992, p. 244.

[3] Ibid., p. 566.

CHAPTER 5

THE CUSTOMER-RESPONSIVE MODEL

Actions are triggered by events. A light causes the pupils to contract; darkness causes them to dilate. An event may cause a single response, or the event may require the person to respond in very different ways. For instance, a telephone call to a manager at work may cause her to attend a meeting, handle a disgruntled employee, or alert her of a sick child. How she, and organizations in general, respond to these events in an effective and efficient manner is the thrust of this chapter. Other examples of how this is modeled in various organizations can be found in Chapter 6.

The customer-responsive model depends on several basic components, as shown in Figure 5.1. First, there is the customer who makes a request (the event). The request is made of the customer contact person (CCP), who diagnoses the need and knows how to match the situation-specific needs with the conditional best-practice guideline. The CCP is the front-line worker who interacts with the customer. If the task is simple, the CCP may perform the work. If it is more complicated, he or she may create a priority dispatch list (a plan for this delivery) that will be used to assign (or dispatch) work to the network of providers. The greater the capability and capacity of the resource network, the more responsive the organization can be to customers. Delivery is made according to the individual delivery plan or to-do list and monitored for conformance to the individual's request.

The use of the scheduling model or the dispatching model is not related to whether the organization is providing a product or a service. It depends on a difference in managerial approach. Consider two companies in the fast-food industry. The first is McDonald's. McDonald's, the world's largest fast-food chain, has been very successful selling very standardized, predefined products. Every Big Mac is virtually identical. One has only to look at Figure 5.2 to see a production line that begins with a sesame seed bun, two all-beef patties, lettuce, tomato, pickles, onions, and special sauce, and the association is immediately made to

The Customer-Responsive Model

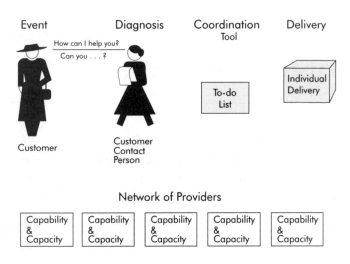

Figure 5.1. A responsive model.

the familiar advertisement. The product is predefined, preproduced, inventoried, and made ready should a customer accept the offer. Special orders, such as "no pickle," take longer to produce because the production line is geared towards a standardized product.

The Subway shop, a delicatessen franchise with the second-largest number of fast-food outlets in the United States, uses a responsive model. In this case, work is not organized as a production line. Rather, a sandwich maker (or "artist," to use the term in a recent commercial) interacts with the customer after he or she arrives to determine that customer's request. Each sandwich maker is able to offer an almost infinite number of sandwiches because of the various combinations of sandwiches that can be made. As shown in Figure 5.3, the sandwich maker can choose from a variety of different meats, cheeses, salads, spices, oil and vinegar, and other condiments (i.e., capabilities and capacities) to meet the individual customer's request. The sandwich maker could work an entire day without making the same sandwich twice. Quality is not determined by conformance to a product standard, as at McDonald's, but rather by conformance to a customer's request. McDonald's goal is to offer a quality product. Subway's goal is to offer a quality response.

This example is illustrative of the fundamental difference between

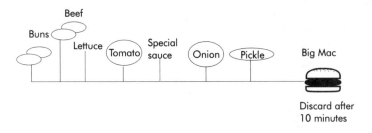

Figure 5.2. McDonald's production line model.

offering-based scheduling coordination and response-based coordination. In the offering-based model, management predefines the details of what, how, when, and where each task is to be done. Definition (i.e., planning) is done in advance of individual customer contact based upon stereotypical customers for each market segment. Offers, be they products or services, are delivered "off the shelf" when a customer arrives. Emphasis is on long-term planning by management and short-run implementation by workers and control by supervisors. The planning focus adheres to the assumptions of economies of scale and specialization of labor. Virtually all decisions occur before and independent of contact with an individual customer.

Responsive organizations emphasize the development of the capabilities necessary to enable the front-line worker to respond to a wide variety of individual customer requests. It is the front-line worker who, in concert with the customer, actually defines the what, how, when, and where of deliveries. Management develops, in the long run, the network of resources that enables the workers to respond when the customer arrives in the immediate run. It is in the short run that resource availability is scheduled. The majority of decisions, however, are made during the customer encounter in the immediate run. This has been defined as the "moment of truth" by Jan Carlzon. It is during the 50,000 customer encounters or moments of truth each day that customer fit, satisfaction, trust, and willingness to return are determined.[1] It is these moments of truth that determine future revenues and profits.

On a daily basis, customer-responsive management has one mission: to develop the resources needed to support the front-line CCPs as they interact with and coordinate the delivery of benefits to customers. Some

The Customer-Responsive Model

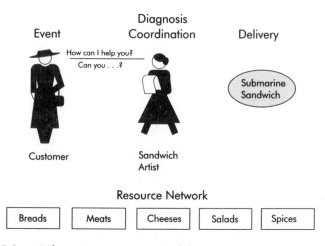

Figure 5.3. Subway's responsive model.

have described offering-based management as "top-down management" and response-based management as "bottom-up management." Whatever terms are used, response-based management recognizes that it is the front-line CCP who interacts with the customer to identify the need and define the details of benefit delivery – not top management, as it has traditionally been with offering-based activities. Management's role is to make sure front-line CCPs have the knowledge, facilities, and tools they need to respond to individual customers on a one-to-one basis.

To be supportive, management must understand the nature of the interactive process that former President of Scandinavian Airline Systems Carlzon calls the "moments of truth." Moments of truth occur in the immediate run, whereas schedules are developed in the short run and resources are obtained in the long run.[1]

The scheduling of offering-based operations is well understood. The organization produces the plan, and the front-line workers are expected to implement the plan according to schedule. Sometimes the plan is operationalized in the form of an assembly line where all tasks are synchronized by the line. In other cases, the organization has very de-

---

1. The long run, the short run, and the immediate run will be described in detail in Chapter 10, where details the economics of response-based management are described.

tailed procedures and policy statements that are used to describe each task. The customer-responsive operational model is much different. As shown in Figure 5.4, there are two interactions that occur: the interactive diagnosis of need during the CCP-customer interaction and the interactive coordination of delivery between the dispatcher and the delivery units.

The Establishment of a Customer-Responsive Strategy

The first step in establishing a customer-responsive strategy is to create a rapport with the customer.

Step 1: Establish a Relationship with the Customer

In the traditional production model, customers go shopping in the marketplace to see what is available and "make do" with what they find. In the case of the responsive or flexible provider, a customer contacts the provider based on a belief that the provider has the ability to meet his or her needs. A potential customer has three basic questions:

- How well will the provider meet my needs?
- How much will it cost?
- How much hassle will there be?

The first question is an attempt to find out about the provider's capability and interest in responding to the customer's needs. The second question addresses the issue of costs. The third question is a measure of how easy the provider is to work with. Hassle includes all of the noneconomic costs – returns, complaints, disagreements, waiting, uncertainty, having to conform to the provider's systems, and disorientation.

The firm's objective is to create a relationship with customers so that they call that firm first when they have needs. As long as a customer calls that firm first, the firm strengthens the relationship by making sure that the customer expects to benefit each time they call. The customer-responsive firm focuses on building long-term relationships with customers by making sure that every customer call is beneficial. The firm is customer focused rather than offering focused and thus more resistant to competition.

A couple went into Nordstrom's department store in San Francisco and asked for a particular video game. It was an item that the store didn't

The Customer-Responsive Model

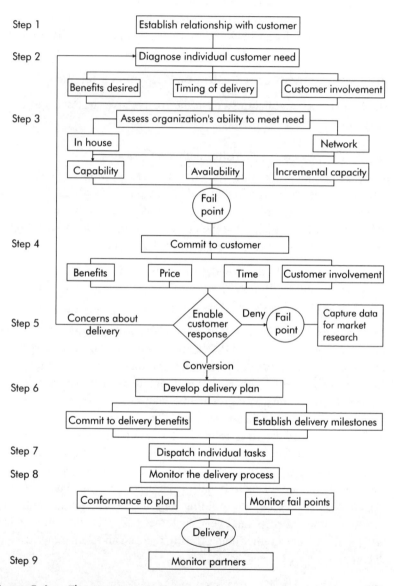

Figure 5.4. The service response model.

sell, but an employee used a computer to locate the nearest dealer, which happened to be Macy's – a Nordstrom's competitor. The employee gave the couple directions to Macy's and told them that the video games were on the fifth floor. He even offered to call ahead to make sure Macy's had the game they wanted in stock.[3]

Step 2: Diagnose the Individual Customer's Needs

After a customer calls, the CCP must determine the customer's need. This diagnosis may be as simple as asking the customer "What would you like today?" or so complicated that it involves a long hospital stay with many screening tests and consultations. Many techniques can be used. In some cases, such as architecture or computer software, prototypic models are created to help a customer visualize options. In still other cases, elaborate profiles are kept on each customer to provide clues as to the customer's needs and expectations.

CCPs must be careful not to let past experiences cloud their diagnoses. Consider the case of an individual seeking a hotel room. On the first night, the guest arrived on an 11:00 p.m. flight and left on a 7:00 a.m. flight. The next time the guest arrived, it was with other family members for a weekend stay in the city. The third time, the guest wanted secretarial and fax support for a business meeting involving local business people. The fourth time, the customer called to book a 500-room convention. In each case, the needs were totally different. If a hotel is to respond effectively to this customer, it must have a network of resources including temporary secretarial service, audiovisual equipment, catering, and conference rooms. The customer contact person must be able to diagnose the needs and determine the availability of the needed capabilities. A vector of typical hotel resources includes:

- Location of hotel
- Time (availability of rooms)
- Bed type and size
- View
- Accommodations for physically challenged guests
- Rate categories
- Clothes cleaning arrangements
- Exercise facilities

- Gift shop
- Work area
- Computer support services
- Cooking facilities in room
- Secretarial support
- Food and beverage services
- Meeting room availability
- Conference room availability
- Block availability for tour groups
- Audio visual equipment support
- Display areas

Step 3: Determine the Organization's Ability to Meet the Individual Customer's Needs

Once the CCP has diagnosed the individual customer's need, he or she must be able to determine the ability of the organization to meet those needs. Typically, fixed-capacity organizations (e.g., hotels, airlines) develop reservation systems, whereas variable-capacity units (e.g., consultants) cultivate networks of support capacity that can be used when needed. Building contractors, for example, depend upon a network of subcontractors and hiring halls for the skills they need.

The ability of an organization to deliver generally is measured in terms of its capability to meet a customer's needs, its ability to schedule capacity to make delivery, and the price of making this delivery.[2] The CCP must be able to contact each member of the network to determine uncommitted capacity and cost so that a commitment can be made to the customer. This step is heavily dependent on guidelines and infrastructure. It is the best-practice guideline that connects need to task and skill necessary to delivery the desired benefits. The information infrastructure is needed to let the CCP know if the capability and capacity are available. It does not matter whether the skill is available in-house or as part of a network of independent providers; it is functionally absent if the infrastructure is not in place to let the CCP know of its availability.

---

2.   This is a potential fail point. If the organization does not have the capability or the capacity to respond to a customer's request, then that customer's data should be captured. These data then become the basis for determining when and how to add future capacity.

Step 4: Commit to the Customer

If the organization has the capability and capacity to provide the desired benefits, the CCP makes a commitment to the customer. This offer is based on the CCP's perception of the benefits desired by the customer, when the benefits are wanted, the degree to which the customer wants to be involved, and the price.

Step 5: Enable Customer Response

Once the customer has approached the provider to see whether that provider can render service and the provider has responded affirmatively, the customer must make a decision. If the customer hesitates, then the CCP may suggest other options. The CCP may check other times, other benefit combinations, different pricing arrangements, or even less involvement from the customer. For example, instead of repairing a defective item, the CCP may suggest examining it and then giving an estimate. Alternatively, the CCP may suggest the pickup and delivery of the defective item instead of having the customer bring it to the shop. An alternative may be to have it repaired at a lower cost if the customer is willing to allow four weeks for repair rather than having next-day service. In essence, the more interactive this evaluation point, the more effective the diagnosis and delivery. The ability of the CCP to interact with the customer is determined largely by the CCP's ability to access protocols and resource availability information.

If the customer "converts" (a term common in the hotel industry meaning conversion from caller to reservation), then delivery is scheduled in Step 6. If the service offer is rejected, this is another fail point.[3]

Step 6: Develop Delivery Plans

Once the conversion has been made, the organization must commit the capacity required to deliver the service and establish delivery milestones. If the organization has standardized units of capacity (e.g., airline seats or hotel rooms), then reservation systems typically are used and the

---

3. Perhaps one of the best examples of market research data is a list of customers whose expectations were great enough to trigger a contact call but for whom the organization was unable to respond. By determining why the organization was not able to respond adequately to meet the customers' needs, adjustments can be made to increase conversion rates.

capacity is committed. If the organization does not use standardized units of capacity, however, then estimates must be made of the time required. Consultants, physicians, attorneys, and others must determine the expected time commitment of each skill area. Unless there is a method for making these commitments dynamically, the CCP will not have current information for providing delivery dates and pricing. This is especially important because pricing is frequently dependent upon capacity utilization. Hotels, for example, charge much higher rates for the Super Bowl week and much lower rates the next day when they have 40 percent occupany.

Step 7: Make the Dispatching of Work Dynamic

Typically, the services will not be delivered by the CCPs themselves. For example, the reservationist may schedule and ticket the passenger, but it is up to food service to make sure that the special meal is available. Information must be communicated in two ways. First, capacity requirements for each unit must be updated continually. This allows the delivery unit maximum advance notice for scheduling capacity. Second, each task is dispatched on a JIT basis as it is needed. In the airline example, the information must be sent to the contract food service and the attendants who serve the meal. If the customer cancels the flight, communication must be made again to change capacity forecasts. Because actual dispatch is made on a JIT basis, the change is made only to the priority dispatch list used for dispatching on an as-needed basis.

Step 8: Monitor the Delivery Process

Mass-production activities can be managed periodically. That is, each month, reports can be generated to see if results conform to the plan and schedule. Reports are typically laced with statistical terms such as units produced, units sold, average cost, average revenue, and variance from plan. Responsive activities are different. They change constantly according to the needs of the individual customers who appear each day. Therefore, each activity must be monitored independently to determine how well each delivery conforms to promise. The customer wants to know when his or her package will be delivered or the results of his or her surgery – not statistical averages about the organization's performance. The organization needs to monitor the following areas:

- Diagnostic effectiveness in identifying customer needs;
- Delivery effectiveness in meeting promised delivery milestones with detection of slippage at the earliest possible moment so corrective action can be taken and/or the customer notified;
- Staffing effectiveness so that there is not too much capacity (results in wasted resources) or too little capacity (which means customers were not able to be served);
- Protocol effectiveness to make sure that conditional best-practice guidelines truly are the most effective way of responding to each customer's request.

Step 9: Mentor Partners

For an organization to be responsive, CCPs must be empowered to respond to the individual customer's needs. This is a skill that must be developed as the employees learn to better define and prescribe solutions for clients. In responsive organizations, managers assume more of a mentoring role than a supervisory role. There is constant emphasis on having front-line employees share new experiences and solutions to expand their ability to interact with customers, diagnose needs, and effect delivery. Employees are expected to become involved, be interested in customers, and take ownership of their areas. Managers are expected to monitor performance and mentor employees and network partners by giving them the support and assistance they need to serve their customers better. Protocols need to be reviewed continually.

An Example of Response-Based Manufacturing

It is easy to see intuitively the need for service organizations to be responsive but also to believe that manufacturing must remain offering based. This is not necessarily true, however. Responsiveness is an alternative approach to management that has applications for both production and services.

Every organization wants to be more responsive to customers. Unfortunately, too many organizations do not consider becoming more responsive because they do not believe it is an option. In many cases responsiveness is not limited because of real limitations but because of the way work is planned and scheduled. Often organizations are so conditioned to focus on their inflexibilities that they strategically limit the options they plan. Consequently, organizations develop operational processes that restrict their activities to a few narrowly defined niches. This is frequently done under the belief that this is the only way to control costs.

There is a difference between the meanings of the words "predefined" and "deterministic." "*Predefined*" refers to the process of defining what is to be done before contact with the individual customer. This can be based on market research surveys or intuition. The opposite of "predefined" is customer responsiveness, where the firm interacts with the customers first so the delivery can be jointly defined.

"*Deterministic*" refers to the process of defining a single "best way" to perform standardized activity. The opposite of deterministic is flexibility. Flexible organizations can do many things in many different ways. This is possible because of a guideline that captures current best practices (benchmarks) but allows for customization of individual deliveries as required. The best-practice guideline can be expanded or modified.

To give a real-world example, Toyota, in an effort to control cost, discovered that the least expensive way to manufacture automobiles was the responsive process. Taiichi Ohno spent 39 years learning the basic principles for controlling costs. To his surprise, he found that the way to reduce the cost of automobile production was to make the system more flexible and responsive. Ohno made his long journey to reduce waste only to find that the same methods that reduce costs also make the organization more responsive. He learned many concepts that are applicable not only to manufacturing but to all responsive organizations. These concepts, therefore, may be considered fundamental to customer responsiveness.

Responsiveness Can Be Increased by Separating the Dispatching of Work from the Scheduling of Capacity

Fundamental to the responsive Toyota process was a rethinking of traditional work scheduling.[2] Traditionally, firms first decide how many units to produce and when they need to be ready. This has typically, at least for mass-production firms, been based on a sales forecast. Once the monthly work decision (i.e., the number and mix of units) has been made, the firm has decided on the best way to meet this production target. The decision has been in the form of a production schedule. Toyota, in an effort to control costs as described in Chapter 2, found that they had to separate capacity scheduling and work dispatching.

Scheduling Plant Capacity. Workers want order and predictability in their lives. They want to have regular work hours and be able to plan off-duty activities. Therefore, they want to know when they will be working. Toyota has developed two methods for forecasting capacity needs. First, forecasts are used to project aggregate capacity requirements so that work schedules can be developed. This predicting process begins with annual, quarterly, and monthly forecasts of aggregate demand by model and type of vehicle. The forecasts do not establish the production schedule, only the expected level of overall activity so that capacity needs can be scheduled.

Second, information systems have been developed to track current customer expectations. These expectations are used to fine-tune the historic forecasts. This information system encourages dealers to submit actual orders ten days in advance for standardized floor plan vehicles. But instead of "freezing" these orders, order changes and specialized customer requests are accepted daily until two days before "line-off." This approach is based on recognition that customers are willing to reveal their expectations as long as they do not feel locked in. The more difficult the decision is to change, the more resistant the customer is to make any type of commitment. By using these two methods, the forecast became so accurate that Toyota has seldom had a capacity imbalance of more than 10 percent.

The customer-expectation system is virtually identical to the reservation systems used by airlines and hotels. By revealing his or her intentions, the customer receives a commitment to capacity and the provider receives an early-warning system of customer intentions. Instead of locking the customer in, as is so often done with scheduling systems, the system is designed to minimize regimentation, thus encouraging customers to provide this information so that Toyota can use it to fine-tune production forecasts.

Dispatching Work. In addition to fine-tuning customer expectations for capacity requirements, the order information system also captures the data needed to dispatch the manufacture of each vehicle. The order file is used in conjunction with a bill-of-material file to specify what parts are needed – and when they are needed – for each vehicle. The bill of material file contains a trigger. The trigger for a fender, for example, may be 37 minutes after production begins. Consequently, the customer-order file and the bill-of-material file totally define all the individual tasks that need to be performed for making each vehicle. Making the bill-of-material file less deterministic and more conditional makes more options can be made available. For example, instead of specifying one system for each model, the bill-of-material file can be set up to trigger the following events:

- If the destination is California, dispatch emission control package 3, 39 minutes after step 1 (the start of production) to location 42;
- If the destination is the United States, dispatch emission control package 1, 40 minutes after step 1 to location 43;
- If the destination is England, dispatch right-hand steering assembly 53 minutes after step 7 to location 52;
- If the destination is not England, dispatch left-hand steering assembly 53 minutes after step 7 to location 51.

By using a conditional instead of a deterministic bill-of-material file, virtually unlimited options can be made available and mixed on each line.

Next, Toyota had to develop a flexible mechanism for communicating the variable dispatches to their suppliers. This was done using a small card called a Kanban. Kanbans specify order requirements as small as five or ten units. Kanbans also specify the sequence in which units are delivered. These information tools were developed because component suppliers, in-house or outside, could not resist the temptation to produce in advance if they obtained copies of forecasts of production needs.

Thus there are four major principles for coordinating for responsive activities:

- Schedule capacity using traditional forecasting methods.
- Develop tools for on-line monitoring of customers' current intentions.
- Use conditional rather than deterministic plans or bills of material.
- Dispatch work on a JIT basis.

Capacity forecasting improves delivery efficiency by eliminating wasted capacity and minimizing capacity shortfalls. Best-practice guidelines improve customer fit and dispatching reduces lead time. Ironically, Toyota's major difficulty in implementing its system was in getting suppliers to shift from the schedule to the dispatch paradigm. When work is coordinated by dispatch, other work habits also need to be changed because they can also limit responsiveness.

Responsiveness Is Limited by Work Quality

When responding to individual customer orders, an organization promises each unit. Consequently, each unit must be deliverable. There is no time or allowance for postproduction inspection, storage, and repair. Each delivery must be right the first time. Toyota used Ohno's principle of autonomation to accomplish this objective:

> In the human body, the autonomic nerve causes us to salivate when we see tasty food. . . . These functions are performed unconsciously without any direction from the brain. . . . An autonomic nerve means making judgments autonomously at the lowest possible level . . . without having to consult the production control or engineering departments that correspond to the brain in the human body.[4]

Automation leads to the following:

- Front-line, continuous inspection;
- The empowerment of each employee to inspect and shut down operations if defects are discovered;
- Information systems that inform all employees of daily goals and progress;
- An emphasis on continuous improvement rather than on annual model changes.

Statistical process-control techniques were developed to shift management's attention from supervision to the development of improved processes that were able to maintain required standards without the physical inspection of each unit.

Responsiveness Is Limited by the Flexibility of the Delivery Units

For Toyota to reduce costs, it had to develop a responsive production process. Instead of being machine oriented, it had to be need oriented. Quick changeover of machines was mandatory. Production lines had to be designed to allow the mixing of models in each run. Employees had to be cross trained to respond to diverse tasks. Not only did Toyota have to learn how to operate responsively, it also had to teach suppliers to be responsive.

Responsiveness Is Limited by the Orientation of the Support Organization

To reduce costs, Toyota realized it had to reorient management from the planning and supervising role to one of facilitating front-line employees as they performed their jobs. Emphasis had to be on doing rather than on desktop planning. Engineers and staff were transferred from planning suites at headquarters to the production area. This enabled them to be closer to and more involved in the production process so they could assist front-line workers when there was a problem. Quality circles were organized so that front-line workers were personally involved in improving the process by identifying problems and focusing on solutions. The technical staff served as advisors, not commanders. During this process, the emphasis shifted from planning to continuous improvement of the process by which organizational resources were used to produce automobiles.

As shown in the Toyota example, responsiveness comes from the development of defining and coordinating procedures that allow the organization to be flexible. The more deterministic the planning and scheduling, the less flexible the firm. The less flexible the firm, the higher the cost and the less responsive the operations. Conditional processes and JIT dispatching increase flexibility. Not only is the planning, scheduling, and control approach to management different from the conditional best-practice guideline, dynamic dispatching, and monitoring approach, the fundamental business philosophy is different for each of the two management methods.

The Effect of Responsiveness on Business Philosophy

When managers operate a business, they develop principles or rules of thumb that reflect perceived reality. Functionally, perception is reality. If a manager does not perceive an option to exist, that option will not be considered. Thus the word "paradigm" has come into common usage. If an option is not perceived as doable (reality) in the manager's mental model (the paradigm), it is not an option.

For this reason it is important to examine some of the basic assumptions about organizational management to determine which are accurate and why they are perceived as true. If the assumptions are changed, reality changes, options expand, and new methods become obvious. Traditional management principles, with explanations, implications, justifications or rationalizations for each, include the following:

1. *Specialization of labor increases efficiency and quality.* The planning process is based on stereotypic standards – standard products, standard processes, and standard employees with standard skills performing standardized tasks.
2. *Organizations cannot be "all things to all people."* Organizations can do a better job if they limit the number of things they do. The planning process defines the "best way" of doing a single or limited number of tasks. Diversity and ambiguity present difficulties in planning. The greater the diversity, the less effective are centralized planning and scheduling. Diversity must be kept to a minimum for the planning and scheduling approach to management to work efficiently.
3. *Mass production decreases costs.* The mass production of standardized products is particularly well adapted to the standardized nature of the central planning and scheduling process. As long as conditions do not change and needs are easy to forcast.
4. *Better (more detailed) planning reduces cost and improves quality.* Planning is effective in analyzing a single standardized task and making the current "best way" better. Scheduling is effective if all delivery conditions are known in advance. Deterministic planning can increase product consistency but not response quality.
5. *Long lead times allow better planning.* Central planning is a time-consuming process and requires extensive lead time. Scheduling works well as long as advance notice of needs exceeds the time required to plan and schedule work.
6. *Quality is conformance to standards.* There are two kinds of standards: standards defined and decided by the firm and standards defined and evaluated by the customer. Mass production excels in producing highly standardized (quality) products. The more diverse customer needs are, the poorer the fit between product quality and response quality.

7. *If something is done for one customer, the same thing will have to be done for everyone.* Customers must realize how difficult it is to modify the planning and scheduling process and not expect special consideration. They must conform to the standardized plan and schedule like everyone else. Organizations cannot take the time to make a special plan and reschedule for each customer.

8. *Customers buy products that organizations define, produce, and distribute in the marketplace.* Products include goods and services. The firm plans and schedules the offering that is distributed to the market for the customers to examine. After all, it is the firm, and not the customer, that has the greatest knowledge and experience about what should be done.

9. *Sales are the best predictor of success.* The purpose of the firm is to produce quality products efficiently and sell them in the marketplace. It is not efficient to cater to individual customers' needs.

10. *Customers want the lowest cost product.* Fit and hassle do not need to be considered. The firm's job is to get quality products to the marketplace in the most efficient manner. It is the customer's responsibility to go to the marketplace and select the product that best meets his or her needs.

11. *Cost is measured in terms of currency (i.e., dollars, pounds, francs, yen).* The hassle of locating, buying, and consuming the product is just part of the normal shopping expense.

12. *There is an arm's-length relationship between the customer, the provider, and the suppliers.* The product is the basis of the relationship. Nothing else matters. The customer wants quality products and low price.

13. *Management plans, schedules, and supervises. Workers perform tasks.* Workers must conform to the plan if it is to be successful. Success is conformance to the plan.

14. *Managers make decisions and workers carry them out.* Qualified managers and planners have researched the "best way" to do each task and should not be questioned, especially by nonprofessionals.

15. *The bottom line on the monthly accounting reports determines the profitability of the organization.* Profitability is determined by the difference between the sales price and the average cost of

making the product. Relationships and customer-retention rates are too vague to be considered. Goodwill is the difference between the sales price and book value of the firm when it is sold. Goodwill, where it exists, should be depreciated so that accounting records show the "real" or book value of the firm.

16. *Organizations must be more productive.* Productive organizations create more output. The purpose of the firm is to produce. Consumers benefit when there is an abundant selection of products in the marketplace.

17. *Profits are increased by cutting costs and increasing productivity.* There are two ways to increase profits: increase sales price or decrease costs. One way to decrease costs is to increase production so that fewer fixed costs have to be added to each unit.

18. *Firms must be market oriented.* Firms become market oriented by basing product design on market research. By developing customer panels and surveys, organizations can design products that customers want to buy. Inside-out companies do not interact and respond to individual customers. They manage by plan and schedule. Therefore, the most they can do to be customer oriented is to sample customers' needs and use this as input to the internally oriented planning process. To these firms, "market oriented" means using market research (i.e., sample data) to define "market niches" and develop "best way" solutions for each market niche stereotype.

Those intimately involved with the deterministic planning and scheduling approach to management may feel quite comfortable with these 18 truisms. Others may feel less comfortable with them. Individuals familiar with customer-responsive management may be more comfortable with an alternative set of truisms. These may include the following:

1. *Customers want benefits.* A product may or may not be involved. The value of the benefits depends upon how well the delivery meets the specific needs of the specific individual.

2. *Benefits have value to customers.* Customers pay for benefits, not the organizational activity necessary to deliver the benefits. Any activity that does not benefit the customer has no value and is wasteful.

3. *Profits are determined by the organization's ability to retain customers.* It costs much more to attract a new customer and satisfy him or her than it does to satisfy an existing one. Existing customers are also more profitable.[5]

4. *Different customers have different needs.* These needs may vary at different times. The depth of the relationship between the customer and the provider is based on the ability of the organization to meet each customer's diverse needs consistently.

5. *There are two costs to each delivery – price and hassle.* Price is the economic cost of the product or service. Hassle includes noneconomic costs such as waiting, experiencing uncertainty, having disagreements, returning to have the delivery corrected, and having to complain. Hassle is frequently the cost that terminates a customer/provider relationship.

6. *Customers interact with CCPs.* CCPs are the ones who diagnose customers' needs, develop solutions, and coordinate deliveries. It is the CCP that determines the value of the benefits delivered. The CCP is the company to the customer.

7. *Management's role is to facilitate the customer-to-CCP relationship.* The CCP's ability to enhance this relationship is influenced greatly by the availability of enabling tools, employee empowerment, delivery monitoring, and expert mentoring.

   a. Enabling is done by providing training, facilities, and tools. Tools that allow the storage and retrieval of data about specific customers and needs are essential. Reengineering is one term currently in use. Enabling tools are object oriented and entity based, not flow driven and application based. Emphasis is on storage and selective retrieval of information rather than inputs and outputs (e.g., reports).

   b. Empowering occurs when the CCPs fully understand that their job is to commit the company to meet customers' individual needs and to make sure that the delivery is made properly.

   c. Monitoring allows employees and management to track delivery effectiveness and identify fail points for each delivery.

   d. Mentoring is specialized assistance and training given to individual employees on a day-by-day basis to help them respond more effectively to their customers.

8. *Training allows employees to be more things to more people.* This means providing more value to more people. Value is what customers pay for. Cross-training results in expansion of the potential customer base and broadening the relationship with each customer. (Broader relationships permit "cross-selling.") Specialized training strengthens customers' confidence in the relationship.

9. *Responsive organizations use forecasting and continual interaction with the customer to reduce unexpected variation.* Unresponsive organizations, in contrast, rigidly adhere to policies, standards, offerings, and rules to reduce variation.

10. *Responsive activity is triggered by a customer's request.* Therefore, organizations must be structured to facilitate rapid and diverse responses and to inhibit anticipatory actions that might restrict future responsiveness. Inventory, for example, is built in anticipation. Once built, it is difficult to change.

11. *Responsive organizations develop networks of providers.* Networks allow an organization to be customer oriented rather than asset oriented.

12. *Responsive organizations develop networks of delivery units to increase capability and capacity.* Strategic planning is used to define the range and depth of skills that should be available in the network. Logistics involves development of methods for coordinating activities among delivery units in response to each request. The network of delivery units includes in-house as well as outside partnerships.

13. *Customized delivery cannot be costed using traditional cost accounting methods.* The more diverse the firm's activities, the more irrelevant the use of cost-allocation methods. Organizational activity must be costed directly. The protocols define activities required to make customized deliveries. Responsive cost systems are thus protocol defined, activity based, and event driven. The emphasis shifts from average costing to costing individual deliveries to maximize contribution. This is called *yield management.*

14. *Quality is determined by customers.* Success is delivering the benefits desired by each individual customer. The role of the CCP is to diagnose need, develop solutions, and coordinate

delivery. Management supports this process by developing enabling tools, empowering workers, monitoring effectiveness, and mentoring so that front-line personnel can be more responsive. The emphasis is on response quality rather than product quality.

15. *Marketing is responsible for strengthening the relationship between the customer and the delivery organization.* When customers could be satisfied only with products, the emphasis was on product planning, promotion, price, and distribution. Today, customers seek to benefit each time they call the organization. In responsive organizations, marketing is no longer limited to offering products in the marketplace; there are many more options for establishing and building relationships. Marketing should be the champion for continual movement of the organization toward increased responsiveness and away from rigidity, bureaucracy, and standardization.

16. *Accounting or information management provides the information required to respond effectively to customers.* It is no longer sufficient to provide after-the-fact, period-end, standardized reports. The CCP (e.g., the airline reservationist) needs certain information to interact with the customer, strengthen relationships, and increase organizational yield.

17. *Responsive activities occur in the immediate run.* Managers must understand the economics of immediate-run as well as long-run and short-run decision making.

18. *Profitability is determined by cost effectiveness.* Delivery effectiveness (i.e., meeting each individual customer's specific needs) increases revenue. Cost efficiency is accomplished by minimizing the amount of time spent waiting on customers and increasing the time spent delivering benefits. This concept goes by various names, such as load factors, percentage billable hours, daily census, percentage deadheading, and room occupancy.

19. *Wealth comes not to owners of production factors (e.g., landlords, factory owners, or capital providers) but to those that have the ability to develop networks, provide enabling tools, and motivate the front-line people to accept empowerment.*

These truisms provide a very different philosophy for conducting business.

Summary

Responsive organizations are built around relationship management. There is one relationship between customers and organizations. This relationship is used for diagnosing needs and defining solutions. There is also a second relationship, the one between the organization and the resources that make the delivery. It is this relationship that is used to coordinate delivery and determine the cost of making the delivery. Coordinators of the first relationship are often called *customer contact personnel* (CCPs). Coordinators of the second relationship are often called *dispatchers*. Collectively, these two relationships were presented in a single service-responsive model.

All organizations want to be more responsive to their customers. Responsiveness is limited by inflexibility. Unfortunately, many inflexibilities are not real but self-inflicted. Self-inflicted inflexibilities are often caused by the time required to plan and schedule work. Although mass-production logic emphasizes the need for deterministic scheduling, Toyota discovered that the way to control costs was to go to JIT scheduling. JIT scheduling is dispatching, whether by computer or Kanban. Many of the principles used to reduce costs for automobile production are the same concepts that increase flexibility and allow greater customer responsiveness. The shift from deterministic work planning and scheduling to flexible protocols and dispatching reflects changes in many of the assumptions or truisms about business.

References

[1] Karl Albrect and Ron Zemke, *Service America!* New York: Warner Books, 1985, p. 27. Carlzon also has written his own book, *Moments of Truth,* New York: Harper & Row, 1987.

[2] Janet Fox, "Want to be Outrageous?" *Amtrak Express,* May-June 1995, p. 8.

[3] The evolution of the Toyota production has been well documented in *Toyota Production System: Beyond Large-Scale Production* by Taiichi Ohno. English translation copyright © 1988 by Productivity Press, Inc. PO Box 13390, Portland, OR 97213-0390, (800) 394-6868. Please refer to pp. 17–74 for a detailed description of this process.

[4] Reprinted by permission of *Harvard Business Review.* An exerpt from "Zero Defections: Quality Comes to Services," by Frederick F. Reichheld and W. Earl Sasser, Jr., Issue 5 (September / October 1990), pp. 105–111. Copyright © by the President and the Fellows of Harvard College; all rights reserved.

CHAPTER 6

EXAMPLES OF CUSTOMER-RESPONSIVE ORGANIZATIONS

The caller's voice was soft, young, and shrouded in fear: "Mommy won't wake up." The 911 operator calmed the child, asking her where her mother was and promising to send help. When paramedics arrived, they found a 29-year-old mother on the floor of the kitchen and a 3-year-old girl holding a phone. The mother had suffered a severe heart attack. Days later, during her recovery, she explained that she had taught her daughter the numbers 9-1-1 and had told her to dial them if there was an emergency. That lesson saved a young mother's life.

At the fingertips of the 911 operator were several suppliers she could have called. Had the little girl said that a man was shooting a gun in the house, the police would have been dispatched. If she said there was smoke in the bedroom, the fire department would have rushed to the scene. The 911 operator's role is to diagnose the need and respond with the appropriate delivery modules (e.g., contact the fire department, police, paramedics, and so forth).

Although it is easy to understand this type of service organization, it is more difficult to see how the responsive model would apply to most businesses that offer products. Software support centers are an example of how a business could use the responsive model. Like the 911 desk, these centers revolve around a telephone help desk. The software support staff has access to computers that capture customer problems and record solutions.

Such software help centers are also prime examples of "dynamic best-practice guideline development." When a problem first occurs, a technical expert will be contacted to track down the problem. After the problem has been identified and resolved, it is added to the dynamic best-practice guideline file. Future references to the problem can then be accessed by the front-line customer contact personnel (CCP). In this way the organization becomes a learning organization – one that is able to respond to each individual customer and to dynamically develop the knowledge base required to effectively do so.

The basic organizational model for customer-responsive organizations is valid whether the firm is a fast-food restaurant, a distribution center, a hospital, or a multinational bank. These businesses are organized for flexibility and responsiveness, not for the routine performance of standardized predefined tasks.

Seven different examples of responsive organizations are presented, each with varying degrees of complexity and objectives. They range from fast-food suppliers (a delicatessen and a pizza restaurant) to distribution centers, hospitals, a military campaign, support services at a multinational bank, and contract logistics services. Each customer-responsive organization uses the basic Subway franchise model with enhancements based upon the complexity of the tasks that need to be coordinated.

The Subway Example

Chapter 5 illustrated the difference in orientation between organizations that deterministically plan and schedule their operations and those that respond using conditional best-practice guidelines and dynamic dispatching. To illustrate these points, Chapter 5 compared the more predefined model used by McDonald's to Subway's more responsive orientation. The Subway model, as shown previously in Figure 5.3, consists of an interactive front-end diagnosis whereby the CCP interacts with the customer to determine his or her preferences and then selects from a number of delivery modules to create the customized delivery. Each delivery module has a capability (e.g., bread, meat, cheese, or salad).

The essential elements of the Subway model are the customer, the CCP, and the delivery modules, which contain a range of options. The CCP (the sandwich maker) interacts with the customer to diagnose the need and selects from the delivery modules (a menu of standard sandwiches) to satisfy those needs. Although there are standard sandwiches (e.g., BLT, meatball, and club), the sandwich maker is encouraged to vary from the menu (the predefined offering) as requested by the customer. Subway's ability to respond to individual customer needs is limited only by the options available from the delivery modules, the CCP's ability to interact with the customer to determine his or her needs, and the processes that guide the CCP's response.

There may be some limitations on the CCP's ability to respond to individual requests. The CCP may not be sufficiently trained to make certain sandwiches. The CCP may not have at his or her disposal the necessary tools, such as a steamer or knives, needed for some options. Third, the management's policy or external regulatory groups may limit the CCP's ability to respond to customers who request certain combinations. Finally, the CCP may be limited by the ability of the resource suppliers to consistently provide the needed meats, cheeses, salads, and other products. These limitations can be described as process constraints, knowledge limits, lack of tools, or the inability (as opposed to the capability) of the delivery units.

In summary, the Subway model:

- Is event driven (customer request);
- Is single level (the sandwich maker diagnoses need and makes delivery);
- Has its flexibility determined by range of resources and its processes developed by management and the skill of the sandwich maker.

The Pizza Hut Example

A slightly more complicated model is used by most restaurants. At Pizza Hut, for instance, the work is divided into two categories – the work of the CCP and the back-room delivery food workers. The front end interacts with the customer to determine customer needs and dispatches the order to the back room for fulfillment. The CCP basically needs to identify the customer and determine his or her order, the price, and process the payment. The back room manages the resources needed to meet the requests of the customer and prepares and delivers the meal (or meals) to the customer.

Interacting with the customer can be done either on site (face to face), or off site (e.g., by telephone or fax). In the case of face-to-face orders, the CCP becomes familiar with regular customers and generally knows their preferences. In the case of off-site orders, a database can be developed by tracking each customer's order and using the customer's telephone number as his or her customer identification number. This identification number is used to access the customer database so that the CCP knows the caller's name, address, method of payment, what he or she ordered the last time, and the customer's delivery requirements. Whether by the CCP's memory and familiarity with regular customers or by sophisticated databases, the emphasis is on building a relationship with the customer and customizing each delivery to meet their unique current needs.

Once the customer's request is understood, a customer order is used to convey the information to the back room, where the work is performed. Back-room workers are dispatched by the customer's order. Once the back-room workers receive the next dispatch, they customize the delivery by selecting from the appropriate delivery module. The specifications of the delivery are on the customer's order. For example, the customer's order can include a wide variety of toppings, crusts, drinks, salads, and the like. In the case of the salad bar, the delivery modules are placed in the front-end area so the customers can select for themselves rather than having to go through the CCP and the diagnostic process. The pick-up and delivery module is separated from the remaining delivery modules (see Figure 6.1) because this module also interacts with the customer and is normally managed (i.e., dispatched) by the CCP. In the Subway example, the CCP handled both front-line and the back-room activities. In the Pizza Hut case, the two activities are separated; most modules are coordinated by the back room.

In summary, the Pizza Hut model:

- Is event driven (per customer request);
- Is dual level (front-end diagnosis, back-room delivery);
- Has its flexibility determined by a range of resources and processes developed by management;
- Is coordinated by dispatch via written order.

Coordination by Prioritized Dispatch List

The Pizza Hut example introduces a key element for coordinating deliveries. Where the delivery is not made directly by the customer contact person, as in the Subway example, there is a need to record the customer's order, identify each work task to be done, assign the work to the appropriate delivery unit, and track fulfillment. Some form of a prioritized dispatch list is used to record this information.

We will use five terms to describe this coordination tool between the

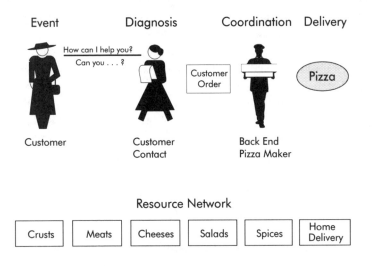

Figure 6.1. The Pizza Hut responsive model.

CCP and the delivery units. In food service, the term "customer order" is well understood. In responsive manufacturing, the term "Kanban"[1] is used. In transportation and many other service industries, the term "dispatch ticket" is used. Hospitals depend on "doctor's orders." Individuals use the term "to-do list."

Whatever term is used, the concept is simple. When activities are responsive rather than scheduled, they must be dispatched dynamically. The customer order, Kanban, dispatch ticket, doctor's order, or to-do list is used for this purpose. To introduce another element of responsiveness, the to-do list can be prioritized with the most critical tasks listed first. This allows the organization not only to dispatch resources dynamically but also to dispatch based on criticality of need. Prioritization allows

---

1. The Kanban is so important to JIT production that Yasuhior Monden devotes two chapters in his book, *Toyota Production System* (Norcross, GA: Industrial Engineering and Management Press, 1983) to a discussion of it.

customer requests to be received in any order but to dispatch work according to priority rules developed by the organization. With JIT scheduling (i.e., dispatching), work priorities can be changed any time before the work is dispatched.

Hyrum Smith, developer of the Franklin Planner, makes a distinction between to-do lists and prioritized daily task lists. A to-do list includes items that must be done on a daily basis just to keep going.[1] The highest priorities in our life can be found on a prioritized daily task list. Smith suggests that time should be spent every day listing what we want to do for that day, placing a value on each task, and ranking each of these tasks by its value. This value provides the priority items for the day.

Prioritized dispatch lists allow the flexible assignment of work. Work can be scheduled for a *specific time* (say, from 10:00 a.m. to 10:30 a.m.), assigned during a *time window* (for instance, between 10:00 a.m. and 3:30 p.m.), or assigned by *priority* (i.e., in order of importance or value rendered). The prioritized dispatch list allows the organization to mix all methods for assigning work dynamically, just as a personal organizer such as the Franklin Planner allows the individual to schedule meetings and prioritize non-time-specific tasks.

United Parcel Service (UPS) understands that management and supervisors must be responsive and also must manage by prioritized dispatch lists. Each manager and supervisor is issued a Franklin Planner and provided at least a day's training on its use. The Franklin Planner has two separate pages for each day; one page includes a list of scheduled events (i.e., appointments) and a prioritized daily task list (i.e., a prioritized dispatch list). The second page provides a list of daily events, including communications exchanged, journal entries, thoughts and ideas, agenda items, and conversations.

Thus the first page of the Franklin Planner recognizes that there are two types of activities: scheduled and dispatched. The second page recognizes the need for developing daily guidelines that allow space to help conceptualize agendas for upcoming meetings, thoughts, and ideas about new initiatives. The Franklin Planner is based on three governing concepts: (1) it is designed to guide, not control, so its use can be customized to each individual's needs; (2) all coordination activities should be based on a single record so all other calendars and lists should be eliminated; and (3) it makes the record central to the individual's operations. (That is, a record is continuously kept at all times and all activities are dispatched from this single record.)

Just as Smith's prioritized daily task list directs an individual's efforts where he or she can do what is most valuable, so a prioritized dispatch list can be used to assign work to large numbers of individuals in an organization to provide the greatest value to the customer. The ability to deliver customer value creates organizational value. The following list includes the headings in a basic prioritized dispatch list:

- CCP ID
- Request time stamp
- Customer ID
- Need
- Desired delivery time
- Individual or group responsible for work
- Dispatch time stamp
- Results
- Completion time stamp

When activities are stable and output standardized, flows can be planned and scheduled, but when there are multiple groups involved in the delivery and each delivery is unique, then dispatch is by the prioritized dispatch list. The prioritized dispatch list defines the parties involved (i.e., the customer, the CCP, and the delivery modules), the work to be completed, and the time when it is to be finished. It also provides the reporting function on the results of the dispatch (i.e., order status and order tracking). Virtually any question can be answered from the prioritized dispatch list. Without this list, work will not be done, no one will know what has happened, and no one will take responsibility for completing the tasks.

Prioritized dispatch lists are the heart of a responsive management approach. When tasks are planned and scheduled, prioritized dispatch lists are unnecessary. Workers simply look at the schedule and complete the work according to the master plan. But can you imagine a manager trying to develop a monthly production and delivery schedule for a restaurant or for an emergency room at a hospital? The manager can schedule work shifts (i.e., capacity), but he or she cannot schedule the actual work until the specific need is defined. The manager would not know where to start because he or she wouldn't know when the customer was going to arrive or what each customer will request from the organization. The manager can only schedule the capacity and capability to be available and take customer orders as they arrive. The customer order, Kanban, dispatch ticket, doctor's order, or prioritized dispatch list is the heart of coordinating responsive organizations.[2]

Whether the record is manual (e.g., a Franklin Planner, a Kanban, or a restaurant customer order ticket) or electronic (e.g., a sophisticated airline dispatching system or Lotus Organizer for the individual desktop), the concept is the same. There is a process for assigning work by schedule and a process for assigning work by prioritized dispatch list. The prioritized dispatch list identifies the parties involved, the work to be done, a time window for doing the work, and a means for reporting completion.

Distribution Center Example

A distribution center follows this same model but with additional dimensions. Figure 6.2 presents the organization of a distribution center.

As with fast-food restaurants, distribution centers respond to individual customer requests. The CCP performs order entry from a menu of available inventory and delivery options. Products offered to the customer may be in stock or available on special order. Items not in stock can be drop-shipped or back-ordered for the customer. The prioritized dispatch list is called a "picking list." The picking list can be dispatched by hand to the warehouse personnel in the back room (in this case, a warehouse) or transmitted by computer to a warehouse at another location. "Pick and pack" workers move through the warehouse selecting the items needed as indicated on the picking list; they either pack the product themselves or give it to another worker to do. What merchandise is to be picked and packaged is determined by the individual customer's needs; there are few orders that are truly standardized for all customers.

---

2. Toyota discovered that if an organization ever makes a production schedule based on a forecast, the workers will produce to schedule. When such an organization produces to a schedule, it creates inventories and becomes unable to respond to individual customer needs.

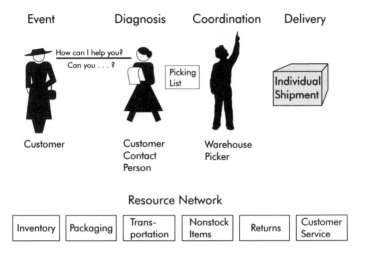

Figure 6.2. The distribution center responsive model.

Just as there are few standardized orders, there is no single way in which a distribution center can be owned or managed. In fact, the distribution center introduces a number of different ownership arrangements, ranging from private ownership and the leasing of facilities from a distribution center operated by a third-party logistician. The transportation delivery module is typically not owned by the distribution center. For many companies, order entry, warehousing, and transportation may all be handled by different independent organizations. In some instances, the interface between the customer and the distribution center may be electronic, thereby reducing costs (both economic and noneconomic) as well as the order cycle time. Such an example illustrates the fact that the responsive model is not limited to operations within a single site or organization. Rather, the responsive model is a method for managing and coordinating many different activities that are basically unique for each individual delivery and that make use of widely differing core competencies possessed by each delivery unit.

125

In summary, the distribution center:

- Is event driven (triggered by a customer request).
- Is dual level (front-end diagnosis and customer service, and back-room picking, packing, and shipping).
- Has its flexibility determined by range of resources (e.g., inventory items and carriers) and management's best-practice guidelines.
- Has information systems that enable and empower the front-line worker to be responsive. (If the order-entry system does not allow for an option, the front-line employee has difficulty providing it.)
- Employs multilevel coordination by Kanban-type dispatch using picking orders, shipping documentation, telecommunication to carrier, the placing of backorders, and so forth.
- Uses in-house and independent delivery units.
- Ensures that delivery can be immediate or time specific.

Military Campaigns

Operation Desert Storm is an excellent example of a modern military campaign based on responsive logistics. It is the ability of the logistics unit to respond to diverse requests that enables various strategies to be operationally feasible for the military commander. Military campaigns are an especially good example of this because each is unique. There are very few strategic similarities between World War II, Korea, Viet Nam, and Desert Storm. No matter how many contingency plans are developed, the conflict is seldom located in the anticipated location, at the anticipated time, and in the anticipated manner. (For example, the contingency plans for cold war battles between superpowers did not prepare the military for hot tribal wars or genocidal civil wars.) The military can only develop a number of scenarios and in so doing train the logistics unit how to develop the capability and capacity to respond to and support the ones that seem most likely to happen. Because ensuring adequate military capabilities and capacity is very expensive, this must be done at a cost that is politically acceptable. Thus, to be effective, the military must develop an organization that is able to respond when the need arises.

At the beginning of every conflict, the key military strategists meet to develop a battle strategy. In the case of Desert Storm, General Norman Schwarzkopf was responsible for the battle strategy. As General Schwarzkopf used a map to define a military strategy, he realized that each part of the campaign needed troops, equipment, and support services such as food, shelter, medical care, and transportation. Unless the support service could obtain the equipment and resources to meet the needs of the front line, the strategy, no matter how brilliant, would not succeed.

Thus the strategic options available to the strategist are determined by logistics. Therefore, the second integral part of the strategy planning process is the logistician, who must determine what strategic options are possible. In Desert Storm the logistician was General William G. Pagonis. Figure 6.3 presents the military responsive model.

In the case of Desert Storm, logistics was handled by the 22nd Support Command. To accomplish this objective, the command grew from 5 to 40,000 people. As General Pagonis later wrote, "The team fed, clothed, sheltered and armed over 550,000 people. They served 122 million meals. . . . They transported and distributed more than 7 million tons of supplies, 117,000 wheeled vehicles, 2,200 tracked vehicles and 2,000 helicopters. They pumped 1.3 billion gallons of fuel."[2]

The military model introduces several variations on the responsive model. First, the diagnostic process is much more complicated. The generals responsible for planning the military strategy do not know specifically what is possible. They may ask the logistician questions such as, "If we plan an assault in a given area, can logistics obtain the support services necessary to sustain a campaign advancing twenty miles per day?" The support services range from food preparation and storage, medical care, sanitation services, fuel, repair parts for the equipment, and even field hospitals and the evacuation capability to handle the wounded. Arrangements often include a level of detail for things that most people would not even think of, such as recreation supplies, religious facilities and personnel, and even mail service.

The military logistician cannot possibly know the answer to all of these questions, but they must be able to quickly assess the ability of the organization to respond. Often the needed capability is not included in the existing network of providers. When this occurs, the logistician must develop the ability to develop the required network capability dynamically so that the resource can be dispatched. In the case of Desert Storm,

Examples of Customer-Responsive Organizations

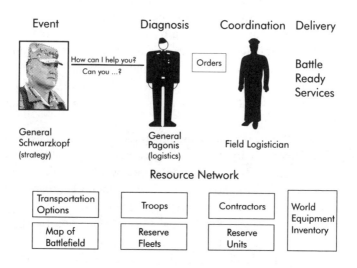

Figure 6.3. The military response model.

the logisticians knew the location of reserve units and their capabilities and capacity. They knew they had inventories of tanks, planes, ships, and other equipment in many different locations around the world. They had a network of transportation facilities including ports, ships, and warehouses that could probably be made available through contract. (The logisticians had to bring ships out of mothballs and even re-enlist retired merchant mariners, one of whom was reported to be 84 years old.)

In the case of a military operation, the diagnosis of customer needs is extensive, interactive, and iterative. Because General Pagonis was personally unable to make all of the inquiries and follow them up, he made use of a logistics support staff and a sophisticated communication system. Once plans are finalized, it is up to the field logistician to coordinate assigned activities according to the time window provided. It is not the field logisticians who necessarily do the work, but they are responsible for making sure that it is done. The field logisticians are not expected to limit themselves to the use of a menu of predetermined delivery modules. Their job is to find whatever resources are needed to do the job in a cost-effective manner.

In the military model, an additional item is added to the prioritized dispatch list – the name of the field logistician who is responsible for coordinating the delivery of that specific task. Tasks on the prioritized dispatch list may include developing new best-practice guidelines and cultivating a network with the required capability and capacity so that delivery is possible.

It can be said in the military that "logistics enables the tactical implementation of strategy." Ironically, in peacetime, when operations are more static and the need to be responsive is reduced, the need for logistics is also less compelling. In fact, there is an old expression that suggests that "in time of war logistics is paramount, but in peace time it is the stepchild of the military."

Even the scope of military logistics is changing. It has traditionally been to support the military troops. The Bosnia, Rwanda, Haiti, and Cuba experiences are rapidly illustrating the added need to support large civilian population groups fleeing their homelands. These refugees need not guns and bullets but sanitation facilities, food, and health care.

In summary, responsive military logistics support:

- Is event driven. (In this case, the event is a request by the general, who wants to know if a specific strategy can be supported.)
- Processes requests that are iterative and that require greater levels of detail as the plan progresses.
- Is dual level (the front-end diagnoses and develops delivery strategies; the back-room researches options, coordinates delivery, and dynamically develops networks of delivery units as needed).
- Has its flexibility determined by the range of resources and the logistician's ability to develop new options with few limits on acceptable options during times of crisis.
- Employees multilevel coordination with continual, two-way communication flow. The first request is typically to determine what is possible, and the second request is to do it. Extensive coordination is needed among many different independent units.
- Includes many activities that are first-time or one-time activities.
- Uses in-house and independent delivery units, with the potential of having only a handful of providers previously enrolled in the network.
- Ensures that new delivery units can be added to the network on a real-time basis.

- Ensures that tracking and monitoring capabilities can be expanded as rapidly as strategic requirements are expanded.
- Ensures that delivery can be immediate or time specific.

The Hospital Example

As illustrated in Figure 6.4, hospitals operate in a similar manner but with some differences. One is the magnitude of the diagnostics portion of the process. Although the field logisticians in the military model need to do extensive research into what is possible, the generals developing the strategies normally know what they want. In the fast-food and distribution center examples, the customers generally know what they want. In the case of the hospital, one of the major – if not *the* major – reasons for admission is to diagnose what is needed so a customized delivery strategy can be developed for each patient.

Before the patient arrives, the admitting physician makes a preliminary diagnosis. This determines where the patient will be located and the type of care he or she will receive. For instance, a patient scheduled for the operating room for a hip replacement requires different care from a patient admitted with a stroke.

Each diagnosis has a conditional protocol that needs to be followed. In the case of an acute myocardial infarction (a heart attack), the conditional protocol is illustrated by the decision tree shown in Figure 4.2. Each point in the decision tree suggests various procedures. Each procedure has a common procedural terminology (CPT) code. For each procedure there is a conditional protocol, as shown in Table 4.2.

Thus, the diagnosis code and the CPT codes are very similar to a multilevel bill-of-material file. The bill-of-material file, for example, may begin with the product, such as a Dodge Intrepid. This file will include a list of all components used to assemble the car, such as five tires, an engine, trunk, and seats. In addition, each component (e.g., the engine) may have a bill-of-material file similar to the CPT protocol that describes the parts that make up the component. In the case of the engine, this file may include crankshaft, block, pistons, rings, and camshaft.

In the case of a hospital, there is the potential for multiple levels of protocols. First, there is a protocol for each diagnosis. The diagnostic protocol will contain a list of the procedures required to confirm the diagnosis or to render treatment. (The term "protocol" is used here

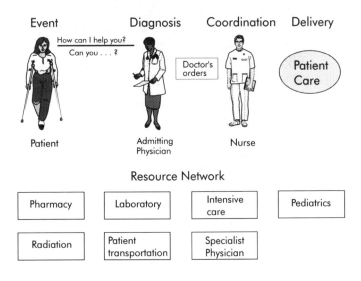

Figure 6.4. The hospital responsive model.

instead of "best-practice guideline" because protocol is the term familiar to hospital staffs.) Each procedure also will have a protocol to be followed for administering the procedure. Each procedure is carried out by one of the delivery modules. In the example shown in Table 4.2, some procedures are performed by laboratory technicians and others by nurses. The physician orders the procedure. The CPT protocol then generates the prioritized dispatch list shown in Table 4.2. The patient's file consists of the doctor's orders, test results, and the patient's history, which are observations and evaluations of this and prior illnesses.

The patient records are very similar to the ever-present prioritized dispatch list that is so essential to the responsive model. The doctor's orders identify the physician placing the order, the time it was ordered, the patient, the procedure, the time when the procedure was completed, and the results. It also records the nurse responsible for coordination activities for this specific patient and the person or delivery module responsible for the procedure. Hospitals are now developing critical pathways that are basically overarching best-practice guidelines (i.e., critical pathways) that show which steps should be taken each day and the expected outcome or results.

A second major difference between the military model and the hospital model is the dynamics of the prioritized dispatch list. Although a diagnosis protocol may suggest a procedure, diagnosis is an iterative process. A lab test or an observation may suddenly change the initial diagnosis and require an entirely different procedure for further screening. Likewise, the nurse may make observations and enter them in the patient record.[3] Thus, the dynamic prioritized dispatch list must allow multidirectional communication between all delivery modules, the nurses, and the admitting physician or physicians. It must allow tasks to be added or deleted depending upon the most recent findings. Without this list, it would be difficult to coordinate patient care.

In essence, as one hospital administrator suggested, a hospital is a large logistics unit. A hospital brings together a large number of independent delivery modules, each with its special core competencies. It provides the facilities to house the patient and working facilities and tools for the delivery units to deliver benefits. It provides the supplies needed by each of the delivery modules. Lastly, it provides the records that allow the integration of activities between the various independent delivery units and coordination to keep the delivery on schedule.

Where do current health care expenditures go?

It is not easy to assign and coordinate work in a large hospital.

Out of every dollar spent on wages, only about 16 cents goes for what most of us would characterize as "medical care." A nearly equal amount – 14 cents – is consumed trying to schedule and coordinate that medical care. The irony is that most of that scheduling effort is a waste of time. The line of gurneys in the diagnostic radiology department probably wouldn't be any longer if we didn't schedule at all.

Where do the really big dollars go? Twenty-nine cents of every wage dollar goes for documentation – two thirds of which is medical documentation, and most of that is by nurses. Nurses produce great tomes of plans and assessments that we know are seldom read by

---

3. In the service logistics study conducted by Arthur D. Little and The Pennsylvania State University for the Council of Logistics Management, it was suggested that the nurse is the logistician in a hospital.

anyone and almost never enter into the real-time clinical care of the patient.

A further 20 cents of our wage dollar pays for structural idle time. Examples abound: phlebotomists with little or nothing to do between their morning and afternoon scheduled rounds, a near-empty recovery room in the early morning, very quiet operating rooms in midafternoon, housekeepers waiting for a patient to finish breakfast before they can clean the room.

The rest of the wage dollar goes for hotel and patient services (8 cents), transportation (6 cents), management and supervision (7 cents).[3]

In summary, the hospital has the following characteristics:

- Is event driven (responds to health problems identified by patient).
- Employs multilevel coordination with continual, two-way communication flow.
- Bases each subsequent diagnosis on the results of preceding tasks.
- Is dual level (front-end diagnosis makes request, analyzes results, and rediagnoses. Support staff performs task specified by front end. Front end selects protocol and support staff makes any changes allowed by protocol).
- Has its flexibility determined by its range of resources.
- Uses dynamic network of in-house and independent providers and delivery modules.

The Union Bank of Switzerland

For several years the Union Bank of Switzerland (UBS) has successfully applied the customer-responsive approach to providing both service to the customer and support service to front-line employees. UBS's approach is rooted in the military logistics model. In the 1970s a Swiss military officer was hired by the bank to help evaluate and improve its operational infrastructure. One of his first actions was to establish a Division of Logistics.

At UBS, logistics is defined as "everything that supports the front line."[4] Logistics, then, is directly responsible for enabling the front line to meet the needs of the customer. This means that logistics supplies the bank with the necessary resources to process the needs of the business in an efficient and effective manner. Logistics can codevelop solutions for the processing of its transactions, as well as help in the implementation of these processes. It can also provide the internal infrastructure necessary for the bank's internal and external functions.[4] These functions include security, training, accounting, personnel, communications, and other internal services.

Figure 6.5 illustrates the responsive model at two levels. First, the bank customer directly interfaces with a particular banking function, which could be provided by any of the front-line divisions. The customer contact person diagnoses the customer requests (i.e., needs) and determines if UBS can meet these needs. In complex financial situations, the customers may not have a clear understanding of all of the options available to them, so the front line must help them develop a clear understanding of relevant options. Second, the logistics department supports the front office by providing the technical and physical infrastructure needed to carry out the business of the organization. When an internal customer (a UBS division or department) has a need, the logistics department is used to supply the needed expertise or support. This may take the form of specialized training or services that may be on an ad hoc basis. This responsive approach can be contrasted to organizations in which a staff function, such as accounting, determines that a new system is needed and proceeds to develop the desired system and train the front line in its use. At UBS, systems are developed in response to user request, not imposed on users.

This example exemplifies the focus of the responsive logistics organization, and that is supporting the needs of the front line. This is done by providing the necessary operational infrastructure to meet the needs of customers and by managing the organizational structure that supports the mission of the organization. Operational infrastructural support provides direct, tangible support of the benefit delivery process. This could be such things as computer lines between UBS and the customer, data service lines such as Reuters, and the information network with UBS suppliers. Organizational infrastructure can include such activities as finance, accounting, human resources, or premises and security.

Thus there are two levels of support provided by the logistics support function. As with the distribution center, the logistics department first provides operational support (e.g., currency clearinghouses) for integrat-

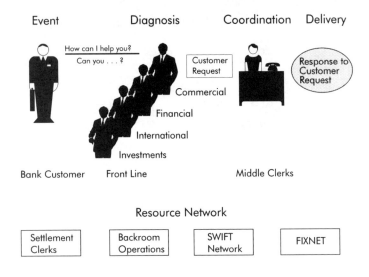

Figure 6.5. The responsive operational model of a bank.

ing with the outside network and then coordinates each delivery promised by the customer contact person. For example, it is the logistics department that operates the information system, which in turn tracks international exchange rates, processes exchange orders, and transmits funds to the appropriate clearinghouses. (Figure 6.5 depicts this organization.) Second, it is the logistics department that develops the supportive infrastructure that allows operators to make requested deliveries. In this case, the request is not made by a bank customer but rather by a front-line department that is encountering new customer needs or desires changes in the infrastructure to make front-line operations more effective. The logistics department is then responsible for making required changes to the infrastructure. This organization is described in Figure 6.6.

In summary, support services in a responsive organization:

- Function at multiple levels to support operations and to maintain the supportive infrastructure.
- Are event driven. At one level, the event is a request for service by the bank customer as diagnosed by the front line. At the

135

Examples of Customer-Responsive Organizations

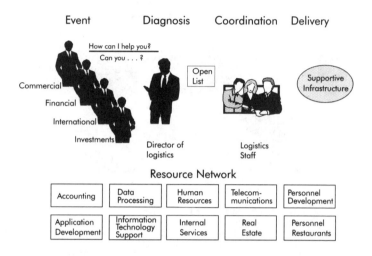

Figure 6.6. The responsive infrastructure model of a bank.

infrastructure level, the event is a request by front-line workers for a change in infrastructure to allow them to do their job better.

- Require multilevel coordination with a continual communication flow between the customer, the front line, and the back office or support services.
- Have their flexibility determined by range of resources in the network.
- Have a dynamic network of in-house and independent providers and delivery modules.

Roadway Logistics Systems

Third-party (i.e., contract) logistics firms specialize in developing and operating responsive organizations. Their use has grown over the last several years. This growth has been fueled by increased competition, the pressure to downsize current work-force levels, and the desire on management's part to concentrate solely on the firm's core businesses. Some organizations, such as Sun Workstations and Reebok, have moved fully to contract logistics firms, whereas others are moving slowly in this area.

Contract logistics firms provide a wide range of services. Perhaps the most familiar are the firms that take total responsibility for physical supply of inbound materials and the distribution of outbound products. There are other contract logistics firms that handle customer-service activities, such as those that handle software support questions for computer firms like IBM or Dell. In one case the request may be for a computer. In another the request may be for technical assistance in using software or the computer.

Contract logistics has had rapid acceptance by corporations. Instead of investing scarce capital in the supply chain or customer service, firms are utilizing contract logisticians who have already developed many of the components of the necessary support infrastructure or delivery network.

One such company is Roadway Logistics Systems (ROLS). ROLS provides services such as purchasing, warehousing, dedicated contract carriage, and less-than-truck-load (LTL) transportation, and has the capability to link rail and air transportation into a single-source logistics management solution. A company's supply chain is managed by one entity, which allows for the optimization of the whole channel, not just pieces of it.

The added value that companies like ROLS provide for their customers is their ability to develop and integrate supply chain components. In the past, each of the activities in the channel was managed separately. Contract logistics has changed the rules of the game by developing a coordinating process for all these activities.

ROLS's primary competency is knowing how to develop and operate responsive infrastructure. It understands how to determine customer needs, develop workable solutions, and coordinate delivery using a wide range of products or services. The clients interact with only one organization, thereby reducing the costs (in terms of both money and hassle) associated with managing multiple suppliers (e.g., warehouses, carriers, exporters).

This process is much like that used by an air-traffic controller, who has a process for coordinating all flights into and out of a particular area. Any small change in the altitude, latitude, or speed of any single flight affects the schedule of other aircraft using the airport.

Like UBS, contract logisticians have two roles. One role is building and maintaining the infrastructure required to support daily operations.

The infrastructure includes the information system, the network of suppliers, and the staff needed to support operations. The second role is to operate the infrastructure that it designs to support the primary purpose of the ROLS client – typically, a manufacturer.

The first role, the infrastructure building, begins with the client contact and a diagnosis of the needs of the individual client. Each client's needs are unique, as are the delivery solutions required. This is managed by a director of logistics development (DLD) who serves as the primary CCP. The DLD will meet with the customers, determine their level of commitment, and identify potential areas of logistical improvement in the organization.

After the contract logistics firm determines that the probability of success is high, a logistics analyst is assigned to the DLD and to the customer. This assignment may be due to the analyst's past work experience or past projects he or she has worked on with the customer. Once the contract logistics firm selects the analyst, the analyst begins the process of developing a feasible solution for the customer using all available resources and staff members, as shown in Figure 6.7.

As in the hospital responsive model, solution development and need diagnosis are iterative processes. At the beginning of the diagnosis, the clients may not know exactly what they want, the scope of services available to them, or the organizational consequences of their choices. For these reasons, the project may broaden or narrow in definition with each iterative step.

After the scope and expectations of the project are finalized, the analyst is responsible for developing an operationally feasible solution (process). The analyst will solicit network partners using requests for quotations (RFQs) on different parts of the process, depending on his or her expertise. ROLS will attempt to use one of its own 20 sister companies, but if the bid is too high or the service does not fit the need, it will use one of over 200 suppliers in its network. The solution (process) developed by the DLD and the analyst is presented to the client.

When the solution, or a modification of the solution, is accepted by the customer, operations begins the process of contacting the network of suppliers and, if the contract is large enough, hiring an on-site coordinator. Operationally, then, the CCP shifts from the DLD to the on-site coordinator. The on-site coordinator is responsible for the day-to-day management of the system, handling customer requests, and managing

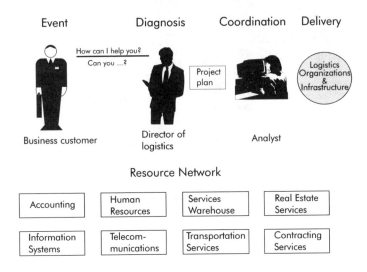

Event	Diagnosis	Coordination	Delivery

How can I help you?
Can you ...?

Project plan

Logistics Organizations & Infrastructure

Business customer

Director of logistics

Analyst

Resource Network

Accounting	Human Resources	Services Warehouse	Real Estate Services
Information Systems	Telecommunications	Transportation Services	Contracting Services

Figure 6.7. The logistics infrastructure development model.

the network of providers that come in contact with the customer. The day-to-day operations, represented in Figure 6.8, are very similar to the operations of the distribution center except that the network of providers may be larger and the coordination and integration processes are more sophisticated. After day-to-day operations begin, it is up to the on-site coordinator to improve the process continually.

There is a significant advantage that can be gained by both the client and the contract logistics firm. The manufacturing firm can focus on product design, production, and marketing. ROLS handles all physical supply and distribution. It focuses on managing the in-house capacity and the infrastructure and coordinating dispatches to the 20 sister transportation companies and the network of over 200 firms they use in the supply and distribution process. It is also easy to expand the range of services ROLS can provide its clients by simply expanding the network to add new capabilities and enhancing the coordination and integration processes.

In summary then, contract logistics:

- Is event driven at two levels. At the operations level, they respond to individual customer needs as they place orders on a daily basis

139

Examples of Customer-Responsive Organizations

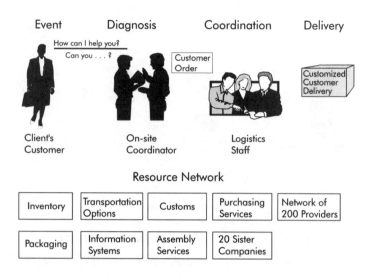

Event   Diagnosis   Coordination   Delivery

How can I help you?
Can you . . . ?

Customer Order

Customized Customer Delivery

Client's Customer   On-site Coordinator   Logistics Staff

Resource Network

Inventory	Transportation Options	Customs	Purchasing Services	Network of 200 Providers
Packaging	Information Systems	Assembly Services	20 Sister Companies	

Figure 6.8. The logistics operational model.

for the client's product. At the infrastructural level, they respond to requests by front-line users or the client. Front-line users may experience new types of customer requests that the existing infrastructure is unable to handle, so they will request changes. The client may decide to make changes in manufacturing processes or product design that will require changes to the infrastructure system to support the new logistics process required. For example, a recall may be an event that requires a unique response and thus modifications to the infrastructure.

- Employs multilevel coordination with a continual communication flow among the customer, the front line, operations, and the network of providers at the operational level and among client, technical staff, provider network, and DLD at the infrastructure level.

- Includes support services that have direct contact with the external customer and the front line.

- Has their flexibility determined by the range of resources available in the network.

- Has a dynamic network of in-house and independent suppliers.

Summary

As we described in Chapter 3, the process used by responsive organizations involves interacting with the customer to determine needs and coordinating with the network of resources to ensure delivery. The organizational structure consists of the front-end diagnosis (CCP), which interacts with the customers to diagnose their individual needs interactively. The back room dispatches a variety of delivery modules, each with its unique core competencies. When the range of responses to customers' requests is fairly limited, the front-end diagnostician creates a customized delivery strategy for each customer. When the range of responses to customers' requests is more diverse, both the front end and the back room may interact to create the customized delivery plan.

It is the front end that interacts with the individual customer to determine individual needs. These individual needs are then used in conjunction with the conditional best-practice guidelines to develop the individual delivery plan. The individual delivery plan becomes the prioritized dispatch list, which itemizes each task, including who it is for and when the work is to be done. The prioritized dispatch list or Kanban is used for dynamically dispatching each task and for recording the dispatch, responsibility, results, and time stamp for each activity. It is the heart of all coordinating, reporting, monitoring, tracking, and measuring quality for the organization.

Responsive management is relationship management. There is one relationship with the customer to identify and diagnose needs. There is a second relationship with the network of suppliers that make the deliveries. The role of the responsive organization is to develop an infrastructure that facilitates the integration of the provider network into the delivery process and the coordination (i.e., the dispatching and tracking) of each delivery.

References

[1] Hyrum W. Smith, *The 10 Natural Laws of Successful Time and Life Management*, New York: Warner Books, 1994, p. 105.

[2] William G. Pagonis, "The Work of The Leader," *Harvard Business Review*, November/December 1992, p. 118.

[3] J. Philip Lathrop, "The Patient-Focused Hospital," *Healthcare Forum Journal*, July/August 1991, p. 18.

[4] Personal conversation with Dr. Heinrich Baumann, First Vice President, Union Bank of Switzerland, October 1992 at the Council of Logistics Annual Conference, San Antonio, Texas.

[5] Karl B. Manrodt, "Service Response Logistics: A Case Study of Financial, Health Care and Contract Logistics Organizations." Unpublished Doctoral Dissertation, College of Business, University of Tennessee, Knoxville, December 1993.

CHAPTER 7

THE CUSTOMER RELATIONSHIP MANAGEMENT TASK

Customer-responsive management is relationship management. As discussed in the last chapter, this involves two relationships. First, there is the relationship with the individual customer. It is this relationship that causes the customer to contact the organization and ask for help. It is this relationship that allows the organization to define the individual customer's need. Functionally, this relationship has the same importance that marketing (e.g., market research, product planning, advertising, sales, and customer service) has to an offering-based organization.

Second, there is the relationship with the resources used to deliver solutions. This is the relationship that allows the organization to satisfy the customer's need. Functionally, this relationship has the same importance that operations (e.g., purchasing, production, supply chain logistics, human resources) has to the offering-based organization.

Four tasks that are essential for managing the relationship with the customer. These tasks are summarized in the familiar customer-process-resources model first presented in Chapter 1 and shown again in Figure 7.1.

Chapter 8 will present the four tasks essential for integrating resources and coordinating delivery. Chapter 8 will also present the primary motivation for managing both relationships with customers and the delivery coordination process – yield on investment to stockholders.

Relationship Management

Customers buy from people they trust. They select providers that they believe understand their needs, can meet their needs, and have their best interest at heart. They patronize businesses where they get the greatest value in return for their expenditure in terms of money and hassle. When this occurs, they continue to return as repeat customers. As shown in Chapter 3, customer retention is the principal predictor of profits.

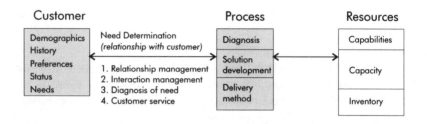

Figure 7.1. Customer relationship management functions.

But how does an organization make the customer comfortable about selecting it as a supplier? If the need is for a product familiar to the customers, they simply go to the marketplace and select on the basis of price or service. The less familiar he or she is with the product, or the greater the risk is of selecting the wrong product, the more searching and studying the customer tends to do. The tangibility of products allows the customer to examine or "test drive" a product. If the product is defective or does not perform according to the customer's expectations, the customer has the guarantee of "customer satisfaction or your money cheerfully refunded."

Customer-responsive organizations, on the other hand, may not be as easy for the customer to evaluate. Frequently, the risk may be high or irreversible. One has only to consider the consequences of risk and permanence of obtaining less than the best in health care, legal defense, or child care. Therefore, customers frequently begin their search by talking with friends and acquaintances to determine if they have had personal experiences with potential providers. When customers are impressed, they tell others. When they are disillusioned, they tell even more people. As Waldrop stated, "Consumers who have a good experience with our company tell an average of five other people, but those who have a bad experience tell twice that many."[1]

Customers develop expectations by listening to others or seeing promotional material. These initial expectations motivate the customer to make the first call to the provider. Because the new customer has had no previous experience with the provider, expectations are frequently based on the personal experiences of others. Expectations typically have three dimensions: delivery effectiveness, price, and hassle.[1]

Most important is expectations about delivery effectiveness. Can you expect the provider to understand your needs and effectively respond? Will the delivery fit your specific needs?

The second dimension is price. Customers seem to expect that some organizations survive by taking advantage of unwary consumers. These feelings can be valid, or they can simply be caused by a lack of understanding what was involved in the delivery process. Regardless of the reason, perception forms the expectations.

The third dimension of expectations is the hassle of interacting with the organization. "Hassle" refers to the noneconomic cost of doing business. Hassle includes uncertainty, filling out duplicate forms, waiting, disorientation, and systems or procedures that are often more important to the provider than to the customer.

Expectations are based on a combination of these factors. A physician may have a reputation of being an outstanding diagnostician, but he or she may have an almost unbearable bedside manner. Many people expect to pay a high hassle cost when purchasing an automobile. To reduce such nuisance, some showrooms now offer "hassle-free" shipping and clearly display the prices of each car. In these situations salespersons can respond to the customer's technical queries, but are unable to negotiate on the price of the vehicle.

Vavra suggests that "relationships are built on familiarity and knowledge."[2] An astute restaurant manager knows his or her regular customers and their preferences. The manager knows where they like to sit, what they like to drink with their meals, and when they miss coming to the restaurant. Mike Connors tells of the manager who notices that a usual foursome is only a threesome on a particular night. The manager inquires and learns that the missing customer is in the hospital but doing well.

---

1. In some instances in this book, the term "delivery effectiveness" will be used. In other cases, "fit" will be mentioned. Both terms refer to the ability of the product or service to meet the needs of the individual customer.

One of the group suggests that the only problem is the hospital food. The manager promptly has the missing customer's favorite meal prepared and delivered to the hospital.[3] With such familiarity, how can the customer not feel that he or she is important and the restaurant is concerned about meeting his or her needs? Not only is the relationship strengthened, but the delighted customer revels in telling others about how "important" he or she is to the restaurant.

Another telling anecdote concerns shoe repair. After purchasing a pair of hiking boots that carried a lifetime guarantee for materials and workmanship, the buyer noticed a small area that had not been completely glued together. He returned the boots. The shoe store manager indicated that it would be no problem to fix the boots in four to six weeks. Because he was leaving on a trip, the customer asked if they could be exchanged. The manager replied that he did not want to get "stuck" with a pair of "repaired" boots.

"I bought these yesterday and I am now stuck with a pair of damaged boots?" the customer responded.

The manager stared blankly and then said that the only option was for the customer to take the boots to a local shoe repair company authorized by the manufacturer, have the boots reglued, pay for the repair, bring the receipt back to the store, and have the money refunded.

The buyer discovered that the store had a policy that the customer must personally perform each of these tasks. The buyer took the shoes to the shoe repair shop, but was not prepared for the following dialogue.

Shoe repairman: "Where did you buy your boots? I sell the same brand and would enjoy your business." The buyer then related his story to the shoe repair owner.

"You should have bought them from me," said the shoe repairman.

"I didn't know you sold them," responded the buyer. "You should advertise."

"Advertise for me," said the shoe repairman.

The buyer (shocked but still remembering his MBA training): "Pay me to advertise for you."

Shoe repairman: "I just did. I fixed your boots for free."

The buyer was amazed at the contrast with his experience at the shoe store, thanked the shoe repairman profusely, and decided to make all future purchases from him. I later hear the buyer tell all his friends that his "wow" experience had made him an annuity (i.e., a continual income stream) for the shoe repair shop.

Where firms are larger, have multiple locations or relationships, or are handled by multiple individuals, the need to maintain databases is essential. Databases typically contain:

- Descriptive data such as the customer's name, address, and phone number;
- The customer's status data, such as outstanding balance, line of credit, and preexisting conditions;
- The customer's preference data, such as meal and seat preferences, preferred newspaper, time and type of bed-time snack, and allergies;
- The customer's history, such as patient history, purchase history, returns, failed deliveries. and any other data that could affect the customer's relationship with the firm.

From these data, the organization can develop solutions tailored specifically for each customer. Mailings can be totally personalized. If purchase patterns increase or decrease, the organization can be aware and contact the customer to express appreciation or determine if anything is wrong.

There is a big difference between individualized databases and statistical databases. For example, health-care providers have typically used the statistical approach. Their first step was to sample a group of people to determine the mean and standard deviation for measures such as blood-chemistry levels. Then normal levels were established, such as plus or minus 2 standard deviations from the mean. When individual blood chemistries were measured, the patient typically was told whether he or she was within the "normal" range.

A more individualized approach would capture the individual patient's measurements. Then when his or her blood chemistry was run, values would be compared to the patient's normal levels. For example, a person's cholesterol level may be well within the normal range but may have increased each time the level was checked over the last five years. By comparing individual data with other readings from the same individual, trends can be spotted that will suggest action to be taken before the patient's test results become "abnormal."

Trust is the basis of a healthy relationship. A customer may continue to use a firm because it is the best option currently available, or the customer may truly develop a strong trust in the provider. Trust comes when the customer believes that the provider is genuinely interested in benefiting the customer. As Buckman summarized, "You cannot empower somebody that you do not trust or who does not trust you."[4] Trust allows the customer to empower the provider to serve him or her.

Trust has varying degrees of importance, depending upon a customer's familiarity and his or her ability to evaluate the benefit being offered. A simple story will illustrate this. If someone told about having a neighbor who was such an effective salesperson that he had sold all of the neighbors new cars, the listener would probably be impressed with the saleperson's ability to help so many friends find selections that met their individual needs. If the listener were also told that there was an attorney in the neighborhood who was so effective that he had gotten all of the neighbors divorces whether they wanted it or not, he or she would probably laugh. If the listener were informed that there was a surgeon in the neighborhood who was so effective that he had given all of the neighbors appendectomies whether they needed them or not, the listener would be horrified. We could not imagine anyone cruel enough to submit individuals to such emotional trauma and personal risk just to "make another sale."

The difference in these three scenarios is that most individuals generally know what they are getting when they buy a car. In the case of the lawyer, it is hard to imagine anyone would be so gullible to be talked into getting a divorce. In the case of the surgeon, where each individual is unable to understand the technical issues, we realize the importance of empowering the provider to make a decision that is in the best interest of the *customer* and not that of the provider.

As shown in Chapter 3, trust develops repeat business. Relationship management is built on nurturing that relationship and never letting the customer feel that the desire of the firm to make another sale is greater than the customer's own interests. Stated another way, the firm would not take any action that would interfere with the customer's willingness to empower the company to solve their needs.

There is also a down side in relationship building. It may be that the company will have to fire customers who take advantage of the company. An effective database can identify those customers who are not profitable or who are abusive of company policies. For instance, one large mail-order company that offers a lifetime guarantee on their clothing started to notice a high rate of returns from one customer for items this customer had never purchased. The company found out that the customer was going to yard sales, buying the clothing, and returning it for new items. When confronted with the facts, the customer ceased. When there is a high incidence of this kind of behavior, the store can call the customers, provide them with the data, and explain that the store's liberal exchange policies were never meant to encourage this type of exploitation. It is simply not fair to other customers. Often this form of honesty can turn a questionable relationship around to one based on a mutual understanding that a relationship must be beneficial to both sides. Information clarifies understanding.

The relationship with the customer is a dynamic process, as shown in Figure 7.2. Individuals first contact an organization based upon its reputation, whether word of mouth or some other source. Each time his or her needs are met, the customer's trust is increased. When the customer has a "wow" delivery, the level of trust jumps even higher and favorably influences word of mouth. If the delivery is below expectations, a gap forms. If the provider accepts responsibility for the problems and makes a good recovery, trust levels are restored. If, however, the recovery is not made, expectations begin to fall and customers become disenchanted until they find an alternative provider. (Eighty-four percent of customers return if their complaints are resolved quickly, but only 15% come back if their complaints are not resolved.[5])

The relationship is important because it establishes customer expectations. When expectations are realistically high, customers call to seek solutions for their needs. Once the customer does call, the provider needs to respond and reassure the customer.

Interaction Management

The way a company responds is determined by the organization's attitude toward the customers and toward its employees. In fact, these were the two basic characteristics of excellent companies described by Tom Peters and Robert Waterman in their book, *In Search of Excellence*. Organizations must truly "love their customers" and believe in "making the average Joe a hero and a consistent winner."[6] These are the two essential ingredients for managing the interaction with the customer. It is the "average Joe" who interacts with the customer. It is this relation-

The Customer Relationship Management Task

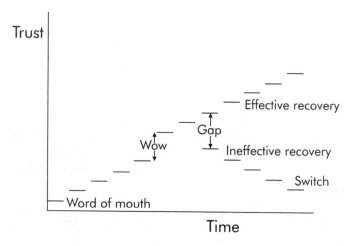

Figure 7.2. The building of customer trust.

ship that builds or destroys the relationship between the organization and the customer. Jan Carlzon has focused on making each "moment of truth" – when customer and airline employee interact – effective.[7] Customers do not interact with corporate officers, planners, or managers. They interact with the baggage handlers, flight attendants, gate agents, and reservationists. These are the individuals that make the trip enjoyable or frustrating.

It is the corporate culture that determines if the customer is viewed as a conquest or a relationship.[2] Offering-based firms have one primary objective: to sell their offering to the customer. The relationship-oriented organization sees the customer not as a single sale but as a long-term relationship in which the *value of future deliveries will always be greater than the value of any existing transaction.* Just as the local dairy will never risk the value of a 25-year relationship with the local grocery chain

---

2. Terry Vavra uses these two terms. "Conquest marketing" is the term he uses to describe a firm that is sale oriented and places a greater emphasis on attracting new customers than on serving existing ones. Salespersons are rewarded for obtaining new accounts. "Relationship marketing," on the other hand, focuses on customer retention. If a customer reduces the frequency of his or her purchases, he or she needs to be contacted so that the firm can determine what it needs to do to be more responsive.

over the quality of a single shipment of milk, so the relationship firm is there to learn and respond to the changing needs of its customers. Terry Varra defines relationship marketing as involving:

- developing an information file on individual customers,
- understanding how customers interact with the organization (blueprinting), and
- developing a dialogue with individual customers (formal, informal, customer service).[8]

An emphasis on corporate culture and relationship marketing is necessary before organizations can become responsive. Until the organization becomes customer-driven, the emphasis will be on the offering, not the response. The customer emphasis is necessary before the organization sees the customer as "a source of stimulation, ideas, and opportunity" instead of someone "to be satisfied at minimum cost" or as "a market segment whose basic needs are (best) understood" by the company planners.[9] Once this transition is made, the emphasis is on maintaining a relationship with the customer and responding to requests and needs.

Organizations cannot be responsive to customers as long as they think of employees as "negative constraints" or as "efficient resources, disciplined, (who) follow procedures."[10] Until the organization recognizes that employees want to serve customers, its emphasis is on developing policies and procedures rather than on providing employees the tools they need to make Peters's and Waterman's average Joe "a hero and a consistent winner" in serving the customer.[11] There is no way that predefined policies and procedures can be broad enough to address each individual customer request. To be responsive, the organization must empower individual employees to diagnose needs and commit the organization to a response when individual customers call. Because the individual employees are in constant contact with customers, managers must recognize that it is they who best know the customers and that they are "innovative, (and should) create procedures."[12] Management must develop an infrastructure that allows the individual employees to be more effective in maintaining their relationships with the customers so that they can diagnose needs, commit capacity, and coordinate delivery. Management becomes the support organization that facilitates the front line while the front line decides what to do and how it is to be done.

This is not a new concept. Peters and Waterman recognized it as a difference in the excellence firms.[13] Chase and Hayes recognized it as the difference between service firms that are simply "available for service" and "world-class service delivery."[14] It is the basis for total quality management (TQM) and of customer-responsive organizations.

Organizations can use many different strategies for improving their contacts with customers. Some organizations, especially commercial banks, have a specific customer contact person (CCP) who always handles a particular customer. This approach allows the CCP to develop an experience base about the customer. The CCP knows the customer's needs, the customer's preferences, and the way the customer likes to interact. Just as an effective family physician knows his or her patients and always has their needs in mind, good CCPs will understand how to apply any new product announcement or capability to the needs of individual customers.

Imagine a restaurant manager calling her customers to tell them when the season's first shipment of oysters will arrive, or the computer salesperson who understands the customer's needs so well that they serve more as a technology scanner for the customer than an order taker. This only occurs when the CCP understands the customer's needs so well that he or she is kept abreast of relevant developments, not just blanket promotions. It is not hard for the customer to know if the interaction is by a CCP who understands the customer's needs and cares and wants to benefit the customer. It is also not hard to understand if the CCP is only following procedures and promoting offerings.

A second approach to providing this understanding and caring interaction is through the use of information systems. In a July 12, 1993, *Wall Street Journal* article, Jack Falvey stated that "Few managers realize that 80% of the sales process is controlled by specific knowledge of a customer's business."[15] Instead of getting information from a personal relationship with the customers, such data is collected and stored electronically. As soon as the customer is identified, whether by the new caller ID service offered by the phone company or some other method, information about the caller is retrieved and presented in a easily recognizable form on the computer screen. Although the CCP for a car-rental agency could answer the phone by addressing the customer by name, referring to his or her last trip, and asking what type of car the customer would like today, he or she will instead say "hello" and let the customers identify themselves. But all the information is available to enable the CCP to interact with the customer the same way a personal, dedicated, and observant CCP could. The implications were identified by Carlzon: "An individual without information cannot take responsibility; an individual who is given information cannot help but take responsibility."[16]

Customers now expect such treatment. We do not expect to give our own travel agent our address, credit card number, seating preference, meal preference, and car-rental needs each time we make an airline reservation. We do not like to provide our complete medical history each time we check into a hospital. We want companies to make it easy for us to interact with each them. When customers call, they should be reassured that they made the correct call by having their needs met. This reassurance occurs when customers know that the firm cares about solving their needs and has made the effort necessary to know and understand them. The next step is to understand the customer need that prompted this call.

Diagnosis Management

When customers know exactly what they want, they may go to the marketplace to shop around to see what is available or they may call a firm and place an order. This works for well-known products and services. But what happens when a customer has a need but has not fully defined a desired solution? Customers often believe that they know what they want but that they are not able to describe it until they see it or experience it. Offering-based firms produce solutions and offer them in the marketplace. It is up to the customers to shop until they find the solution that best meets their needs.

There are many different approaches that can be used to diagnose the needs of the customer. The appropriate approach is determined in part by how well the customer understands his or her own needs, the lead time needed to deliver the benefit, and the amount of customization that must be done.

If customers know what they want, then the diagnosis process is simple. Take, for example, the customer who purchases a gallon of bleach at the grocery store. The product is familiar and the quantity is known. The retailer makes the product (i.e., offering) available, and the customer responds to past experience or advertising and purchases it.

Suppose a customer asks a custom home builder, "Can you build me a dream home with big white columns in front, a cathedral ceiling, and an atrium room on the side?" In this case, the customer knows what he or she wants but is only looking at three of thousands of details that must be defined before the home can become a reality. Details such as site, floor plan, type of roof, floor covering, and even building material must be decided. Unless such details are correctly decided upon, the customer will not be satisfied by even the best delivery of the three criteria.

Several approaches can be used to diagnose needs. These include diagnoses based on listening, displays, questions, or prototypes.

Listening-Based Diagnosis

Listening-based diagnosis occurs when customers know what they want. The CCP simply listens to the customer explain his or her need. Individuals who use this approach have often been labeled "order takers." Many salespersons at one time viewed their job to be to drive to the customer's site and wait in the purchasing office until the purchasing agent gave them a verbal order that they faithfully recorded on the appropriate order form and mailed to the factory. In similar vein, how many realtors view their job as being taxi drivers and door openers who have a key to the front door?

A step up is the auto salesperson, who may see his or her role as listening to the customers describe the model they want and showing them where to find it on the lot. A more astute salesperson will listen to the customer's stated desires and attempt to show the customer options that he or she may not have considered.

A more sophisticated listening-based approach is exemplified by having information systems placed on the customer's site so that the customer can place an order without having to interact with a salesperson. In the 1970s, American Hospital Supply replaced the traditional salesperson with a computer terminal located in the hospital so that hospital employees could place orders when they needed the products without having to contact a salesperson. Banks have introduced the automatic teller machine, which works very well when customers know what they need.

A still more sophisticated version of the listening model was pioneered by Wal-Mart. Because all products have bar codes and are scanned at the point of sale (POS), this information can be used to automatically replenish stock. POS data are gathered each evening, transmitted to the corporate offices, processed, and retransmitted to the appropriate vendor the next morning. The vendor thus knows what has been sold and can immediately replenish the shelves. This electronic listening system eliminates the hassle of salespersons, purchasing, travel, waits, mail, and long lead times. Retailers use this type of information system to reduce stockouts and increase inventory turns. This increases sales by having the product available when requested by the customer, and also allows inventory not only to pay for itself but also to help finance the cost of the retail facility.

Consider a retailer balancing two cash flows. The first is payments for the inventory the store purchases. The second is the cash flow that results from the sale of goods. If purchases have to be paid for in 30 days and the inventory turns 12 times a year (i.e., takes 30 days to sell), then the merchant is paid for the goods by the time payment is due for the purchase. If the inventory turns only six times a year, the merchant must have 50 percent of the purchase price of the inventory in working capital to pay for inventory. If inventory turns 24 times per year (i.e., takes 15 days to sell), then the inventory generates cash flow fast enough to provide its value in working capital to help finance the building of the store. Inventory turns of 48 to 96 times a year could easily finance aggressive expansion.

Regardless of how simple or how sophisticated, the simple listening approach to diagnosis assumes that customers know what they want and that the CCP is simply there to record the order, locate the desired items, and process the transaction. Within firms that use the more sophisticated listening systems, CCPs have learned to listen to the description given by the customer and convert the customer's description to a specific model number or a more tailored description of the desired delivery.

Display-Based Diagnosis

Display-based diagnosis is another method of helping the customer visualize potential solutions. A display is designed to show various options and thus help the customers visualize ways of solving their individual needs. Sears Roebuck introduced the catalog that became a household standard in much of America. Individuals could look through its pages to see what options were available. Even individuals who made their own clothes could use the Sears catalog to stimulate their imaginations. As individuals looked at the pictures and descriptions, they began to visualize what products they would like. Travel brochures have long used this method to help individuals visualize how they might like vacationing at a particular location. Magazines supported by vendor advertising use this same method to show how individuals have remodeled their homes, sometimes with the same products found advertised a few pages away.

Question-Based Diagnosis

Question-based diagnosis is interactive. The organization does not expect the customers to know exactly what they want. Therefore, the firm develops a series of questions to help diagnose needs. The customer's response to these questions will help the CCP define these needs so that the delivery can be responsive to them.

Consider the request for telephone service in the post-Ma Bell environment. The traditional question that differentiated service had always been "commercial or residential?" In an era of telecommuting in which salespersons, programmers, and consultants work out of their homes with the help of answering machines, modems, and faxes, this question is less meaningful. Is the truck driver who is always on the road a commercial account? Is the telecommuter a residential account? Such questions were not designed to diagnose customer needs but rather to meet regulatory requirements for charging higher rates to commercial users.

Instead of having the CCP read a menu of 50 different services and products offered by the telephone company (which the customer probably could not remember anyway), the CCP could instead ask a series of questions.

"Do you have teenagers at home?" "Do you plan to connect a modem or fax to the computer?" The first question may suggest two telephone lines while the second question may nullify the value of call waiting. "Do you expect to have many long distance calls?" "Will they be calls to this phone or calling close friends or relatives out of state?" These questions may suggest electronic mail, calling cards, various types of long-distance charging plans, or the identification of referrals. "Do you have individuals who may need emergency assistance yet are unable to get to the phone?" Question-based diagnostic systems are designed to diagnose customer needs so that the CCP can provide the best possible fit.

Question-based approaches are typically designed by gathering a group of experts. These are the individuals who best understand how to ask questions that accurately define needs. These experts each contribute questions that they want to ask customers and explain why. Next, they are asked to show how they use the customer's responses to diagnose needs.

The result of this exercise is called an "expert system." The expert system can be disseminated to CCPs through training or information systems that embody the expert system. These systems enable relatively new CCPs to interact with customers and diagnose needs just as capably as the mature, experienced experts. Expert systems are typically based on "if" logic. That is, if the customer gives one answer, question 2 will be asked. *If* they give a different answer, a different question will be asked.

Whirlpool has made a major investment in a question-based system for diagnosing customer problems with their appliances. A customer history file is developed either from the customer's calls to a nationwide customer assistance center or from warranty cards that they have returned. Using this information, Whirlpool can develop a very extensive customer history showing appliances owned and problems. Whirlpool uses a question-based expert system to diagnose problems and determine if the customer or a service representative should make the repair. For example:

Customer: "I am having trouble with a film on my drinking glasses when they leave the dishwasher."

Whirlpool: "Can you wipe off the film?"
  If the answer is "yes," the phosphate level in the soap is too low for the water hardness. If it is "no," the customer is using a detergent with too much phosphate that is permanently etching the glasses.

To determine if customers might be able to make the repairs, the Whirlpool CCP asks if the customer has a volt-ohm meter. If he does not, he is probably not the home repair type and should rely on a technician. If he does have a volt-ohm meter, he will probably have the ability to do some voltage checks to assist in the diagnosis. If the customer seems to understand the suggested checks, the part can be sent for customer installation. If not, a technician should probably be dispatched. If a service call costs $50.00 and the phone assistance is only $5.00, an expert system can not only expedite solution of the customer's need but also save expensive service calls. This is especially important if the system can reduce warranty repair service calls. Now Whirlpool provides another option. The CCP will take the do-it-yourselfer through the repair for a fee.

Prototype-Based Diagnosis

The prototype approach to diagnosis is used when individuals have trouble visualizing what they want. The prototype is a tool to help the individual visualize possible solutions. Prototypes (and portfolios) have often been used by creative individuals to convey their ideas. For example, architects develop drawings and even three-dimensional models of proposed buildings. Such prototypes can help the client visualize how the proposed building will look, fit into the environment, and be used. Commercial artists develop prototypes of advertising copy for review by customers. Designers build clay mock-ups of automobiles and other products. Computer programmers build prototypes of screens so that customers can respond to the look and feel of the programs under development.

A prototype process begins by interacting with the customer and understanding the customer's vision (as far as it is developed). Then a designer creates a prototype that reflects the customer's ideas. The customer then responds to the prototype. Prototyping is an iterative process. The prototype may be modified many times before concensus is reached between the involved parties.

One group that has used prototyping very well has been custom log-home manufacturers. Log-home producers have been very aggressive in customization because such homes are self-supporting and do not need internal load-bearing walls. Catalogs published by such firms typically include pictures of different roof designs, floor plans, windows, doors, and other features of the building. Customers are encouraged to sketch out their own floor plans on graph paper that is provided. In addition, many different types of questions are asked about housing preferences. Within a very short time, customized plans are developed and prices are calculated. The customized plans may be sketches or plans made with a computer-aided design (CAD) system. Next, the design data are entered into an estimating program that calculates costs.

It does not matter how prototypes are created. What is important are that the customer and the designer interact, that ideas are shared, and that the designer develops a prototype to help the customer see the final results.

A new prototyping concept is being pioneered in barber shops and beauty salons. A video camera can be used to record a person's picture so that alternative hair styles can be electronically simulated before a single hair is cut. This concept could also be extended to other fields, such as the automotive industry. The individual could select the model, color, and interiors and then view computer-generated pictures illustrating the desired options and the resulting price and monthly payments. This could substantially reduce the need for planning for a large number of vehicles to be displayed on the showroom floor. In fact, the computers could even be located at banks, credit unions, or other unconventional outlets, and the cars could be custom ordered and financed at one location. Once the need is defined, the order can be transmitted to the manufacturer, and within a short time the customized product could be delivered to the customer.

Seiko is developing a very sophisticated prototyping system to replace many of the traditional market research methods. Now the firm does test marketing by simply producing small lots of many different new products. The products are then placed in stores. By monitoring point of sale (POS) data, Seiko can easily tell which products are selling and which colors and styles are achieving the greatest customer acceptance. This information is then returned to the factory, and the products are changed, dropped, or modified based on this continuous flow of data.

Screening-Based Diagnosis

In many cases, customers do not know what they need and would not recognize it if they saw it. This is especially true for extremely technical benefits. The obvious example is in health care. When the patient responds to the physician's query "How can I help you?" with "I don't feel good," the provider must develop methods for screening out various options. Much of this screening can be done with expert systems that ask the patient questions to determine when the symptoms began, how they are changing, and their nature. The expert-systems approach is used to screen out as many areas as possible. Blood tests, X-rays, pathology, vital signs and many other techniques are used to further screen out various options.

The medical field is not the only one to use screening methods. Consultants interested in the financial or environmental health of an organization may conduct audits, analyze reports, or make air or soil tests to determine radiation levels or to screen out other potential problems. In fact, the purpose of this type of research is to examine a number of options to determine which ones seems to be causing the problem facing the organization. Statistical tests are often used to determine if there is a causal relationship between the measure under question and the problem. Whether it is the geologist taking core samples to determine geological suitability for construction, the statistician taking readings to determine upper and lower process control limits for a production process, the auto mechanic taking readings on the diagnostic computer, or the oncologist sending specimens for biopsy, each is using screening methods to diagnose needs.

Screenings can also be done electronically. Health-care providers could send lab technicians and nurses into work sites to collect blood samples and gather information deemed to be important for screening purposes. This could be done on an annual basis, and the results could be recorded electronically. Test results from employees working in similar sites could be screened to provide an early-warning system for detecting environmental hazards before they become a crisis for the employers. It would be better for the employer to have such workplace hazards identified by the screenings rather than be notified of the problem by an attorney representing an ill employee.

However needs are diagnosed – whether through listening, questioning, prototyping, or screening – there is one main purpose to such exercises: to understand the customer's need so that a solution can be developed. The fourth management area is slightly different. The first three identify strategies used to 1) build relationships, 2) interact with the customer, and 3) diagnose the need. The fourth area looks at the types of business events that a CCP can expect to encounter.

Customer-Service Management

"Customer service" is the term used to describe the ongoing dialogue between the customer and the organization (i.e., CCP). The answers provided to a customer's many questions give the reassurance the customer need. The questions can occur as part of the relationship-building process, as part of the diagnosis process, as part of the delivery process, or at any time after a delivery is made. In general, customer questions can be divided into the following five categories, which are applicable to any organization:

1. "Can you . . . ?"
2. "Will you . . . ?"
3. "Did you . . . ?"
4. "Why did you . . . ?"
5. "Why should I . . . ?"

"Can You . . . ?"

This question represents the effort made by the customer to determine if the organization is able to meet his or her needs. This is the customer's way of testing the organization to see if it has the ability to diagnose needs and the capability and capacity to respond effectively. This is the individual's effort to determine if the organization should be considered as a potential provider. The more unique the customers' needs, the more common this question. When the firm produces and promotes a single product, all the customers have to do is determine if the product can meet their needs. In the case of a responsive organization, customers may suspect that their requests can be served by the organization's competency area, but they are unsure.

For example, a person may call and ask, "Can you get me from Knoxville to St. Louis for a 7:00 a.m. meeting on April 12?" To answer this question, the on-line CCP must have access to capability, capacity, and commitment data from each of the delivery units. For example, the reservationist must have access to all flight schedules and information about the available seats on each flight. This information is needed for company flights as well as for interline carriers. If the information is not available to the reservationist, it is not an available option for the caller.

"Can you . . . ?" is at the heart of market research for the responsive organization. The firm should capture all cases in which it was unable to respond to a customer query. The customer had enough confidence in the organization to call, but the organization did not have the capability to respond. This effort identifies the customers who had needs, expected the organization to be able to meet them, and were motivated to call. There is no better indicator of potential market opportunities. These data should be captured using dynamic Pareto charts. A Pareto chart is simply a listing of attributes (e.g., size, color, complaints, reasons for failure) ranked by frequency of occurrence. Pareto charts can help an individual focus on the most important attributes. A dynamic Pareto chart is one that allows data to be continually added to the list and tracked. (See Figure 7.3.) For instance, if a shirt is returned to a store because it was the wrong color, the Pareto chart will be updated to reflect this new data point. If the reason for the failure is not listed on the Pareto chart, the CCP should be able to add that reason to the list. Marketers should constantly monitor the dynamic Pareto charts to identify potential areas for expanding capabilities.

The following example illustrates this concept. A CCP for a local lawn-fertilizing service complained bitterly about how "stupid" the people were in her market area. She explained that she must get ten calls a day from individuals wanting to have their yards reseeded. She complained that she was tired of explaining that the promotional material plainly stated they were a fertilizing service and not a reseeding service. It is important to ask, "Who are the dummies?" After the firm wisely added reseeding service, the CCP again began to complain bitterly that the dumb people did not understand that they fertilized and reseeded lawns and that she must have 30 calls a day from people wanting to know if they could mow lawns. Again, unfulfilled customer requests are the best source of market research data and should be captured dynamically on a continual basis by the CCPs as they interact with customers.

This helps explain a fundamental difference between product-based and response-based firms. *The difference is basically a result of organizational inflexibilities.* If a firm is very limited in what it can do, either by capacity or production constraints, then it tries to do that one activity for as large a market as possible. For example, if a firm can only produce one product, it attempts to sell as many of that product as it can produce. This approach focuses on the limitations of the production process.

The response-based organization seeks to increase flexibility so that it can strengthen the relationship with the customer. It seeks to respond to more needs from existing customers as well as reach out to new customers. The customer-service group interacts with existing customers

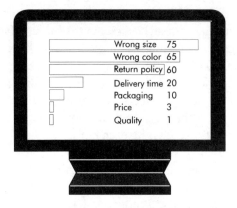

Wrong size	75
Wrong color	65
Return policy	60
Delivery time	20
Packaging	10
Price	3
Quality	1

Figure 7.3. A computerized, dynamic Pareto chart showing the reasons why customers were dissatisfied with the firm's performance.

and marketing reaches out to new customers. Existing customers are already in the habit of doing business with the organization, and a level of trust has developed. Such customers are already identified. It is often easier to get existing customers to try new capabilities than to locate new customers. The firm will typically link failures shown on Pareto charts with the specific customer experiencing the failure. The cost of contacting these customers, researching their needs, and getting them to begin using new services is minimal compared with new product-development and roll-out costs.

"Will You . . . ?"

This question is much different. It indicates that the customer is satisfied with the diagnosis and the firm's ability to deliver. The hotel industry calls this a "conversion" – that is, the inquiry is converted into a room reservation. Once a conversion has occurred, the delivery coordination mechanism is initiated.

The request must first be checked against the best-practice guideline. In a hospital, as shown in Chapter 4, there is a best-practice guideline for each diagnosis and procedure. This guideline determines the tests that should be run, whether the patient should be admitted to the hospital, and the specialist that should be called in.

The Customer Relationship Management Task

If you ask Federal Express to ship a package for you, they must schedule a pickup and commit capacity in the form of the plane that will take the package to a distribution center, the distribution center itself, and the plane that will take the package to the destination city. It must also determine the delivery truck that will deliver the package.

In essence, the best-practice guideline creates a new item on the priority dispatch list for each task that must be undertaken. It also commits the capacity required by each delivery module to perform that part of the delivery. Each task on the priority dispatch list also contains a time window for completing the task. Sometimes the time window will be absolute (e.g., "by noon on the 14th") and sometimes it will be relative (e.g., "as soon as task A and B are completed"). Other times it will be conditional (e.g., "if test A is positive, do B"). Thus the question, "Will you . . . ?" is the event that triggers the scheduling of all the tasks necessary for the delivery of the desired benefits. It is the event that initiates the entire delivery process.

"Did You . . . ?"

When the customer asks this question, he or she wants reassurance. The customer is apprehensive and wants to make sure everything is on schedule. Perhaps Harry Dalton, vice president of technology integration at Federal Express, has described this process best. During a presentation at The University of Tennessee, Knoxville, he told the following story to help students understand the motivation for Federal Express's very large investment in its COSMOS 2B tracking system. It was nearly 11:00 a.m., and a hospital patient was prepped and the medical staff scrubbed, but the implant the patient was scheduled to receive had not yet arrived. Someone suggested calling Federal Express to see if they could find the implant. Because the COSMOS 2B system tracks each package at each point in the system, it was easy for the CCP to check the to-do list, determine when each task was completed, locate the package, and identify the next step in the delivery process. In this particular case, a call to Federal Express resulted in a trace that indicated not only that the package had been delivered, but where, when, and who had signed for the package.

As this example shows, tracing is typically not used when Federal Express is at fault but when there is breakdown in communication. No one cares whether Federal Express did not deliver as promised or whether there was a breakdown in communication at the receiver's site. All they want is to have the implant when they need it. It is not important who is at fault, only that the customer trusts that delivery will be effective and the problem solved.

"Why Did You . . . ?"

Customers ask this question when they are trying to reconcile what happened with their original expectation. This has been defined as "perceived quality." Perceived quality is a "comparison of expectations with perceptions of performance."[17] Was the expected service actually delivered? Were the actual charges consistent with expectations? Although disappointed customers may become irate, most are simply trying to retrace events to understand the original agreement. If the customer and CCP can clearly remember what happened, most conflicts can be resolved. Where both parties have very different understandings of what happened and why it happened, a conflict remains. When both parties harden their positions around conflicting understandings, feelings become intense and relationships deteriorate.

To maintain a positive relationship with a disappointed customer, the CCP must be able to retrace all contacts and show why the actual delivery was made. Perception gaps may be caused by two types of errors: *diagnosis error* and *delivery error*. Diagnosis error occurs when the CCP did not diagnose the customer's need correctly. With today's emphasis on quality, this can be called "diagnosis quality." A delivery error occurs when the delivery did not conform to the promise made during the diagnosis process. This can be called "delivery quality."

Delivery quality is a dynamic concept. The most effective organizations may deviate from the original delivery strategy because of additional information. For example, a package may have been addressed to a specific room, but if the delivery person realizes that the recipient is not in and the door is locked, he or she may notice that it is 10:30 a.m. and think to check the cafeteria to see if the person to whom the package is addressed is on break. Or an auto repairperson may notice an additional item that needs to be repaired while the car is in the shop.

The CCP must be able to retrack activities with the customer to determine the reason for the perceived gap between delivery and expectation. Sometimes it may simply be a matter of accessing and presenting conditions that occurred during the diagnostic stage. This may help both the customer and the organization remember the original conditions and the decisions that were made early in the process. Frequently, this information is enough to help both parties remember the original agreement and resolve the conflict.

If there was agreement over definition, then delivery activities must be tracked. If the delivery was made according to original definition, then something must have happened to change the customer's expectations. If the delivery was not made according to original definition, then either the provider was in error or additional information was received so that a "good-faith" change was made because the provider thought it would be in the best interest of the customer. If this was done, then the customer needs to understand why the change was made. Such an understanding may actually increase the customer's appreciation and trust and strengthen the relationship.

If the customer disagrees with the change that was made, then the provider should realize that he or she made a judgment call. In such cases, there is always the possibility of making a wrong choice, but good judgment and experience typically result in a strong, overall gain. If the customer is upset, the provider must go into the recovery mode. The decision on judgment calls is to maximize the "wows" and enter recovery mode when the customer is unhappy.

"Why did you . . . ?" calls are heavily dependent upon access to the priority dispatch list and the customer's history. The customer files contain customer preferences and information about what to do when judgment calls are required. The priority dispatch list establishes each task that was performed and the results. Because all transactions are time stamped, a great deal of information is available to answer customer requests.

"Why Should I . . . ?"

This question is especially important when the customers do not know what they want. The more technical the problem, the less familiar the customer with the situation or the provider, and the greater the risk to the customer, the more important this question becomes. The way this question is answered will determine whether the customer feels the provider is primarily interested in his or her needs or just selling. The last thing the provider wants to do is give a very condescending, "Honey, this is too technical for you to understand. Just trust us and everything will be all right."

To answer this question, the provider needs to be able to explain the reason for selecting the guideline that is being used. Why is this medical test being run? Why is this spray being used? Why is this route being taken? Why is this repair being made? Unless such questions can be answered, the customer does not know what to expect and cannot justify doing business with the organization.

This question explains how new customers can drive up a firm's costs. If the customer has a long history with the provider, a trust develops, but until that trust is firm the customer must understand what is happening and what to expect. There are many ways of answering this question, but the answer must be related to the diagnosis and the delivery guideline selected. To paraphrase a statement by Robert H. Buckman, customers empower people and organizations they trust. Without trust, customers do not empower people and organizations and customers begin to ask questions.[18]

Summary

The first four management areas discussed in this book have focused on the customer-provider relationship. Relationship management focuses on building trust and expectations so the customers call when they have a need. *Interaction management* focuses on the interaction that takes place once the customer calls. Customers need to be reassured that the firm is more interested in meeting their needs than in just making a sale. The interaction should also minimize the hassle involved in the interaction. *Diagnosis management* focuses on developing best-practice guidelines for diagnosing customer needs when the CCP is interacting with them. This is accomplished by having experts (individual CCPs who are very effective in diagnosing customer needs) develop methods for defining what the customer really wants. *Customer-service management* is the ongoing dialogue that occurs when service is requested during and after delivery. The next four management tasks that we will discuss are directed to the delivery process itself.

References

[1] Judith Waldrop, "Educating the Customer," *American Demographics*, September 1991, pp. 44–47.

[2] Terry G. Vavra, *Aftermarketing: How to Keep Customers for Life Through Relationship Marketing*, Homewood, IL: Business One Irwin, 1992, p. 27.

[3] Mike Conners, presentation to MBA class (BA 506), Spring semester, 1994.

[4] Robert H. Buckman, Speech given to Anderson Partners, Chicago, October 25, 1995.

[5] Norman E. Richard, "Customer Satisfaction – Repeat Business," *Creating Customer Satisfaction*, New York: The Conference Board, Research Report No. 944, 1990, 41–44.

[6] Thomas J. Peters and Robert H. Waterman, Jr., *In Search of Excellence*, Cambridge, MA: Harper & Row, 1982, p. 29.

[7] Jan Carlzon, *Moments of Truth*, New York: Harper & Row, 1987.

[8] Vavra, op. cit., p. 62.

[9] Richard B. Chase and Robert H. Hayes, "Beefing Up Operations in Service Firms," *Sloan Management Review*, Fall, 1991, p. 17.

[10] Ibid., p. 17.

[11] Ibid., p. 17.

[12] Ibid., p. 17.

[13] Peters and Waterman, op. cit., pp. 13–15.

[14] Richard B. Chase and Robert H. Hayes, "Beefing Up Operations in Service Firms," *Sloan Management Review*, Fall 1991, p. 15.

[15] Falvey, Jack, as cited in speech by Buckman, ibid.

[16] Carlzon, Jan, as cited in speech by Buckman, ibid.

[17] A. Parasuraman, Valarie Zeithaml, and Leonard L. Berry, *Servqual: A Multiple-Item Scale for Measuring Customer Perceptions of Service Quality*, Cambridge: Marketing Science Institute, 1986, p. 3.

[18] Buckman, op. cit.

DELIVERY COORDINATION MANAGEMENT TASK

Four tasks are essential for managing resources and coordinating their efforts to effect delivery. These tasks are summarized in the familiar customer-process-resources model first presented in Chapter 1 and shown again in Figure 8.1. This is the relationship that allows the organization to satisfy the customer's need. Functionally, this relationship has the same importance that operations (e.g., purchasing, production, supply-chain logistics, human resources, and finance) has to the offering-based organization.

Best-Practice Guideline Management

Best-practice guideline management is to the response-based firm what strategic and tactical planning is to the offering-based firm. Best-practice guideline management is the management of the organization's knowledge base. It is not conducted by having a handful of experts plan how something should be done and then training the front line how to do it. Rather, it is the process of collecting new needs encountered by the front line, recording solutions developed by the front line, and disseminating that information to all front-line workers on a continuous basis. It is also the process of facilitating communication among workers so that when a new problem is encountered, the workers can consult with others in real time to develop required solutions.

A good example of this would be the private practice physician who encounters a new ailment and desires to be able to consult with respected colleagues or specialists who can help confirm the diagnosis and prescribe a solution. The colleague or specialist probably will not be located at the same site. The communication will include not only dialogue but also lab results, a view of the patient or specimen, and anything else that would help communicate the physician's understanding of the problem. Once a diagnosis is made and the solution prescribed, it becomes part of both physicians' informal knowledge database (i.e., experience), or if the

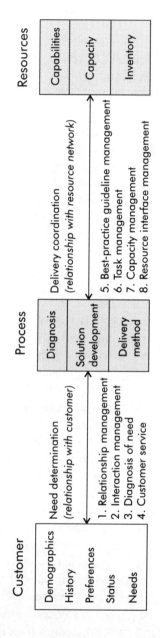

Figure 8.1. Back-room management functions.

organization has a formal database, it is captured so that it can be retrieved upon demand by other physicians when they experience the same problem. Periodically teams of physicians should review the conditional best-practice guidelines to see if new knowledge dictates that the guidelines should be updated. The process is no different if the front-line worker is a computer operator, an automobile mechanic, a consultant, a meeting planner, or even a strategic planner for a major firm. Individuals responsible for solving problems and developing customized plans go through the same process. It is the way knowledge workers work.

There are two best-practice guidelines. The first is used to diagnose the need. That was part of the need diagnosis task in Chapter 7. The second is used to define work, identify resources, and coordinate delivery.

The best-practice guideline defines:

- How a firm approaches each delivery (the list of tasks required to perform the delivery);
- How resources are integrated into the delivery process (who or what skill level should perform the task);
- The sequencing of each task (the time window and the lead time required for each task);
- The capacity that needs to be committed to perform each delivery;
- When the task should be performed relative to the customer request and the dispatching of other tasks.

Best-practice guideline management is based on understanding synergistic interaction among resources.[1]

There are three steps to best-practice guideline management:

- The development of new best-practice guidelines when new resources become available;
- The dynamic modification of existing best-practice guidelines when new situations are encountered;
- The periodic review of existing best-practice guidelines to see if they can be improved (i.e., continuous improvement).

---

1. The shift from vertically integrated firms to the use of organizations such as those described by Peter Drucker in his book *Post Capitalist Society* will be discussed in Chapter 14.

Best-practice guidelines must be developed when the organization is totally redesigning a new or existing process. For example, at one time kidney stones could only be removed surgically. When the lithotripter was introduced, many stones could be broken up by ultrasound. When the hospital invested in a lithotripter, it dramatically changed the procedure. When the equipment was received, it required extensive facility and staff to support its operation. The equipment was so expensive few hospitals had it. Therefore, the hospital that had the lithotripter could plan on having many referrals from surrounding physicians and other hospitals. The equipment was the catalyst for completely reengineering many processes involving kidney stones.

In this case, the hospital went through all of the planning and analysis required by any other firm making a new offering. The offering was a service (i.e., kidney stone shattering), not a product. The new processes had to be conditional to make allowances for patients with widely differing preexisting conditions and needs. (Nature does not facilitate the deterministic planning process by giving all individuals standardized dimensions, challenges, or infirmities that fit neatly into target market strategies.) Process development will consist of extensive testing with different approaches to determine which process results in the best outcome.

After the best-practice guideline is in place, conditions will arise that are not covered. In these cases, special procedures must be developed by the attending physician or customer contact personnel (CCP) to cover the new situation. These modifications are captured and recorded.

Results (i.e., outcomes) must be tracked on a regular basis to determine the impact of best-practice guideline changes. If a process is modified – even if only one step is changed – it is important to understand the effect of the change on results.

Federal Express has a point system for measuring results. Every day points are accumulated and conspicuously displayed to front-line workers so they can understand system performance. This point system is shown in Table 8.1.

Processes are under constant review because they currently represent best-practice methodology. It is the best-practice guideline that defines how various delivery units are utilized to deliver the desired benefits. It is best-practice guideline management that determines the cost-effectiveness of benefit delivery (i.e., quality). There is perhaps no

Table 8.1. The Federal Express Point System

Outcome	Points
Late delivery – wrong day	5
Late delivery – right day	1
Invoice adjustment	1
Traces (subsequent)	1
Missed pickup	10
Complaint rehandled	5
Lost package	10
Damaged package (taken to rewrap desk)	10
Over good (no address on package)	5
Abandoned calls (customer hung up)	1
Missing proof of delivery	1
Late delivery – international	1

Measure	Year 1988	Year 1991
Daily package volume	877,543	1,246,311
Monthly SQI	152,000	125,000
Points/package	.0078	.0045

more important operational management task for the responsive organization.[2] Measurement indicates results, but it is up to the most knowledgeable staff members to modify best-practice guidelines to make delivery more synergistic and cost-effective. This is the basis of the critical pathway studies currently under development in hospitals.

Task Management

Just as the best-practice guideline defines the process for developing individual delivery plans for each customer, it is the prioritized dispatch list that is used to assign and coordinate the work necessary to make the delivery happen. It is the best-practice guideline that determines individ-

---

2. The new informational modeling practices (e.g., neg entropy) are especially effective for monitoring the effectiveness of best-practice guideline changes. This technique avoids the necessity of the traditional experimental design, sample size constraints, and confidence intervals required by traditional statistical methods.

ual delivery tasks for each customer. Each time a customer calls and asks for a delivery, the CCP follows the best-practice guideline to define the work that needs to be done. Each work task is placed on the priority dispatch list so that it can be dispatched to the appropriate resource group when needed.

When work is coordinated by dispatch, task management is performed through the to-do list. Because work has not yet been assigned, the only change required to modify the delivery plan is to modify the next undispatched item on the to-do list. Task management is virtually identical to project management. The only difference is that many different projects have to be managed at the same time. It is very analogous to the job of the custom home builder with dozens of homes under construction at the same time. The coordinator must determine the availability of carpenters, masons, electricians, drywall installers, and painters and assign them to work on projects on a real-time basis in a way that delivers the greatest value to the customer while recognizing that the weather does not always cooperate. It is also like the traditional job shop, except that many job shops simply schedule on a first-in, first-out basis. Remember the print shop sign that said "Procrastination on your part does not constitute an emergency for us." The US Postal Service, on the other hand, is now learning that procrastination on the customer's part will make him or her select more responsive options such as fax, UPS, and Federal Express – even though they are more expensive.

Each delivery has a critical path. If there is delivery slippage along the critical pathway, delivery will not be on time unless other tasks are expedited. Perhaps the most familiar example of this occurs when manufacturing is delayed and shipments must be made by air instead of by truck to meet promised delivery. Expediting typically involves additional cost. Therefore, critical pathways are monitored closely and standard expediting practices are developed when there are unavoidable delays.

Sometimes work is assigned to maximize current capacity utilization. Airlines, for example, place stringent limits on itinerary changes for discount fares. (The reasons for this will be discussed in Chapter 11.) One such restriction is the inability to change flights. But if a customer with a discount ticket for the 5:00 p.m. flight arrives in time for the 1:00 p.m. flight, he or she will probably be able to get a seat, because the airline would much rather use the 1:00 p.m. seat that would otherwise be empty and create additional capacity on the 5:00 p.m. flight in case another customer arrives to use it. Future flexibility is always enhanced by performing the work as soon as capacity is available, unless this would decrease delivery effectiveness.

Thus, best-practice guidelines must be developed to guide the dispatching, tracking, and delivery process. Ticket agents must have principles or best-practice guidelines for accepting passengers on earlier flights, front-end managers for opening checkout lines, and construction superintendents for deciding which houses crews should work on first. When there is plenty of lead time and all conditions are static, the work can be scheduled. The more dynamic and variable the customer request, the more variable and dynamic the resource capacity, the more different the deliveries and tasks, and the more important the development of dispatching best-practice guidelines. These best-practice guidelines must consider the integration of all tasks and resources. That is the role of task management.

Capacity Management

In offering-based organizations, the major emphasis is on managing production and inventory. In a responsive organization, where there is no inventory, the emphasis is on capacity management. The responsive organization schedules capacity and then "waits on customers." If customers appear, the organization responds. If the customer is "converted," capacity is used to provide benefits. If capacity is not used, it cannot be inventoried for later resale; it is forever lost or wasted. Capacity management is the process of maximizing capacity utilization to deliver benefits. Stated another way, it is the process of minimizing wasted capacity because delivered capacity generates revenue, whereas wasted capacity creates only additional cost.

Capacity management is well understood by most service organizations. Profits are determined by capacity utilization. Consulting firms focus on "percent billable hours." Transportation companies want "load factors" up and "percent deadheading" down. For hospitals, it is the "daily census." Hotels refer to the "occupancy rate." It does not matter what it is called. Capacity is scheduled in the short run and sold in the immediate run. Unsold capacity is wasted and can never be recovered.

Capacity managers develop many different methods to keep capacity utilization high. There are basically three ways of doing this: better forecasting of capacity needs so extra capacity is not scheduled in the short run, cross training employees so capacity can be used for a wider variety of tasks, and developing cooperative networks so that extra capacity can be obtained on an as needed basis.

Improving the Forecasting of Capacity Needs in the Short Run

There are two types of forecasting: periodic forecasting and event forecasting.[3] Periodic forecasting is used to make preliminary projections of capacity needs. Traditional methods may be used. Trend analysis can show whether capacity needs are growing at a rate of 10 percent per year or declining at 5 percent per year. Although this method may be sufficient for firms that produce inventory, it is not sufficient for activities that cannot be inventoried. When the results of the activity cannot be inventoried, unused capacity is wasted. If the organization is concerned about capacity utilization, it must match capacity scheduling to capacity utilization. Consequently, it is important to identify cyclical changes. Fast-food restaurants, for example, will experience wide variations in demand based on the month, the day of the week, the time of day, the weather (e.g., temperature and precipitation), school schedules, and holidays. Therefore, they develop indexes so they can accurately forecast capacity needs (e.g., when the schools have a snow day on the Thursday before Good Friday).

Event forecasting involves pre-event activity tracking to predict event demand. Hotels and airlines solicit reservations. Conference planners seek advance registrations. Physicians encourage the making of appointments. If the organization knows the patterns of pre-event activity, it can be a good predictor of event demand. For example, if conference planners know that 50 percent of conference attendees usually preregister and that 30 percent of the preregistrants do so three months prior to the conference, they can develop an early-warning system to predict confer-

---

3. Taken at its limit, any continuous activity can be converted into period data. Computer screens have lines drawn using discreet pixels. A continuous line can be plotted using numerous points. The phrase "periodic versus dynamic" is used to distinguish the process of decision making by large time periods (i.e., monthly or quarterly) versus the continuous tracking of ongoing activities. Inventory and standardized activities allow periodic management.

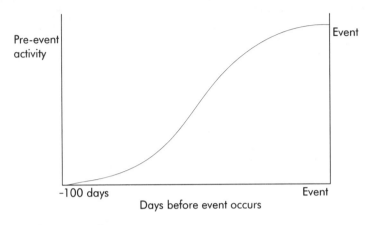

Figure 8.2. Event forecasting.

ence attendance. Figure 8.2 illustrates an example of an event forecast based on previously identified patterns of advanced activity.

Airlines and hotels use reservations to predict demand for capacity. It is not expected that everyone will keep a reservation, but reservations do provide a good predictor of future activity. The first step is to record the advance notices given by the number of days received in advance of the event. This step usually provides extensive insight into customer behavior. Some individuals will always register early, and others will habitually register at the last moment. The airlines, for example, find that trips to vacation sites such as Orlando are invariably booked one or more months in advance. Trips to business sites such as Washington, D.C., are almost all booked during the last several days before departure. Thus each site and each flight have different usage patterns.

Once a pattern is established, this can be used to forecast ridership on future flights. The mean and standard deviation for each event (i.e., flight) can be calculated, and threshold curves can be drawn at one, two, or three standard deviations from the mean. (See Figure 8.3.)

Airlines and hotels use these methods to forecast expected demand levels not only by flight but by each fare class within each flight. John Carmel used these methods to forecast registrations at the Duke Diet and Fitness Center sessions.[1] Based upon 20-day forecasts, he could modify prices and take other actions to increase capacity utilization when advance bookings were low.

Delivery Coordination Management Task

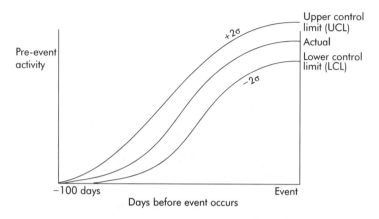

Figure 8.3. Event forecasting using two standard deviations for rescheduling capacity.

These methods are not limited to events. Toyota has dealers submit orders ten days in advance of production. The dealers are allowed (even encouraged) to make any changes up to two days before the vehicle is actually produced. Althouh dealers (and customers) perceive the providers to be responsive to individual customer needs, in reality it is in the best interest of the supplier to encourage the customers to reveal their true intentions. Allowing the customer to freely make changes reduces the customer's reluctance to make an early commitment. The earlier the order, the more advance notice the provider has. The easier it is for the customers to make changes, the more likely they are to indicate their changing plans. The more likely they are to reveal plan changes, the more accurate the forecast. Therefore, the best forecasting methods are based on building a relationship with customers so that they notify the organization when they make their plans and when their plans change. When this approach is used, responsiveness is not only easier but also more cost-effective than rigid, long-term scheduling that "locks" the customer into the schedule and prohibits changes.

Once capacity needs have been forecast, the organization may modify schedules to minimize excess capacity. Hotels may shut down floors during periods of low occupancy. Hospitals may close wings on weekends or during holiday seasons such as Christmas. After these patterns have been identified, they can be used in several ways. The first approach is used to forecast future activity levels. If booking levels have been consistently running above normal, then actual bookings can be expected to be higher than normal. Normal forecasting techniques can be used to predict how much final demand is expected to vary from average demand. This forecast will be made using percentage of normal rather than absolute levels. For example, if class registrations are running 40 percent higher than normal 70 days before the class starts, this is an early warning that attendance may be high.

Cross Training Employees

The second approach to capacity management is the cross training of employees. The traditional approach to coordinating activities was based on a belief in the specialization of labor. Each employee was given a limited number of tasks to perform so that the employee could be very efficient with a minimum of training. The cross-training strategy is built on the concept of economies of scope. That is, the greater the breadth of training, the more things the individual can do. An attorney, for example, would not be able to specialize in adoptions and expect to have demand for all of his or her capacity. By being cross trained in litigation, divorces, and criminal defense, the attorney may be kept busy even in a relatively small town.

Cross training also allows the organization to combine rush jobs with space-available deliveries. This allows greater utilization of capacity just as space-available freight or standby passengers keep the planes full. In a similar manner, different types of jobs allow the organization to increase capacity utilization.

Although more accurate forecasts allow the organization to better match capacity scheduling with ultimate demand, the queuing of less time-sensitive jobs provides work when excess capacity is available. Where variation in capacity needs are too great to be managed through forecasting and cross training, the organization will develop networks of outside providers. Because networks are familiar in practice but not in theory, more background is needed to place networking in context.

Developing Cooperative Networks for Immediate-Run Flexibility

There are two ways in which resources can be organized. The multidivisional, mass-production firm of the twentieth century emphasized vertical integration of resources within the same organization. The firm was viewed as a self-sufficient unit. It performed its own purchasing, production, distribution, and promotion functions and often owned its own retail outlets. It also owned and operated all staff areas such as accounting, information systems, legal, transportation, and finance. The reason given for using in-house resources for all activities was the belief that it was less expensive to "do it yourself" than to use an outside organization.[4]

The total quality management (TQM) movement has challenged this belief. Central to this challenge was the concept that the organization has to operate in an adversarial relationship with other parties, each trying to extract concessions from the other. The TQM movement identified new methods of controlling costs that had long been ignored. It recognized that manufacturing costs were heavily influenced by the quality of purchased materials and that some activities added value for the customer but others did not. Thus TQM focused on avoiding costs that did not add value for the customer and minimizing costs that did add value.

Juran developed a cost-of-quality accounting system to show how total costs were affected by quality.[2] This system as described in Chapter 2 included *appraisal costs, internal failure costs, external failure costs,* and *prevention costs*. Crosby emphasized that "Quality is Free" if you organize to avoid defects.[3] If the purchasing process is tightly controlled so that no defective parts are received, many of the four costs just mentioned could be eliminated. According to his estimate, defects accounted for between 15 and 20 percent of total production costs. As long as you paid less than 20 percent more for zero-defect products, "quality is free." Deming used statistical process-control methods devel-

---

4. This concept was presented in Chapter 1. Oliver Williamson has described transaction costs. These include the cost of processing transactions (e.g., ordering, receiving, billing, payment) and the cost of control (e.g., contracts, inspection, litigation). As long as it was assumed that intrafirm activities had to have substantially fewer controls than interfirm activities, it was logical to be vertically integrated. Now that firms have found it easier to minimize interfirm transaction costs and are adapting a more collaborative posture, there is less need for vertical ownership of resources. With decreased need for costly control, emphasis can shift to networking resource capacity so resource capability will be available when needed.

oped by Walter Shewart at Bell Labs in the 1930s to show that 85 percent of all errors were not caused by the workers but by the processes designed by management.[4] He emphasized the need for consistency in processes and continual improvement.

Because consistency in process requires consistency in input, Deming emphasized that the need for continual improvement is the relationship between the buyer and the supplier. The provider must know and understand what the buyer wants and how they want to use the product. He believed that customers should not select suppliers solely on purchase price but on the total cost of using the supplies. He encouraged the cultivation of long-term relationships with fewer suppliers so that each supplier could be trained to better understand the needs of the customer. In addition, because there is greater variation in the parts provided by multiple providers than there is in parts obtained from a single supplier, he advised firms to limit the number of suppliers.

A second contribution TQM made to supplier relationships was to recognize that the relationship between supplier and customer is not a one-time, zero-sum activity. Suppliers do not just supply raw material, components, and services – they supply knowledge and expertise that can dramatically enhance their value to the purchaser. Thus, as purchasers extend their focus from a single transaction to a longer term relationship, many more options become available and the supplier becomes more valuable. When the supplier better understands the customers' needs and sees an advantage in helping the customers solve their needs, this enhances the value it delivers to the customer. The more valuable the supplier is to the customer, the more stable and profitable the relationship. When this happens, the customers are no longer limited to their own resources. They now have access to the know-how and technology of their suppliers to help design their offerings to their customers. As this happens, the relationship shifts from adversarial to cooperative.

In the cooperative model, both parties see the long-term value of future business being so much greater than the value of any current transaction that they both have a strong incentive to cooperate (i.e., "work it out") and preserve the relationship. They also recognize the importance of understanding the purchaser's needs so that they can make suggestions to improve the relationship. This requires that the relationship between supplier and purchaser be based on mutual trust.[5] As suppliers and purchasers work together, both parties obtain value from the relationship:

the supplier by obtaining a steady reliable customer (and thus a cash source) and the purchaser by decreased quality costs (and thus increased total profits and satisfaction to its customers). The value of a relationship is determined by the ability of both partners to make collective innovations that increase market share by better serving final customers.

Cooperative Supplier Strategies. There are two conditions under which cooperative relationships are important: in organizations involved in steadystate, standardized activities and in organizations involved in responsive activities. The term "partnership" has typically been used for steady-state activities, whereas the term "network" is used for responsive activities.

Cooperative Partnerships. The selection of cooperative partners is based on the expectation that the supplier can be the most effective contributor to the cooperative effort and not focus only on the one-time cost of a single component. The selected supplier is expected to work with the purchaser to evaluate and modify both the provider's and the purchaser's production processes and operating procedures to increase customer value. The provider is expected to provide solutions, not just things (i.e., products).

As firms began to work more closely with suppliers, they discover it takes effort to create an effective relationship. Because of this effort (and the belief that variation among suppliers is greater than that within suppliers), purchasers have begun to reduce the number of suppliers. As the number of relationships is reduced, both supplier and purchaser become more dependent upon each other. Thus the selection process must be carefully made. No longer is the purchasing department simply buying a part; they are entering into a long-term, cooperative effort to compete for long-term customer satisfaction and retention. The success of the purchaser will be enhanced or limited by the partner selected.

One approach to selecting suppliers is to categorize them into various tiers based on a wide variety of factors. Examples of the possible categories within this type of tiered system are the James River Corporation's approved, qualified, preferred, and certified suppliers[5]; the Carrier Corporation's unacceptable supplier, normal supplier, long-term

---

5. See Chapter 14 for a discussion of relationship principles and methods for strengthening relationships.

contract, alliance, and partner[6]; and the Tenant Corporation's non-qualified, qualified, preferred, and select suppliers.[7]

Typically, the top tier of suppliers is assured of a continuing relationship with the purchaser as long as they continue to be so classified. The second tier can expect to receive contracts with the provider as well as assistance and training to become a top-tier provider. The third-tier organizations know what is required to obtain a first- or second-tier classification but cannot expect extensive purchaser assistance in reaching it. Such a tiered system encourages suppliers to make changes in order to be moved into a higher tier.

A tiered system is not sufficient to shift relationships from adversarial to cooperative. The shift is determined by the criteria used to classify suppliers into the categories. If the selection criteria are cost, technical, or management issues only, the relationship remains adversarial. If the criteria are expanded to include factors such as organizational compatibility (e.g., culture, information), vision, stability, and innovativeness, then it becomes more cooperative.[6]

Cooperative partnerships with a limited number of providers are appropriate where needs are standardized and predictable. Cooperative partnerships are oriented toward long-term, steady-state, continuous relationships. This allows the supplier to depend on the continued business, and the purchaser to depend on a consistent, reliable supply of know-how and materials. But what about response-based organizations? How do response-based organizations develop cooperative relationships?

Cooperative Networks. Cooperative relationships are also applicable for firms that provide products or service in a more dynamic or responsive manner. Response-based firms put less emphasis on limiting the number of suppliers and more on developing a large network of providers to increase the range of capabilities it can use to meet its customers' needs. Instead of emphasizing steady-state relationships, the emphasis is on making it as easy as possible (instantly, costlessly, seamlessly, and frictionlessly) to have access to a variety of resources when needed.

---

6. For further discussion of these concepts, see Al Cole and John Kamauff, "A New Agenda for the Purchasing Professional," unpublished manuscript, Knoxville: University of Tennessee Management Development Center, 1993, and Lisa M. Ellram, "The Supplier Selection Decision in Strategic Partnerships," *Journal of Purchasing and Materials Management*, Fall 1990, pp. 8–14.

Delivery Coordination Management Task

Response-based organizations must network resources for two basic reasons. First, responsive organizations do not know customer needs until their customers call. The responsive firm can be no more responsive to its customers than its delivery units are to it. The firm's ability to respond is determined by the capability and capacity available for dispatch. Therefore, response-based firms constantly seek to expand the core competencies (i.e., capabilities) and capacity (i.e., availability) for dispatch to serve customers. The more capability and capacity available, the more customers can be served. Because various delivery units tend to specialize around their core competency, the responsive organization obtains a greater diversity of capabilities by developing a broader network of delivery units that are available for dispatch. For example, it is not unusual for a large hospital to have 600 to 1,000 different physicians, each with very different skills, on its staff. The hospital does not need many of the specialists full time, but it does need rapid access when the specific skill is needed.

Because customer requests are not controlled, *demand levels may vary dramatically over time*. For example, security companies need a large work force during surge periods such as sporting events and rock concerts, but may have very limited requirements at other times. Therefore, a responsive organization will expand its capacity by developing a network of providers with the same capability (i.e., core competency) to provide peak-capacity needs. One might suggest, "Why not simply obtain the maximum capability and capacity needed so it will be available in house when needed?" The answer to this question should be based on the economics of responsive capacity.

The economics of response-based firms is significantly different from that of firms that produce a product to inventory. Without inventory, unused capacity is wasted. Typically, there are three categories of costs for these organizations:

- *Fixed capacity costs* (FCC) – long-term costs incurred in order to be in business (e.g., airport facilities or airplanes);
- *Scheduled capacity costs* (SCC) – costs incurred when the capacity is scheduled and whether or not it is used (e.g., flight crews, fuel, or maintenance);
- *Service delivery costs* (SDC) – costs incurred when the customer

actually uses the service (e.g., in-flight meals and travel agents' commissions).[7]

Typically, the service delivery costs comprise less than 10 percent of the total cost of delivering the service to the ultimate consumer. The remaining 90 percent is incurred whether or not a service is delivered. Therefore, the profitability of the firm depends on reducing the fixed and scheduled capacity costs and maximizing the *percent utilization.*

The organization can be no more responsive to its customers than its resources are to the organization. And to control costs the firm must maintain a high percentage of utilization. To accomplish both of these objectives, the firm must establish a network of suppliers who are always on call and can be made use of when needed. From a cost perspective, it may be more efficient on a per-hour basis to have the resource in house, but on a per-use basis it is more efficient to network. That way the purchaser pays the supplier on a per-use basis. Thus the network approach to cooperation allows the accomplishment of two basic goals: a greater ability to respond to customer needs and a reduction in the cost of the response.

Partnerships are ideal where two firms are matched and balanced. That means the provider has the full range of skills needed by the user and that the user is able to make use of virtually all of the provider's capacity. When the provider and customer are not matched and balanced, firms tend to network. If the customer requires more competencies and capacity than the provider is able to supply, the customer will network with multiple providers. If the customer cannot use all of the provider's capacity, then the provider will network with other customers.

The more diverse the final customer needs, the broader the network necessary to provide access to more core competencies (i.e., capabilities). The greater the variation in capacity needs, the greater the depth of the network to allow the capacity required for each core competency. For each need (capability or capacity), the basis for selecting network members is similar to those for cooperative partnerships. The larger the network for both provider and customer, the greater the number of interfaces. Interface management's responsibility is to simplify the process.

---

7. These cost concepts will be described in more detail in Chapter 10.

The challenge to cooperative networks is to make interface management more cost-effective. Examples of this include:

- *Searching procedures.* When its customer has a special need, the response-based firm – as was the case with Desert Storm and ROLS – must find a supplier with the appropriate capabilities. Most response-based firms will have a knowledge base of potential providers showing their capabilities, capacity, responsiveness, effectiveness, and costs already available to minimize search time when the need arises. Trade unions fulfilled this function by reducing the search effort required for a contractor to obtain pipefitters, carpenters, masons, and electricians. Now temporary employment agencies meet this need for a variety of firms.
- *Start-up procedures.* Any time a new relationship is established, many details must be worked out and understandings reached. This takes time and effort but must be recognized as an investment in establishing capability and capacity, just as investment in plant and equipment are necessary for an inventory-based firm. Typically, lawyers work on retainers, consultants establish letters of agreement, trade unions establish rates and work rules, and carriers maintain tariffs. Once these are in place, getting delivery of services can be as simple as a phone call.
- *Transaction procedures.* A responsive organization cannot be any more responsive than its resources. Thus response-based organizations must develop dispatching, reporting, and billing methods that can be activated at any time with virtually no transaction costs. Toyota uses Kanbans to let its suppliers know what is wanted and when. Wal-Mart uses scanned data to transmit requests to distribution centers each morning. These procedures not only make interaction virtually instantaneous, but also almost costless and seamless between organizations. It is the seamless, boundary-spanning activity that makes networks workable.
- *Coordination procedures.* In cooperative partnerships, there is a limited number of organizations involved. In cooperative networks many organizations may be working on a single project. It is very important to establish procedures for ensuring that functional groups from each organization are working together. It is the task management (i.e., dispatch) based on best-practice guide-

lines, project management techniques, and dispatching methods that allows this interface to occur.

- *Communication procedures.* There must be a point person. Someone must take responsibility for processing communication and overseeing activities in a cooperative network. Consultants identify project managers; vendors may have a representative on-site; and hospitals use an admitting physician for each patient. This individual is the CCP for need diagnosis activities and the logistician for delivery coordination activities.

There are many examples of cooperative networks. FTD, for example, has developed a network of florists who sell and deliver floral arrangement over widely scattered geographical areas. Hospitals typically develop a network of labs, physicians, pharmaceutical distributors, therapists, and other suppliers to provide a wide range of services to patients when needed. In each case, the purpose of the network is to make service easy to obtain when needed to serve a customer but to avoid the cost of idle capacity when it is not needed. The network members actually become additional delivery units and interface with the response-based organization just as in-house delivery units do.

Capacity management is the process of coordinating capacity scheduling, training, and networking to keep responsive capability high and wasted capacity low. That is necessary if delivery is to be effective and costs are to be controlled.

Resource Interface Management

Oliver Williamson, as mentioned in Chapter 1, described governance as a major function of the firm.[8] Governance is the process of controlling transaction costs. Transaction costs occur when two organizations interface. They are the boundary-spanning cost of interacting together. For organizations to be flexible, they need access and the ability to integrate core competencies into a unified delivery process. They also need the ability to coordinate the delivery. This role of interface management is to facilitate intraorganizational relationships so that work can be seamlessly assigned (i.e., dispatched) and coordinated (i.e., tracked) at a very low cost. When interface management is inefficient, firms are forced to vertically integrate and limit options to the capabilities (i.e., competency) of the in-house group. When interface management is effective:

- The firm can focus on meeting customer needs unconstrained by the need to find a use for existing in-house capacity;
- The firm has virtually unlimited capability and capacity at its disposal to serve its customers' diverse needs;
- Virtually all organizations can become part of the delivery network;
- The cost of wasted capacity can be dramatically reduced.

Interface management requires conditional best-practice guidelines to define needs and define what resources to use in the delivery. Dispatching and task management coordinate the assignment of work and monitoring results.

In the product field, interface management was known as "channel management." Because interfaces incurred transaction costs, the purpose of channel design was to reduce the number of interfaces. The purpose of the intermediary (e.g., the broker, wholesaler, or rack jobber) was to reduce the number of customer interfaces for the manufacturer. By setting up intermediaries in each area, the firm only had to interact with each of the intermediaries, who in turn interfaced with each customer. It also reduced the number of interfaces for the customer because each intermediary represented multiple product lines and the customer did not have to have interfaces (i.e., contact) with every manufacturer.

Wholesalers and intermediaries who take title to goods (as opposed to brokers who only take orders) were established to reduce the cost of transportation. The wholesaler was large enough to receive shipments in rail car-load (CL) lots because freight rates were only a small fraction of less-than-truck-load (LTL) shipments. The transportation rate savings more than justified the break bulk activities of the wholesaler. As firms become able to economically ship in smaller and smaller sizes, there is less need of the wholesaler. As firms are able to develop CCPs and effective need diagnosis systems, there is less need for the local intermediary to interface with the customer and provide an assortment of products for the customer to scan in finding a solution to his or her needs. The dramatic decline in local grocery wholesalers and brokers and the move toward Efficient Consumer Response (ECR) in the grocery field is a prime example of this, as is the popularity of the mail-order computer distribution chains. If the CCP can diagnose the need over the phone and if express delivery service can provide overnight delivery, it is easier to buy direct than through a local outlet. It also reduces inventory and the expense of operating the retail facility, and increases the options available to the customer.

Just as distribution channels could make just about any product available in the community, so interface management, best-practice guideline management, and task management can integrate and coordinate virtually any organization's capability and capacity into any single delivery. Interface management allows an organization to be a resource if best-practice guideline management can determine how to integrate it into the delivery process and task management can determine how to dispatch and coordinate the delivery.

Delivery Coordination Summary

Firms have traditionally used demand forecasts and product planning to design an offering and to define how much should be produced and sold. Planning was based on identifying those factors that were inflexible, such as limits on what could be produced and how long it took to change over to producing a different product. The emphasis was on determining the best, most profitable way to use inflexible resources to bring an offering to the market.

Responsive management takes a different tack. Its objective is to identify and eliminate obstacles that cause inflexibilities so that the firm can be more responsive to customers. Interface management reduces the interorganizational barriers to the use of resources. Best-practice guideline management defines the process for integrating resources to make responsive deliveries. Task management develops processes for reducing coordination barriers to their use. Capacity management develops methods for forecasting aggregate capacity needs and identifying customer intentions so that information can be used to minimize wasted (i.e., unused) capacity. Delivery coordination management allows customer-responsive delivery in a cost-effective way, just as need diagnosis management allows the relationship with the customer to be comfortable and effective. Collectively delivery effectiveness and cost-efficient use of capacity make the delivery yield long-term profits. Profits are not measured by markup or by contribution to capacity, but rather by the overall coordination of delivery-effectiveness and cost-efficiency. This is called yield management and is illustrated in Figure 8.4.

Yield Management

When firms produce standardized outputs, they can price by output. First, they calculate costs. Costs can be calculated by adding direct costs and indirect costs. *Direct costs* are the costs of raw materials and labor used to produce each product. *Indirect costs*, such as for plant and equipment, cannot be identified with a single output unit, so these costs are collected, aggregated, and divided by the units produced. The sum of direct and indirect costs equals total costs. Sales price less the average total cost equals markup or unit profit. It makes no difference whether the product is sold today or tomorrow because its value can be maintained in storage (i.e., inventory). The only difference is that the indirect costs may be higher in one period or another based on the number of units produced during that period because the indirect costs are allocated by a smaller or large number (i.e., units produced or sold for the period).

When a firm produces different products, the same procedure can be followed, except that some method must be developed for allocating indirect costs. It is necessary to avoid the rabbit-steer stew problem. When the cook adds 1 rabbit and 1 steer, the result is not 50 percent rabbit and 50 percent steer meat in the stew. To develop a more rational allocation of costs, we generally use a direct variable, such as direct labor hours or direct machine hours, for allocating indirect costs. When this is done, the total costs are as accurate as the allocation method for indirect costs. Still, output can be priced based on unit cost of production to give the desired level of profitability.

Unfortunately, the cost-allocation method selected can have a major impact on market strategy. For example, if a trucking company uses shipments as a means of allocating costs, it will be very competitive in the market for hauling a few large shipments long distances. If, on the other hand, the company uses ton-miles to allocate indirect costs, it will be very competitive in the market for many small shipments shipped short distances (few ton-miles). This is understandable because shipments that require a minimum of the resource used to allocate indirect cost will be underpriced.

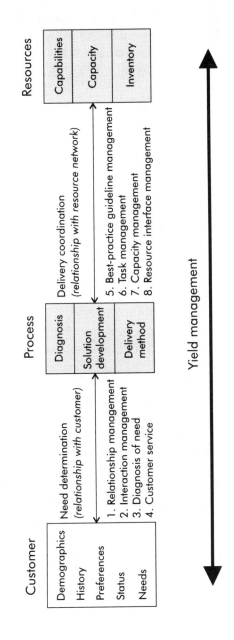

Figure 8.4. The yield management function.

Delivery Coordination Management Task

When the firm is involved in activities that use dramatically different units of indirect costs, activity-based cost-accounting methods are more accurate. For example, less-than-truck load (LTL) transportation makes extensive use of terminals for pickup and delivery, break bulk, and consolidation of freight; in contrast, truck-load trucking (TL) picks up the load at the customer's dock and delivers it directly to the delivery site without ever using terminal facilities.

Activity-based cost accounting requires that indirect cost be aggregated based upon the perentage of the activity that output uses. In the trucking case, terminal costs would be included in the LTL indirect costs but not in the TL indirect costs. This way, only the indirect costs relative to that output are included in the allocation.

Cost-allocation models work well where outputs are uniform, production is stable, and indirect costs are low. These conditions are the antithesis of customer-responsive activity. Output is not uniform. A moving van moves a young, single college graduate with 500 pounds of stereo equipment and 300 pounds of personal effects to the first job 200 miles away; a senior citizen from a single-family house with a life-time collection of furniture and personal effects three blocks away into a condominium; and a 40-year-old executive with eight children, a van, a half-dozen bicycles, beds, playpens, board games, a ski boat, and swing sets across country. How do you allocate costs? What is the average cost of each activity? How do you allocate costs for using a fairground that is vacant most of the time but has occasional activities ranging from a sold-out rock concert to a Boy Scout parade to a horse show?

It is not sufficient to price by average markup, for there is no effective way to allocate costs. It is not sufficient to use total-cost pricing, for the lower valued activities would not be able to afford the costs and the facility would remain vacant generating no income. With fewer groups able to afford to rent the facility, there would fewer groups over which to allocate costs so the allocated cost would increase. When the allocated costs increase, rental rates must be increased until no one can afford to rent the facility.

Likewise, it is not sufficient to use contribution to margin pricing because everyone will want to minimize his or her contribution. If everyone only makes a small contribution, the total contribution will not be sufficient to cover total costs, and the facility will go out of business. It is not sufficient to price high at the beginning of the season and liquidate unsold items at the end of the season, for the value of unused capacity cannot be stored in inventory. Furthermore, not all the customers that can afford to pay top dollar move to the front of the line and rent the facility early in the season. Highly profitable events and sentimentally valued events are intermixed. Yield management is the process of maximizing return on investment (ROI) by responding to diverse needs on an irregular schedule and using a network of independent resources. Yield management will be the subject of Chapter 11 after the economics of customer resonsive organizations is introduced in Chapters 9 and 10.

Summary

Manufacturing activities have traditionally been product focused. This was necessary when production was inflexible. Inflexibilities occurred because it was difficult to use the production facilities to make multiple products. When multiple products could be produced, it was difficult to shift from the production of one product to another. The shift typically involved large set-up costs.

As firms begin to organize to eliminate inflexibilities instead of simply working around them, this will change the organization of the firm. Rather than being organized by type of skill (e.g., production, distribution, marketing, or accounting), the firm will be organized by activities. The activities consist of need-diagnosis activities that focus on customer relationships and delivery coordination activities that integrate resources and coordinate delivery. The collective purpose is to maximize long-term ROI (yield management).

Chapters 9, 10, and 11 will describe the economics of customer-responsive activities in which the emphasis is on capacity management rather than the production, distribution, and storage of a tangible product.

References

[1] Stephen N. Chapman and Jonathan I. Carmel, "Demand-Capacity Management in Healthcare: An Application of Yield Management," *Health Care Management Review*, Vol. 17, No. 4, Fall, 1992, pp. 45–54.

[2] Joseph M. Juran and Frank M. Gryna, Jr., *Quality Planning and Analysis*, New York: McGraw-Hill Company, 1980. Reproduced with permission of the McGraw-Hill Companies.

[3] Philip B. Crosby, *Quality Is Free*, New York: McGraw-Hill Company, 1979. Reproduced with permission of The McGraw-Hill Companies.

[4] Reprinted from *Quality, Productivity and Competitive Position* by W. Edwards Deming by permission of MIT and The W. Edwards Deming Institute. Published by MIT, Center for Advanced Engineering Study, Cambridge, MA 02139. Copyright © 1982 by The W. Edwards Deming Institute.

[5] Shirley Cayer and James P. Morgan, "What It Takes to Make World Class Suppliers," *Purchasing*, August 15, 1991, p. 69.

[6] Shirley Cayer and James P. Morgan, "True Believers?" *Purchasing*, August 13, 1992, p. 61.

[7] "Carrier Qualification and Evaluation," Publication 10191290R (Tenant Corporation).

[8] Oliver E. Williamson, *The Economic Institutions of Capitalism*, New York: The Free Press, 1985, p. 13.

CHAPTER 9

CUSTOMER-RESPONSIVE DEMAND ECONOMICS

Customer-responsive economics is different from traditional production economics. In traditional production economics, both buyers and sellers have a common denominator to focus on: the product. The demand curve illustrates the buyer's focus and the supply curve shows the seller's focus. The common denominator of both the demand curve and supply curve is product quantity.

The concepts of supply and demand form the very foundation of the current thinking about production and microeconomics. The universal acceptance of these two concepts is mirrored in an anonymous quote used by Samuelson, "You can make even a parrot into a learned political economist – all he must learn are the two words 'supply' and 'demand.'"[1]

This is not the case for customer-responsive activities. Customers are looking for benefits. Organizations schedule capability and capacity. Organizational capacity can be used to provide many different types of benefits. Thus customers and providers have a very different focus. Customers want benefits and providers sell capacity. Organizations can sometimes be so strongly focused on selling capacity that they forget that there is no direct demand for capacity. There is only a demand for capacity when customers perceive that they can derive a benefit from its use.

Benefits versus Capacity Orientation

A person having problems with a new pair of glasses calls the optometrist for help. The receptionist answers, "Hello, how may we help you?"

The customer responds, "I am having trouble with my new glasses. I can't see to drive my car, read the paper, or work at my computer."

The receptionist asks, "Do you want a vision exam or do you want the optometrist to check your glasses?"

The customer replies, "I don't know. I just want to see. I am calling you because I thought the optometrist could tell me what I need to do

195

to be able to see so I can drive my car, read my paper, and work at my computer."

The receptionist defensively answers, "I understand, but it is important that I know what procedure you want so I know how much of the optometrist's time to schedule."

Customer-responsive activities require a different type of economic analysis. Customer-responsive economic analysis must be focused on the link between benefits desired by customers and the capacity scheduled by providers. This link is cost-effectiveness. This compound term has two dimensions. The first is delivery effectiveness. Delivery effectiveness is determined by how well the benefits delivered by the organization meet individual customer's needs. The second is cost efficiency. Cost efficiency is a measure of the resources required to deliver benefits to the customer. This is not a simple cost measurement. Some costs are incurred to deliver benefits and others are incurred to "wait on customers." Since capacity cannot be inventoried, unused capacity spent waiting on customers to arrive is wasted. Therefore, cost efficiency mirrors how well the organization can schedule and utilize its capacity.

This chapter will address the concept of providing customers with benefits that they value. It will also show how customer value can be converted to demand for capacity. Chapter 10 will look at capacity costing. Chapter 11 will show how customer value and capacity-costing concepts are used to maximize organizational yield. Before introducing the concept of customer value, the structure of traditional demand curves will be introduced to show that all demand curves begin with individuals and that demand curves were only meant to apply to things.

Demand Curve Construction

Traditional production demand curves exist at three levels: the individual's demand curve for products, the industry's demand curve for products, and the organization's demand curve for products. All demand curves begin with individual demand curves. These are a measure of the number of product units that an individual would buy at various price levels. The industry demand curve is simply the summation of all product units demanded by all individuals at each price level. The industry demand can then be divided by each organization's market share. The subdivided demand is the organizational demand curve. This concept is presented in Figure 9.1. The organization's ability to differentiate its product will determine not only market share but also slope of the individual provider's demand curve.

All Demands Are Derived from Needs of Individuals

All demands are derived from needs of individuals. Individuals have needs (or wants) and seek solutions to these needs. Demand is a measure of what individuals are willing to pay for a given solution. Some customer needs have high value. In other words, customers are willing to pay dearly for a solution. Some needs are time sensitive. Some needs are relatively unimportant to the customer and thus their solutions have low value. Thus *customer value* is a measure of the importance of the solution to the customer. It is the value that the solutions provides to the customer.

Providers deliver solutions. Some solutions are effective (e.g., the solution effectively solves the problem and requires a minimum of hassle to acquire and use). Other solutions are ineffective (e.g., the solution does not solve the need very well or is a major hassle to use or acquire). Customer value is what the individual customer is willing and able to pay to solve the problem. Solution value is determined by how effectively the solution fits the individual customer's need and how much hassle is involved to obtain it. If the fit is 100 percent, and there is no hassle, the solution value is equal to the customer value. Delivery effectiveness is a measure of how well the solution fits the customer's need. Delivery effectiveness is a measure of how much of the customer value the solution can capture. Following are the definitions of some key economic terms.

Customer value is what the customer is willing and able to pay to solve a need.

Fit, or *delivery effectiveness,* describes how closely the proposed solution meets the customer's need.

Hassle is a measure of effort that the customer must exert to realized the proposed solution.

Solution value is the value of the solution offered by the provider. If the solution meets 80 percent of the customer's need, he or she will not be willing to pay as much as if the solution met 100 percent of their need. If the solution requires extensive customer involvement, solution value is less than it would have been if there was less hassle involved.

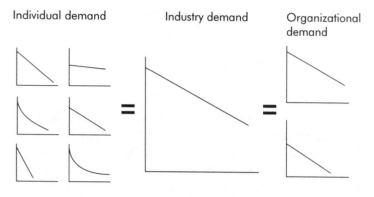

Industry demand = Sum of individual demands
Organizational demand = Industry demand x market share

Figure 9.1.　Demand curve relationships.

Solution Value = (customer value × fit) – hassle

The demand for provider capacity is determined by the organization's efficiency in converting capacity into benefits that provide value to customers. The economist's task is to develop a method for defining the customer value of the solution to the individual and converting that to a measure for determining the demand for the provider's capacity to deliver solutions to multiple consumers.

Customer Value

The demand for solutions is unique to each specific individual. Even a very standard service such as a plane ride from Knoxville to Atlanta has a different value to each passenger. One individual may be making the trip to close a very large contract. A second individual may be attending a wedding. The third passenger, a teenager, may have the day off and want to do some shopping in Atlanta. Each has a very different reason for going, and the value of the benefit is different to each one. Customer value can be conceptually plotted as in Figure 9.2. In the airline case, the capacity required for each passenger is identical – one seat on a flight between Knoxville and Atlanta. But what happens if a different amount of capacity is required for each customer?

Figure 9.3 presents this concept. The Y axis is labeled *customer value*. In this case, the units of capacity needed to develop or deliver the

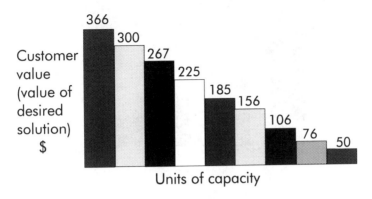

Figure 9.2. Customer value expressed in equal capacity units.

solution are different. For example, say that our three passengers headed for Atlanta have decided to travel by automobile instead of by air. The business person may need to have the fan belt replaced so that he or she can get to Atlanta and close the contract. The individual going to the wedding may need his or her water pump replaced. The teenager on a shopping trip may need to have his or her car's automatic transmission overhauled. In these cases, not only are the customer values different, but the amount of capacity required to deliver the benefits is also different. A different customer value schedule must be considered for each of the three cases. As shown in Figure 9.3, not only is the customer value for each individual different, but the amount of capacity required to deliver that benefit is different as well.

It is important to note here that customer value is a demand schedule, not a demand curve. To understand the difference, one must understand the following three terms.

A *demand point* is what one individual is willing to pay for a specific solution at a specific point in time. The demand point can change dramatically if the individual changes, the service changes, or the situation changes. Demand points are independent and have no relationship to other demand points.

A *demand curve,* as defined by Albert Marshall, is "the demand prices at which various quantities of a *thing* can be sold in a market during a given time and under given conditions."[2] A demand curve exists when there are many people, many units, or many people and many units.

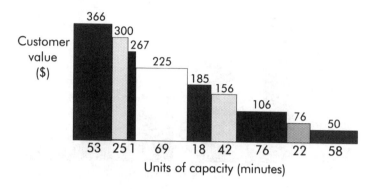

Figure 9.3. Customer value expressed in unequal capacity units.

Regardless of conditions, a demand curve is always for various quantities of a *thing*. Points on a demand curve are not independent because the demand is for the same thing.

A *demand schedule* is made up of many different independent demand points where there is no commonality among points. For example, in the automobile-repair example, how do you compare the demand for a transmission overhaul and a fan belt replacement? The only commonality is the units of capacity required. The units of capacity required provide many different benefits that are totally independent of each other.

The more unique the deliveries, the more important to understand why solutions provide different levels of customer value, which is determined by the individual customer's intensity of need and the customer's ability to pay. In the example of the three travelers, the business-person has an intense need to get to Atlanta to close the deal. Assuming that the contract would be lucrative, the willingness and ability to pay for this intense need to replace the fan belt was high. The individual attending the wedding likewise has a strong need, but the ability to pay for the water pump may be substantially less. The teenager who needs the car to go shopping in Atlanta has a low intensity of need, at least in his or her parent's eyes, and probably a limited ability to pay.

The Demand for Capacity. The customer value schedule is much different from demand for the provider's capacity. Capacity demand is a measure of the revenue that can be obtained from various units of capacity. The term "yield" is often used to describe capacity demand. There are two different yield measures: *potential yield* (*customer value divided by the units of capacity required to make the delivery*) and *actual yield* (the *solution value* or units of capacity required to make the delivery). The difference between potential yield and actual yield is determined by how well the solution fits the customer's individual need and by the amount of hassle required to receive the benefits.

Yield is a demand curve; each point on the curve is related. Common to each point on a yield curve are the units of capacity. Capacity units are homogenous. For example, as will be shown in the next section, providers know what it costs to provide units of capacity. Trucking companies know how much it costs per hour and per mile to schedule a truck. Airlines know the cost of scheduling an airline seat between any two points at a given time. Hospitals know the cost per hour to schedule operating room use. Thus the yield curve for organizational capacity is the revenue that can be generated for each unit of capacity.

A yield curve is derived from the customer value schedule in two steps:

Step 1. Calculate potential yield from each delivery.

$$\text{Yield}_i = \frac{\text{solution value of delivery}}{\text{capacity required to deliver benefit}}.$$

This indicates the yield from using capacity to make a specific delivery. Figure 9.4 shows the yield from the customers in Figure 9.3. (Notice that the units of capacity are the same for each individual and the order of the individuals is the same as in Figure 9.3. The only difference is that the Y axis is the yield per unit of capacity rather than the solution value of the benefits.) Figure 9.4 indicates a wide range of yields between the different customers. The customers who had the highest value of benefits do not necessarily provide the highest yield for the capacity required to serve them. It depends upon how much capacity is required to deliver the benefits.

Step 2. Rearrange the yield schedule to form a demand curve for service capacity. (See Figure 9.5.) The word "demand" is used to

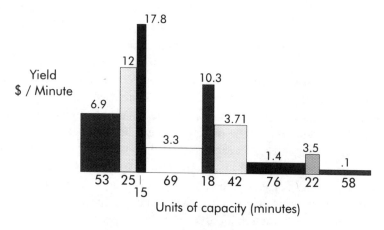

Figure 9.4. Capacity yield for service shown in figure 9.3.

emphasize that this schedule truly shows the price at which various levels of organizational capacity will be demanded. In essence, it shows how many minutes of capacity can be used to generate the indicated yield. It is not a continuous demand curve, however, because each delivery is unique and discreet. A dentist, for example, may have 15 patients a day, with some receiving high customer value deliveries and some receiving low customer value deliveries.

The Factors that Affect Yield

Organizational yield is affected by fit, specialization, scope, and delivery efficiency. The word "fit," as described previously, refers to how effectively the provider is able to deliver the benefits specifically desired by the customer. Fit determines how much of the customer value can be captured by the proposed solution. The more accurately the provider can diagnose the individual customer's needs and develop customized deliveries to meet these needs, the more customer value can be captured. Customer delight is a different concept. Customer delight occurs when delivery effectiveness exceeds the customer's expectations – that is, when the solution value comes much closer to customer value than the customer ever expected.

In some cases, specialization may allow the organization to increase yield. James Heskett, for example, describes the Canadian hospi-

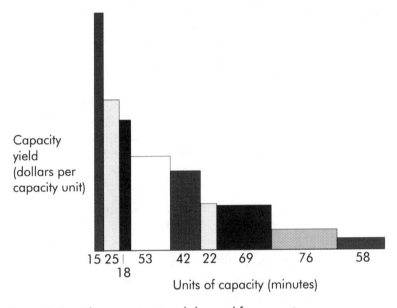

Figure 9.5. The organizational demand for capacity.

tal, Shouldice, that specializes in performing 7,000 inguinal hernia operations annually.[3] Individuals may be willing to travel great distances and pay very high fees because they expect that the specialist will be more effective. In other cases, where the need is not quite so specific, customers may prefer scope. Many transportation companies, for example, develop extensive route structures so they can provide single carrier responsibility for virtually all shipments. A specialization strategy tries to be "something special to more people," whereas a scope strategy seeks to "be more things to some people." A combination strategy is one in which the firm cross trains so it can be "more special things to more people." Specialization seeks to provide higher customer value. Scope allows greater capacity utilization. Yield management uses capacity first to meet high customer value needs and second, to find revenue-generating uses for the remaining capacity so it is not wasted.

Organizations will typically pursue both a specialization and a scope strategy at the same time. A local tailor shop, for example, may develop a specialty in designing and sewing costumes for wrestlers and other performers. Because of this specialization, the shop is able to reliably fit the special needs of this very demanding group. Because of this specialization, the shop is able to receive a very high yield from this business. Imagine the first bar in Figure 9.5 representing the value of the costume to the professional wrestler, the second bar the value to the skater, and the third bar the value to the actor. Although these specialized activities provide a very high yield, they do not fully utilize the organization's capacity. Therefore, the tailor also pursues a scope strategy. Bar 4 might represent the alteration of suits, and the last bar may be the hemming of pants. Collectively, there is enough business to fully utilize the organization's capacity.

The last measure, delivery efficiency, is a measure of how efficient the organization is in converting capacity to benefits. If one barber takes 10 minutes to give a haircut that another barber takes 30 minutes to deliver, they will have vastly different yield curves.[1]

For this reason, the service firm makes tradeoffs between specialization and scope to improve yield. Specialization improves revenue for each unit of capacity sold, and scope increases the percentage of capacity used to obtain revenue. Yield is managed by simultaneously pursuing both strategies. Specialization capabilities are developed to enhance revenues but through cross training (i.e., scope), otherwise wasted capacity is able to be used to generate revenue.

Direct and Derived Demands. There is another distinct difference between demand for products and the demand for organizational capacity – that is, there is a direct demand for products and an indirect demand for organizational capacity. A direct demand for something exists when individuals desire it. There is a derived demand when the thing is not desired for itself but because it is a means to a desired end.[2] For example,

---

1. There is another factor to consider: capacity management. Although this is covered in more depth in the next chapter, capacity management is the balancing of scheduled capacity and utilized capacity, with the critical success factor being the percentage of utilization.

2. Marshall clearly defined the difference between direct and derived demand. He stated there was an indirect demand for factors of production such as land, labor, and capital. This demand was derived from the direct demand for those products that they helped to produce. (See [2], p. 453.)

there is no demand for chemotherapy. It is painful, unenjoyable, and harmful to the body. The desired benefit is to be free of cancer cells. If chemotherapy were not one means for destroying cancer cells, there would be no demand of any kind for such treatment. Thus the demand for chemotherapy is derived from the desire to have the cancer cells destroyed. In a similar manner, there is a derived demand for most services. Take the transportation of textbooks, for example. Customers will not pay more for a textbook because it has been transported a greater distance. The textbook has a time and place value. The demand for transportation is derived from the difference in value of the textbook when it is located at the publisher's warehouse and when it is in the location desired by the customer.

Perhaps a better indication of direct and derived demand is the way that customers respond to the purchase of additional units. In the case of direct demand, customers will pay more for more units. In the case of derived demand, they will pay more for less as long as the goal is achieved. As in the case above, the cancer patient would pay much more for less chemotherapy if the remission goal is achieved. In the case of productive service, such as transportation, the value of the service is derived from the value that the service delivery adds to the product.[3]

There is a direct demand for benefits; customers are willing to pay for benefits. Customer value is the amount they will pay for the desired benefits. There is a direct demand for solutions because customers are willing to pay for solutions to their needs. There is a derived demand for organizational capacity. Customers do not pay for capacity because they want the capacity but because that is the only way they can receive the desired benefits. The less capacity they have to pay for, the better. This is not just because customers do not want the benefits. In fact, they will often pay more to get the same benefits if they require less capacity. A direct flight, for example, is worth far more than a longer, indirect flight. The customer only wants the benefit of being there. The hassle of having to be present and interact with the provider is a cost of receiving

---

3.   Economists have typically defined two types of service: productive and nonproductive. Productive services, such as transporting, repairing, and financing, add value to a product. If there is no product, the service is nonproductive. Adam Smith, Karl Marx, and Alfred Marshall all agreed on this concept.

benefits. Consequently, customers will typically pay more if the benefits can be delivered with less capacity and less hassle.

An excellent example of how improved deliveries are frequently associated with less capacity and less hassle can be seen in the old "Star Trek" television series. This series used hassle-free service delivery to give the viewers a feeling of a futuristic setting. Travelers used Scotty's transporter, which allowed instantaneous travel without seat belts, airport transfers, and fast-food outlets. Likewise, Bones always had a meter that could diagnose and repair aneurysms, clots, broken bones, and any other illnesses without surgery, hospital stays, bed pans, or extended periods of convalescence. Applying this concept today, can you imagine what Canadians would pay to have Scotty instantly beam them directly to south Florida in February rather than to have to travel many hours and miles by taxis, limousines, planes, airport shuttles, jumbo jets, moving walkways, and rental cars?

In a few cases, there may be a direct demand for a service delivery in which the customer will pay more for more. In these cases, the delivery process itself (e.g., attending a concert, ball game, or a cruise to the Bahamas) is typically enjoyable. The terms "event" or "happening" are often used to describe a service delivery in which the process itself is desirable. In these cases, there is a direct demand for the delivery process itself.

Individuals typically do not want to buy a product. It can be said that the demand for products is derived only from the benefits the individuals expect to receive from consuming the product. Thus the demand for products would also be indirect were it not for the ability to store and resell products. Philip Kotler has written that "in thinking about physical products, their importance lies not so much in owning them as in using them to satisfy our wants."[4] There is a direct demand for loaves of bread because they can be bought for future use or resold. The user is willing to pay more for 2 loaves of bread than for 1 loaf, more for 10 loaves than for 5, more for 100 than for 50. Because value can be stored in the loaf of bread, it can be purchased by the individual consumer, stored in a freezer, and consumed at will. As long as the loaf can be stored and the cost and hassle of storage and obsolescence is not too high, the buyer will purchase more bread. Another option is to resell the bread. If the price drops sufficiently, the buyer may buy loaves in hopes of reselling them. Thus there is typically a direct demand for products when the product can be purchased for multiple future uses or for speculation.

How a Demand Schedule Affects Pricing and Organizational Revenue. When benefit delivery is customized and cannot be resold, it dramatically changes a firm's pricing and revenue structures. Standardized, resellable products have a market price. If a different price is charged to different customers, the customers paying the lower price will resell it to the customers paying the higher prices. As long as the products are standardized, the customer will see no difference between the products purchased from the manufacturer or the reseller. The concept of a market price introduces the concept of the marginal revenue curve and the consumer surplus, as shown in Figure 9.6.

The marginal revenue curve is below the demand curve because to sell additional units, the price must be reduced to all buyers. As the price is dropped from P_0 to P_1, revenue is decreased by $(P_0 - P_1) \times (0Q_0)$ but increased by $OP_1 \times (Q_1 - Q_0)$. Although the market price has dropped to P_1, there are still individuals who are willing and able to pay much more for the product but who do not have to because the market price is below what they are willing to pay.

The area under the demand curve but above P_1 represents the consumer surplus that customers receive because they do not have to pay as much as they are willing to pay to receive the product. The *consumer surplus* is the difference between *customer value* and *market price*. When benefits can be traded, prices stabilize around a market price and customers obtain the consumer surplus. When benefits are customized and are not tradable, there is no market price. In the customer value schedule shown in Figure 9.7, the marginal revenue schedule is the same as the solution value schedule because each benefit delivery will be uniquely priced. Customer 1, for example, can be charged P_1 for a service that requires 15 units of capacity to deliver, Customer 2 can be charged P_2 for a service that requires 25 units, and so forth.

No one would expect a carpenter to contract for the same amount to build a deck on one house and install kitchen cabinets in another. The work is not comparable. Where deliveries are customized, customer value pricing is logical. When customer value pricing is used, customer value becomes the potential marginal revenue for each delivery. Where

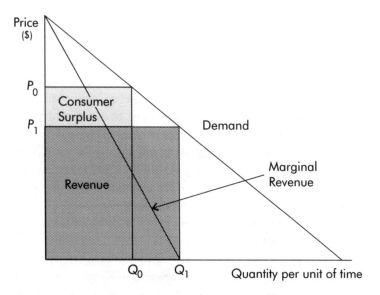

Figure 9.6. A product demand curve.

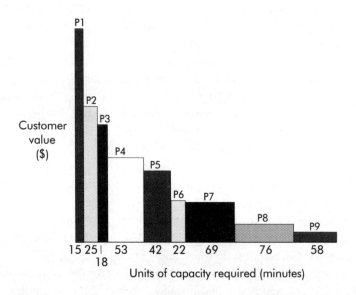

Figure 9.7. Marginal revenue for benefits that cannot be traded. *Note: Capacity demand schedule equals marginal revenue schedule.*

customer value is the marginal revenue, marginal revenue never becomes zero. Additional revenue can always be generated by serving additional customers (unless the service is given away). Therefore, total revenue is equal to the summation of customer value. Thus customer responsiveness increases revenue in two ways. First, it improves delivery fit and reduces hassle so solution value is greater (i.e., so that the solution value captures more of the customer value), and second, it allows solution-value pricing rather than market pricing.

The Determinants of Customer Value

Customer value is determined by the characteristics of the customer's need. Individuals have three types of needs: current needs, future needs, and speculative needs.

Current Needs. Current needs are those that require immediate solution. Current needs are frequently *binary* because they can be satisfied. A person may have a strong need for food, transportation, or security. Once that need is satisfied, it may cease to exist.

Needs also vary in *intensity*. One minute a person may be intensely hungry. A few minutes later, after having eaten, his or her hunger may be partially satisfied. After a large dessert, that person is not interested in another bite.

Current needs are also *situation specific*. For example, most individuals have no immediate demand for automatic transmission repair, ambulance service, spare tires, or legal representation. If, however, their personal situation were to change, these benefits could be of great value to them. Situations can change instantaneously and dramatically. The solution must match the current need. When people are commuting to work, they want transportation from their current location to the work site. They want to be delivered a few minutes before work begins. Bus service at the right time on the right route but in the wrong direction has no value. Bus service that arrives five minutes after work begins is also of no value. The benefits must meet the specific needs of the individual.

Often the need is for *discreet* solutions. That is, they cannot be partially met. Likewise, satisfaction cannot be improved with multiple deliveries. One half of a plane flight has little value. Even though styles vary, few people want three-quarters of a haircut. The demand is to have the need satisfied – no more and no less.

Thus current needs tend to be *highly erratic* for the individual. Although aggregate current needs for large groups may be predictable, they vary widely over time for each individual. Group needs may be erratic or stable. If individual needs are independent, group needs will be stable. The group need for adult eye exams, for example, may be relatively stable. On the other hand, if there are factors that synchronize individual needs, group needs may be equally erratic. Eye exams for children, for example, may be synchronized to school schedules just as commuter transportation needs are synchronized to employer work schedules.

Consequently, current solution demand tends to be *highly inelastic*. When a person is hungry, food has great value. Likewise, when people have a current-use need for health care, auto repair, or the services of a police officer, the need is often so intense that they would be willing to pay a very high price to have it satisfied. Afterwards, the demand for a solution may cease to exist. Both products and services can be purchased for current needs.

Future Needs.   Individuals may purchase a product to satisfy expected future needs. This is typically done when the current price of the item justifies storage and expected spoilage or obsolescence. Purchases for future needs are also made where the hassle of continually buying to meet current needs is too great. Products (i.e., prepackaged benefits) can be inventoried and thus can be purchased for future use.

Future solution demands are usually much more stable than the current solution demands. Unless people are terminally ill or expect a sudden change in their lives, they always expect to have more needs in the future. Thus future solution needs are seldom satisfied. If a "bargain" is found on an item that may be needed in the future, the customer may buy it. Thus future-use needs are continually on people's minds, and they are usually willing to make purchases for future use if the price is right.

Future-use purchases are almost always larger than purchases for current use, because future use purchases are typically for multiple future uses. In fact, a major pricing consideration is the price discount required to induce the future-use buyer to increase the size of the purchase. Grocery stores often have regular size, family size, and giant economy size packages, each successive size having a slightly lower cost per ounce. Even if the product is packaged into individual serving sizes, the individual packages are bundled into six packs or assortments or priced to encourage larger purchases for multiple future uses. Convenience stores, for example, which cater to current-use needs, typically have higher prices and smaller sizes than grocery stores or warehouse outlets such as Sam's, which cater to future needs. It is typically more difficult to buy a service for future needs because the intangible service cannot be inventoried for use in the future.

Speculation. Tangible products, which can be bought, sold, and transferred, also lend themselves to speculation. Speculative needs normally do not result from individual users but from intermediaries who buy for resale. They expect the benefit from the purchase to be profit. Their purchases are motivated by expected resale opportunity, the ability of the product to maintain value, and the cost (in terms of storage, transportation, or financing) of reselling. The speculator is not particularly concerned about the nature of the benefits to be derived from consuming the product (i.e., customer value), only about market value and potential resale opportunities. This is especially true for middlepersons, such as brokers or wholesalers.

Speculative demand is typically stable and very elastic. Because speculators are always looking for a "deal," it is they who stabilize prices over space and time.[5] Speculative purchases tend to be quite large, and a small price change can make or break a large sale. A 10 percent change in the price of an item to a grocery store chain may be a strong incentive where profit margins hover near 2 percent of sales. Thus, price elasticity of speculative demand is greater than price elasticity of demand for future solutions, just as the demand for future solutions is much more elastic than demand for current solutions.

How Benefit Value and Capacity Are Determined for Customer-Responsive Activities

There are four characteristics of activities that determine the value of the benefits and the demand for the organization's capacity. These are standardization of output, the ability to inventory benefits, the ability to trade and resell, and the presence of synchronizing factors. These factors are summarized in Table 9.1.

Standardization. Whenever an organization provides a standardized offering, whether a tangible product or an intangible service, it moves to standardized or market pricing. When the organization has the ability to customize, it customizes benefits to each person and price according to the benefit to be received.

The Ability to Inventory. When an organization has the ability to inventory, it encourages customers to purchase for future needs and typically practices seasonal pricing. Under seasonal pricing, the firm prices the offering at a high price at the beginning of a season and has a clearance sale for the excess inventory near the end of that season. Without the ability to inventory, customers buy for current needs. Without the ability to inventory, capacity continually perishes with time. Therefore, firms use both specialization and scope strategies simultaneously so that high prices "beginning of season" and clearance sale prices "end of season" are continually in effect.

The Ability to Trade. When the product can be traded, it has the potential for speculation. It can be distributed through a supply chain to resellers. These resellers compete and move toward a standardized market price. Without the ability to trade, the benefits can only be delivered to the beneficiary. (An appendectomy, a plane ride, or a hair cut, for example, can only be delivered to the beneficiary and cannot be traded.) The inability to trade allows customer value pricing because different customers cannot trade benefits.

Synchronizing Factors. If there are synchronizing factors, demand will have substantial peaks and troughs. When this variation in demand is for products, it is compensated for through inventory. When the variation is for a service that cannot be inventoried, then alternative strategies for varying capacity or finding alternative uses for scheduled capacity are persued.

The Methods for Changing the Characteristics of Activities

There are three methods for changing the characteristics of intangible services. These are reservations, tickets, and insurance.

Reservations. Reservations allow a purchase for a future need even though the benefit cannot be inventoried. Reservations typically are for a specific amount of capacity (e.g., a hotel room, an airline seat, or teeth

Table 9.1. The Effect of Benefit Characteristics on Demand

Standardization	Customization
Market (group) pricing (i.e., the same price for everyone)	Customer value pricing
Reduced fit – solution value is less than customer value for most	Improved fit – solution captures more of the customer value

Ability to inventory	Inability to inventory
Customers buy for future needs	Buy for current needs
Market pricing	Customer value pricing (e.g., different prices simultaneously)
Seasonal pricing (e.g., high price at beginning of season; clearance price at end of season)	Economics of specialization (e.g., high prices for high customer value deliveries)
	Economics of scope (e.g., low prices for low customer value deliveries)

Ability to trade	Inability to trade
Speculative demand	Customer value pricing
Single market price	Direct relationship with customer
Use of market intermediaries	

Synchronizing factors	No synchronizing factors
Results in demand peaking for products that can be inventoried	Results in stable demand for capacity
Use inventory to respond to demand fluctuation	
Use flexible manufacturing to be more responsive for services that cannot be inventoried	
Vary capacity scheduled for service delivery	
Develop resource network that can be used as needed	

cleaning). Either the customer must be able to define his or her need in advance or the interactive diagnostic process must occur before the reservation can be made.

213

Tickets.   A ticket is generally different from a reservation. Tickets allow speculation in benefits that cannot be inventoried. A ticket can also be used for a specific benefit at a specific time. The difference between the ticket and the reservation is that the ticket can be resold. Tickets can be bought and sold through various distribution channels. Speculators can even buy and sell tickets, as is obvious to any college football fan who is familiar with the ever-present "scalpers."

Tickets may also take the form of token or passes. Tokens are generally used for benefits for which there is surplus capacity, such as for general admission rather than for a specific capacity (specific seat at a specific time). Bus tokens, for example, let a person use the service whenever it is available and do not specify a specific seat on a specific vehicle. Passes, on the other hand, allow benefit delivery (e.g., admission) over an extended period of time.

Insurance.   Insurance allows individuals to purchase for uncertain future needs, especially when the need may be very large.[4] Individuals may buy insurance for automobile repair (extended warranties), health care, towing, bail bond, or many other predictable but uncertain events. In each case, the insurance consists of paying a guaranteed premium so that a large probabilistic expenditure will be covered, if it occurs.

Summary

The concept of supply and demand applies when there is a direct demand for products that can be inventoried and resold. Traditional economic analysis, which was built on supply and demand curves, was developed to apply to activities involving the production of products that could be inventoried and resold. Traditionally, economics focused on the product, the marketplace, suppy and demand, and market pricing.

Customer-responsive economic concepts focus on customized deliveries, the interaction with individual customers to better fit needs, and customer value pricing. Its emphasis is on improving fit and reducing hassle so the solution delivered by the provider better meets each customer's need and is thus able to capture more customer value. Firms

---

4.   Insurance generally requires that the specific risk, as well as the maximum level of risk and the time period, be specified at time of purchase.

develop specialization strategies to better fit high customer value needs and scope strategies to use otherwise wasted capacity to generate revenue. Collectively, these strategies increase yield. Yield is a measure of the revenue that can be generated from a delivery and/or the scheduling of units of capacity to provide deliveries.

References

[1] Paul A. Samuelson, *Economics*, New York: McGraw-Hill, 1970, p. 55.

[2] Alfred Marshall, *Principles of Economics*, London: MacMillan & Company, 1898, p. 174.

[3] James L. Heskett, *Managing in the Service Economy*, Boston: Harvard Business School, 1986, pp. 27–29.

[4] Philip Kotler, *Marketing Management*, Englewood Cliffs, NJ: Prentice-Hall, 1988, p. 4.

[5] Samuelson, op. cit., pp. 399–405.

CHAPTER 10

CUSTOMER-RESPONSIVE COST ECONOMICS

Traditional economics addresses fixed and variable costs. There are two decision-making periods – the long run and the short run. In responsive organizations, however, there are the three types of costs and three decision-making periods.

Role of Inventory

Inventory greatly simplifies the task of managing an offering-based business in which products are involved. In many cases, however, inventory can carry a large cost. Inventory allows the business to manufacture products and ship finished goods to the marketplace in anticipation of demand. If the demand forecast is low, additional units can be produced and shipped on an expedited basis. If the demand forecast is high, production and shipments are decreased for the next planning period to absorb the excess inventory. Alternatively, the product can be discounted to stimulate future use or speculative purchases. Inventory also provides longer lead times and desensitizes decision making. Inventory allows management to virtually ignore daily variation in demand and production because it buffers the effect of short-term variation. It is the buffer between different activities in the value chain.

Where there is turbulence, inventory reduces flexibility. The organization is not able to respond to changing needs if it has large inventories for disposal. When this happens, even production organizations realize there is a large cost involved with holding inventory. Consequently, the field of business logistics stresses the efficient management of inventory, and offering-based firms are using just-in-time (JIT) and quick-response techniques to reduce inventory to a bare minimum. As the quantity of inventory decreases, however, the complexity of coordinating activities increases.

Customer-responsive activities where there is no inventory present in the process are the extreme cases. The absence of inventory does offer an advantage, however. Without inventory, organizations can be both fiscally leaner and easier to coordinate but organizations must change the way they coordinate activities to realize these benefits. They must shift from the deterministic planning and scheduling management approach to the protocol and dispatch method of coordination.

When interest rates jumped to over 18 percent during the 1970s, business recognized that inventory carrying cost was high. Chrysler discovered when it was left with a large inventory of large cars in a small-car market just how expensive inventory could be. As Toyota refined the concept of just-in-time (JIT) manufacturing, firms recognized that inventory could create major inflexibilities in the production process. In the late 1980s, Wal-Mart illustrated that inventory could change from being a large user of capital (because inventory turns slower than payment terms) to a source of capital for financing retail outlets by dramatically increasing *inventory turns* to *inventory spins*.

Customer-responsive businesses and service organizations do not have the luxury of inventory to reduce management complexity. Responsive organizations schedule capacity in anticipation of customer requests. The use of this capacity, however, cannot be scheduled until after the customer request is received. If the provider schedules too much capacity, the excess is wasted; its value cannot be preserved in inventory. Empty airplane seats cannot be inventoried and liquidated at a later date. A hotel cannot close down during the winter season so it will have more rooms to rent during the peak tourist season. The unused capacity is totally wasted without the ability to recover any cost at a later fire sale or liquidation.

On the other hand, if inadequate capacity is scheduled, the user cannot be served. No one likes to be denied service because a hotel, airline, hospital, or college class overbooked and is unable to provide someone the desired benefit. Even more distressing is the realization that a fire department, ambulance service, police department, or the military may not have adequate capacity and cannot respond to peak emergency needs. In fact, one reason for the high cost of government is that politicians usually find it much easier to justify extensive wasted capacity than to explain capacity shortages in an emergency. They simply react to criticism about emergency service employees not doing anything of value much of the time with the question, "Would you rather they be responding to a need at your home?" Capacity management is the balancing of capacity scheduled and capacity utilized, with the critical success factor being percentage of capacity utilization.

What Is the Cost of Capacity?

When a firm produces a product, cost measures are expressed in terms of the offering and stated as average costs. When someone asks what it costs to produce a product, the implication is the average cost. There are two components of average costs: costs that are fixed regardless of production levels and costs that vary according to the number of units produced. Production economists use the terms "fixed" and "variable" costs to describe these two costs.

Average costs are the sum of variable costs plus fixed costs divided by the number of units produced. If fixed costs are large, average cost will be strongly influenced by output (e.g., number of units produced).

Although this dual classification of cost may be satisfactory for costing products, it is too limited when applied to responsive services. How do you determine the number of units produced? Is it the number of problems solved, or is it the amount of capacity scheduled to solve problems? In the case of mass transit, is it the bus miles scheduled or the number of passengers carried? How costs are calculated will vary, based on how output is defined. For responsive activities, costs vary with both the capacity scheduled and the customers served. Costs vary by the number of flights scheduled and by the number of people actually transported.

Consequently, there are three levels of costs for responsive services. These are fixed capacity costs, scheduled capacity costs, and service delivery costs. Therefore, a three-level classification system must be used based upon the types of decisions that must be made.

Capacity acquisition costs or *fixed capacity costs* are incurred to acquire or develop facilities, tools, and skills that will be used for multiple scheduling periods. In the case of an airline, capacity acquisition costs include the purchase or lease of planes (i.e., the tool), the training of pilots (i.e., skills), the acquisition of terminal and baggage facilities (i.e., facilities), and the development of the reservation system (i.e., another tool). Once the decision has been made to obtain capacity, acquisition costs are irreversible and do not vary regardless of the number of flights scheduled or passengers carried on each flight.

Scheduled capacity costs are incurred when the facilities, tools, and skills are scheduled so that they will be available to serve customers. Scheduled capacity costs are incurred by an airline when flights are scheduled; they include the costs of fuel, flight crews, landing fees, and maintenance. Once made, scheduled capacity costs do not vary regardless of the number of passengers served. These costs will be the same whether the flight has one passenger or the flight is full.

Service delivery costs are the costs incurred when the benefits are actually delivered to the individual customer. Service delivery costs are those that vary when a passenger sits in the airline seat. To continue with the airline analogy, it is the difference between flying with a full seat versus an empty seat and includes costs such as the travel agent's commission, in-flight snacks, and a slight increase in fuel costs.

From these three costs, two additional categories of costs can be calculated: total capacity costs and total service delivery costs.

Total capacity costs consist of both capacity acquisition and scheduled capacity costs. Total capacity costs are fixed during service delivery. Total capacity costs are incurred when the capacity is scheduled to serve the customers. Total capacity costs are unchanged whether the hotel spends the entire day waiting on guests who never arrive or whether the hotel is fully rented with multiple occupancy in every room. Total capacity costs are incurred whether the hospital wing is full or has only one patient and whether the truck is full or deadheading. These costs vary by the number of solutions delivered.

Total service delivery costs are the sum of total capacity costs and service delivery costs. These costs are summarized in Table 10.1.

Table 10.1 also indicates the approximate magnitude of these costs. John Dearden has suggested that fixed costs for most products range between 10 and 20 percent, whereas variable costs range from 80 to 90 percent.[1] These same values were applied to responsive service costs. Fixed capacity costs are between 10 percent and 20 percent. Scheduled capacity costs are between 70 percent and 80 percent, and service delivery costs are typically less than 10 percent of the total service delivery costs.

Capacity Management Is Immediate-Run Management

A three-level classification of costs is not new to economics. Alfred Marshall described them in 1898.[2] Paul Samuelson describes the time periods developed by Marshall as "(1) momentary equilibrium, when the supply is fixed; (2) short-run equilibrium, when firms can produce more within given plants; and finally (3) long-run equilibrium . . . when firms

Table 10.1. A Summary of Cost Terms for Responsive Organizations

Cost Category	Description	Characteristic	Percentage of cost
Capacity Costs:			
Fixed capacity costs	Multiperiod acquisition costs of knowledge base, tools, facilities, and infrastructure	Fixed whether or not capacity is scheduled to serve customers	10%–20%
Scheduled capacity costs	Incurred when capacity is scheduled to be available to respond to customers	Fixed whether or not any customers are served	70%–80%
Total capacity costs	Total cost of making capacity available to serve customers for that period	Incurred when doors are opened for business	≈90%
Delivery Costs:			
Service delivery costs	Out-of-pocket cost of making delivery	Specific to each individual delivery	≤10%
Total service delivery costs	Total cost of providing all benefits for period	Not applicable to any single delivery	100%

can abandon old plants or build new ones and when new firms can enter the industry or old ones leave it."[3]

Although Marshall used these terms to describe equilibrium time periods when supply and demand were equal, management decisions are also made during each of these time periods.

Although Marshall recognized "momentary-run" equilibrium, he thought that momentary changes occur too erratically for management to respond, because conditions change too quickly to change production schedules or to influence plant size. In fact, the term "ceteris paribus" ("all other things being equal") has been used to assume away such irrelevant momentary variations. The reason that these momentary variations have not been important to management is that inventory has been the buffer to mitigate the impact of immediate-run variation. Without inventory as a buffer, immediate-run management becomes the heart of capacity management. Capacity is committed in the immediate run.

This work uses the word "immediate run" in place of Marshall's "momentary run." The reason for using the term "immediate" is that according to *Webster's New Universal Unabridged Dictionary*, "momentary" means "continuing or lasting for a very short time."[4] In Marshall's world, momentary changes in supply or demand were simply irrelevant, although expected – "noise" in the system that should be ignored. The manager might say "Why worry? Tomorrow conditions will return to normal." In the case of responsive activities, however, capacity is routinely committed in the immediate run.

The word "immediate," however, means "occurring or acting without any perceptible duration of time." "Immediate run" refers to the continual stream of commitments being made to individual customers right now. An attorney may accept a client, an airline may accept a reservation, a contractor may accept a new project, or a taxicab may pick up a fare. Each of these decisions is made in an instant but may affect the organization for an extended time period before the delivery is completed.

In the immediate run, decisions are continually being made to match scheduled capacity with expectations about the arrival of customers. Should an airline call freight brokers and offer them a discount on freight for the 5:00 p.m. flight to Tokyo, or should they wait and risk holding the capacity for less freight that would pay full rate if it materializes? It is in the immediate run that the response-based organization interacts with the customer and makes many decisions that influence capacity utilization.

The terms "long run," "short run," "and "immediate run" imply time dimensions. Perhaps Marshall could have been more selective in his choice of terms; they refer not to chronological time but to the types of decisions that are made. Lest these terms be taken too literally, let's remember Marshall's admonition: "Of course there is no hard and sharp line of division between 'long' and 'short' periods. Nature has drawn no such lines in the economic conditions of actual life; and in dealing with practical problems they are not wanted."[5]

Immediate-Run Decisions Determine the Revenue Generated from Scheduled Capacity

Albrecht and Zemke, in their book *Service America!*, allude to the immediate run by emphasizing that the basis for successful service delivery is in managing "moments of truth."[6]

According to Jan Carlzon, former chairman of SAS airlines, such moments occur thousands of times a day as each front-line service provider interacts with the customer and commits not only themselves but also the organization to meet the customer's needs on a real-time, immediate-run basis. There is no time to get approval from multiple levels of management, conduct studies, pore over reports, or examine the impact of each customer's request on the organization's strategic plan. The customer has a need: he or she wants to know whether the organization can deliver the desired benefits and, if so, what the cost of the delivery will be. It is in the immediate run that the service promise is made. Immediate-run decisions are typically made by the front-line workers based upon the information and policies they have been given. Just as decisions to acquire, modify, or abandon plants and facilities are based on long-run economic analysis and just as decisions to schedule capacity to provide services are based on short-run economic analysis, so decisions about interaction with individual customers are based on immediate-run economic analysis.

In general, long-run decision making influences multiple scheduling periods and is based on an analysis of long-run trends. Short-run scheduling tends to coincide with the accounting periods because the accounting data provides information on sales, production, costs, revenue, and inventory upon which schedules are based. For the scheduling to be done other than during the accounting periods, management needs another set of data upon which to base schedules. Immediate-run decisions, consequently, are not based on accounting period data but on real-time operational data.[1] These operational data may be from reservation systems, tracking systems, project management systems, first-hand experience with irate customers, reviewing priority dispatch lists, and observing queue lengths. These information sources are not part of the normal financial reporting system. Immediate-run decisions must be

---

1. Product firms must also make immediate-run decisions, but inventory has been used to disconnect production, distribution, marketing, and financial decisions in the immediate run. Thus, inventory is used to "damp out" the "noise" of day-to-day fluctuations; it also makes the organization numb to changes in the marketplace. This is not a problem as long as operations remain relatively steady state and there is a limited need to make market, competitive, or environmental changes.

based on current data about capacity availability and commitments for that capacity rather than historical data about financial transactions. But as Carlzon discovered, short- and long-run financial results are determined by making sure that in the immediate run "you're selling what the customer wants to buy"[8].

How Are Costs Used to Make Decisions?

In many cases, costs must be classified to determine how costs are impacted by the decision at hand. For instance, in the short run, only variable costs are changed by the decision. Fixed or unavoidable costs are said to be "sunk." For example, when a college was approached about letting senior citizens audit classes at reduced tuition rates, there was concern that regular students who were paying full tuition would be excluded. Once it was decided to limit this option to classes on a space-available basis, there was no more concern because there is little if any cost incurred when senior citizens sit in an otherwise empty seat.

For decision-making purposes, then, it is important to understand which costs are fixed and which costs are variable, because it is the variable costs that are influenced by the decision. In the long run, all costs are variable. New planes can be purchased, new factories can be built, and new employees can be hired and trained.

Capacity is scheduled in the short run. Here capacity acquisition costs are fixed, but scheduled capacity costs and service delivery costs are variable. The cost structure for short-run capacity scheduling is shown in Figure 10.1.

Service commitments are made in the immediate run. For these decisions, all capacity costs are fixed. Only service delivery costs are variable. The cost structure that is faced during service commitments is shown in Figure 10.2.

Is There a Relationship Between Fixed and Variable Costs?

The relationship between fixed and variable costs has been one of the major focuses of production economics. Production planners are continually looking for ways to use long-term, fixed investments in plant and equipment to reduce variable production costs. Because long-term costs were traditionally capital and short-term costs were largely labor,

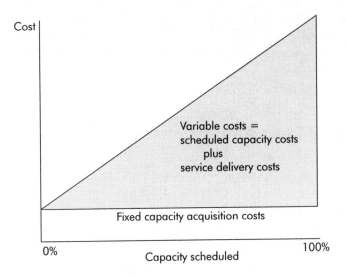

Figure 10.1. The cost structure facing short-run decision makers.

this was described as substituting capital for labor. Whatever tradeoffs are made, the goal of the production economist is to reduce the average cost of producing a product.

$$\text{Average cost of product} = \frac{\text{Fixed capital costs}}{\text{Units produced}} + \text{variable production costs.}$$

There are two ways to reduce average product costs. One method is to make a larger investment in fixed capital costs that will dramatically lower variable product costs. If capital costs are 10 percent of the total costs of the product, the firm can justify increasing its capital cost by 100 percent (from 10 percent to 20 percent of its total costs) if it will reduce production costs by 11 percent (from 90 percent to 80 percent of its total costs). This multiplier creates a strong incentive for capital investment.

The second way to reduce average product costs is used when increased capital investment allows the construction of a larger plant that can produce so much more output that fixed capital costs per unit drop dramatically. Economists call this "economy of scale." (The larger the production facility, the lower the average cost of production.) Because

225

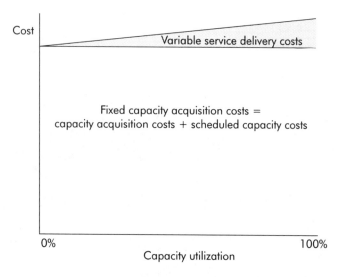

Figure 10.2. The cost structure facing immediate-run decision makers.

of this principle, it is not unusual to have all production, whether designed for national or global markets, for a given product performed at a single site.

Although there may be economies of scale in the scheduling of capacity, service organizations are faced with different considerations. Because of the need to facilitate the interaction with customers, service organizations tend to be small.[2] Although there are large service organizations such as ARA or Service Master, actual service delivery activities tend to be made at decentralized sites. Large service companies develop the infrastructure necessary to support a large number of small franchises

---

2. Exceptions do occur. Public utilities tend to be quite large because they were required to own their own rights-of-way. Thus railroads, pipelines, and power companies are very large and capital intensive. On the other hand, many local phone companies, power distribution companies, and cable television companies are quite small. These firms would often buy power and television programming or enter into partnerships with a major phone company. An argument can be made that these industries would be much different today had government regulation not determined their organizational structure.

or service delivery organizations located close to their customers. They are large only in that there are many local delivery organizations. For example, maid service, hospital meals, transportation, and funeral services are not provided nationwide from a single large facility. Motels, consultants, system designers, and CPAs may have a central office to which they report, but the service is provided in the field where the customers are located. Thus economy of scale is not an option for many service delivery activities. An exception to this occurs when telecommunications enable customer-assistance centers, 800-number help desks, and order-entry desks to interact with customers and make overnight delivery of packages.

Customer-Responsive Relationships Between Fixed and Variable Costs

There are two major differences between production and customer-responsive economics. First, averages have no meaning for responsive activities. As shown in Chapter 8, it is difficult to determine average moving costs when one customer is a recent college graduate moving to his or her first job 200 miles away with 500 pounds of stereo equipment and 300 pounds of personal effects, one is a senior citizen moving 20,000 pounds of household goods three blocks to a condo, and another is an executive moving 30,000 pounds of household goods plus six children and four cars 2,000 miles away after a promotion to a new position. How do you average the costs of a tonsillectomy, a coronary bypass, and long-term chemotherapy? Each delivery is customized, and the variation by individual needs can be dramatic.

However, averages do have meaning for scheduling capacity. Capacity costs are more homogenous. The mover can give you a per-mile cost to operate the moving van and a per-hour cost to provide packers. A physician can tell you what it takes to keep the office open per hour or day. The cost of the individual service delivery will depend upon the amount of each type of capacity required.

Second, responsive organizations do not have a standardized output (product) to manage. Offering-based firms can focus on common output – the product. Responsive organizations schedule the capacity to serve in the short run but make service commitments in the immediate run. Because capacity cannot be inventoried, it perishes with each tick of the clock. Capacity spent waiting on customers rather than on *serving* customers is wasted and can never be recovered or used to generate revenue. Therefore, these differences create a different operating strategy for customer-responsive organizations. Customer-responsive organizations seek to increase yield. That means they try to use the capacity scheduled in a way that will generate the greatest possible amount of revenue. This can be done in three ways.

First, the organization seeks to utilize every unit of scheduled capacity to generate revenue. Expressed another way, the organization wants to minimize the amount of non-revenue–generating, wasted capacity. The term "economy of use" can be used to describe this concept.

Second, the organization seeks greater flexibility to schedule capacity. This is done by developing modules so that less capacity can be scheduled when the demand for benefits is expected to be light. The term "economy of modularity" is used to describe this concept.

Third, the organization seeks to minimize its exposure to inflexible, fixed commitments. The customer-responsive organization's prime commitment is to the customer. If the organization has large investments in fixed facilities, long-term contracts with resources, or large staffs of highly specialized workers, it can be caught between wanting to respond to the needs of the customer and facing the need to find a revenue-generating use for those resources. Therefore, responsive firms will typically acquire resources where expected demand is stable and continual. Where there is greater variation in the expected capacity and the capability needs, the firm will network with resources on an as-needed basis. The term "economy of networking" is used to illustrate this concept.

These three concepts are discussed more fully in the following sections.

Economy of Use

The actual cost of providing service is primarily determined by capacity utilization. If it costs $100 to schedule a bus run and the bus transports 50 people in each direction (for a total of 100 riders), the cost per ride is $1 per ride. On the other hand, if only one person is transported, the cost for the ride is $100 per ride. Although the bus company can change costs slightly by changing operating procedures, the primary method for controlling costs is by managing capacity utilization. Thus the actual cost of each unit of capacity actually delivered can be calculated as:

$$\begin{array}{l}\text{Average} \\ \text{cost of} \\ \text{capacity unit}\end{array} = \dfrac{\text{Total capacity cost}}{\text{\% capacity utilization}}.$$

This relationship is shown in Figure 10.3.

Figure 10.3 shows that the unit cost of the service capacity delivered varies dramatically with capacity utilization. If the utilization ratio is only 50 percent, the average cost of delivered capacity is twice as much as if all capacity is utilized. At a utilization rate of 25 percent, the cost is four times as great.

Consider the city government that purchases a fleet of school buses to transport school children. The buses may be utilized two hours each morning and two hours each evening for 180 days a year to transport students; the rest of the time the drivers and vehicles are not delivering benefits. Thus the majority of school bus capacity is spent parked at the county garage. Even part of the scheduled hours are spent driving empty to and from the beginning of the route. This means that much of the cost of providing school bus service is not the cost of service delivery but costs resulting from extensive, wasted capacity.

Because of this, the primary determinant of the cost of delivery is capacity utilization. Although purchasing departments may make minor reductions in their operating costs by buying less expensive tires for the airline or less expensive sutures for the operating room, dramatic changes in delivered capacity costs are possible by even slight changes in utilization rates. Therefore, *the focus of management must be on increasing capacity utilization.* This is the reason that managers of responsive organizations continually monitor percentage of billable hours, percentage of load factors, percentage of deadheading, percentage of occupancy, or any other measure of capacity actually used to deliver benefits.

In fact, increasing capacity utilization is a primary focus of responsive management. But how is capacity utilization increased? Chapter 8 described capacity management as one of the key management responsibilities in a responsive organization. Chapter 9 described the economy of scope approach that allows the provider to do more things for each customer through cross training and more flexible capacity. In the following

229

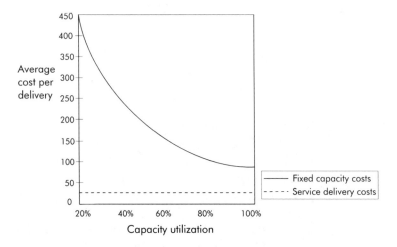

Figure 10.3. The relationship between delivered cost and utilization.

sections, two methods of obtaining resources are given that dramatically reduce the cost of capacity required to delivery solutions to customers.

Economy of Modularity

One method of increasing capacity utilization is to develop the ability to schedule capacity in modules. Organizing work groups by modules allows the organization to schedule less capacity during periods when organizational demand is expected to be low. Figures 10.4 through 10.6 illustrate the economy of modularity concept.

Line OA in Figure 10.4 represents the theoretical range of expected organizational demand. During some periods, such as a hotel on Christmas Day, the organization may expect only 10 percent of its potential capacity to be required. On other occasions, it will be able to deliver all the capacity it can possibly schedule. Line OC in Figure 10.4 represents the amount of capacity that must be scheduled if the organization is not designed for module operations. In this case, the business is either open or closed. The entire area above line OA represents wasted capacity that will have to be scheduled but not delivered under various capacity utilization scenarios. Expressed another way, if only 50 percent of capacity is utilized to deliver a benefit, the remaining 50 percent is wasted waiting on customers who do not arrive.

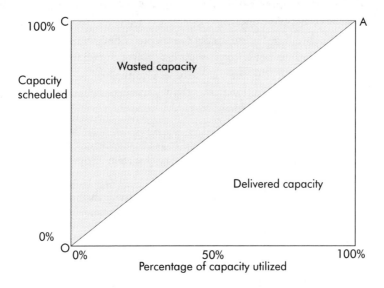

Figure 10.4. Delivered versus wasted capacity at varying levels of utilization.

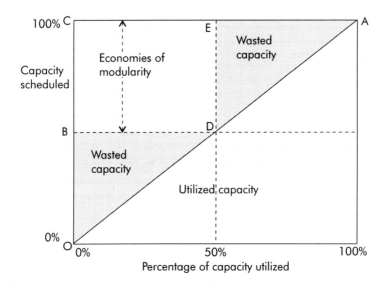

Figure 10.5. Economies of modularity (with two modules).

231

If the organization is designed for modular scheduling, one module, OB, can be scheduled anytime expected organizational demand is less than 50 percent. (See Figure 10.5.) If expected demand is expected to be greater than 50 percent, two modules, OB as well as DE, can be scheduled. The line BC indicates the economies of modulation when expected capacity utilization is less than 50 percent because capacity BC does not have to be scheduled.

But modularity is not limited to two modules. Figure 10.6 shows an organization that has been organized to schedule capacity in up to eight modules. The more modular the organizational structure, the more efficiently the organization can respond to variations in expected capacity utilization. In the eight-module case shown in Figure 10.6, the expected wasted capacity is reduced to the shaded area, or about 6 percent, as compared to 25 percent in the two-module case and 50 percent in the one-module case.

Modularity holds not only for the organization but for each individual service delivery. For example, if a carrier only has 45-foot trailers, that is the smallest module that it can assign to a truckload shipper. If the shipper has only 24 feet of freight, the carrier must either assign an entire trailer or use local pickup, freight consolidation, line haul, break bulk, or local delivery. The only options will be extensive wasted capacity or extensive extra handling. If, instead of operating only 45-foot trailers, the carrier began to offer the smaller 27-foot "pups," the carrier could more economically serve smaller customers with direct-haul service. It is easy to understand why truckers lobbied to get permission to operate double and triple trailers. By using a tractor to pull two or three small trailers rather than one or two big ones, the carriers could achieve the economies of truck-load movements with smaller and smaller modules.

Economy of modularity strategies motivate hospitals to schedule by work station. During the period between Christmas and New Year's, for example, when people prefer to avoid elective surgery, the hospital may close down several wings to reduce costs. Fast-food restaurants schedule employees in 15- to 30-minute increments and are anxious to use part-time employees on whatever basis they are available. Airlines may use smaller planes with more frequent schedules to serve smaller cities.

However the organization does it, the purpose is still the same. The most effective way to control costs while responding to varying customer needs is to organize by modules so that wasted capacity is minimized.

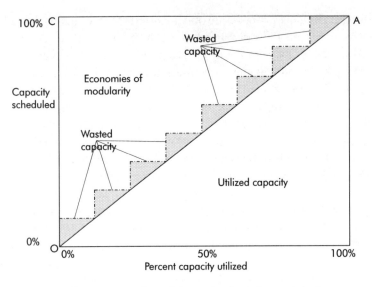

Figure 10.6. Economies of modularity (with eight modules).

Whereas production economics emphasizes economies of scale, responsive economics stresses economies of modularity. One way of increasing modularity is through networking.

Economy of Networking

Networking is a method for obtaining resources to deliver benefits to the customer. Resources can either be acquired or networked. (Production firms typically use the terms "make" or "buy.") Acquisition occurs when the resource is owned or employed by the organization. Acquired resources become capacity costs. Facilities become fixed capacity costs. People become scheduled capacity costs. Networking occurs when the organization obtains the service of the resources on a use-by-use or short-term basis. Networked resources are variable service delivery costs because they are paid for on a per-use basis.

The purpose of a network is to provide the organization with the range of capabilities and capacity it needs to serve its customers' diverse needs while at the same time keeping the cost of the resource a service delivery cost, which is variable in the immediate run, rather than a capacity cost, which is fixed in the immediate run. This is important

233

because service delivery costs are only incurred when a delivery is made. Capacity costs, on the other hand, are scheduled in advance and are wasted whenever they are not needed to provide benefits to a customer. For example, a nursing home could hire a full-time physician and acquire laboratory facilities to take care of residents, or it could negotiate with a network of physicians and labs to provide services on a per-need basis. If the nursing home acquired its own in-house resources, these costs become part of fixed capacity costs, whereas if they are obtained as part of a network, there is only a charge when the resource is needed.

Figure 10.7 compares the cost of these two methods. The dotted line OG indicates the unit cost of obtaining resource capacity by networking. It begins at the origin where the resource is not needed. The 100 percent level indicates that the resource module would be busy 100 percent of the time. The 125 percent level indicates capacity needs must be expanded by 25 percent. Thus the outsourcing or networked line is straight, indicating that the rate per delivery is the same whether the resource delivers one unit of capacity, 100 units of capacity, or 125 units of capacity. The cost per unit of network capacity is shown as the slope of the dotted line (E).

The lines HI and JK represent the cost of scheduling in-house resources to provide the delivery. These lines are similar to the line CA in Figure 10.4. Line HI is flat, indicating that once capacity is scheduled, capacity costs are fixed in the immediate run. Line HI could be stepped as shown in Figures 10.5 and 10.6, depending upon the firm's ability to modularize capacity. Whatever the shape of HI, capacity costs are incurred when they are scheduled. The service delivery costs are not incurred until the capacity is used to deliver the benefits. Line JK represents capacity cost to expand capacity by 25 percent.

If capacity utilization is below point A, it is less expensive to outsource or network. If the organization routinely experiences stable demand for capacity levels between A and B, then in-house provision of capacity is most economical. If, however, capacity demand is frequently below point A, it is more economical to obtain capacity on a per-use basis from the network (i.e., outsourced) rather than in-house.

This analysis is very similar to that made by a production firm to determine if it should buy its own trucks or use contract or common carriers to deliver its products. If distribution patterns are such that the trucks would have few deadhead miles and would be in constant opera-

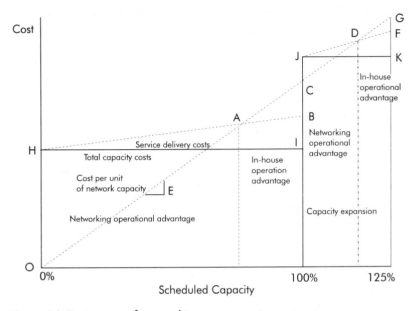

Figure 10.7. Impact of networking on capacity cost.

tion, it may pay to acquire the trucks. If, on the other hand, demands are seasonal and there are few reverse hauls, it would probably be less expensive to use a network of contract or common carriers. If all shipments are to a single site and one carrier can meet all needs, the firm may select a single trucking company to provide the service. If, on the other hand, shipment needs are diverse and to many different destinations and of many different sizes, the company will need a network of carriers that can be available to delivery with a simple phone call.

If demand for capacity exceeds the 100% level, the network can still provide additional capacity at rate E. For example, a firm may expand, but FedEx and UPS will still be able to meet their needs at the same rates. If the service is provided in-house, the firm must incur the fixed capacity cost and scheduled capacity cost to add an additional module, such as an additional truck and driver. If demand for capacity is stable between AB and DF, in-house provision of capacity is most economical. If, on the other hand, the firm experiences varying capacity needs including periods with demand below A or between CD (as is typically the case with most responsive organizations), networking becomes much more attractive.

235

Customer-Responsive Cost Economics

One excellent example of the principle of networking is illustrated by the growth in temporary employment services. Rather than hire employees full time, firms with varying demands for capacity often hire individuals on a temporary basis. This occurs not only for laborers and secretaries but also for physicians to staff emergency rooms and nurses to staff hospital wings and adjunct faculty to teach university classes.

Unfortunately, traditional production economics has not only ignored immediate run variation but has given limited attention to even the dynamics of short-run decisions. Marketplace demand has been thought to be relatively stable. In reality, it is not unusual for hotel occupancy to vary between 50 percent and 100 percent. Consultants are frequently happy with 70-percent billable hours with substantial variation around that average. Even less familiar are the rigidity of capacity costs.

The Capacity Inflexibility Dilemma

In-house organizations frequently are very inflexibile. However, mass-production approach to management is so thoroughly ingrained in our society that even service organizations are typically managed to be steady-state operations. In these organizations, flexibility is all but eliminated. Perhaps one of the best examples is a public agency such as a county school system. These are actual budget figures from a county school system are shown in Table 10.2. This budget illustrates the lack of flexibility in changing levels of operations. Virtually all school expenditures are set in the spring before the fiscal year begins. In the late spring, the school must forecast the number of students by grade and class and decide how to staff classes. Because 80 percent of the budget is salaries and benefits and the staffing level is decided in late spring, there is little flexibility once school starts in the fall. Supplies make up only 7 percent of the budget and include all textbooks, which are ordered in the summer. Also included is about $100 per teacher per year for other supplies. Virtually all of this is committed before school starts.

Contracted services, which make up 10 percent of the budget, include bus transportation (based on the number of routes, the number of miles, the number of buses, and so forth), which is virtually 100-percent committed before the year starts. Small changes in routes are made after the year starts, but almost everything is fixed without knowing the actual enrollment or needs. In schools where bus service is provided in-house,

Table 10.2. The 1992–1993 Budget for a County School System

Budgeted Expense	Amount	Percent
Salaries and benefits	$25,691,768	79.7%
Contracted services[a]	3,195,033	9.9%
Supplies and materials	2,266,447	7.0%
Other charges[b]	1,065,965	3.3%
Total expenditures	$32,219,213	100.0%
Budgeted Revenue		
Property taxes	$ 6,591,475	20.5%
Local sales and other taxes	5,605,992	17.4%
State and federal funds	18,659,846	57.9%
Other charges and fund balances[c]	1,361,900	4.2%
Total revenue	$32,219,213	100.0%

[a]Includes about $1.7 million in bus transportation and most maintenance to school facilities.
[b]Includes an Insurance Premium and Trustee Commission.
[c]Includes cafeteria collections and the use of fund balances or savings from prior years.

this part of the budget would not be listed as contract services but lumped in with salaries, repairs, and fuel. Purchase of new buses would not be part of the budget but would require an additional appropriation for capital equipment. Building maintenance is also include in contracted service. The only way to get any flexibility in the budget is to delay building maintenance until the end of the school year. Because of this, about 75 percent of all maintenance occurs in the months of May and June after the administration is reasonably sure the school will make it through the year on its budget.

This creates a problem. If expenses are high, the only area in which administrators can save money is to eliminate the purchase of maintenance supplies and materials. Thus the building maintenance personnel are paid salaries, but without supplies and materials they are not effective in repairing or cleaning the building.

The other charges include the County Trustee's Commission, which by state law requires the county to keep about 1 percent of revenues to help offset the administration of the tax-collection and bill-paying process. Also included in the "other" category is the insurance premiums, which are committed before a single school door is opened.

On the revenue side, about 21 percent of revenue comes from property tax. The sales and other local taxes (17 percent) are collected by the state and distributed according to the location of the business collecting the tax. These taxes are totally dependent upon the local economy. The largest source of revenue is federal and state aid, but this is allocated by the state and federal political process. When budgets become tight at these levels, they expect the local systems to pay a larger share.

Virtually the only flexibility available to the administration is to reduce the purchase of supplies. All other expenses are fixed. Ironically, supply expenditures must be totally stopped to achieve a very small savings. Without supplies, the employees do not have anything to work with and organizational effectiveness is drastically diminished. If the administration wants to do more, its only flexibility is to greatly increase property taxes. Because property taxes represent only 21 percent of revenue, a 10 percent increase in the budget requires a 50 percent increase in property taxes. Thus public schools, like most planned and scheduled activities, have virtually no flexibility and must focus attention on steady-state production of standardized activities rather than on respond-ing to the needs of individual customers (e.g., students). Because of organizational inflexibilities, stability of the system become more im-portant than the needs of the customers (e.g., students, parents, and community). Administrative sanity depends upon maintaining stability.

This concept can be illustrated graphically by reviewing Table 10.2. An immediate need to reduce the budget by five percent will actually lower operating level costs (service delivery costs) by around 50 percent. This is because the only variable costs are the service delivery costs, which represent less than ten percent of the total service delivery cost.

Summary

In summary, all organizations have three levels of decision making: long run, short run, and immediate run. Inventory allows managers of produc-tive organizations to virtually ignore immediate-run variations, but that is not the case for responsive service organizations. For the responsive organization, revenues are determined by immediate-run decisions when the organization interacts with the customer. Almost all costs, on the other hand, are determined in the short run or the long run.

The objective is to minimize wasted capacity. This can be done by making scheduling more flexible. Several methods are available to allow more flexible scheduling in the short run and higher utilization in the immediate run. Economies of scope allow greater utilization of capacity. Economies of modularity allow the organization to minimize the amount of wasted capacity that must be scheduled. Networking is a method for allowing firms the flexibility to focus on changing customer needs rather than to be burdened with finding a revenue-generating use for the inflexible resources.

While these concepts address capacity utilization, they do not address pricing decisions, which determine the financial yield of scheduled capacity. Chapter 11 describes the process of pricing benefits and scheduling capacity to maximize yield.

References

[1] John Dearden, "Cost Accounting Comes to Service Industries," *Harvard Business Review*, September–October 1978.

[2] Alfred Marshall, *Principles of Economics,* London: MacMillan and Co., 1898, p. 442.

[3] Paul A. Samuelson, *Economics,* New York: McGraw-Hill, 8th edition, 1970, p. 365.

[4] Webster's *New Universal Unabridged Dictionary,* Deluxe Second Edition, New York: Simon & Schuster, 1983.

[5] Marshall, op. cit., p. 450.

[6] Karl Albrecht and Ron Zemke, *Service America!* New York: Warner Books, 1985, p. 27.

[7] Jan Carlzon, *Moments of Truth,* New York: Harper & Row, 1987.

[8] Ibid., p. 21.

CHAPTER 11

CUSTOMER-RESPONSIVE PRICING

There are two primary pricing models presented in traditional production economics. This section will present a third pricing model that is applicable when customers are looking for solutions and providers are selling capacity. It will compare and contrast the three pricing models and show the assumptions for each. The three models are the product-based model, the public-good model, and the customer-responsive model.

Product-Based Pricing

Traditional product pricing is based on several basic assumptions, including:

- There is a standardized, homogenous product. Thus average price and average cost are meaningful and can be calculated for the product.
- The product is transferable among customers. Because customers have the ability to buy, sell, and trade the product, there is a market price for the commodity.
- Short-run production costs are assumed to be a large part of total costs – approximately 80 to 90 percent. Thus variable costs are high.
- The product can be inventoried. If it is not sold one day, it can be sold the next, so analysis can be in terms of quantity rather than capacity or time. Consequently, immediate-run variations can be ignored.

When these assumptions hold, the familiar product pricing model presented in Figure 11.1 is appropriate. But why are these assumptions important? How do they effect the supply-and-demand pricing model?

These assumptions are important for several reasons, including:

Customer-Responsive Pricing

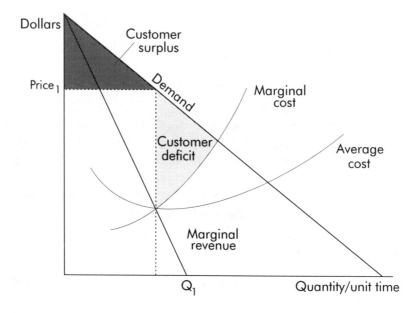

Figure 11.1. The high variable cost product-pricing model.

- If there were no standardized products, averages would have no meaning.
- If variable costs were not so considerable, marginal costs would not play a significant role in determining what quantity to produce.
- If the product were not transferable, the emphasis would be on solution-value pricing, and the marginal revenue curve would not be a continuous function and would never be zero.
- If the product could not be inventoried, cost would be a factor of capacity and time, not quantity.
- If the benefits (i.e., the product) could not be transferred, the emphasis would be on customer-value pricing, not market pricing. When the product can be transferred, all customers pay approximately the same market price for the product. This means that those who are willing to pay more do not have to do so.

Economists use the term "consumer surplus" to refer to the difference between solution value (i.e., what each customer is willing to pay) and the market price.[1] Those who are unable to pay the market price have their needs unsatisfied. This occurs even though they are willing to pay more than the marginal cost of producing the product. This book uses the term "customer deficit" to describe the difference between customer value and the marginal cost of providing the good when these values are below the market price. The reason these individuals' needs are not satisfied is that if you lower the price for one customer, you end up lowering the market price for all customers. This means that where there is a consumer surplus, there is also a customer deficit. The larger the customer surplus, the more the marginal revenue curve is to the left of the demand curve, and the larger the customer deficit. The concept of "one price for all" is the basis for maximizing the consumer surplus, the customer deficit, and the location of the marginal revenue curve to the left. Where there is totally individual pricing, there is no consumer surplus and no customer deficit, and individual solution value is the marginal revenue.

Where the traditional product assumptions hold, the familiar supply and demand curves are appropriate. When these conditions exist, firms operate where marginal revenue equals marginal costs. This means that if they produce less, revenue will be reduced more than costs. If the firm produces more, costs will increase faster than revenue.

The high variable cost product-pricing model leads to three consequences.

First, firms operate where marginal revenue equals marginal price. As long as the firm can generate positive contributions (i.e., marginal

---

1. The term "customer" is used here instead of "consumer." The word "consumer" may be appropriate when used for products. Ironically, the principle in physics that "matter can neither be created nor destroyed, only converted in form" was developed soon after the word "consumer" began to be used by economists. The consumption of staples such as bread, meat, and fuel is intuitive. The purchasing of automobiles, movies, and education is less so. It is not intuitive when used for funerals, hazardous materials cleanup, lighthouses, or highways. For these reasons, the terms "customer surplus" and "customer deficit" will be used. We have generally avoided using the word "consumer" throughout this book because only products need be consumed to obtain benefits. Services are delivered directly to the beneficiary without ever having existed in the form of a product that must be consumed.

revenue greater than marginal costs) to fixed costs, it is beneficial to increase production. Therefore, firms operate where they can maximize contributions to fixed costs and profits.

Second, where products are standardized, there is a standardized market price. In fact, the definition of fair pricing is that everyone is expected to pay the same market price for identical products. Expressed another way, those that receive a higher solution value from use of the product and are willing and able to pay more do not have to. In fact, that is the very definition of the consumer – or customer – surplus.

$$\text{Customer surplus} = \sum_{i=1}^{N} (\text{solution value } i - \text{market price}) i$$

where solution value is above market price.

But what happens if customer value is below the market price? This situation illustrates a third point. The firm is unable to sell to individuals where customer value is greater than marginal cost but is below market price. As shown in Figure 11.1, when there is a customer surplus, there is also a customer deficit. The reason that these individuals cannot have their needs met is because of the customer surplus. If the price is dropped below the market price, the market price must be dropped for everyone. That is the definition of a market price.

$$\text{Customer deficit} = \sum_{i=1}^{N} (\text{market price } i - \text{solution value}) i$$

where customer value is above marginal costs but below market price.

Public-Good Pricing

Public-good pricing is a special condition usually mentioned only as an aside in microeconomics texts. The following quotation illustrates an economist's view of public goods.

> A *commodity* is called a "public good" if its *consumption* by any one person does not reduce the amount available for others. Or putting it another way, a good is "public" if providing the *good* for anyone makes it possible, without additional cost, to provide it for everyone. . . . The traditional example is the lighthouse. [Emphasis added][1]

Comments such as these show how ingrained the concepts of "product," "good," "commodity," and "consumption" are in economic thought. It is difficult to understand whether the "commodity" is the lighthouse, the light, or the warning to the ships regardless of how provided.[2] It is also hard to understand if it is the lighthouse, the light, or the warning that is being consumed or even how it is being consumed. Even though the terminology may not be clear, one basic concept is. That is, for public goods, there is no additional cost to making the benefit available to more people. This means that the marginal cost is zero.

The public good pricing model can be presented in two ways. First is the case of a public good that can be inventoried and traded, as shown in Figure 11.2. If the public good can be traded, there is a market for that good. Where there is a market, market pricing takes precedence over solution-value pricing. Because the marginal cost for a public good is zero, the market price will be OP. Again, as shown in Figure 11.2, there will be a customer surplus for individuals where customer value is greater than market price. There is also a customer deficit for individuals when the customer value is greater than the marginal cost (zero) but lower than the market price.

The second example of the public-good pricing model is more typical. It is the case of a public good that cannot be inventoried or traded. The word "service" is often used to describe nontradable items; this term draws on the definition that a service is an intangible good. If it cannot be inventoried or traded, customer value pricing is more appropriate as long as it is politically acceptable (i.e., understood by customers).

Take the example of a highway bridge financed with a bond issue that is to be retired by collecting tolls. In this example, the bond issue represents the fixed costs of building the bridge. Once the bridge is built, there are virtually no additional costs for additional users, at least until the bridge's capacity is reached. If the bridge district elects to price each user the same amount, then Figure 11.3 would apply. This would mean that commercial trucks, buses, and high-solution-value individuals would use the bridge, but others (i.e., lower-solution-value users) would not use it, even though there would be extensive excess capacity and no

---

2. This work would suggest that the benefit is the warning. The lighthouse is the capacity scheduled to provide the light (i.e., the capacity to serve).

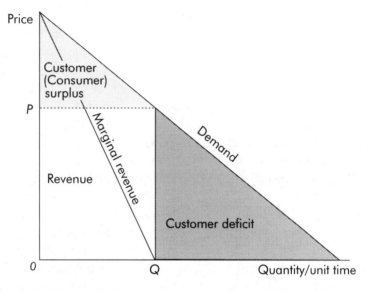

Figure 11.2. The public-good pricing model for tradable goods.

additional costs for them to do so. Revenue ($P * Q$) would be available to pay off the bond issue.

Because the bridge crossing cannot be inventoried or traded, the bridge district could explore the use of customer-value pricing (Figure 11.4). A survey of potential users suggested that trucks benefited P_t from crossing the bridge, commercial vehicles benefited P_c, and so on with pedestrians benefiting P_p.[3] The bridge district proposed a customer value pricing scheme in which each group pays according to the benefits it receives. Many argued that it would not be fair to charge different prices. Then someone else argued that there might be a difference in the cost of long-term maintenance based on vehicle weight.[4] Once that argument

---

3. Even within each group each individual receives a different level of benefits and is thus willing to pay a different amount, but for simplicity a very familiar and accepted example is used.
4. It may be understandable that a large truck might cause more damage than a pedestrian, as the truck is nearer the design limit for the bridge. It is more difficult to see how a pedestrian, a bicycle, and a compact car could create different levels of damage. In effect, the large truck versus pedestrian

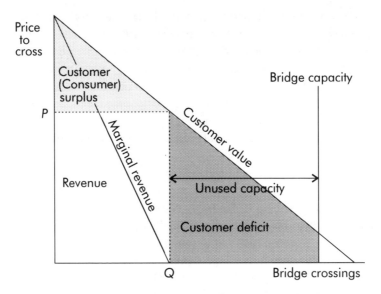

Figure 11.3. A public-good pricing model for a highway bridge.

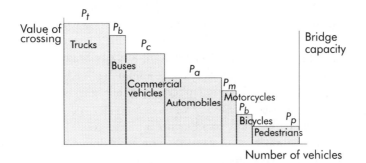

Figure 11.4. Customer-value pricing for a highway bridge.

was accepted, a new benefit or customer value toll structure was implemented with each class of vehicles paying a different rate, as shown in Figure 11.4.

---

argument is used to establish the justification for value of service pricing. Once the principle is accepted, it is only logical to implement for each weight-class difference.

Now the bridge is used to capacity. Everyone pays according to the value he or she places on the crossing. The bridge provides much greater benefit to the community and to many more people. Costs do not increase because the incremental costs of each additional use is zero for a public good, but the revenue available to retire the debt is dramatically increased by each additional user. By removing much of the consumer surplus and the customer deficit through customer-value pricing, the bridge is now affordable and available to all users and no one pays more than he or she is willing.

In Figure 11.4, the demand schedule under customer value pricing is represented by P_t multiplied by the number of trucks that want to cross plus P_b multiplied by the number of buses plus P_c multiplied by the number of commercial vehicles plus P_p multiplied by the number of pedestrians. Because each individual pays the customer value, the marginal revenue schedule is the same as the demand schedule. Each additional customer pays what the solution value is to him or her. Figure 11.4 groups customer by vehicle weight because it is more familiar to readers. The grouping could also be done by time sensitivity – for example, the need of having overnight packages costs more than next afternoon or second-day service. In Figure 11.4, the marginal cost is zero, which is the definition of a public good.

The term "public good" does not refer to the provider of the service. Radio and television broadcasts, for example, have a marginal cost of zero because the cost is incurred to broadcast the signal not by how many people tune in. Costs do not vary whether 5 people or 5,000 people tune in. Education, on the other hand, is not a public good. Educating 5,000 people will cost much more than educating 5. Although broadcasting is a public good and education is not, public policy in the United States has decided that the government should not control broadcasting but should provide education. Thus a public good can be provided by the public or private sector.

This raises an important question. Does customer-value pricing result in subsidies? Do the high-solution-value individuals paying high rates subsidize the low-solution-value users? Under the assumptions of the product-based model, (market price, average unit cost, and ability to inventory), this would seem to be the case. But for a public good, conditions are different. By definition, costs do not change whether no one uses the service or it is used to capacity. Consequently, only revenue varies with use. The question becomes about who you prevent from making a contribution to the operation of the bridge. Tolls from trucks alone may not be sufficient to sustain bridge operations. Even the tolls (contributions) made by both truck and bus users may be insufficient to sustain operation. In many cases, operations can only be maintained if all are invited to use the service and all contribute the value of the solution to them. If any group does not contribute its part, or if market pricing is used, the revenue is reduced and bridge operation may not be feasible. Only if each group cooperates and pays according to customer value can the service be available to anyone.

Public-good pricing is based on yield pricing or pricing to maximize revenue from the capacity available. Yield pricing has two objectives: to use customer value pricing so that each customer will pay the value of the service (solution) and to use all possible capacity to generate revenue.

Although the rule that marginal revenue equals marginal cost does not apply to public goods, there is a common principle that does applies to both the product-pricing model and the public-good pricing model. That is, both groups price so that they maximize contribution (i.e., marginal revenue minus marginal costs) to fixed costs and profit. In the public good model where marginal costs are zero, contribution is maximized when revenue is maximized. In the product model, in which marginal revenue decreases as marginal cost increases, contribution is maximized when marginal revenue equals marginal cost.

Responsive Activity Pricing

The pricing of responsive activities is a hybrid of both product and public good pricing. Its differences and similarities occur because of the following assumptions:

- There is no standardized product for which there is a market price. Because the delivery is customized to each individual customer's need, each delivery must be priced separately. The value of the delivery is defined by how well the delivery solves the customer's need.
- Deliveries are not tradable. Consequently, there is no market price for the delivery. Customers may, however, perceive deliveries to

be the same if standard units of capacity, such as airline seats, are used for the delivery.

- Commitments to customers are made in the immediate run. Variable costs in the immediate run are very small (less than 10 percent). Consequently, the immediate-run cost structure is similar to the one presented in Figure 10.2. This cost structure is very similar to the one used for a public good. The difference is that the variable costs for a public good are theoretically zero, whereas the immediate-run variable costs of a responsive service are usually less than 10 percent.

- There are no products to inventory, only capacity that continually perishes if it is not used to deliver benefits. Thus emphasis must be on pricing in the immediate run to maximize the yield that can be obtained from the capacity scheduled in the short run. Yield maximization requires minimizing wasted capacity and maximizing the customer value of capacity delivered.

Because of these conditions, customer-responsive pricing has its own models. First, customer-responsive pricing is similar to public good pricing because it has a customer-value schedule and very limited variable costs, at least in the immediate run, when there is interaction with customers.

Second, it is like both product pricing and public-good pricing in that it is still based on the same principles: maximizing contribution to fixed costs and profits. Figure 11.5 presents the basic responsive-service pricing model.

The responsive-service pricing model recognizes that the customer is buying a benefit and that the provider is selling capacity. The customers know the value of the benefit to them and but want to maximize the customer surplus (i.e., get the benefits at the lowest possible price).

The provider knows the out-of-pocket cost (i.e., the service delivery costs) of proving benefits but wants to maximize yield. Yield is maximized by capturing as much of the customer surplus as possible and using all capacity to generate revenue. Figure 11.5 illustrates this point. Customer 1 is willing to pay P_1 but, to maximize his or her customer surplus, tries to negotiate down to the service-delivery cost of the delivery.

The provider, on the other hand, wants to generate revenue from the scheduled capacity but in most cases may only be able to charge what

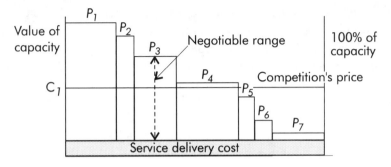

Figure 11.5. A responsive-service pricing model.

the competition is charging at C_1. To be able to charge more than C_1, there must be a very strong relationship to induce the customer to have much higher expectations of the firm. The key point is that the provider will a) make individual service deliveries as long as the service-delivery costs can be covered, b) must collectively cover capacity costs and profits through contributions from customers, and, c) desire to capture as much of the customer surplus as possible. Therefore, in terms of pricing, the customer value is the upper limit and the service delivery cost is the lower limit. In between these two values is the negotiable range. The final price for each customer will be somewhere within the negotiable range.

If the firm has built a relationship with the customer so that the customer calls the firm first, competitors may not have an impact on pricing if the customer-responsive firm is able to fit the customer's needs well, if the price seems reasonable, and if the hassle level is acceptable. If the interactive diagnosis of need is not satisfactory or leaves the customer with doubts, the customer may begin to shop around.

There are actually two upper limits to pricing. The first upper limit is customer value – what the customer is willing to pay for solving his or her individual need. The second upper limit, solution value, is determine by delivery effectiveness (e.g., how well the solution solved the customer's need) and hassle (the noneconomic cost of obtaining the solution). The price paid will be determined by the negotiating strengths of the customer and the provider. Negotiating is a hassle many individuals will not tolerate.

At this point in the discussion, some readers may counter with the argument that the service must cover their average cost or it will go out of business. Average cost is a concept that is only meaningful for standardized activities. Average revenue is a market price, not a customer-value concept. There is no such thing as the average cost of an activity unless utilization ratios are constant. What is the average cost per hotel room when occupancy will vary from 20 to 100 percent? The average cost is simply the total cost divided by capacity utilization. The average cost is simply a substitute measure for capacity utilization. High average cost simply means low capacity utilization. Low average cost simply means that capacity utilization was high.

The real question must be asked differently: "Pricing at out-of-pocket costing is scary because the firm will not generate sufficient revenue to cover total costs. How do you avoid that trap?"

The answer is very simple. Measure what you want to accomplish. The objective is to generate enough revenue to cover all out-of-pocket expenses and all fixed capacity costs and to contribute to profit. Therefore, the objective is to maximize contribution to fixed capacity and to profit from each sale. This can be done for any time period (e.g., hourly, daily, monthly). But this is irrelevant to the front-line workers who interact with customers, price services, and commit capacity. Front-line workers need to know how to interact with customers. They need to know how to commit the organization. They need to know when to commit capacity and how to price it. They need to know how to negotiate service deliveries with each customer.

Negotiating strength is determined by several variables:

- If capacity utilization is expected to exceed scheduled capacity, the provider will restrict service to those that provide the highest yield.
- If the provider has extensive wasted capacity, services will be provided to any customer who makes a contribution to capacity costs and profits. But even when low-value solutions are provided, customer-value pricing still will be used to minimize the customer surplus for all deliveries.
- If the customer's need is not time critical, he or she can postpone delivery until the provider has scheduled excess capacity and a lower price can be negotiated.

- If there are competitors who provide comparable solution value, there is a second upper limit on pricing. Providers continually try to increase delivery effectiveness and reduce hassle so that the competitor's solution is never solicited nor comparable. This is especially true for high-risk problems. In a high-risk trial not all attorneys are seen as providing comparable delivery effectiveness. In the case of a life-threatening illness, the patient wants the best; the second best is not in the running.

Thus there are four critical pieces of information needed to implement customer-value pricing.

The Value of the Benefits to Customers

Customers do not have easily readable labels that indicate what they are willing to pay for each delivery. Therefore, it is important that the organization know the customers well enough to understand their special needs, their expectations, and what they are accustomed to paying. Physicians continually test the reasonable and customary rates allowed by insurance companies by periodically increasing charges to determine if they will be accepted. As soon as the new rate is accepted, then fees increase. (The patient is frequently oblivious to fee changes because the payments are made by insurance.) Airlines know that business travelers typically have less advance notice for scheduling and are unwilling to stay over the weekend just so they can save their employers money. Therefore airlines separate business and vacation travelers by advance notice and weekend stay. Hotels know that government travelers will not spend money out of their own pockets just to stay at a different hotel; therefore, virtually all hotels honor General Services Administration (GSA) and state government rates. Customer-responsive firms develop databases to collect information that will be helpful in analyzing the value of the benefits to the customer.[5] In fact, one of the advantages of repeat business is the mutual understanding about rates as well as procedures.

---

5. For an excellent discussion of customer databases, see Terry G. Verra, *After Marketing: How to Keep Customers for Life Through Relationship Marketing*, Homewood, IL: Business One Irwin, 1992.

The Out-of-Pocket Cost of Providing Benefits

The out-of-pocket cost of providing a delivery forms the lower bound for pricing decisions. However, the accounting systems used by most firms do not provide these costs, for the following reasons:

- Traditional accounting systems are too aggregated. Once data are aggregated into the standardized chart of accounts, they cannot be disaggregated for decision making about individual deliveries.
- Accounting reports are designed to provide averages. Capacity costs are aggregated and are allocated by measures such as machine or labor hours. The results are then divided by output to provide average costs. But average costs have no meaning for customized solutions.
- Traditional accounting systems were not developed to assist in determining the cost of providing individual deliveries but for external users and for internal purposes to allocate resources between various divisions and groups within the organization.[6]
- Accounting systems were designed when data were scarce, expensive, difficult to process, and primarily paper oriented, so many compromises were made to facilitate collection and storage of paper data.

Responsive organizations develop processes for pricing jobs. These processes usually identify the specific materials required for a job and the capacity required to complete delivery. Automobile body repair shops, for example, have books that list each type of repair for each vehicle and list the parts, the prices, and the standard hours required to perform the repair. From this data, the estimator knows the out-of-pocket costs and can mark up materials and charge the labor rate necessary to provide the desired yield. Hospitals, on the other hand, charge all identifiable costs directly to the patient's account, and capacity costs are billed according to procedural allowances. However it is done, responsive service organizations must develop methods of identifying out-of-

---

6. For an in-depth discussion of these concepts see Denna, Cherington, Andros, and Hollander, *Event Driven Business Solutions*, Homewood, IL: Business One Irwin, 1993, and Johnson and Kaplan, *Relevance Lost: The Rise and Fall of Management Accounting*, Boston: Harvard Business School, 1987.

pocket costs so they know how to price the delivered benefit. The implementation of event-driven business systems will greatly facilitate costing of individual deliveries.

Competitor Charges. A constraint on customer-value pricing is competition. If a competitor is willing to provide similar services for lower prices, then the limit on customer-value pricing is the degree to which the customer's trust in the provider's greater effectiveness in solving the need and/or minimizing the hassle of delivery justifies the higher price. This is another reason trust and length of relationship reduce price sensitivity.[3]

Alternative Uses of Capacity. Because customers do not cooperate by queuing up according to customer value or yields, providers must forecast the expected demand. Once the expected demand has been forecasted, the firm will accept customers who will provide higher yields and reject lower yield customers if there is inadequate capacity. This forecast will vary day by day and often hour by hour. (Airlines forecast expected demand for each passenger category for each flight segment each night.)

It is said, for example, that hotels will allow a customer to select either the rate or the date, but not both. If the guest selects a low rate, Christmas is always available. On Christmas, expected occupancy is so low that the only thing the hotel will turn down is the sheets. If the date is the day when the big football game is in town, the hotels will turn down everything except the highest rate. (There are some exceptions to this rule, such as the regular customer who stays in the hotel every week. The hotel does not want to spoil a long-term relationship. The value of the long-term relationship is worth more than a single night's rate differential.)

With these four pieces of information (customer value, out-of-pocket cost of delivery, competitors charges, and alternative use of capacity), the front-line customer contact person (CCP) (i.e., the reservationist or the desk clerk) can make a pricing decision. In fact, it is these four pieces of information that allow pricing decisions to be made under any condition. The authors typically use the following example in their classrooms to illustrate this concept.

Imagine a church that was only interested in maximizing profits and that had no spiritual, service, or moral concerns. (A church is used for the example because it seems to eliminate the resistance to the word "contribution." There is no intention to alienate anyone by using this

Customer-Responsive Pricing

example, but classroom experience indicates that readers cannot identify with making contributions to a firm.) Suppose the church has a chapel with a capacity of 1,000 people per service that costs $1,000 per service to operate. The question is, how would you decide who would be able to attend? There are four different scenarios under which decisions would have to be made.

Less-than-capacity attendance. In this case, anyone who was willing to make a contribution would be allowed to attend because the incremental costs would be virtually zero. Some might argue that because the fully allocated cost to service 500 people is $2.00 each, anyone who did not pay $2.00 should be excluded. This might eliminate 100 attendees who would have made a combined contribution of $100 to cover costs. There would then be only 400 people to cover the cost, so the fully allocated cost would go up to $2.50 each. If this happened, another 50 to 75 people would be excluded and the fully allocated cost would go up again. And because the church was now specifying how much should be paid, those that contribute $20 or $50 would also feel taken advantage of and reduce their contribution to the $2.50 market price. It would not be long before the church would no longer exist. It is best, therefore, to encourage everyone to contribute as much as possible but to allow all to attend as long as they make some kind of contribution.

This logic has interesting implications for hospitals that are operating below capacity. Although publicly financed patients pay less than the fully insured patients, it is hard to argue that the Medicaid patients are being subsidized by the fully insured patients. If a hospital admission is worth $3,500 and the out-of-pocket cost is approximately $350 (10 percent), the admission contributes $3,150 to the bottom line. That is the difference between a full bed and an empty bed, especially because all directly identifiable costs are billed directly to the patient. Even if the hospital only receives $2,000 for the stay, it will be $1,650 better off than if it did not have the patient. Of course, every effort will be made to negotiate for more if the hospital thinks there is a possibility of getting it.

Operating at capacity. When the church operates near capacity, it attempts to place the lower contributors on standby so that capacity is reserved for the higher contributors. If there are not enough higher contributors, the standbys are allowed to enter. If the minimum is set too high, there will be empty seats. If the minimum is set too low, the greater contributors may not be able to be seated. In Shakespearean days, those making minimum contributions were relegated to the worst seats – the pits.

Operating where demand occasionally exceeds capacity. In this case, the church would forecast expected demand and develop cut-off points. Anyone unwilling or unable to contribute at that level would be denied admission.

Operating where demand continually exceeds capacity. In this case, there are two different pricing decisions. The first is the immediate-run decision: who to allow in. This decision is reached as described previously. The second decision is whether or not to expand capacity by adding another service. This decision is made by comparing the contributions that are now lost but could be received by expanding the facilities so that the additional attendees could be accommodated.

Implicit in the yield-pricing model is that customer-value pricing is rigidly adhered to. Yield pricing is not total cost pricing (i.e., fully allocated cost pricing), nor is it contribution to margin pricing. It is not total cost pricing because the total cost has no meaning. Without a product, there is no link between the capacity used and the benefits delivered.

Yield pricing is not contribution to margin pricing. Both full-cost pricing and contribution to margin pricing only look at half of the picture. Yield pricing must consider both simultaneously. True yield pricing maximizes contribution by using customer-value pricing to maximize yield from each customer. Consider the case of a hotel. One month the corporate manager complains that room rates are too low because they are not covering fully allocated costs and admonishes the local manager to get room rates up. The manager complies, but the next month the corporate manager acknowledges that room rates are good but that more rooms must be rented if they are to make a profit. The local manager talks to the sales team, and occupancy rates go up, but the corporate manager complains that the hotel can't stay in business "giving rooms away." In reality, neither approach is sufficient where capacity perishes over time.[7]

---

7. For an excellent video on this concept, see "Yield Management" by the American Hotel and Motel Association's Educational Institute, E. I. Video Productions, 1990.

Yield pricing combines these two approaches. First, it develops a theoretical or "ideal" yield. In the case of hotels, utopia would be to have all rooms rented at the "rack" (highest) rate. Ideal revenue would be rack rate times the total number of rooms available. That is the theoretical maximum revenue the hotel could generate. Actual revenue will be the sum of the revenue generated from each room. If out-of-pocket cost is zero as in the public good case, then the organization would attempt to maximize revenue. Because out-of-pocket costs are not zero in most cases, it must be considered. Therefore yield (contribution to capacity costs and profit) is calculated as:

$$\text{Yield} = \sum_{i=1}^{n} (\text{Revenue } i - \text{service delivery cost } i)$$

where n equals the total number of rooms rented.

The objective is to maximize this value. Where there is a standardized product with standard market pricing (i.e., where there is a customer surplus and customer deficit), this occurs where marginal revenue equals marginal costs. If these assumptions do not hold true, the yield approach must be used. Fully allocated costing and incremental capacity costing are both insufficient.

Pricing Implementation

Pricing implementation typically revolves around the following equation:

Price = customer value × fit − hassle
where customer value = f (intensity of need, ability to pay).

Pricing techniques are built on this model.

Fit

Where fit (i.e., delivery effectiveness) is an important benefit, the emphasis is on customizing individual deliveries. This usually requires that the customer and provider interact, that the need is diagnosed, and that an individualized estimate is given. Because each job (i.e., delivery) is unique, comparison is difficult and thus customer value pricing is typical. Classic examples of this include home repairs, automobile body repairs, construction projects, and consulting efforts.

Intensity of Response

Where delivery response is important, organizations develop pricing methods based on the response. These include:

- *Time-of-day pricing.* When demand is much greater during certain time periods, higher prices are charged. This can be done to increase yield or to shift demand to off-peak periods. Examples of this approach include transit companies charging commuters higher fares, restaurants charging more for dinner meals than for luncheons, telephone companies reducing rates for evening and weekend usage, and fitness centers offering lower rates for daytime use only.
- *Lead-time pricing.* When quick response has high value, pricing can be based on response rate. Freight sent on the next flight out and passengers who want the ability to change flight plans at will can expect to pay more. Field-service repair rates are typically based on response time. For instant response, personnel and supplies can be kept on site. The primary response may be within two hours. The regular response may be next-day repair. Each will have its own pricing structure.
- *Response-level pricing.* When the customer has widely fluctuating needs, he or she can expect to pay higher rates. For example, if a shipper's needs vary from zero to 50 trucks a day, this shipper can expect to pay more than organizations that require ten trucks every day. The greater the variation in response level, the more standby or safety capacity required to cover the delivery.
- *Guaranteed-response pricing.* When organizations expect the provider to guarantee a response, they can expect to pay more. When government, for example, negotiates for GSA hotel and airline rates, the rates are on a space-available basis. If the hotel or airline is fully booked, there is no obligation to provide the service. If the customer expects to be guaranteed service, especially on short notice, then rates will be expected to be higher and justified by the excess capacity that must be maintained to guarantee the response.

Hassle

No organization attempts to sell hassle; rather, it uses hassle to build fences to protect the rate structure (i.e., increase yield). The hassle is used to separate those that can and will pay more from those that cannot afford to pay the higher rate but require basically the same delivery. Airlines are perhaps the classic example. They know that business travelers do not want to stay over a Saturday to save their employers' money. The employees are protective of his or her personal time. Therefore, the requirement that the passenger stay over a Saturday night forms a fence to separate those who are willing to let their employers pay more from the personal travelers who are very cost conscious. Likewise, the hassle of having to book in advance or not be able to change flights are techniques used to build fences around the higher priced customers.

Pricing can be done in many different ways. Pricing can be posted, experienced based, negotiated, or packaged.

Posted Pricing

So many customers have been conditioned to paying posted prices in retail stores that the posting of a price seems to reduce negotiation. Although automobile dealers have sticker prices, few customers pay sticker price. Even with the trend to one-price selling pioneered by Saturn, there is still great variation in trade-in and financing charges. In a similar vein, hotels, hospitals, fitness centers, and other responsive providers conspicuously present price lists to give credibility to their pricing structure, but frequently few pay the posted price.

Experience Pricing

In many cases, it is almost impossible to predict the amount of capacity required to respond to some needs. Automobile insurance is a prime example. Some drivers are more prone to have an accident than are others. Thus base rates are set statistically so that the anticipated payouts will be approximately 64 percent of the total premium dollar. (The remaining 36 percent goes to pay sales commissions, administration costs, and so forth.) If a driver begins to have claims, especially multiple claims, a surcharge will be levied.

The maintenance of industrial or construction equipment is also heavily dependent upon each situation. The anticipated repairs for tracked vehicles operating on clay is much different from those operating on rock. The individual operator will also make a difference. The provider may begin with a base rate and have quarterly adjustments based on experience. This approach can be very effective because it provides the customer with feedback for identifying the operating practices that could be changed to improve the experience rate.

Negotiated Pricing

Regardless of technique used to peg pricing (i.e., posted or experience), virtually all pricing between out-of-pocket cost and customer value is negotiable. The primary limitation is the empowerment of the employee doing the pricing. The negotiation can take many forms. The rate can be lowered, but response may be limited. Or hassle factors may be introduced: "We will fix your television at a lower price, but you will have to bring it to our shop and it will take three weeks." The rate may be held but "something extra" can be included. The manager of a hotel with excess capacity, for example, might suggest, "Pay the regular rate, but I will put you in a suite rather than a regular room."

Package Pricing

Tour groups, hotels, amusement parks, and so forth develop packages that include rooms, travel, means, and entertainment tickets or passes which they can sell as a total package. Various modifications can be made to the package, such as the type of room, type of seats, or arrival and departure times to reduce the price and make it acceptable to the customer.

Summary

The pricing strategies used by responsive organizations are much different from those used for standardized products. Responsive deliveries are not predefined; thus, neither delivery nor price is standardized. Because each delivery is – or can be – unique to varying degrees, price is determined on a case-by-case basis. Because capacity cannot be inventoried, its value cannot be preserved if it is not sold. The role of the manager is to maximize the yield obtained from the capacity scheduled. Because it is the CCP who interacts with the customer and defines what activities are to be performed and when, the CCPs must have the tools they need to price individual deliveries. Not only are they pricing individual deliveries, but each delivery influences the long-term relationship with that customer. If all customers are given the lowest price, the firm will not generate enough income to stay in business. If all customers are charged the highest rate, utilization rate will be so low that the firm will not remain viable.

References

[1] Jack Hirshleifer, *Price Theory and Applications*, Englewood Cliffs, NJ: Prentice-Hall, 1988.

[2] Eric L. Denna, J. Owen Cherrington, David P. Andros, and Anita Hollander, *Event Driven Business Solutions,* Homewood, IL: Business One Irwin, 1993, pp. 47–50.

[3] Reprinted by permission of *Harvard Business Review*. An excerpt from "Zero Defections: Quality Comes to Services," by Frederick F. Reichheld and W. Earl Sasser, Jr., Issue 5 (September / October 1990), pp. 105–111. Copyright © by the President and Fellows of Harvard College; all rights reserved.

CHAPTER 12

THE CUSTOMER-RESPONSIVE ORGANIZATION

Chapter 2 traced the history of business and economics through three eras. The third era was the free enterprise economy. One of the stages in the free enterprise economy was the growth of mass production. Mass production was enabled by Eli Whitney's concept of standardized parts; the Ford production line, which standardized production flow; and scientific management, which standardized each process along the production line. With standardized products and processes came the centralized planning of products, work, and processes. This centralized planning of standardized activities differs, however, from the planning and management of responsive activities.

Planning the Responsive Planning Process

Centralized planning and decision making typically leads to the development of standardized offerings, not customized deliveries for individual customers. To get customized solutions, individual delivery planning must occur at the front-line level after interaction with the individual customer. Flexible management's role is to develop the protocols, the network of resources, and the information infrastructure necessary to enable front-line workers to plan individual deliveries. Front-line planning is not reactive. It does not eliminate planning. It amplifies planning. More planning is done by more people, and more people have ownership in the planning process. What is different is that not all organizational activity is covered in a single plan developed by a central planning group.

Responsive organizations require a different organizational structure and a different approach to planning. Toyota's Ohno led the way. Since then, there have been many books and articles written on the steps needed to become responsive. Topics include staying close to your customer, lean manufacturing, virtual corporations, hollow corporations, team building, quality circles, downsizing, the avoidance of activities that do not deliver customer value, customer satisfaction, the reduction of complexity, reengineering, and efficient customer response, just to name a few.

Whatever terminology is used, the fundamental concept is that to be responsive, the organization must interact with each individual customer to diagnose individual customer needs before the work is planned. Solutions defined before any interaction with the customer takes place can be responsive to target groups' in stereotypes but not individual customers. The detailed planning of the work must be done at the front line. The front-line worker's role is to define the customer's need and how the work is to be done. Management's role is to enable and empower the worker to define, plan, and perform work tasks. Management accomplishes this by (a) providing a process for guiding the workers in defining and planning each individual delivery, (b) providing the resources needed to make the delivery, and (c) providing the infrastructure needed to coordinate work between workers.

Process

In his book *Mass Customization*, Joe Pine emphasizes the importance of separating process from product to achieve flexibility. Traditional mass-production managers considered process to be the way to produce a product. The flexibility for mass customization is obtained by viewing the process as a way of converting resources into products so that a single process can be used to produce many different products. The mass-production process focuses on limitations (e.g., setup time, resource availability, capability of the existing workforce) and develops the most efficient process that can function within the constraints. To gain greater flexibility, mass customizers develop processes to minimize or eliminate limitations (e.g., reduce setup time, locate alternative resources, expand capabilities of current workforce, develop a network of additional resources). Customer-responsive management develops numerous best-practice guidelines to guide front-line workers as they interact with customers to plan deliveries and expect them to modify the guidelines, if necessary, to improve customer fit.

Resources

Front-line workers can be no more responsive or capable than their resources allow them to be. Consequently, management must continually develop and expand the network of resources available to support the workers. Unfortunately, a resource is not a resource until it is readily available for integration into the delivery process. Therefore, the resource is not a resource until it is part of the best-practice guidelines and the infrastructure allows easy, two-way communication for coordinating (i.e., dispatching and tracking) work.

Infrastructure

Dramatic new developments in information systems have made responsive management possible. In a responsive organization, the front-line customer contact person (CCP) has a need to have access to relevant customer information (i.e., to the customer database) so that they better understand the customers better, have access to the best practice methods, and have the ability to capture and organize customer requests. They also need to know what resources, including the capability and capacity to respond, are available. They need the ability to communicate and commit resources and track delivery performance so they can take personal ownership of the delivery process. Responsive information systems are designed to facilitate work, not control or restrict workers.

If the CCP encounters a need for which there is no guideline, he or she is frequently encouraged to develop one on the spot, often by adapting an existing guideline for a similar need. The solution may not be optimal, but the customer was served, and the first delivery occurrence serves as a learning process for new guidelines that will need to be developed. The delivery may have been expensive, but it was probably less expensive than the traditional deterministic planning and approval process and it did provide the first data point for monitoring future delivery effectiveness and mentoring future employee activities. The organization thus becomes a dynamic learning organization by providing (a) the front-line worker with the ability to experiment and innovate when a process is not in place, (b) a mechanism for capturing the results of the innovation, and (c) the continual analysis and review of innovations, with the most successful becoming part of future best-practice guidelines.

In addition to making the organization responsive and to providing a mechanism for being a learning organization, there is one other advantage to this approach: it creates relevance and ownership. When employees are assigned work by an impersonal plan, often the only perceived relevance is their periodic evaluation (e.g., salary, title, or perks). If they vary from the plan or if quality is poor, many workers may believe it does not matter unless they get caught. In case they may get caught, they want to have all decisions documented and approved by someone above them or by a committee to spread the responsibility in case of criticism. It is also important to inspect (i.e., measure) everything to make sure it meets the quality standard or specs.

In a responsive organization in which each order is for a specific customer and the customer gives a personal response when it does not measure up, the activity itself becomes more relevant. Both the customer and employee become inspectors. The more the employee personally identifies with the customer, the more relevant the work. When employees make a personal commitment to the customer, they begin to take ownership of the commitment, especially if subsequent customer calls are routed to them. Ritz-Carlton has made this concept an integral part of their "ladies and gentlemen serving ladies and gentlemen" program. Any employee who receives a request from a customer becomes the owner of the request and is expected to follow up to make sure it is resolved.

This relevance also provides a focus to the work. When employees are simply performing a routine task for another internal group or producing to inventory, it is easy for the response to be less than enthusiastic. When cooperation is required to accomplish a specific customer request, it seems more relevant because someone (the customer) cares about the benefits they receive. It is not just another task to be done because it is on the schedule.

There is, however, one major disadvantage of enabling and empowering front-line workers to commit the organization. People are comfortable when the entrepreneur, possessing a proven ability to start and grow an organization, is firmly in charge and the workers follow his or her commands. It is easy to have faith in the proven judgment of the professional manager. People are also comfortable when there is a plan, carefully reviewed by an approved process, and when the organization is operating according to that plan. Results are predictable. We understand what to expect and we trust the ability of the organization to control implementation. On the other hand, people are often not comfortable with front-line employees committing the organization without someone being *in charge* and reviewing each decision.

A classic example of the concern that occurs when no one is in charge occurred at a meeting with a group of transportation officials from eastern bloc countries at the World Bank in the late 1970s. The subject was how to promote ride sharing and increase private transportation operations. The audience's main concern was over who would plan routes and schedules and set fares for each car pool or van pool. When the speakers explained that these decisions were inconsequential and would be worked out by the drivers and riders and tried to explain how the free-market system worked, the audience then asked who appointed these individuals to the free-market committee that set prices, routes, and schedules for each car pool. The eastern Europeans understood centralized domestic planning but not the innovative operation of the free-enterprise market system. Nor could they tolerate the uncertainty that occurred when no single individual had the power to define and control activities for each and all car pools. To let individual riders and drivers work out their own schedules sounded to these eastern bloc planners like total chaos. How would the central transportation managers know what was happening in each car pool? The presenters explained that instead of microplanning the detailed operations of each car and van pool, an infrastructure was set up that freed the pool operators from government regulation, used a computer system to match riders and drivers and provided referrals, helped the driver solve insurance difficulties, and even arranged to help drivers obtain loans to purchase vehicles. To these transportation officials, it sounded like utter confusion to let drivers and riders make their own decisions.

As explained to the eastern bloc transportation ministers, in a free-market economy the role of government is to plan the development of an infrastructure that enables each individual the freedom and flexibility to experiment with new ideas and innovative ways of relating to and benefiting others. People go to great lengths to identify the most successful innovations and to publicize them widely so that other individuals can emulate them and hopefully improve on them. For example, the Department of Agriculture hires county agents to demonstrate new concepts to farmers. The purpose of flexible planning, then, is not to plan all the details of the work but to plan the infrastructure that is necessary to enable and facilitate individual innovation.

It is often as disconcerting to let individual workers commit the organization as it was for the eastern bloc transportation ministers to let individuals operate car pools and van pools without some agency being in charge of setting rates, routes, and schedules. Ironically, what people are comfortable with (e.g., someone in charge, standardization, or centralized planning and review) appears to be the basis for the decline and fall of nations. The recent decline and fall of the centrally planned and controlled Soviet bloc is still familiar. Paul Kennedy suggests that Ming China, the Ottoman Empire, the Mogul Empire, Muscovy, and Tokugawa Japan "all suffered from the consequences of having a centralized authority which insisted upon a uniformity of belief and practice, not only in official state religion but also in such areas as commercial activities and weapons development."[1] When authority is centralized, there is no training ground for new leadership. When all activities are standardized, there is little tolerance for innovation.

Ironically, while U.S. business leaders confidently watched the self-destruction of the centrally planned and controlled eastern European nations, they stared in disbelief when the centrally planned and controlled businesses they managed saw their markets defecting to more responsive Japanese competitors. Their first reaction was to credit the Japanese successes with free-trade violations such as import trade restrictions, rigidly controlled Keiretsu, or other noncompetitive practices. The next step was to credit the Deming-inspired quality methodology that increased quality and lowered production costs. Both responses contained some truth, but each failed to take into account the importance of being flexible to the needs of individual customers and of giving front-line workers more responsibility and authority so that they can innovate.

It is easy to think that the opposite of someone being in charge is no one being in charge. It fact, it is just the opposite. As in the car pool example, each person is in charge. Each driver is in charge of picking up people according to a planned schedule. Each rider is in charge of being at the pickup point at the required time. It is the individual ownership of each step that makes the market system and free enterprise work. It is free enterprise, not control, that allows the individual decision making that encourages the development of leaders and innovation. (It could also be countered that when one group is responsible for central planning of activities for a business or family, it is easy for everyone else to abdicate responsibility so that little planning is done. *But isn't order more important than responsiveness?*

Stalk and Hout of the Boston Consulting Group discovered that responsiveness made firms (manufacturing as well as non-manufacturing) more viable:

Many closely held assumptions as to how costs and customers behave have been altered. Instead of costs going up as run-lengths are reduced, they decline . . . [and] instead of costs going up with increasing variety and response time, they go down. Further, instead of customer demand being only marginally affected by expanded choice and better responsiveness, it is astoundingly sensitive to this better service – with the company that is able to set customers' expectations for choice and response very quickly dominating the most profitable segments of demand.[2]

For firms to be more responsive, they must follow the autonomous nervous system principle of more decision making at lower levels in the organization that was first advanced by Toyota's Ohno. Stalk and Hout studied Wal-Mart, Atlas Industrial Doors, Ralph Wilson Plastics, Thomasville Furniture, and the Citicorp mortgage department and found that these firms responded to customers one-third faster, grew three times as fast, and were two to five times as profitable as their competitors.[3]

Businesses, like nations, thrive when they are responsive to customers and empower individuals (i.e., citizens or employees) to experiment and innovate. This is an incubation process for future leadership and allows learning to occur. To be successful, however, leadership needs to facilitate the responsive process. This infrastructure is created by cultivating networks of resources, developing flexible process (i.e., protocols), and creating information infrastructures that allow delivery coordination. This approach creates a very different view of the firm.

A Biological Analogy for Organizations

Early economists compared the economy with the human body being nourished by the bloodstream.[1] Just as there is a constant flow of fresh oxygenated blood from the heart and lungs to the body and a return flow of metabolized waste, so there is a constant flow of goods, services, wages and interest from firms to households and a return flow of money and capital from the households to the firm. This flow analogy has

---

1. For a discussion of Quesnay's ideas, see Robert Heilbroner, *The Worldly Philosophers,* New York: Simon and Schuster, 1967.

become the basis many use to think about business. Many would say that the role of business is to manage flows (e.g., cash flow, product flows, information flows, even work flows). Physical supply coordinates inbound material flows and distribution channels are designed to handle product flows from production to consumption. Even Porter's competition models were built on flows.[4] But are flows the only way of viewing the organization?

When he described the Toyota production system, Ohno also made an analogy to the human body. His analogy referred not to blood flow but to the autonomous nervous system. Ohno explained that if the hand touched a hot surface, response time was too long if all information had to be transported to the brain for a decision before action (i.e., removing the hand from the hot surface) could be taken. Thus front-line employees were expected to shut down the production line when they encountered a problem.[5] Ohno's metaphor was apt. The blood system analogy works well when describing relatively stable flows associated with tangible products that can be inventoried, but it is the nervous system that determines responsiveness.

The central nervous system analogy also provides a relevant insight into responsive organizations. Just as the eyes and ears sense events and alert the brain, so the front-line employee, who interacts with the customer, senses events for the organization. These events include activities such as customer requests or unmet delivery milestones. These events are captured as they occur by the information infrastructure (corresponding to the nervous system), which compares what is sensed with existing experience (e.g., the customer database) to define how the body should respond. This response is guided by prior organizational experience, which is captured in the best-practice guideline files.

Imagine a rabbit sensing a moving object with its eyes. Experience tells the rabbit that that image is a fox and that the best course of action after observing a fox is to hide or run. When the rabbit makes a decision, its central nervous system then directs (i.e., coordinates) various body parts (e.g., the heart, lungs, blood vessels, and legs) in responding. Likewise, the employee of the responsive organization senses a customer request, uses the information infrastructure (i.e., the central nervous system) to review the situational history (i.e., the customer database and the best-practice database), and decides how to respond. Each step in the response plan is sent to the prioritized dispatch list. This list is used by the information infrastructure to direct (i.e., coordinate or dispatch) the resource network to make the responsive delivery. As the rabbit flees, each part of the body performs its assigned task and reports back. The central nervous system thus provide a continuous, biological feedback loop.

So it is with the information infrastructure. As each member of the resource network completes his or her tasks, he or she reports back the results to the prioritized dispatch list. This provides a continuous monitoring system for tracking delivery. If the rabbit tries a new evasive maneuver and it works, this technique becomes part of its experiential database (its best-practice guidelines) stored in its brain. So as the organization tries new delivery methods, its effectiveness should be evaluated and its improvements captured in the protocol file. Thus the responsive firm is always learning.

When the central nervous system (the body's information infrastructure) does not function well, activities are erratic, uncoordinated, and unpredictable. When the central nervous system functions smoothly and is well coordinated, the body can forget about the need to sense, define, respond, and assign responsibility to each individual body part. It happens almost unconsciously. The well-functioning nervous system thus allows the body to turn its primary focus outward to interact with others, interact with the environment, and enjoy new experiences. When the central nervous system (the body's information infrastructure) is not functioning well, a person has a major challenge just getting the eyes to focus, the legs to walk, and to keep in balance. Much of the individual's time is spent trying to plan how to cope with normal biological functioning and mobility needs. The more time and effort required to plan and coordinate routine tasks just to exist, the less time and energy there is available to observe, interact, and learn from the environment and personal experiences. However, too many firms become so obsessed about the need for centralized planning and controlling of the most routine ordinary internal operating functions that they do not have the time or energy left to observe, interact, and learn from their customers and the environment. The focus is on coping with internal limitations (often self-inflicted) instead of on becoming more responsive to customers and the changing business climate. The emphasis is on control rather than performance.

When one watches Olympic sporting events, it can be safely assumed that central nervous systems of each of the participants are functioning well. In fact, there are Special Olympics for athletes who may have even more drive, courage, and determination than those in the regular Olympics but who may have less efficient central nervous systems that make them unable to compete on the same basis. Observers admire the performances of the first group and become awed by the courage and raw determination of the Special Olympics athletes.

When we observe a Federal Express driver pick up a package from a business person at a little league ball field with 45 minutes notice or watch two FedEx drivers hand off packages to each other as they pass through an intersection without stopping, we are impressed by performance. We do not know whether the packages were placed on the wrong truck or whether the actions observed were made to expedite a local delivery. Whatever the reason, the transaction probably occurred because the FedEx information infrastructure, developed by Harry Dalton's group, enabled the front-line workers to interact with each other and to easily respond to an individual customer's need. It probably did not occur because Fred Smith called a central planning meeting of top-level managers to develop a strategic plan on what to do with that particular package.

In all probability, no memos were written, no turf battles were waged, and no financial impact statements had to be developed. The CCP and the drivers, the eyes and ears of the organization, had an infrastructure that allowed them to focus on building relationships with customers and they did it. In all probability no one will know or comment on the well-coordinated package hand-off, but it was as impressive in its own area as any Olympic performance.

Chapter 13 will describe the process for building information infrastructures that allow firms to be responsive. As the information infrastructure becomes more effective, it allows the firm to shift attention from the centralized planning and control of routine internal operations to the real purpose of the organization – building relationships and meeting customer needs. The role of management becomes the design of the best-practice guidelines and the information infrastructure that enable relationship building with the customer by front-line workers. Relationship building occurs because the customer is viewed as being one of the most important assets of the firm. One measure of the importance of this relationship is its economic value. Carl Sewell, the Texas Cadillac dealer, suggests that the value of a customer is $332,000.[6]

The value of a Domino's Pizza customer in Montgomery, Maryland, has been estimated at more than $5,000 over the life of a ten-year franchise.[7]

A second measure of the value of a relationship is the positive value of the word-of-mouth promotion provided by a satisfied customer. This can be very effective in attracting new customers. The customer base is the net of customer attraction (i.e., new customers) less customer defections. Organizational revenue is determined by the customer base and the frequency of purchase. Firms that provide Olympic quality performance focus on removing barriers to their responsiveness to customers. When firms are so focused on centralized planning and cost control that customers come second, they induce self-inflicted inflexibilities. When that happens, customers learn not to expect high-level performance in meeting their needs. With time, the customers seek such performance elsewhere.

The central nervous system analogy does not replace the traditional flow analogy. It complements it. Perhaps the best way of explaining the need for a more sophisticated information infrastructure can be seen by understanding the coordination needs of the individual. When an employee works on the mass-production line doing the same task all day long, there is little need to keep a personalized calendar. If, however, the individual becomes a salesperson who regularly calls on customers, it is important for that individual to identify customers, schedule calls, and develop work plans to make sure that all customers are contacted.

Many aids have been developed to support the individual, such as week-at-a-glance appointment books. As the individual becomes even more responsive to customers (as might be required of on-call computer support personnel, for instance), their coordination needs become more complex. Some requests are by time (e.g., a schedule). Others are by a time window (i.e., by a specified time range), and others are by priority (e.g., a dynamic dispatch list). The individual is constantly in communication with customers and suppliers and needs access to phone numbers and the ability to record his or her expenses and the parts used. There is also a need to visually organize the day's work. These needs exceed the capabilities of the appointment book, and new tools, such as the Franklin Planner and computerized organizers have evolved.

This same analogy can be used for the firm. When the firm produced a single product and there was such scarcity that customers would buy what was available, there was no need for extensive coordination, planning, and scheduling. Inventory was used to buffer purchasing, production, and sales. As organizations became larger (i.e., became vertically integrated and multidivisional, producing multiple products), there was extensive need for elaborate planning and scheduling mechanisms to coordinate the flow of products, cash, and work. As the organization becomes more responsive, a different infrastructure is needed to dynamically coordinate the responses. These differences are summarized in Table 12.1.

A Generalized Responsive Model

Chapter 6 presented six responsive organizations ranging from fast-food restaurants to health care to Operation Desert Storm to banking and introduced a generalized model of the firm. This model was based on customers with different needs, resources with different capabilities, and the process of integrating these resources to coordinate the delivery of the desired benefits. Each of the six responsive organizations followed this model in varying degrees.

Implementation of this model requires two levels of activity: the individual delivery process and the enabling infrastructure process. The individual delivery steps are performed by front-line workers as they interact with individual customers. The infrastructure process must be championed by management to support the front line.

Individual Delivery Process

The individual delivery process is the most visible component of the organization to customers. At this level, there are basically four steps:

1. *Diagnosing the customer's individual delivery needs.* This can be done in many ways, from the "What kind of bread? . . . meat? . . . oil? . . . vinegar?" dialogue at Subway to the iterative approach used during Operation Desert Storm. In Desert Storm, a desired strategy was visualized and logistics determined if it had the ability to support the strategy. The most effective, supportable strategy was the one ultimately followed. This process continued throughout the campaign as battle plans and support options changed and new support needs were realized.

Table 12.1. Alternative Management Emphasis.

Emphasis	Focus	Physical Analogy	Purpose
Entrepreneurial	Manufacturing Purchasing Sales	Muscle	Product flow
Professional management	Accounting Finance Marketing Supply-chain logistics	Skeleton	Structure, coordination, and control
Customer response	Mass customization Lean production Service-response logistics Relationship management Responsive information systems	Central nervous system	Responsive delivery Relationship building Flexible intergration of resources Dynamic learning by the organization

2. *Developing an individual delivery plan.* Again, there are many ways of doing this. The pizza store may have a simple order pad and have the waitperson write down, typically in a form of shorthand, the customer's request. The hospital may have an elaborate set of procedures (i.e., critical pathways or protocols) to complete each diagnosis. FedEx may only have 14 steps between pickup and delivery. However it is done, each delivery is unique and thus requires a customized delivery plan.

3. *Dispatching the work dynamically.* The simplest methods may be used by the fast-food shop in which each request is placed on a wheel so the cooks can process them in a first-in, first-out (FIFO) fashion. The most effective methods involving a system for dynamically dispatching requests to various parts of the organization and assigning work when capacity is available. The Kanban system developed by Ohno at Toyota is an example of such a methodology. Ideally, the dispatch system will be based on a maximum preservation of capacity method consistent with customer requirements.

Maximum preservation of capacity is a means of increasing the efficiency of capacity use. Because the capacity to provide benefits cannot be inventoried, unused capacity perishes with each tick of the clock. For example, when a plane takes off with empty seats, they are forever wasted. If a passenger is scheduled for a 5:00 p.m. flight but is willing to use an empty seat on a 2:00 p.m. flight, this preserves capacity on the later flight so it is available should an unexpected passenger arrive. With maximum preservation of capacity, that it is always better to use existing capacity rather than waste it. This gives the provider more uncommitted capacity for future use. The limitation is, of course, customer need.

4. *Monitoring the work dynamically.* Each task has a time window. Frequently, there are milestones. When a milestone is not achieved on schedule, delivery will be delayed. By monitoring milestones, the firm has an early-warning system so that corrective actions can be taken. The corrective action may be notifying the customer (e.g., "Because of the rain, we have rescheduled the mowing of your yard"), expediting procedures, or rediagnosing the need, as may occur when a patient does not progress as expected on the critical pathway. No matter how it is done, the emphasis is always on maintaining the relationship with the customer (i.e., meeting the customer's needs and expectations).

Infrastructure Development Plan

At the organizational level, responsive organizations develop a supportive infrastructure that allows the front line to respond to requests as they are received. This infrastructure consists of three components. These are:

1. *Best-practice guideline development.* Guidelines are the processes used by responsive firms to create individual delivery plans. They consist of a list of the steps required to make the delivery. Guideline development occurs in several ways. First, a new guideline must be developed each time a new need is encountered. Thus the steps used by the front line to respond to the new need should be captured so that a new guideline will be in effect the next time that need is experienced. Second, the front line should be able to deviate from the best-practice guideline if conditions indicate the need to do so. These deviations should also be captured so that a guideline will exist when these conditions are experienced in the future. Third, such guidelines should be constantly reviewed to deter-

mine if they should be modified. This can be accomplished in two ways. One way is to encourage front-line workers to vary from the guideline and experiment with alternatives. Informational modeling techniques (discussed in Chapter 15) provide a good means for benchmarking innovations. Existing guidelines can then be modified to reflect best practice. This allows the organization to become a learning organization. A second and more traditional method is to periodically bring together the most effective front-line workers to review existing guidelines to determine if new developments or technology make protocol changes desirable. This is the approach used when hospitals bring physicians together to review current practice for responding to a particular diagnosis.

2. *Network development.* The ability of an organization to deliver is determined by the resources available and the process for integrating these resources to effect delivery. The guidelines are the processes for integrating these resources and coordinating deliveries utilizing them. Network development is the process for identifying resources and developing relationships so that the resources are available when needed. This usually requires that agreements be reached and communication established (frequently by tying computers together). When ROLS sets up a logistics system for a client, the normal order-processing system includes a package for selecting the best carrier and automatically dispatching the shipment to the carrier for pickup.

Mark White coordinates the construction of customized homes for a building contractor in Knoxville, Tennessee. In an ideal world, the customer would approach him with a well-thought-out set of building plans, prepared by an architect, that specifies all the details required for construction. In the real world, new home buyers have an abbreviated view of their dream home. They may be able to visualize large, white columns in front, a living room with a cathedral ceiling, a bedroom with a skylight, and a large deck in back. They have not even begun to think about the thousands of details required to complete the house and will not be able to begin thinking about them until the house begins to evolve.

Mark begins the design process with a rudimentary sketch illustrating the key features that the customer has thought about. Each line on the sketch directs the customer's attention to additional details that need to be considered. Within less than an hour, the vision materializes sufficiently so that Mark can provide a list of existing homes with the desired features. The customer then begins to tour homes with similar features. Because the owners of these homes went through the same process earlier, they identify with the customer and are willing to share feelings about what they like about their homes and what they wish they had done differently. In this case, the builder helps define needs and points the customer to homes where the diagnostic process can be continued. The builder does not need to be involved in the actual visits, only in pointing to and making contact with the existing homeowners, who are part of the resource network.

Once the basic building plan is defined, financing is arranged. Mark realizes that the customer is probably not yet able to visualize interior details such as carpets, sinks, and lighting fixtures. Therefore, standardized allowances are calculated for each of these, loans are obtained, and construction begins. Mark originally tried to keep samples of carpets, plumbing fixtures, paint colors, and lighting fixtures, but this took too much time, the customers always wanted something different, maintenance of inventory was a hassle, and he had to maintain a staff that was knowledgeable about each option. Therefore, he developed a network of supply firms. The supply firms are given the allowance on each house. Customers are encouraged to visit supply firms, ask questions, and examine samples as part of the diagnostic process. The only requirements are that the customer is happy with the selection, that any deviations from the allowance are covered by the customer or added to the construction line of credit, and that a decision is made by the time the construction workers are ready to install the fixtures. Mark frequently does not know what fixtures will be installed until they arrive at the construction site.

If the customer is unhappy, it is up to the supply firm to make him or her happy. Thus the supply firms, the financial institutions, the existing homeowners, and the construction crews are all part of Mark's network. Each network member has coordination meetings with Mark on at least a weekly basis. (Mark's cellular phone is always ready at other times.) Attention is focused on milestones, progress, process, and resolving problems. Each individual network member is responsible for performing the work and, if the customer is not happy, for doing what is necessary to rectify the dissatisfaction. Customer responsiveness and flexibility direct all activities.

3. *Information infrastructure development.* Fundamental to the difference between offering-based and response-based activities is the

integration and coordination of the infrastructure needed to support them. Chapter 3 described how offering-based activities use periodic planning studies to anticipate customer needs and periodic scheduling to define how activities between various groups should be integrated and coordinated. Responsive organizations, on the other hand, require on-line communication and a method for organizing requests to facilitate dynamic dispatching and monitoring.

Because the purpose of the responsive organization is to build a relationship with customers by being able to respond when the customer makes a request, the emphasis must be on the customer and on delivery, as shown in Figure 12.1. The individual delivery tasks performed by front-line workers are presented above the line shown in Figure 12.1. The organizational tasks conducted by management are under the line, showing that they support the benefit-delivery process.

The resource block, a sublayer of Figure 12.1, represents the network of resources that can be used as building blocks to deliver benefits. Resources typically provide functions such as movement, storage, security, or processing. Because responsive organizations typically deliver benefits to people, in the form of information, money, and products, there can be a wide range of resources used. Resources range from satellite networks (for information movement) to truck lines (for product movement) to airlines (for people movement). Storage resources can be hotels (for people), electronic mail or answering services (for information), or warehouses (for products). Security may be provided by storage vaults or refrigeration units (for goods), escort services or perimeter watch (for people), or underground storage vaults (for the long-term storage of computer tapes). Processing may include order fulfillment centers (for products), janitorial services (for facilities), health-care providers (for people) or data processing centers (for information).

In addition, there are many different resources, ranging from telemarketing firms to physician groups to medical labs to consultants to finance companies. Each resource has its own core competency. To make responsive deliveries, the organization must be able to build the network, develop guidelines that allow the integration of the resources into the delivery task, and information systems that allow the coordination and dispatching of work. Figure 12.2 illustrates the network of resources available to the responsive firm. Resource units may be owned by the responsive firm or the relationship may be collaborative. The relationship

The Customer-Responsive Organization

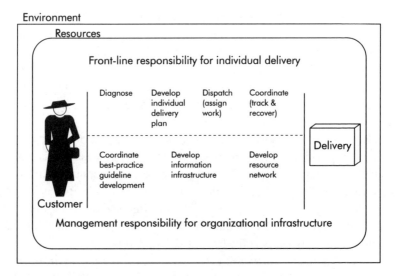

Figure 12.1. A customer-responsive management model.

may be an exclusive partnership (i.e., continuous use) or network (i.e., continual with intermittent use). The legal nature of the relationship is based on expected use patterns (i.e., make versus buy). The critical parts of the relationship is that it is collaborative, that it is on-line (i.e., available when needed), and that it has the capability and capacity needed to respond to the responsive firm's dispatch.

Although the emphasis is on the customer and delivery, the organization also must realize that it operates in an environment that imposes considerations such as those shown in Figure 12.3. Operations must respond to the environment. Military logistics may be in Korea, Viet Nam, or Saudi Arabia. Each situation presents a new situation, such as hurricane recovery efforts in south Florida; flood relief in Iowa, Nebraska, and Missouri; or posteruption activities near Mt. St. Helens. Distribution centers face different environments in New York City, Mexico, Las Vegas, and Russia. Central-city hospitals and suburban and rural hospitals operate in very different environments. Environmental laws and issues will be different in Boston, Louisiana, and Saudi Arabia.

Customer and network expectations will be influenced by the environment. The role of the facilitating infrastructure builder is to develop methods that allow the organization to be responsive within these

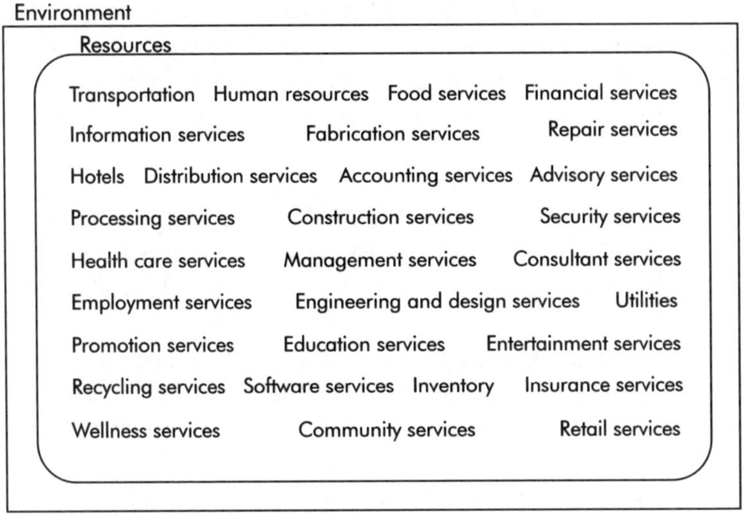

Figure 12.2. A customer-responsive resource network.

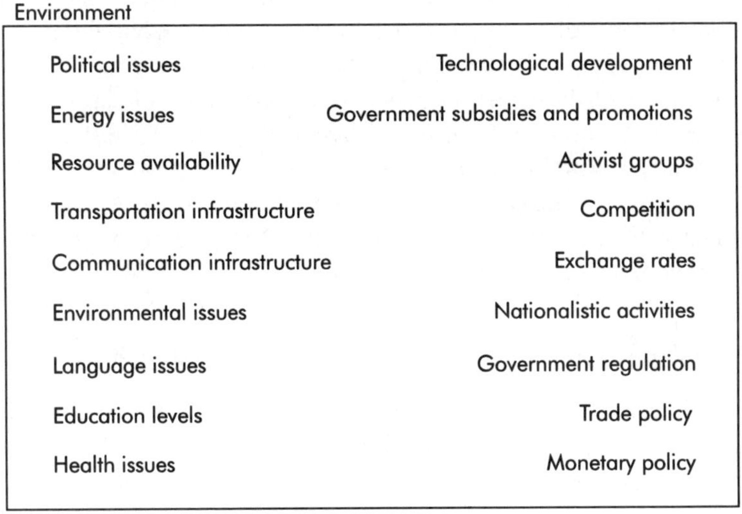

Figure 12.3. Customer-responsive environmental considerations.

environments. If the Mexican telephone system is unable to support the transmission of scan data, the retail chain may develop satellite capabilities. If each country requires a different certification procedure for pharmaceutical drugs, the guidelines must be modified to include country-specific requirements. Every environmental difference is simply another issue to be resolved.

At the heart of the model depicted in Figure 12.1 is the primary purpose of the responsive organization: to relate with the customer and make deliveries that respond to the customer's request. Although the delivery is represented in Figure 12.1 by a box, this does not imply that delivery must include a product. To be able to respond, the organization must first create an organizational infrastructure that includes best-practice guideline development, network development, and an information infrastructure that integrates and coordinates individual deliveries. With the infrastructure in place, the organization is able to make individual responses. Each individual response requires diagnosis, development of an individual delivery plan, a dispatching system, and coordination.

The line between customer and delivery in Figure 12.1 is dashed to illustrate two basic concepts. First, it is not a flow but rather a process – the responsive delivery of benefits, tangible or intangible. Second, it does not imply a separation between the development of organizational infrastructure and individual deliveries. Just as Toyota's Ohno felt it important to bring support staff out of their isolated offices and into close proximity with the factory floor, so the organizational infrastructure staff is there to support the front-line delivery of benefits. The support staff constantly reexamines guideline effectiveness and the ability to respond to customers to make changes in network development, information infrastructure, and protocols. It is a continuously improving, continually learning process.

Logistics is the Management of Responsive Activities

Even in centrally planned organizations, there were many activities that had to be responsive. Order fulfillment, for example, could not be predefined. Orders, by definition, could not be filled before they were received. The group traditionally responsible for responsive activities was logistics. Logistics, in concert with sales, interacted with customers to take orders and coordinate delivery. Likewise, logistics interacted with suppliers to coordinate the delivery of supplies. Frequently, logistics was also responsible for customer service.

The term "logistics" was first used in a military context in the early 1800s to describe the efforts made to support Napoleon's military conquests. The military used the term to describe all the support services required by personnel, facilities, materials, and services. It included everything from communications to the provision of health and food services to the movement of troops to the supply of ammunition.

In the 1960s, many of the former military personnel who had been involved in logistics during World War II began to apply these concepts to support business operations. Because employees were responsible for their own housing, health care, and feeding, the primary application of logistics principles was in physical distribution. Here the request was an order from the customer, and the delivery was the delivery of a product. The Council of Physical Distribution Management was formed in 1963. Membership grew rapidly, and in 1968 its concepts began to be applied to physical supply. Here the request was a production plan and the delivery was the delivery of raw materials required to support production. In 1985, the National Council of Physical Distribution changed its name to the Council of Logistics Management to reflect its broader mission. Before long, many firms began to assign other responsive activities, such as customer service, to the logistics department.

This evolution was natural and logical. The firm focused on its primary mission and core competency – producing predefined offerings that were distributed to the marketplace for sale. There were groups that were responsible for planning and producing products and other groups that were responsible for managing responsive activities. Logistics was responsible for the responsive activities.

Unfortunately, because the primary support service provided by business logistics was physical supply and physical distribution, logistics began to be equated with the management of product flows, transportation, inventory management, packaging, and order entry. Today the term "supply-chain logistics" is used to describe these activities. The term "service-response logistics" is used to describe customer-responsive activities in which a product is not the primary focus. For example, sutures may be involved in surgery, but they are not the primary reason for the surgical process. Logistics, as a field, consist of both product-focused supply-chain logistics and benefit-focused service-response logistics.

If the management of responsive activities has historically been considered to be logistics, Figure 12.1 could be considered to represent the customer-responsive management model or the logistics management model. It would apply not only for service-response activities such as a hospital, a bank, or Operation Desert Storm but also for supply-chain activities, whether for a distribution center or a contract logistics firm, such as ROLS. Currently contract logistics firms are experiencing dramatic growth. Supply-chain logistics firms, such as ROLS, have grown dramatically and are starting their own national associations. Likewise, contract service-response logistic firms are one of the fastest growing segments of the information technology field. For example, many large firms have contracted with firms to provide customer software support and hardware repair. Although these firms, which equate logistics with supply-chain logistics, do not identify themselves as logistics firms, the management model is identical. The growth in contract logistics is caused, to a large degree, by the difficulty management has in knowing when to apply offering-based management and when to apply the responsive (i.e., the logistics) management style. Therefore, they contract with logistics management firms to manage responsive activities.

One of the problems with disciplines such as marketing and logistics is the tendency of many to think of them in terms of function. Marketing, for example, may be confused with advertising. Even marketing books may describe current buying, storing, advertising, order-processing, financing, and billing procedures. A marketing text may describe the current approaches to managing market research, pricing, and product development. Such works rapidly become dated as new data collection methods (e.g., surveys to scanning), advertising outlets (e.g., newspaper to interactive TV to Internet), and new statistical approaches (e.g., sampling to information data modeling) become available. What stays constant is the concept.[2] The market concept, for example, is basic. When customers will not buy items simply because they are available, the best way to achieve the organization's performance objectives is by a) examining people's needs and wants as the basis of deciding what the business

---

2.   The authors are indebted to a colleague, Mary Holcom, for this concept.

should do, and b) selecting the best way to meet consumer's needs targeted by the firm.[8]

Traditional marketing management assumes that it is more economical to base all activities on extensive preplanning than on experimentation because (a) there are extensive economies to large-scale mass production; (b) the firm has the ability to design production lines and distribution channels for virtually any product, but midcourse changes are difficult and expensive; and (c) transaction costs, using Williamson's definition, are high.

Like marketing, logistics is often seen in functional terms such as "the process of planning, implementing, and controlling the efficient, cost-effective flow and storage of raw materials, in-process inventory, finished goods, and related information from point-of-origin to point-of-consumption for the purpose of conforming to customer requirements."[9] The logistics concept, however, is not restricted to specific functional activities. The logistics concept is based on the following principles:

1. Coordinating deliveries in response to individual customer requests.
2. Integrating the capabilities of a network of resources to enable deliveries within virtually any environment.
3. Developing the flexible processes and information infrastructure needed to support delivery coordination and resource integration.

The logistics concept may be stated as *coordinating deliveries responsive to individual customer requests using a network of resources and integrated by flexible guidelines (i.e., processes) and communications.*

The degree of responsiveness may vary, but delivery must address what, to whom, when, and how. "What" may include products, services or benefits. "How" may include the Pony Express, trucks, airplanes, telegraph, or the Internet. The what, to whom, when, and how options will vary depending on location, technology, and the environment, but the basic concepts will not change. Logistics is the management of responsive activities.

Responsive management is relationship management and infrastructure management. There is one relationship with the customer to identify and diagnose needs. There is a second relationship with the network of suppliers who make the delivery. The role of the responsive organization is to develop an infrastructure that facilitates the integration of the provider network into the delivery process and the coordination (i.e., the dispatching or tracking) of each delivery. Chapter 13 will describe infrastructure (i.e., information and communication) design and Chapter 14 will describe relationship management.

Summary

Offering-based organizations are based on centralized forecasting and planning of needs and the scheduling of production and distribution to meet these needs. Work is organized on a flow basis. Customer-responsive management, on the other hand, is based on front-line diagnosis of need, the development of individualized delivery plans, the dispatching of work, and the monitoring of work. In offering-based organizations, the role of management is to plan work and processes and to supervise and control the implementation of the plan. In customer-responsive organizations, the role of management is to coordinate the capturing and monitoring of protocols (i.e., the knowledge base) and to locate resources and make them accessible for the front line. Production management has used central planning, implementation, and control of activities. Responsive activities require front-line planning and the monitoring of activities. Centrally planned and controlled activities are reassuring because they are predictable. Front-line planning, on the other hand, encourages not only customer responsiveness but also innovation and the development of new leaders.

Production-management techniques can be effective for relatively steady-state production and distribution flows. Customer-responsive activities require an on-line information and communication infrastructure for integrating resources to make the delivery and coordinating the assignment of work. Traditionally, customer-responsive management has been the responsibility of logistics. However, business logistics has to often limit its scope to coordinating inbound and outbound production flows. In reality, logistics responds to requests (e.g., customer orders or material requirements plans), develops methods for finding and using resources to meet the requests, and coordinates deliveries by dispatching and monitoring work. The front line is responsible for doing this on a request-by-request basis. Logistics planning is responsible for developing the organizational knowledge base (i.e., protocols), developing the resource network so it is accessible by the front line, and developing the infrastructure necessary to support the front line and facilitate their interaction with customers and resources.

Chapter 13 will describe the infrastructure-building process. Chapter 14 will describe the attributes of win-win partnerships.

References

[1] Paul Kennedy, *The Rise and Fall of the Great Powers*, New York: Random House, 1987, p. xvi.

[2] George Stalk and Thomas Hout, *Competing Against Time*, New York: Free Press, 1990, p. ix.

[3] William H. Davidow and Michael S. Malone, *The Virtual Corporation*, New York: Harper-Collins, 1992, p. 23.

[4] Michael Porter, *Competitive Advantage: Creating and Sustaining Superior Performance*, New York: The Free Press, 1985.

[5] From *Toyota Production System: Beyond Large-Scale Production* by Taiichi Ohno. English translation copyright © 1988 by Productivity Press, Inc., PO Box 13390, Portland, OR 97213-0390. (800) 394-6868, pp. xiv–xv.

[6] Carl Sewell and Paul B. Brown, *Customers For Life: How to Turn That One-Time Buyer into a Lifetime Customer*, New York: Doubleday Currency, p. 161.

[7] Reprinted by permission of *Harvard Business Review*. An excerpt from "Zero Defections: Quality Comes to Services," by Frederick F. Reichheld and W. Earl Sasser, Jr., Issue 5 (September / October 1990), p. 110. Copyright © by the President and the Fellows of Harvard College; all rights reserved.

[8] David W. Cravens and Robert B. Woodruff, *Marketing*, Reading, PA: Addison-Wesley, 1986, p. 19.

[9] "What It's All About?" Council of Logistics Management, Oak Brook, IL, 1992, p. 2.

CUSTOMER-RESPONSIVE
INFORMATION INFRASTRUCTURE

This chapter will describe the information needs of customer-responsive organizations. The migration to customer-responsive management is typically limited by three factors:

- The organization's ability to comprehend the business processes that compose the organization's knowledge base;
- The organization's ability to use technology that gives the front line access to this knowledge base as they interact with customers and coordinate delivery;[1]
- The organization's ability to add to and modify the organization's knowledge base.

These three areas cannot be considered in isolation. Business processes are the knowledge base of the organization and need to be supported by an information and communication infrastructure to be useable. Business processes and technology must be used by the front-line workers before they are effective. Change must be experienced, embraced, and integrated into the technology and business processes before they change the organization. Thus customer-responsive management requires the integration of all three areas.

Traditional business processes have been based on a communication infrastructure of paper, telephones, and meetings. Telephones typically have been used to track and expedite activities (e.g., to determine the

---

1.   When the term "front line" is used, it is not only referring to customer contact personnel (CCP) but to any individual who is receiving requests, developing solutions, and responding to new situations. These are the people who organize the work, commit organizational resources, satisfy the customer, and are constantly learning from the new situations they encounter. The front line includes CCPs; customer service personnel; and even engineering, production, logistics, and other departments if they interact with customers to resolve delivery, technical, availability, or other issues.

status of an order, to find out if a task has been completed, or to see if a person's schedule is open for a meeting). Meetings have been used to disseminate information to groups of people. Paper has been used for two purposes.

1. To transport information horizontally across departments. Paper notified departments that work was coming so that they could plan work schedules. Paper notified departments when work arrived so that they knew what to do and could begin work.

2. To transport information vertically. Once the work was completed, the paperwork was filled out to report results and to show that the work had been completed. This paper traditionally went to the accounting department, where it was processed and from which periodic reports were generated. These reports were designed to measure actual work performance with planned worked performance for the period. That is, the monthly reports were used to periodically check that the work was on schedule and on budget.[2]

The traditional role of management was to review reports and studies and to develop work plans. These included long range plans, production plans, market plans, product plans, distribution plans, and financial plans. Paper traditionally transmitted the plan to the workers, and periodic reports indicated whether or not the planned results had been achieved. It was not unusual to take longer to process the paper than to do the work itself. Reports provided after-the-fact information that was used to modify the plan for the next period.

Computers have traditionally been programmed to "automate" the reporting function within these traditional information and communication flows. A much different approach must be used to develop the horizontal and networked systems required for customer-responsive systems.

The Basis for Customer-Responsive Infrastructure Design

Front-line workers and management must be involved in customer-responsive infrastructure design. Management is responsible for the

---

2. For an excellent discussion of the inflexibilities inherent in the traditional financial control process, see Eric L. Denna, J. Owen Cherrington, David P. Andros, and Anita Sawyer Hollander, *Event Driven Business Solutions,* Homewood, IL: Business One Irwin, 1993.

strategic vision but front-line workers possess and develop the knowledge base (i.e., the customer knowledge base, the best-practice guideline knowledge base, the customer service knowledge base, and the resource knowledge base). Both perspectives must be integrated into information system design. The success of the system design will be determined by how well system design and technology support the front-line workers in carrying out the organizational vision and sharing information. As Robert H. Buckman said in 1995, "Today we at Buckman have an objective to have 80 percent of our company effectively engaged on the front line by the year 2000."[1] There are five key elements of the strategic vision. Each can be characterized by a set of questions that are important to the customer-responsive organization.

Customer Relationship Strategies

How do I want to interact with customers? How do customers want to interact with my organization? How can I make it easy for customers to do business with me? How can I be more effective in diagnosing individual customer's needs? Where are the potential fail points of our relationship? Who are the buying influences in the organization? Are there technical decision makers, economic decision makers, and gatekeepers? If customers call me with a need, how can I make sure that I meet or exceed their expectations? How can I strengthen and maintain their trust and earn their repeat business? How do I monitor delivery activity so I can take corrective action before problems arise? How do I determine when I need to mentor my employees to help them be more effective in solving customer needs? What information do I need to have about my customers so I can be more effective in meeting their needs and reduce the hassle of doing business with me?

Resource Relationship Strategies

What range of resources do I expect to need to meet customer needs? What is the expected utilization of each resource? Should the resource be networked or owned? How can I use infrastructure to reduce the cost of using resources and having the resource network available in the immediate run? How do I determine resource capability, capacity, and availability? How do I minimize lead times for use of resources? Can infrastructure be used to allow the use of different types of resources that are not cost-effective using existing methods? What information do I need to have about my resources so I can use them more effectively and efficiently? How can I make the interface with resources "instant, costless, seamless and frictionless?"

Knowledge-Base Development Strategies

How can I formalize the required corporate knowledge bases and share them with the appropriate workers when they need it? When CCPs encounter new needs, how do I facilitate the development of new protocols to meet these needs, measure the effectiveness of the delivery, and capture the new protocol so that it can be integrated into the corporate knowledge base? How do I monitor deliveries so I know when to change process protocols? How do I evaluate the effectiveness and efficiency of each protocol change? What information do I need to capture about processes so I can develop more effective and efficient protocols?

Operating Strategies

How can need diagnosis be improved? What types of questions do customers ask? What information do our customers need to get more value from our products or services? What types of questions must employees be able to answer? Do we currently collect the information needed to answer these questions? How can I use this information to enable employees to do their jobs better? How can I improve the dispatching of work? How can I improve work monitoring to anticipate and avoid delivery failures? How can we increase capacity utilization? How can we price to increase yield? How can I better schedule capacity to meet actual demand? When should I network resources and when should they be provided in-house?

Information Infrastructure Strategies

How can the interaction between users and knowledge bases be improved to enable employees to do a better job of responding to customers and coordinating resources? How can I minimize the information they must enter to get the response needed? How can the retrieved information be presented in a more understandable way? How can I improve the interaction between the users and the computer? How can I make sure that information is available to all involved parties? How can expert systems be developed to enhance the employee's ability to diagnose needs, define delivery plans, and coordinate delivery?

These are the strategic questions for customer-responsive organizations. It is the information infrastructure that enables the first four strategies to function, just as the central nervous system does in the body. Thus the information infrastructure becomes a central issue in strategic planning. It is not a function that can be performed by the information technology (IT) staff. It is knowledge-base dependent, and a critical component of this knowledge base resides with the front-line workers, who are constantly encountering new conditions, situations, and requests.

Most knowledge bases do not reside with central planning or even functional planning groups. Therefore, two groups must be involved in information infrastructure building. First, management must understand the potential and capability of technology and create the strategic vision of how the firm could relate to its customers and the resource network. Second, it is the front-line workers who understand the range of support needs required of the information infrastructure. Thus customer-responsive information systems development must be driven by users, front-line workers, and managers – not the technical staff.

Second, the systems development methodology must change. Information systems were traditionally developed using classical planning methodology. This method, often called the "waterfall" approach, required that every detail of the need definition had to be determined before the system could be designed. Next, every detail of the system design had to be completed before programming could begin. Likewise, all programming had to be completed before testing began, and all testing had to be completed before the system was operationalized.

There are two problems with the traditional planning approach to infrastructure development. First, it takes so long to complete each step that by the time the system is developed, current industry dynamics will dictate that it is no longer what the organization needs and major changes are required. The second problem is that users know what they want but will not recognize it until they see it. Thus it is virtually impossible to get a meaningful definition of needs during the definition sessions because the users do not truly know what they want until they can see it and use it in their individual jobs.

Thus the key to developing customer-responsive systems is to find methods of quickly and accurately defining the infrastructure needed to maintain relationships. There are some fundamental questions that need to be answered in the infrastructure building process.

1. What are the key relationships that determine the success of the organization? For example, retailers are dependent upon customers, employees, and suppliers. The success of a university is determined by the relationships with students, faculty, alumni, and industry. True, there are other relationships, but these are the most important.

2. What interactions occur as part of these relationships, and who are the individuals who are responsible for these interactions?

3. Who is involved in these relationships? What kind of responses do these individuals need to make to strengthen these relationships? What are the customers' perceptions of these responses?

4. What information do these individuals need to enable them to respond to requests? How will this response change customers' perceptions?

5. What information is already available, what information must be captured for each interaction with the customer, and what information should the organization begin to capture so it does not have to ask again?

6. How should this information be captured for storage and retrieval, and for facilitating the interaction between user and computer? Is it the same if the user is the customer or a customer contact person? For example, should orders be entered directly by customers, or should the order be given to a CCP, who in turn enters the order?

7. What are the business rules and best-practice guidelines for interacting with customers?

8. Are there are steps in the process that do not create value to the customer? How can customer hassle be reduced? For example, should Domino's Pizza be able to respond to the telephone customer by simply asking if the customer wants a large, double-cheese pizza delivered to 306 Oak Street and charged to the VISA card just the way it was done last Wednesday, or should the customer be required to restate the new order?

No one individual possesses the complete knowledge base to answer questions like these. These questions require consensus building within large groups of people.

Consensus-Building Concept Room

Walt Disney developed a method for developing consensus when he developed animation films. He recognized that a picture is worth a thousand words, so he developed a method that would allow the large teams to visualize ideas that were the basis of an animated feature. Without these visualization techniques, it would have been virtually impossible for groups working on stories, character development, voices, layout, background, animation, and recording to have worked together as a team to coordinate all of the detail of such a voluminous task.[3]

A Disney feature begins with an idea or vision. The idea can be presented in a few sentences.

Jealousy leads a vain queen to threaten the life of a young princess, who flees into the woods where she is befriended by seven dwarfs. When the queen, in disguise, tricks her into eating a poisoned apple, the girl is thought dead and preserved in a glass coffin until a prince awakens her with love's first kiss. . . .

A baby elephant is considered to be a freak because of his enormous ears, until an enterprising mouse discovers a way to turn this liability into a startling asset.[2]

Next, the idea is expanded in sequences. A list of 10 to 15 major concepts to be communicated during the feature is prepared. Each is developed into a separate sequence.

Once the sequence is generally developed, the team begins developing sketches of each characters. As each sketch is developed, it is posted in the "concept room." The concept room is a room where all of the team

---

3. It takes over 2.5 million drawings for an 80-minute feature. Each arm movement in each drawing must be coordinated with the preceding drawing and every lip movement must be synchronized with the sound track. For a reference, see Frank Thomas and Ollie Johnston, *Disney Animation: The Illusion of Life*, New York: Abbeville Press, 1981, pp. 185–243.

meetings are held. The walls of the room are designed so that it is easy to post drawings on the wall. The walls of the concept room contain the latest version of the story, the sequence, the story line, each character, and each setting. Each is shown in the form of a picture or outline so that all the members of the team are looking at the same visuals. The visuals are in the room where the teams have meetings, eat lunch, or take coffee breaks. Therefore, anyone who has an idea or question can go to the appropriate visual and suggest changes. If the rest of the team likes the changes, the visual is updated. If not, the idea has been presented and processed.

Once the plot, character, and setting have been roughed out, it is time to begin putting these pieces together with the story line. Major turning points in the story are sketched showing the interaction of the characters, the setting, the plot, and the script.

The concept room has several strengths:

- It is always accessible to all team members.
- The sketches make it easy for everyone to visualize the other team members' ideas.
- It is easy to make changes.
- The visuals always reflect the most currently accepted changes.
- Design risk is reduced because any idea is easy to present so that others can visualize and respond to it.
- It allows all components (e.g., plot, character, setting, and script) to be seen in context.

Just as the concept room is extremely valuable to the Disney design team, it can also be valuable to the infrastructure design team. It should:

- Always be accessible;
- Contain visualization tools that make it easy for everyone to visualize other team members' ideas;
- Make it easy to make changes;
- Always reflect the most current version of the infrastructure vision;
- Make it easy to experiment with changes so that team members can brainstorm on various ideas and do "what-if" experiments;
- Allow all components of the organization to be visualized in context.

The design teams need members to fill several roles:

- *Front-line team members* are knowledgeable workers who have first-hand experience diagnosing customers' needs, developing solutions, and coordinating delivery.
- A *facilitator* is a person who understands business process development and has some familiarity with the activities of the front-line workers. The facilitator's role is to keep the project focused and moving toward consensus.
- A *recorder* is a person or a recording device that captures the essence of the group's decisions. If the visuals can be created easily enough, the recorder's job may be to develop prototypes or visuals as the group discusses them.

In addition, each group should be supported by people in two additional roles:

- A *leader* is needed. This might be a visionary senior executive who authorizes, champions, funds, protects, and motivates the group effort.
- A *process owner* might be a manager with responsibility for a specific business process and the infrastructure needed to support it. This is the individual with the operational vision of what the team is trying to do. The process owner needs to understand business process development.[4]

Design Criteria for Responsive Information System

A responsive information system, based on the central nervous system concept described in Chapter 12, coordinates activities between the customers and various work groups. The system is designed to facilitate responsiveness and network building. The organization can function no better than the infrastructure enables it to function.

---

4. Adapted from Michael Hammer and James Champy, *Reengineering the Corporation: A Manifest for Business Revolution*, New York: Harper Business, 1993, Chapter 6.

As shown in Figure 13.1 the responsive process consists of the following components:

- Diagnosing customer needs;
- Developing customized solutions (i.e., delivery plans) based on the organizational protocols (i.e., the application of a knowledge base);
- Dynamically assigning (i.e., dispatching) work to the appropriate delivery units;
- Tracking performance as each task is completed.

Infrastructure development should never be the objective of the development team. The team's objective should always be to accomplish one of the strategic tasks identified earlier in this chapter – that is, improve relationships with customers and resources and develop the knowledge base and the processes needed to coordinate deliveries. The infrastructure that evolves is simply a means of enabling organizational strategy. Thus, infrastructure development is a means to an end, not an end in itself. The way an organization changes is to change the information infrastructure.

Managers and employees are not interested in infrastructure for its own sake; they are interested in tools that allow them to reduce work hassle and job stress. They are not interested in an information system as a project that needs to be defined and then built; they want tools that allow them to do their jobs more effectively. They do not think in terms of infrastructure; they think in terms of facilitating the interaction (i.e., the relationship) between customers and resources, capturing and retrieving information from the knowledge base, and improving diagnostic and delivery processes.

Infrastructure development is not a one-time planning process. It must evolve as it is needed to enable employees to do their jobs better. As new customer needs evolve, infrastructure must change to enable these new needs to be satisfied. As new resources become available, the information system must be modified to integrate the new resource into the delivery process. As new technology develops, the system must be changed to allow new options for relating with customers and coordinating deliveries. As new measurement techniques become available, infrastructure changes can incorporate them to allow better delivery

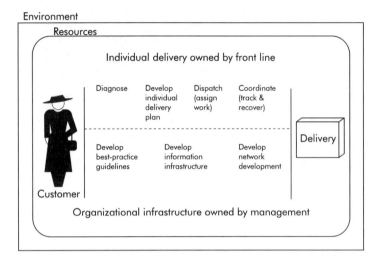

Figure 13.1. A customer-responsive management model.

coordination. The infrastructure must continually evolve to allow the organization to stay ahead of competition and keep pace with technology and environmental changes. Thus infrastructure development must begin not by defining current processes but by asking strategic questions.

The Customer-Responsive Process

By "responsive," we mean that the organization is structured to respond to customer requests. These requests reflect the customers' specific needs and contain all of the conditions that are specific to those requests. Next, there is a series of business processes (i.e., best-practice guidelines) for converting customer-specific needs into an individualized delivery plan. The information in the request, when matched with the best-practice guidelines, specifies each individual work task that must be performed for that delivery. Each work task will specify what is to be done, who it will be done for, the capability and capacity required, when the work was dispatched, and when it was completed.

The responsive process is supported by a responsive information system presented in Figure 13.2. The boxes represent information areas that will eventually become information files. The text on the

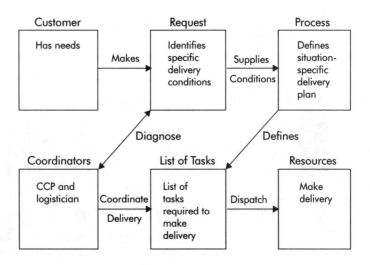

Figure 13.2. The information components of a responsive organization.

connecting lines shows relationships. This can be read as follows. The *customer* has needs and makes a *request* to the firm. (In many cases, the firm knows the customer so well that it notifies the customer when it discovers solutions that may be of special interest to him or her. But even when the firm notifies the customer of the option, the customer must take the next step by making a request.) The request identifies all conditions specific to the request and supplies the input conditions required by the conditional guidelines to define the individual delivery plan. The individual delivery plan consists of a *list of tasks* required to meet the customer's specific need. The list of tasks is then used to dispatch the work to the various *resource groups,* based on capacity and capability available. The *coordinators* consist of customer contact personnel who interact with the customer to diagnose needs and define deliveries and logisticians who coordinate delivery through dispatching and monitoring of work.

For example, a hotel could have a deterministic policy of delivering copies of *USA Today* to every hotel guest. In the responsive organization, the CCP (i.e., the desk clerk) could ask whether the customer's preferred newspaper is *USA Today, The Wall Street Journal,* or some other publication. (Alternatively, the return guest could be asked if he or she still wanted *USA Today,* as they did last time.) For the request to be an option, the hotel must have a resource to make the delivery. In this case, there are two resources: the supplier of papers and the person who delivers the paper to the hotel-room doors. If the resources are available, delivery must then be coordinated. Coordination requires interaction with the customer and the resources necessary to make the delivery. The customer interaction is necessary to make sure that for each new stay, the guest still prefers *USA Today.* Interaction with the resource is required to order the correct number of copies of each newspaper and to provide the delivery list (dispatch) for the carrier. Interaction can be performed by a person (face to face or telephone) or mechanized (fax or EDI). However it is done, this interaction is information based.

The role of infrastructure in a responsive organization is to collect, store, retrieve, and communicate the information necessary to facilitate operations. When the infrastructure works, the relationship is effective and hassle free. When the infrastructure does not work, the relationship is frustrating and unresponsive. When the infrastructure works, the delivery is efficient and coordination cost is low. When the infrastructure does not work, delivery is late and ineffective, and special recovery mechanisms such as expediting, inspection, signoffs, and approvals must be implemented to work around the inadequacies of the infrastructure. These recovery mechanisms unduly increase expense, slow delivery, and make the organization inflexible and unresponsive. Workers become controlled by the inflexible systems and are unable to respond to customers, no matter how much they desire to serve. Systems take precedence over customer needs, common sense, and getting the job done, and the firm's response to the customer is unconvincing.

The Requirements of a Customer-Responsive Infrastructure

A responsive information should be able to accomplish the following:

The Capture, Storage, Retrieval, and Sharing of Customer Information

The capture, storage, retrieval, and sharing of customer information is necessary to improve delivery effectiveness and reduce relationship hassle. This occurs when the organization has the information necessary to understand the customers and their special needs. Hassle is reduced when the organization captures the information when it is given the first time, so that the customers do not have to give it again each time they do business with the organization. (For example, a frequent user of a hospital who is given a new patient history form for each admission experiences this as hassle.) *Customer information* needs can be subclassified into six categories.

- *Descriptive data* such as name, address, phone, birthdate, and so forth. This is the data that identifies and defines the customer.
- *Status data* such as credit limit, account balance, existing medical conditions, academic standing, current medical diagnosis, and any other data necessary to indicate the individual's current status at that point in time. Status items can change in an instant but are important for interacting with the customer. Status items are typically used by the organization to define how it will respond to the individual. Status variables, used or created by the diagnostic process, select the protocol that will define delivery. For example, a guest's status changes when he or she makes a reservation, checks in, checks out, or notifies the hotel that he or she is responsible for selecting a site for a 3,000-person convention.
- *Special needs or preferences* such as preferred newspaper, preferred in-flight meals, existing medical conditions (e.g., diabetes, hemophilia), preferred billing date, allergies, style or color preference (e.g., spring, summer, fall, or winter typing), preferred delivery time, or any other data that help diagnosis needs and preferences. Special needs data are different from status data in that they are used to identify long-term desires, preferences, and needs. For example, the preference data may describe the hotel guest's choice of newspaper, credit card, and room service requests. It is often these special needs that provide the conditions that are used by the conditional protocol to customize the delivery to the individual's needs.
- *Historical data* on prior relationships with the customer. Historical data may give medical history; purchases, payments, and returns; product usage; academic record; or any other data that help define the nature of the long-term relationship between the customer and the organization. This record should include organizational failures as well as successes. It is these data that allow the relationship to be placed in context. Does the customer return

every article of clothing he or she buys on a Friday on the next Monday morning? Has the company repeatedly missed delivery dates? Should the organization suspend the relationship, continue in a protective mode, or go the "extra mile" to make amends for past mistakes?

- *Relationship-specific data* such as the CCP assigned, the date on which the relationship began, EDI codes for intercomputer communication, account codes for electronic funds transfers, and other data used by the organization to facilitate the relationship and reduce hassle and transaction costs.

- *The individual responsible for decision making.* In many cases, especially when customers are organizations, there are many individuals involved in the decision-making process. Some individuals are concerned about technical issues, others about economic issues, and still others about availability and coordination. Therefore, it is necessary to identify the individuals involved in the buying decision, their roles, their concerns, and their needs so that all needs can be addressed as part of the relationship development process.

The Storage, On-Demand Retrieval, and Evaluation of Processes

There are two types of processes: guidelines that define the activities and bills of material that define the supplies required. These types serve different functions for the organization.

- Guideline management requires that it be easy to add new guidelines or to modify existing guidelines. For example, if a physician reads about a new oncology protocol, he or she should be able to enter it one time and have it on call whenever needed. Entry should be as easy as possible. Once it is entered, the physician should have the option of selecting the new protocol or continuing with the old one when new patients arrive. Effectiveness data should be collected so that the staff can compare the effectiveness of each guideline. If the group believes that a combination of the two guidelines would be more effective, they should be able to modify one of the guidelines or create a new one and collect data to compare relative effectiveness.

- Guidelines should be able to be modified "on the fly" to add new conditions that had not be considered before.[5] For example, if a patient with an unusual complication, such as hemophilia, requests treatment under an established protocol, the physician would alter the existing protocol to address the special conditions. The alterations should be captured and added to the existing protocol so that it will not have to be redeveloped when the next patient with this need arrives. By integrating protocol development and operations, the protocol files always show current practice.

- The guideline should identify each task required, the skill needed to perform that task, the timing of the task (absolute time or relative to another task), the conditions under which the task should be performed, and the capacity required to perform the task.
- Bills of material (e.g., ingredient or recipe lists) files are used to define supplies needed to complete any given task. For each task, they include the supply needed, the quantity needed, when needed, and where needed. For example, if the task is to produce a specific automobile, the bill of materials would require, among other supplies, four P185/70R14 tires at station 57 one hour and 43 minutes after production for that unit began. It would also show when the dispatch ticket (i.e., the Kanban) should be issued and which supplier to issue it to.

The Identification of Resource Ability and the Capacity for Responding to Customer Needs

The identification of resource ability and the capacity for responding to customer needs allow the CCP to determine what resources are available and how much is available to serve customers. Resources can be categorized into products and services.

1. *Product resources* are maintained in the form of inventory. When the customer calls, the CCP needs to know if the product is available and, if so, how much is available. In addition, it is

---

5. This is now required of the physician when he or she writes orders for the patient. If the protocol is not captured, it must be rewritten each time it occurs or it must be added to the printed protocol currently distributed by many physicians.

helpful to know how to access the product (e.g., the warehouse, bin, or factory), the supplier, and the lead time. If this information is not available, the CCP needs to know when it will be available. In addition other information, such as cost, description, vendor, size, weight, and so forth, would also be helpful.

2. *Resources that cannot be inventoried will be in the form of capability and capacity.* Capability and capacity collectively describe resource availability.

- Capability is a measure of what the delivery unit can do with the skills, tools, and facilities that it has. For example, the radiation department of a hospital may have X-ray machines, MRI devices, and other equipment. Each of these pieces of equipment represents a different capability. Likewise, a trucking company may have many different types of equipment, ranging from flat bed trucks to vans to refrigerated vehicles. A consulting firm will have individuals with different skills, such as civil engineers, radiation monitors, lawyers, and project monitors. Each has his or her own capabilities.

- Each capability will have a schedule for responding to customers that shows when capacity is available. This schedule is a function of time. For example, the December 24th schedule may be different from the January 16th schedule. Once capacity is scheduled, it becomes available for commitment. A commitment is for a specific time period.

Typically, delivery units manually schedule deliveries. This may work well if conditions are very static, but imagine the X-ray room technicians who have 30 percent of their work scheduled at the beginning of each day. Some of the rest of the work that comes in during the day are emergencies. Others are not emergencies but may result in physicians waiting until X-rays are completed before they can perform their tasks. When this happens, the schedule becomes decimated as all requesters struggle to get to the front of the line and those with less bargaining power wait in line. This creates a "stat" crisis in which everyone wants the work done immediately and the workers become so desensitized that "stat" ends up meaning next to nothing. The capacity files keep track of the capacity scheduled and the capacity committed so that work can be accepted and assigned on a schedule, by a time window, or on a priority basis. This allows the delivery units to manage capacity on a weekly or daily basis; individual work tasks are dispatched on a just-in-time (JIT) basis to maximize flexibility and capacity utilization.

The Ready Identification of Individuals Responsible for Coordinating the Relationship

Allowing for the ready identification of individuals responsible for coordinating the relationship with the customer as well as the individual responsible for coordinating delivery is a key principle. In a hospital, these individuals may be the admitting physician and the nurse. In a truck line, they may be the salesperson and the dispatcher. In a consulting firm, they may be a principal and the project manager. Whenever there is a problem, anyone must be able to identify and get in contact with the individual responsible for working with the customer and coordinating the actual deliveries. If that person is not available, it must be clear who is covering for him or her. If the customer calls, he or she should be routed to the correct person automatically. It is this part of the infrastructure that is responsible for making sure that all questions can be resolved by the first person contacted, who is the right person to solve the request with a minimum amount of run-around or hassle. The Whirlpool Customer Assistance Center does this by recording the customer contact person for each customer and using the customer's caller ID (i.e., his or her telephone number) to route the call to the same CCP each time that customer calls.

As firms move away from the single point of contact (e.g., the salesperson and the purchasing agent) to a multifunctional relationship with the customer, it will be necessary to identify the key contact points that are part of the broader relationship. Who in the delivery organization is coordinating technical issues on various products with the customer? Who coordinates availability, accounting, or warranty issues with the customer? How does the organization make sure that all necessary parties are notified?

In addition, there are two other needs that must be supported by the infrastructure. They are the current request and its individual delivery plan. The request is the event that triggers the delivery. The individual delivery tasks are the steps that need to be taken to effect delivery customized for that particular request.

The Capture, Storage, and Retrieval of All the Information Necessary to Completely Define the Request

The information system must allow the capture, storage, and retrieval of all the information necessary for total definition of the request. As a minimum, this should allow the identification of the customer, the coordinators, the need, the time of the request, the desired delivery time, the price agreed upon, and any other information required to describe the request.

The Capture, Storage, and Retrieval of All the Steps Necessary to Dispatch the Delivery

The capture, storage, and retrieval of all steps necessary to dispatch the delivery must be included. For example, when Federal Express receives a request to pick up a package, it must pick up the package, transfer it to an airplane, sort it at the Memphis hub, transport it to the destination airport, transfer it to the deliver truck, and make the delivery. There may be special conditions that require additional steps, such as customs declarations. Just as the decision to make a product requires the ordering of all the components, so the request for a delivery requires the dispatching of all of the tasks required to effect delivery.

At an automobile dealership, the job may require frame alignment, the replacement of body parts, front-end alignment, sanding, painting, and detailing. Each of these tasks must be identified, captured, and placed on the prioritized dispatch list. The work can then be dynamically dispatched as each prior task is completed.

The infrastructure must be able to capture, store, and retrieve all of the information necessary to dispatch the work, such as who the work is for, what should be done, when it should be done, who should do it, when it is to be dispatched, when the work was completed, who did it, and the results. With this information, each delivery becomes a project and traditional project management methods such as PERT and CPM can be used.

Developing Visualization Tools

The concept room can provide a setting for bringing front-line workers with their knowledge base and managers with their strategic vision together to define the support system they need to build relationships with customers and coordinate delivery. The concept room, whether a physical location or a virtual location created by groupware, provides a means for developing consensus and commitment to implement the changes developed. But what types of visualization tools does a firm use in a concept room?

Four general categories of visualization tools may be considered.

1. A context diagram to identify the organization's customers and determine the relationships that the system is trying to support.
2. Entity relationship diagrams to define what entities (e.g., person, place, thing, or activity) are important to the organization and the information that should be captured and retained for each entity.
3. Business event tables to identify the events that are expected to occur and the business processes that should be used to respond to the request.
4. System windows to show how the worker wants to interact with the computer.

Each of these visualization tools will be described in turn.

Context Diagrams

Context diagrams have been used by many groups. They basically start with two bubbles connected by lines. These bubbles identify the parties involved in the relationship, and the lines indicate the relationship itself. Businesses may label the lines to show events (i.e., transactions) that may occur between the two parties. Figure 13.3 shows an example where the lines show interaction. Responsibility for each type of event can be different. The purchase can be made by having customers enter their desires into the computer themselves. The purchaser can check inventory and availability, material specifications, and EPA ratings on their own or go through a customer contact person in customer service. Who and how each event occurs will determine the customer's perception of the organization.

Figure 13.4 presents a bubble chart in which the emphasis is on the perceptions of the relationship. This approach to bubble diagrams has been used by the social scientists.[6] In this case, each party sends a

---

6. For an example, see C. Terry Warner, *Bonds of Anguish, Bonds of Love*, 1992 draft, Moral Studies Group, 3196 JKHB, BYU, Provo, UT.

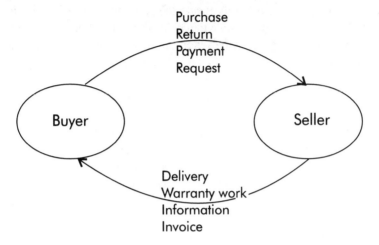

Figure 13.3. A transaction context diagram.

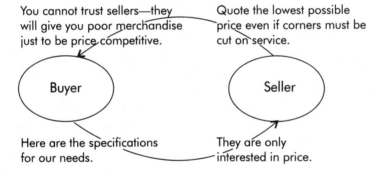

Figure 13.4. A perception context diagram.

message and the other party perceives the message. Perception diagrams have two dimensions. First one party sends a message. Then the other party receives the message. The message perceived by the second party may be very different from what the sender thought he or she was sending.

The buyer issues detailed specifications for their needs (see Figure 13.4). The seller perceives that as long as it meets specifications, the buyer is only interested in the lowest possible price. The seller then provides a product that barely meets the specification and prides itself on its low price. The buyer then perceives that it must be very careful to fully specify needs because the seller will do anything possible to barely meet minimum specifications just to get a lower price.

In Figure 13.5, the buyer asks for a solution to its problem and provides the seller with the goals it is trying to achieve. In this case, the buyer seeks a solution, not a completely defined product. The seller perceives the request differently. The buyer perceives the response differently. Both parties seek a win-win solution.

Perhaps it would be helpful to present two additional context diagrams, one for a university and one for a supplier of industrial chemicals.

A Context Diagram for a University. Although universities are often very large, with many departments and administrative groups, organizational success revolves around four entities: students, faculty, industry, and alumni. Successful university functioning is highly dependent upon the needs of these four groups being met.

The student wants to be recognized by the faculty member and known as a person, not just as a number or a nameless face. Students want to know what to expect and how they are doing on their work. This includes grades and comments on their work. They want to know that they are important and that their time in school has meaning. Students want to learn how to find jobs and which student and professional organizations to participate in.

The faculty wants some way to know students and know something about them. They want to be able to communicate with them. Faculty members would like to be able to share articles that they have read and to notify students about news events, internships with industry, job opportunities, changes in course assignments, and even review problems with exam questions or other assignments. If industry asks for recommendations, faculty members want to have access to student information such as student goals and work experience.

Industry wants to know the availability of students for jobs or summer internships – or even if there are students who could work on special projects that their current professional staff are too busy to address right now. Industry would like to be able to promote its organizations so that they are attractive to potential employees. Industry would

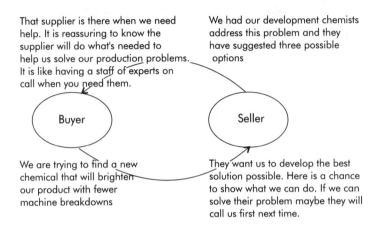

Figure 13.5. A perceptual context diagram in which the customer seeks a solution.

like to be able to establish relationships with faculty members. They would like for the faculty to understand their specific needs so that professors will recommend students that might be particularly attractive to them.

Alumni also have needs. New employment patterns (e.g., rightsizing and downsizing) means there are many alumni looking for job opportunities. They would like to network with friends with whom they went to school. They would appreciate job referrals and aptitude testing as they reconsider new career paths. Some may be freelancing and want to know how to network with former friends they went to school with. Alumni may be happy to be mentors to students who are working in their firms as summer interns or as new employees.

This could create a context diagram as shown in Figure 13.6. The needs and perceptions have been left off this figure and included in the text. The text could easily be written on an enlarged diagram posted in the concept room. It is not the form of the context diagram that is important but only that front-line workers and managers understand what each entity needs and how each perceives what it is receiving.

A Context Diagram for an Industrial Chemical Company. An industry context diagram may be slightly more complex. Consider an industrial chemical company that has salespersons calling on many different

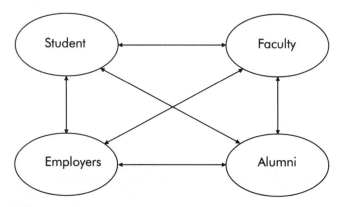

Figure 13.6. A context diagram for a university.

accounts. When the salesperson calls on the account, there are typically many different people at the buyer's site who have questions. The chemist working in product development has very different needs from in-bound logistics, purchasing, or a person responsible for environmental issues. The salesperson needs to collect lists of the individuals who have questions and begin to develop context diagrams for each type of person at the customer's site. Figure 13.7 illustrates the salesperson's objective of creating a network where people at the customer's site know who to contact in the seller's organization.

The seller may believe that price, quality, and availability are the only important issues but eventually discover that the buyer is actually looking for responsiveness. However the context diagram is drawn (whoever the entities are in the bubbles; whether the lines represent perceptions, needs, thoughts, or transactions), the purpose of the context diagrams is to make relationships explicit and to bring them to the attention of the front line and management groups as they discuss business processes in the concept room. Context diagrams should also focus attention on the diversity of needs and away from a single determinant "best way" of relating to all individuals.

Entity Relationship Diagrams

Entity relationship diagrams (ERDs) are used to focus attention on information needs about each entity. ERDs have their own symbols. A

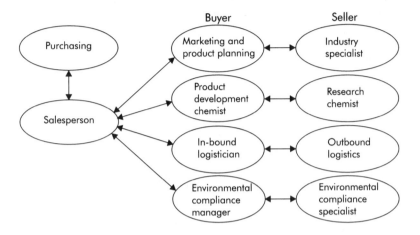

Figure 13.7. A context diagram for an industrial chemical salesperson.

box is used to define an entity such as students, faculty, alumni, or employers. It can also be used to address activities such as requests, sales, or job listings. Inside the box is information that is needed about the entity. Lines join the boxes to show the relationship. A company, for example, may have many departments, and a department may have many individuals making requests of the salesperson. Figure 13.8 shows a sample entity relationship diagram for the chemical company salesperson.

The ERD shown in Figure 13.8 shows the entities and information about each entity that may be important for customer tracking for a chemical company salesperson. Typically, information about each person, place, or thing is captured at the first encounter. For example, the first time the customer contacts the firm, information about that customer will be collected. During subsequent encounters, the only information that will be collected will be changes in the customer's records and event-specific information. The event-specific information will be linked to the entities in the organization so that it can be referenced in many different ways. For example, the salesperson will want to know requests by company, by each department within each company, and by each individual within each department.

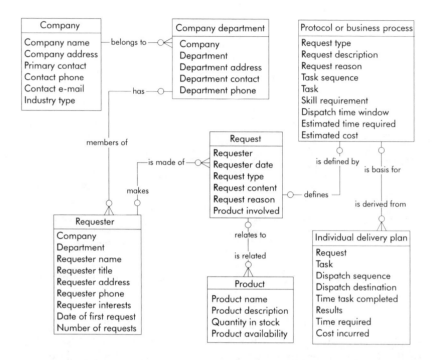

Figure 13.8. An entity relationship diagram for a chemical salesperson.

The company will probably want to be able to have separate business processes for each type of request. The process may also be different not only for each type of request but also for each type of request for each product and perhaps even for the reasons behind each request. For example, if a request were for a chemical sample for a new product, the protocol may be different than it would be if the sample request were to eliminate a production problem with an existing production process.

A similar diagram can be developed for a university (See Figure 13.9). Relationships in a university revolve around *departments*, which have *staff* who offer *courses*. A course, especially the basic courses, may have many *sections* scheduled. *Students* enroll in these sections. Their enrollment is manifest by their presence on a *roll*. Inside each entity is a list of attributes or information that one would want to know about each item.

The purpose of an entity relationship diagram is to identify the things

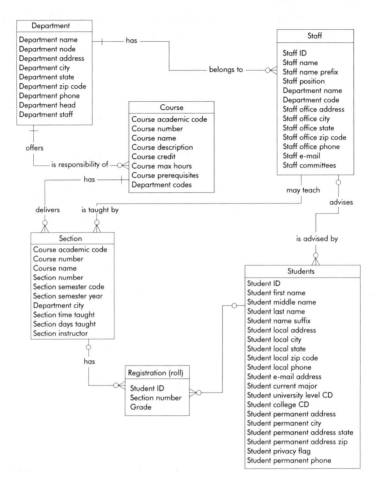

Figure 13.9. An entity relationship diagram for a university.

that are important to the organization and what information is needed to manage those things. The ERDs should be prominently displayed in the concept room so that front-line workers always know what information is available and can constantly seek ways of using that information to improve their relationships with customers (both internal and external). Unless front-line workers know what information is available, they will not be able to think of ways to use that information to interact with customers and the resource network. The ERD can be thought of as an inventory map for the information stored in the organizations data warehouse. If you don't know what you have in inventory, you don't know how to use it to create value for customers.

Business-Event Diagrams

The context diagrams define the entities, their relationships with the organization, and the person responsible for strengthening each relationship. The ERDs describe the information needed about each entity. The business-event tables identify routine events to which there must be a response. There will be a separate business event for each type of request made of the front line. Although this may seem daunting at first, most needs can be quickly categorized.

The business-event table can take many forms. Table 13.1 simply shows one way of making a table that identifies the primary parts of the process of enrolling and registering a student at a university. The first column identifies the customer request. The second column identifies the key pieces of information that can only come from the customer. The third column identifies the business process for responding to this business event.

The lines shown in italics represent decisions that need to be made. Is the individual a student? Have all past charges been paid? Does the student meet acceptance criteria? These questions require the organization to define the rules for making these decisions. Thus, for each italicized line, the organization will need to specify all business rules for making these decisions. For example, student acceptance may be made on the basis of grades, major, and recommendations. Financial aid decisions may be made on the basis of grades, family income, employment status, or some other criterion.

The lines shown in bold are for items that provide value to the customer. It is these events that justify all of the other steps. The students want to know if they have been accepted, if they can receive financial aid, and obtain the classes they desire.

The lines shown in regular type represent the necessary steps that must be taken to make the process work. For example, it may be necessary to collect demographic information such as address, phone number, and reference identifications. These are simply pieces of information that must be captured. The role of the design team is to maximize the ratio between the bold lines (events that provide value) and the regular lines (necessary steps to acquire information needed to satisfy business rules).

316

It is not sufficient just to look at the steps made by the organization; the hassle required of the customer must also be considered. For example, the university may require that each applicant write a letter requesting an application form that must be completed and returned along with two certified copies of official transcripts and three letters of recommendation from high school teachers. An alternative would be to have high school guidance counselors transmit at the applicant's request his or her student records electronically at the end of the junior year. This would eliminate sending a letter requesting an application, completing the application, mailing the application, obtaining the official transcripts, getting the three letters of recommendation, and entering the information into the student's record at the university. Not only would this reduce hassle for both parties, but it would also remove many potential fail points. Failure at any point could prevent the relationship from occurring. Also, many applications can also be automatically approved based on grades, test scores, and courses taken.

By thus reducing the hassle to both the student and the admissions office (which does not have to collect, compile, file, and track the information), attention can be redirected to having students write letters defining their goals and the reasons they want to attend that particular university. The admissions office can spend time advising and counseling the potential students it wishes to attract. The admissions office might even use the time saved to identify alumni who graduated in the student's desired major and promote a mentoring program so the student can get a first-hand feel for his or her chosen major.

Granted, the steps presented in the "Process" column of Table 13.1 represent a very simplified view of the business process. It is much like looking at the process from an altitude of 50,000 feet. It allows a big-picture view of the process. It makes a distinction between steps that add value and organizational overhead steps. It also identifies key decision points and allows the design team to begin to identify organizational decision rules. It is frequently at this level where the design team sees the objective of each step without being encumbered by detail. At the 500-foot or 15-inch views, the tendency is to get too involved in the details of keeping track of the number of copies of the transcripts that have been received and whether they are official transcripts rather than considering various ways of obtaining the student's academic history.

Table 13.1. A Business-Event Table.

Business Event	Input Needed	Process	Display Window
Student request to register for classes	Student ID	*Student is enrolled.*	Registration window
		Payments are current.	
		Display available courses for declared major	
	Course ID	**Have student select desired course**	Selection box
		Student meets prerequisites.	
		Register student for course	
		Student does not meet prerequisites.	
		Explain prerequisite requirement	
		Continue until selection complete	Message box
		Process fee payment	
		Payments are not current.	
		Display list of outstanding charges	Fee box
		Student is not enrolled.	
		Perform student application	
		Individual is enrolled.	
Student request to enroll	Student ID	**Perform student registration**	Enrollment window
		Individual is not enrolled.	
	Demographic data	Get demographic data	
	School ID	ID prior schools	
	Release consent	Provide approval for transcript release	
		Request transcript information from prior school	
	Selection of major	Display majors for selection	
	Financial aid needs	Display financial aid information	
	References ID	Request references	
		Contact references	
		Route application to approval committee	
		Collect committee reaction	
		Applicant accepted.	
		Notify student of acceptance	
		Notify student of financial aid	Letter, e-mail
		Applicant not accepted.	
		Notify student of denial	
		(Suggest options)	

The "Display Window" column simply allows the design group to conceptualize this diagram by beginning to design windows to visualize what the interaction would be between the user and the computer screen. The window should allow basic functions such as selecting stored information, entering situation-specific information, displaying key information, and communicating relevant information to others. For example, a salesperson should be easily able to identify any customer or individual involved in a buying decision. The salesperson should not have to remember a name or identifying number. He or she may want to be able to select the individual by company, department, function, or even the type of benefit desired. This is typically implemented by allowing lists of individuals to be filtered by familiar variables such as the firm, department, function, or desired benefit. This can be done in many ways, including the use of list boxes or simple, full-screen views. The choice is up to the user.

This chapter has suggested that infrastructure be defined by design teams composed of knowledgeable front-line workers and visionary managers in concept rooms using visualization tools that depict relationships, the information needed to manage the relationship, and the events that the front-line must be able to respond to. It has also suggested that the logistics model can be used to allow diverse responses. This model captures the organizational knowledge bases in protocol files and uses it to develop customized delivery plans. Once the organization develops a strategic vision for maintaining relationships with customers and the resource network and has developed an overview of its business process, it is ready to select and apply the implementation strategy that best enables it to do so.

Implementation Strategy

There are basically three different approaches to selecting an implementation strategy. The strategy selected will be determined by several factors.

The Structure of the Information Required

Some applications, such as order entry for a grocery store chain, are highly structured. That is, all information such as store ID, product ID, and quantity desired are either numeric, text, date, or time data. The form of the data fits carefully defined ranges and structure. Medical records, on the other hand, include fields such as EKGs, X-rays, pictures of specimens, or even sound or video clips. Such data are considered to be unstructured and are not suited for many relational database applications.

The Linking of the Processes

Some processes are closely linked. An order-entry process, for example, identifies the customer, does a credit check, identifies the products and quantities desired, calculates charges, and processes payments as parts of the same process. All steps are closely linked together. Whether the processes are batched or on-line, synchronous or asynchronous, they are still closely linked together.

The process of writing a proposal or strategic plan, on the other hand, is a much different process. It will typically have several people writing different parts of the document at the same time. After the lead person makes the first draft, he or she will want other people to make suggestions and editorial comments. The review process may occur at different locations and at different times. Each document may require different people to review it. The preparation and review process is not closely linked.

The Structure of the Process

Some processes are highly structured in that the same information is required for each business event, the same business rules apply, and the same questions are asked. Again, order entry for familiar products is highly structured and standardized. It does not matter whether the information is given to a CCP who enters it into a computer or whether the customers enter the information themselves, the process is highly structured.

Other processes are much less structured. For example, a lawyer doing research for a particular case may search through many different cases using key words and categories to find relevant precedents. Each such search may be very different. Unfamiliar key words may often be encountered. Cases may be cross-referenced. The selection of the cross-referenced materials will depend upon the context of the search. The search process is much less structured.

The Importance of Authentication

Authentication is the process of ensuring that the users are who they identify themselves to be. In some cases, this is important. For example, if a student's phone number is changed, it is important that only the students himself or herself be allowed to make the change to avoid practical jokes or harassment. A grade change must be made by the faculty member responsible for the class. On the other hand, if individuals are searching public documents from the library or a bulletin board, it really does not matter who the users are. All people are free to read the material.

The Importance of Information Security

Security involves ensuring that the information is not accessed by someone for whom it is not intended. If the system is an isolated unit and there is only a single user, security is not an issue. If, however, many different individuals can intercept information from the phone lines or a network or even access the computer, then security may be important. Information such as legal searches, class syllabuses, or dispatches for wreckers may not be critical. The transmitting of competitive information, the dispatching of trucks carrying high value shipments, or the storing of military intelligence data may be very sensitive. When the information is very sensitive, various methods of encrypting the data are used to prevent outside access to information.

The methods used to implement the business process will depend upon these characteristics. There are several general approaches to developing the information infrastructure.

Gopher, Browsing, or Surfing Tools. The availability of the public Internet computer network has fostered the development of community bulletin-board discussion groups and e-mail. Individuals or organizations can connect a server to the network. They can then place one or more files on the server with the information they wish other networkers to access. Whenever the server is accessed by a "surfer," the surfer is routed to the home page. The home page typically explains the rationale for the database. Some of the words in the home page are typically highlighted. When the word is highlighted, it means that that word is cross-referenced to another file. When a key word is selected, the user is taken to a cross-referenced area of the database. Thus key words allow the browser to navigate through the entire database. These applications were primarily designed to allow the posting of data on a computer network. The design of the database is critical if it is to be easy to use. The home page should be designed to provide a quick, intuitive overview of the subject. The key words and the linkages should be obvious so the user can easily navigate through the organization's presentation.

Although browsers can allow the surfer to supply information such as to request catalogues, they are used primarily for one-way communication. This is quite obvious because the browsing software does not provide the authorization and security required of important information. For example, if an organization's home page allows the surfer to browse through a variety of items and place orders, it will be difficult to determine if the persons placing the order are truly who they represent themselves to be. Unhappy football fans, for example, could request a moving van in the coach's name after a disappointing loss. The browsers are excellent for promotion, catalogues, posting of community activities, and anything else that the organization wishes to disseminate. The browsers are able to handle text or pictures and other unstructured data very well.

Groupware Tools. Groupware was primarily designed to allow individuals to work collaboratively on activities although separated by time and space. It enables the integration of activities by large numbers of users. Groupware is network oriented. It can function over a network (e.g., local, wide area, or occasional). The network can be the Internet, a long-distance carrier, or an Ethernet system. Groupware is client-server based. The server is like a post office with each user (i.e., client) having his or her own box. The user can send or receive containers of information to and from the box. The user sends containers of information to the post office box. The container can hold structured data (e.g., text, numbers, date, time) or unstructured data (i.e., pictures, video or sound clips, spreadsheets, word processing files). The package can be labeled for any delivery schedule – immediately, hourly, or after hours. The label can specify that the package can only be delivered to a specific person or to some category of people. The package has a method of verifying the signature of the sender of the information so that the receiver is assured of the identity of the sender. (If the post office had this capability, it could dramatically reduce the number of package bombs sent.) The package can be addressed to a single person or to many different persons. The delivery addresses can even be set up to require that the first person receiving the package approve or respond to it before it is routed to the next recipient, who must then respond before it is routed ahead. (This can be used to review design or contract change orders.)

The post office analogy does not hold true for all functions, however. Post offices deliver packages. Groupware can either deliver packages according to the instruction on the address or it can allow access to the package without letting it leave the first server. For example, if ten people are working on a budget, each person can access the package containing the budget and make the changes he or she desires. When they finish, it can be the original that is updated, not a copy of a copy. There is even the ability to keep track of versions so that the person accessing the package knows who has already looked at the package and made changes.

Groupware not only has the ability to deliver and provide access to the information in the package, it also has a method of displaying and working with the information in the package. If the package contains many items, a *view* can be created to see each of the items in a view or list. By selecting an item of information from the list, the details of that specific item can be displayed. Detailed information about a single item or document in the package is displayed in a *form*. Detailed information about a group of items is displayed as a list in a *view*. Extreme flexibility is provided by linking views, forms, and multiple packages together.

For example, by looking at a computer view entitled "class sections by departments," a user can locate specific university class section. The selection of a specific class can then lead to display of a form with detailed information about that specific section. Action buttons on the section form can then provide the user access to the class syllabus, reading list, and roster and to send mail among class members. If the class roster button is chosen, a view of all students in the class will be shown. By selecting an individual from the list of students, detailed information can be provided by displaying the student form. Buttons on the next form can allow a view of the student's transcripts (with access to transcripts limited to the student's advisor or the student himself or herself), picture, resume, personal goals, extracurricular activities, and any other information helpful to the faculty. Selecting a student and an address of an employer could allow that student's resume to be immediately sent to a potential employer soliciting names from a faculty member. All of the files necessary to support such a system can be stored on different computers using different operating systems and located at different sites.

Structured Systems. Structured systems evolved in an earlier era than browsers and groupware. They were conceived in the 1970s and 1980s, when disk storage space was very expensive. Structured systems used relational databases that were designed to minimize the storage of redundant data. Relational database systems were designed to handle structured data in a most efficient manner. All customer data were in the customer file and referenced by a customer identification number. All inventory data were kept in the inventory file and referenced by a part identification number. All files were *normalized* so that data would be stored at the most disaggregated level. Normalization was simply a process for defining what data went in what files. Each file had an identification number such as a customer ID, product ID, vehicle ID, or employee ID. Information was placed in a file that totally defined the value of the information. For example, an individual's ID totally defined an individual's birthdate because each individual can have only one birthdate.

Structured systems not only have structured databases but also structured programs for responding to highly structured and defined business events. Structured systems are developed using computer-assisted systems engineering (CASE) tools. Perhaps the easiest to use are "upper CASE tools," which allow for the conceptual definition of systems. The entity relationship diagrams in Figures 13.8 and 13.9 were developed using an upper CASE tool. This tool allows each file to be defined and each field in each file to be totally defined using visual tools that make it easy to see the relationships among the files. Lower CASE tools provide visualization tools for defining specific business events, drawing the required windows, and programming the business rules and data manipulation processes.[7]

7. For an outstanding example of visualization tools used to design object-oriented, event-driven, structured systems using CASE tools, see Ed Yourdon, Katharine Whitehead, Jim Thomann, Karin Oppel, and Peter Neverman, *Mainstream Objects: An Analysis and Design Approach for Business*, Upper Saddle River, NJ: Yourdon Press, 1995.

Structured systems are very effective when there is a limited range of business events, each process is highly structured, all activities are closely linked, and data needs are limited to structured data. However, most business systems will require a combination of implementation methods. In fact, vendors of structured systems are desperately trying to add more of the messaging capacity of groupware to their systems. In a similar vein, groupware vendors are aggressively adding more relational capabilities and browser capabilities into their software. Likewise, the browser software developers want to enhance the authorization and security capabilities of their offerings.

Summary

In summary, there are several key concepts that should be gleaned from this chapter. First, any group that sits down to design or select a computer system has already limited its success. The first step is to define a strategy for relating to customers and to the network of resources. The second step is to define business processes (i.e., an organizational knowledge base) and operating strategies for applying the knowledge base to improve relations with customers. The information infrastructure that evolves should be designed to enable the front-line workers to do their job better.

Second, no one individual is able to develop the ideal system. The organizational knowledge bases reside not with centralized planners but with the many front-line workers who continually interact with customers and the network of resources. They are the only ones who intimately understand what tools they need to enable them to do a better job. The key is to find the most effective front-line workers and make them part of the infrastructure design team. It is these expert front-line workers (as defined in the beginning of this chapter) that make the information infrastructure an expert system. This does not mean that management does not have a role. Management must have a vision and disseminate any information such as market research data to expand the front line's perception.

But even the best front-line worker possesses only a limited part of the knowledge base. A cross section of front-line workers and managers needs to have a place and methods for visualizing needs and for communicating those needs to each other. The visualization tools may reside in

325

a central place or in a virtual place where information can be shared over the information infrastructure. The term "concept room" was used to describe this place. Only when members of the development team clearly understand each other and feel free to express ideas and critique each other can the group come to a consensus on the approach to use. Several visual tools are available. It is not the specifics of the tools that are important but the concepts that the tools convey.

Third, there are many different implementation strategies that can be considered based upon the characteristics of each individual process. Many business processes will require a combination of methods.

It is a mistake for an organization to start with a hardware or software technology and then design a system to use it. Customer-responsive firms must begin with the desired relationships and design an infrastructure that enable that relationship to evolve. Software selection should only occur after the organization knows what is needed. Now that so many vendors are offering platform-independent software, the hardware is the last and most inconsequential decision of all. The success of the software development team is only determined by how well the front line can respond to customers. Infrastructure development is not a one-time project. It is an iterative process. The infrastructure should be constantly improved to allow the CCP to respond to more diverse needs with more effective deliveries.

References

[1] Robert H. Buckman. Speech given to Anderson Partners, Chicago, IL, October 25, 1995.

[2] Frank Thomas and Ollie Johnston, *Disney Animation: The Illusion of Life*, New York: Hyperion, 1981, pp. 368–370.

[3] Adapted from Michael Hammer and James Champy, *Reengineering the Corporation: A Manifesto for Business Revolution*, New York: Harper Business, 1993, pp. 103–109.

CHAPTER 14

RESPONSIVE RELATIONSHIPS[1]

The transition from the third era, when the emphasis was on the production of products for the marketplace, to the fourth era, when the focus shifts to providing solutions to customers is profound. During the production era, it was assumed that everyone knew what they wanted. The manufacturers knew what they wanted to produce and offer to the marketplace. The customers knew what they wanted when they went to the marketplace. Marketing focused on product planning to plan the offering. Retailers developed assortments of products and methods to attractively display their offerings. Employers wrote job descriptions specifying their job offerings. The entire focus of the production era was on the offer and the acceptance of the offer. Even business law has been based on the offer, the counteroffer and the acceptance of the offer. Offers and acceptance of offers implies that the buyer knows what they want.

The fourth era – the customer-responsive era – is focused on long-term relationships between partners. The strength of the relationship is determined by a continual stream of responsive, effective deliveries in the immediate run. In essence, the customer says, "I don't care about promises or promotions. Just effectively meet my needs when I call and I will keep calling you first. Let me down and I will go elsewhere." Each request occurs in the immediate run and begins with the identification of the customer's problem. It ends with a solution delivered. To understand the difference, consider a dialogue between a third-era firm looking for a predefined product and a fourth-era customer contact person (CCP) trying to explain his or her capability.

> 4th-era CCP: How can I help you?
> 3rd-era buyer: What are you selling?
> CCP: We have a number of resources that we can use to provide solutions to your problems.

---

1. The authors are indebted to Rosalie Risley for her significant contribution in the writing of this chapter.

Buyer: What kinds of resources are these?

CCP: We have access to a number of equipment providers, reengineering coordinators, software writers, network administrators, and other groups to help you implement and maintain information infrastructure that enables you to interact with your customers the way you desire.

Buyer: How many people do you have in your company?

CCP: We only have a staff of 10 people, but we have a network of 4,000 individuals working with us, and that number changes daily.

Buyer: What software do you sell?

CCP: We don't sell a specific package; we do have many modules or objects that can be used to develop software that meets your specific needs.

Buyer: How can I see what the software can do?

CCP: We would be happy to provide a list of clients and have you contact them.

Buyer: How much will it cost me?

CCP: First we have to determine what you want done. We will be glad to meet with you and outline your needs so we can give an estimate.

Buyer: Why can't you tell me what you sell and how much you charge?

CCP: When we better understand your needs, we can then suggest alternative solutions.

The third-era buyer is looking for a predefined offering! The fourth-era CCP is trying to identify need and then define solution.

Solution-based activity is based on long-term relationships, not on individual transactions. Individual transactions may be effective when they involve well-understood needs and offerings. The more complicated the need, the less both parties clearly understand what is involved in the solution, the more the customer needs to rely on the provider's specialized knowledge base, and the more important it is that organizations develop interactive relationships for defining and solving needs.

But what is a relationship? Is it the same as an industrial partnership? Does it mean staying with a supplier regardless of quality and price? Does it mean signing contracts with individuals who can't show you what they have to offer or give you a price before they start?

Relationships Defined

In essence, traditional relationships have been based on the unilateral offer and its acceptance. Firms have been expected to know what they wanted and to buy from willing suppliers. Labor has been purchased by employment, and supplies have been purchased by procurement. Firms have planned an offering that they distributed to the marketplace.

As firms become more flexible, they can be more responsive to customers. Firms cannot be more responsive than their resources enable them to be. Therefore, resources must also be responsive. Customers, whether individuals or firms, do not want products, services, or employees. They want solutions to their needs. Lewis Stern has described the customer's wish for *stress reduction*.[1] Customers want to avoid the stress of defining needs, ordering, reordering, tracing shipments, maintaining inventory, cleaning buildings, processing IRS forms, paying invoices, and all of the other hassles necessary to do our jobs and live our personal lives. Customers (whether external, internal, firms, or individuals) want to develop relationships with those they can trust to meet their needs at a reasonable cost and a minimum of hassle. Minimizing hassle reduces stress. Ronald Henkoff has described this phenomenon in the following words:

> Welcome to the front line of the new American economy, where service – bold, fast, unexpected, innovative, and customized – is the ultimate strategic imperative, a business challenge that has profound implications for the way we manage companies, hire employees, develop careers, and craft policies.
>
> It matters not whether a company creates something you can touch, such as a computer, a toaster, or a machine tool, or something you can only experience, such as insurance coverage, an airplane ride, or a telephone call. What counts most is the service built into that something – the way the product is designed and delivered, billed and bundled, explained and installed, repaired and renewed. Product quality, once a competitive advantage, is now just the ante into the game. Eric Mittelstadt, 58, president and CEO of Fanuc Robotics North America, says, "Everyone has become better at developing products. In robotics, the robot itself has become sort of a commodity. The one place you can differentiate yourself is in the service you provide." . . .
>
> Says Patrick Harker, director of the Wharton School's Fishmand-Davidson Center, which studies the service sector: "Once you start

thinking of service as a process instead of as a series of functions, the old distinction between the front office (the people who did the selling) and the back office (the people who pushed the paper but never saw the customer) disappears."

The changing nature of customer relationships demands a new breed of service worker, folks who are empathetic, flexible, informed, articulate, inventive, and able to work with minimal levels of supervision . . . .

Says President (Merry Maids) Mike Isakson: "We used to focus on the process of cleaning, making sure the home was free from dust. Now we understand that the ultimate benefits to the customer are peace of mind, security, and stress reduction."[2]

Customer-responsive management is relationship management. First, the organization develops an infrastructure so it can relate rather than worry about internal coordination. Second, it builds relationships.

When P&G discovered Total Quality Management, it attempted to share it with its major customers. One customer was Wal-Mart. A number of Wal-Mart employees, including Sam Walton, flew to P&G headquartes to attend training. After a short period listening about SPC, Fishbone chart, and other TQM concepts, Sam Walton interrupted by saying this was too complicated. All he wanted was to have P&G keep his shelves full and send him a bill at the end of the month. Out of deference to who Sam Walton was, a short discussion ensued and then the instruction into TQM continued. Within a short while, Sam again interrupted by saying that this was too complicated. All he wanted was for P&G to keep products on his shelves and send him a bill at the end of the month. This time attention turned to solving a Wal-Mart need, and the now legendary P&G-Wal Mart partnership began. Such partnerships have changed American industry dramatically.

What Is a Relationship?

"Relationship" is a term used to describe how two or more people interact with each other. It describes how they communicate, how they handle conflict or differences of opinion, how comfortable or protective they are, how well they understand each other, and the degree to which they have common goals. Relationships determine expectations. Relationships do not just happen. Just as in a marriage, a relationship begins with an introduction and includes an acquaintanceship period, the courting period, and, finally, a more permanent relationship. As the two parties move through these phases, they learn how to work with each other and what to expect from each other. Relationships range from the extremely open, trusting, mutually beneficial win-win partnerships full of high expectations to the very impersonal, arm's-length win-lose transaction relationships to the very stormy, turbulent, lose-lose, codependent relationships.[2]

During the cold war, Roger Fisher and Scott Brown, two members of the Harvard Law School faculty, were concerned that conflicts between the Soviet Union and the United States were determined more by the process used to resolve such conflicts than by the issues themselves.[3] They sought to understand the relationship between the two superpowers. Their work is also applicable to the relationships between parents and children, husbands and wives, buyers and sellers, and employers and employees. In the following sections many of the concepts of Fisher and Brown are adapted to customer-responsive business relationships.

Why Cultivate Relationships?

Relationships are cultivated because they allow us to obtain benefits we need. Good relationships allow us to obtain substantial, beneficial outcomes with a minimum of effort (i.e., cost and hassle). Economists would say that relationships minimize transaction costs.[3] In more personal terms, the ideal marriage (or other personal relationship) is one in which both parties totally understand each other's needs, have a strong desire

---

2. "Codependent" is a term used in the mental health field to describe a person "who has let another person's behavior affect him or her, and who is obsessed with controlling that person's behavior." (Melody Beattie, *Codependent No More,* New York: Harper/Hazelden, 1987, pp. 27–34.) An argument can be made that businesses have become so obsessed with dishonest and negative behavior from customers, suppliers, and employees that their primary emphasis has been on controls and supervision and the delivery of benefits (i.e., value) to customers has often become secondary.

3. Here the term "transaction cost" is used as defined by Oliver Williamson (see Chapter 1).

and ability to support each other, are totally trustworthy and predictable to each other, and communicate easily. Such a relationship minimizes transaction costs in several ways:

- *They already understand each other.* They know the other person's history, special needs, and current status. There is no need for the awkward introduction, familiarization, and courtship periods. One has only to reflect on the time required for a new physician to give a second opinion or the new consultant going through a familiarization (i.e., fact-finding) process with a firm. When there is a strong relationship, each knows the other and how to place their advice and promises in context. (A child soon learns what a parent means when he or she says, "I'll play with you in just a minute.") Each knows how the other will respond to various suggestions. Each knows the other's allergies (a firm can have an allergic (i.e., a knee-jerk) reaction to certain types of recommendations.) Each knows the other's style.[4] (A consultant's recommendation must fit the corporate management style (i.e., the corporate culture) to be accepted and used.) Each knows the other's abilities (e.g., financial, physical, organizational).

- *It reduces the time it takes to make a diagnosis.* Only information on new conditions needs to be collected. Where there is a close relationship, one only needs to communicate such new information and allow the other party to put it into context. Close couples, for example, may read each other's body language (e.g., a frown, a glance, or a wink) or even each other's thoughts and understand them. A "close" consulting firm may need only a one- or two-sentence description of a new problem, whereas a new consultant will first have to spend enough time (i.e., a courtship period) to get to know the firm before he or she can place its requests in context. The close consulting firm may be able to initiate delivery before the new consultant even receives directions, arrives at the facility, and has the familiarization tour.

---

4.   For a discussion of individual styles, see Isabel Briggs Myers, *Gifts Differing*, Palo Alto, CA: Consulting Psychologists Press, 1980 or David Keirsey and Marilyn Bates, *Please Understand Me: Character and Temperament Types,* Del Mar, CA: Prometheus Nemesis, 1978.

- *It reduces diagnosis error.* The close firm already knows the customer. Thus it can avoid all of the stutter steps required for the new firm to learn about the special characteristics of the new customer.
- *It reduces the need to take defensive (i.e., protective) steps.* In any new relationship, there is always the fear or suspicion that the other party, intentionally or unintentionally, may not behave as one would desire. One or both groups may fail to perform or live up to promises. One party may be trying to take advantage of the other. For example, it is conceivable that sometimes unnecessary auto repairs or surgeries may be performed to generate revenue rather than to benefit the customer. It is also conceivable that customers may want the work done but may try to develop schemes to avoid having to pay for them. Many attorneys spend hours developing contracts, hoping to foresee all possible outcomes and defining the responsibility of each party in each eventuality. It is often as difficult for a new business relationship to be open and responsive as it is for a couple to be relaxed on a first date. It takes time before the parties are comfortable enough with each other to be able to openly focus on substantive issues rather than on protecting themselves from possible unwanted behavior.
- *It makes working together easier.* Any relationship begins with each party trying to understand the way the other works. A visit to a physician's office often begins with the completion of insurance forms and the identification of billing procedures and scheduling methods. Some parties have a very structured and defined organizational style. Other individuals are more flexible and spontaneous. The better we understand the other side of the relationship, the easier it is for us to interact.
- *It allows us to integrate schedules.* As the relationship develops, we begin to be able to anticipate not only how but when the other party will contact us. We all develop habits or patterns for doing things. Regular customers have patterns for having their teeth cleaned, their yards mowed, their cars serviced, and even their businesses reorganized. If we know the habits of regular customers, we can almost predict their needs. This ability to predict allows us more lead time for forecasting capacity needs. As described in chapter 8, airlines use these habits to forecast capacity needs dynamically.

- *It provides greater comfort.* When we are dealing with known parties, we know what to expect. We know how they will respond to special conditions. We know their competence and capacity. We know their motives in working with us. The more we know, the more confident we become of the outcome. Confidence creates comfort. The more uncertain we are about eventual outcome, the less comfortable we will be. "**We also want:** *inner* **peace**. We want a relationship that leaves us feeling positive. If we don't feel positive after the last transaction, we may dread the next and have more difficulty dealing with it."[4] If we feel comfortable and confident of the other person's response, it is much easier to call him or her the next time we have a need.

What Makes Relationships Work?

Relationships involve the interaction between the two parties. When relationships are positive, deliveries are effective, and the effort (e.g., the hassle, stress, or transaction) required to make the deliveries is reduced. There are characteristics that make relationships work, just as there are characteristics that make relationships fail. Relationships are more cost effective when the following conditions exist:

- *The parties are trustworthy.* When both parties are confident of their ability to trust each other, communication can be taken at face value. There is no need to suspect ulterior motives, look for hidden meaning, or constantly be afraid of one's vulnerability. Perhaps most essential is for the customer to perceive that the provider is sincerely interested in meeting his or her needs and is not just trying to sell capacity. If the customer believes that the provider is primarily interested in maximizing sales rather than providing benefits of value to the customer, the relationship can quickly end.
- *The parties are predictable to each other.* Unwanted, unexpected, and unpleasant surprises are anathema to relationships. Unexpected, pleasant surprises create the "wow" factor (i.e., customer delight) described in Chapter 7. Unexpected, unpleasant surprises can be tolerated occasionally if the provider has a good recovery program.
- *The parties have shared values.* In general, the more both parties share the same perceptions and values, the easier it will be for

them to relate. Shared values typically reduce the number of differences and make it easier to have a common basis for the relationship. On the other hand, diversity in values and perception may provide a broader base upon which to benchmark final solutions.

- *The parties have the ability to resolve differences.* Relationships are easy as long as there are no differences. The ability to deal with differences determines the strength of a relationship. Relationships are almost always based on competing interests. The buyer wants benefits and the provider is selling capacity. The buyer wants to pay a low price for the benefits. The provider wants to maximize yield from capacity. If there is an efficient way of dealing with these legitimate differences so that each party is satisfied, the relationship will be strong and lasting. If resolving these differences requires too much hassle (i.e., stress or control), the relationship quickly disintegrates.

There are some basic characteristics of a healthy, positive relationship. Fisher and Brown identified the following:

- *Balance emotion and reason.* Emotions are an important part of any relationship. The passion to achieve desired results motivates us to find a way to obtain resources and make relationships work. Also present are the disappointment of failure, the excitement of winning, and the camaraderie of working together on a successful team. Emotions help us communicate and show a depth of feeling and conviction. Emotions motivate. On the other hand, when emotion and reason are not balanced, communication suffers. Logic alone is not sufficient for solving problems and developing solutions. "We need both reason informed by emotions and emotion guided and tempered by reason."[5]
- *Understand the other party.* Although we may not agree with the other party, we still need to understand his or her interests, perceptions, and notions of fairness. Only if we understand can we create solutions acceptable to both.
- *Communicate clearly.* "The more openly we communicate, the less basis there is for suspicion. And the more we believe the other side has heard and understood our views, and we theirs, the more

likely we will feel that an agreement is fair and balanced. Within reasonable limits, the more communication, the better the working relationship."[6]

- *Be reliable.* Trust increases when we perform as expected by the other party. Thus "commitments entered into lightly or disregarded lightly are often worse than none."[7] Both reliability and trust are determined by making sure each party understands what is expected and that performance is according to expectations.

- *Be totally accepting of the other party.* Everyone wants to feel that he or she is an equal partner in a relationship. The person needs to feel accepted, worthy, and valued. The more accepted and valued he or she feels, the more cooperative the relationship. Acceptance does not necessarily mean agreement. You can accept the other person but realize that you may have valid disagreement on issues. It is often easy for professionals to look down on individuals who do not speak the same jargon or have the same status in the profession. When this occurs, the relationship suffers. The person is coming to the professional for a solution, not a procedure. The solution typically includes providing some degree of understanding or education about both the problem and the solution.

- *Be persuasive rather than coercive.* No one likes to feel pressured, and a person who experiences this will not be comfortable continuing the relationship. Coercion usually occurs when one party is more interested in the immediate outcome rather than the long-term relationship. A typical ploy used by conquest marketers is to tell the potential buyer that if he or she does not accept the offer immediately, the deal is off. Coercion may occur through worsening alternatives, scare tactics, warnings, threats, extortion, or physical force. The greater the coercion, the more one-sided the outcome. The less coercive, the more likely it is that differences will be resolved and that the outcome will be mutually beneficial.[8]

One major criticism channel members have had in working with large customers or suppliers has been defined as "being in the ring with a 2,000-pound gorilla." The perception (perception is reality in the mind of the beholder) is that the parties are adversaries and the only communication is "do it my way or else." This conveys the feeling of never being accepted as an equal and of the relationship being coercive.

What Makes Relationships Fail?

There are other actions that cause relationships to fail (i.e., result in ineffective outcomes and become costly). These actions include:

- This occurs when differences are denied or interpreted as failures in the relationship. One party may continually gives in to keep the other party from becoming upset. There will always be legitimate differences in any relationship. If these differences are legitimate, they improve the outcome by becoming a benchmark with which to test the final solution. A party who continually gives in is not helping develop an effective solution, only minimizing the dialogue that could help to develop a mutually acceptable solution.

  The greater the legitimate differences, the more important it is to have an effective process for evaluating options and making sure that the best solution is chosen. The more important the solution to the various parties, the more important the dialogue and benchmarking. On the other hand, if one party creates differences simply to get his or her way rather than working toward a better solution, that is coercive and counterproductive. Taken to the extreme, one of the parties may equate dialogue and legitimate differences as antagonism and put those with differences on an "enemies" list.[5] This adversarial, "us versus them" approach can then be used to justify breaking up the relationship rather than finding a solution to the problem. This virtually ensures that win-win relationships will not develop. Too often managers use this approach with employees and wonder why workers lose heart. Too often firms take this stance with customers and wonder why they don't return. Too often firms follow this approach with suppliers and wonder why suppliers perform according to the letter of the contract and don't recommend innovations that could be more effective. This does not mean that parties should not ever give in on differences. Both parties must agree to disagree, with each party giving in sometimes if something is especially important to the other party. When one party is forced to do all the giving

---

5. This is a view that often is taken by political groups. Those with legitimate differences may be seen as enemies.

in, especially when that party has few options, he or she can become embittered with the 2,000-pound gorilla who always wants his or her way.

The objective of the relationship is to develop solutions. As the various parties interact to develop the solution, the vision must always remain to achieve the most cost-effective solution that provides the greatest value to the customer. Sometimes the consensus will favor one party and sometimes the other. The most important thing is the relationship itself. As long as both parties see the value of the relationship as always being greater than the value of any single transaction, it will be advantageous to cooperate. That is the reason it is so important for firms to understand the value of a retained customer. This can be expressed mathematically:

Value of resolving issue = value of retained customer − cost of resolving issue.

Therefore, if the value of a Domino's Pizza customer is $5,000 and the conflict is over a $20 transaction, it is worth $4,980 to resolve the issue in a way that preserves the relationship. On the other hand, if Domino's always gives on every contested order, it may begin to establish a behavioral norm in which there is a different operable equation:

Value of giving in = value of retained customer − future cost of behavioral change.

If giving in reinforces a behavior that creates a $20.00 conflict every week, then the value of giving in is $5,000 − $20.00 × 52 weeks/ year × 10 years = $5,400. Thus the front-line individual responsible for handling the transaction may be making a $10,380 decision. That is the reason it is so important to have databases designed to track activities and profitability by customers, not just products.

It is in the interest of all parties to develop solutions that maximize the value of the benefits to the customer in a way so that everyone benefits. If the customers do not benefit, the providers may find they are without customers (and revenue). If the providers do not benefit, the buyers may soon find themselves without a supplier of solutions.

- *Partisan perceptions are maintained.* It is often easy to forget how differently people see things. A young single parent with two primary-school-aged children may view school board funding policies differently from a 45-year-old working couple with one teenager or a person who has never married. Orientals may place more importance on relationships, whereas American businesses may compete primarily from a price perspective. Older workers in middle management may see things differently than young workers with strong computer skills do. Unless we understand the other party's perspective, we will have difficulty developing solutions that are mutually beneficial.

- *Parties rely on reciprocity.* It is easy to expect that others will follow our lead. We may lead off with what we perceive as a "peace offering" so that others will follow suit and do something that we desire. When they do not, there is a tendency to believe that the other party is not trying to be constructive. What we seek is reciprocity, but in reality "two people will deal more skillfully with their differences if both behave rationally, both fully understand each other's perceptions, both communicate effectively, both are reliable, neither tries to coerce the other, and each accepts the other as someone whose interests and views deserve to be taken into account."[9]

Steps to Build a Strong Relationship

There are some steps that can be taken to build relationships. Foremost is to be unconditionally constructive in pursuing the relationship. "This means that in a relationship with you, I should do those thing and only those things that are both good for the relationship and good for me – whether or not you reciprocate."[10]

Fisher and Brown also provide a checklist that we can use to determine our relationship-building capability. Their view of unconditionally constructive behavior is summarized in Table 14.1. The first response to these relationship principles may be to suggest that they may work well in a family setting or even when negotiating between nations, but not in the normal business world. That is because we are accustomed to thinking that business is unilateral decision making. A person decides

Table 14.1. Unconditionally Constructive Behavior (from [9]).

Unconditionally constructive advice:	Good for the relationship because:	Good for me because:
1. Even if they are acting emotionally, balance emotion with reason.	An irrational battle is less likely.	I make fewer mistakes.
2. Even if they misunderstand us, try to understand them.	The better I understand, the fewer collisions we will have.	The less I shoot in the dark, the better solutions I can invent and the better able I am to influence you.
3. Even if they are not listening, inquire, consult, and listen to them before deciding on matters that affect them.	We both participate in making decisions. Better communication improves them.	I reduce the risk of making a mistake without giving up the ability to decide.
4. Even if they are trying to deceive us, neither trust them nor deceive them; be reliable.	It tends to build trust and confidence.	My words will have more impact.
5. Even if they are trying to coerce us, neither yield to that coercion nor try to coerce them; be open to persuasion and try to persuade them.	If people are persuaded rather than coerced, both the outcome and compliance are better.	By being open, I keep learning; it is easier to resist coercion if one is open to persuasion.
6. Even if they reject us and our concerns as unworthy of their consideration, accept them as worthy of our consideration, care about them, and be open to learning from them.	To deal well with our differences, I have to deal with you and have an open mind.	By dealing with you and reality, I remove obstacles to learning the facts and to persuading you on the merits.

what he or she wants and goes out and finds someone who has it for sale. An employer decides what he or she wants done and hires someone to do it. Decision making is at the top. We hire people to do, not to decide what to do. As soon as we shift our thinking to buying solutions and not things (or hands), we must shift thinking to getting both parties involved in defining needs and developing solutions. Unfortunately, when we think about defining needs (or relationships) the tendency is to think contracts.

How Good Is Our Relationship? A Checklist[11]
1. Goal
   - Am I trying to win the relationship or improve it?
   - How well do we resolve differences?
   - How often do I think about improving the process for working together over the long term?
2. General strategy
   - Do serious substantive issues disrupt our ability to work together?
   - Do I tend to retaliate by doing things that weaken our ability to deal with each other in the future?
   - Do I ignore problems or sweep them under the rug rather than deal with them?
3. Balance of emotion and rationality
   - Awareness: What emotions, mine and yours, are affecting our interactions?
   - Effect: How are emotions helping and hurting our decision-making?
4. Degree of understanding
   - How well do I empathetically understand your perceptions? interests? values? motivations?
   - How well can I state them to your satisfaction?
   - How well do you understand mine?
   - Can you state them to my satisfaction?
5. How effective is our two-way communication?
   - How regularly do I consult you before making decisions?
   - What important subjects don't we discuss? Why?
   - How extensively and frequently do we communicate? Do I listen?

6. Reliability: How much confidence do you have in my future conduct?
   - Might I be more reliable? How?
   - How could I be more worthy of trust?
   - Do your perceptions suggest some changes I might make?
   - What risks do I see in relying on you? Are those risks well founded?
7. Persuasion or coercion
   - Do I try to persuade you on the merits?
   - Could I be more open to persuasion? How?
   - How well do I avoid threats, warnings, and commitment tactics?
   - How extensively and frequently do we communicate? Do I listen?
8. Degree of mutual acceptance
   - Do I fully accept you as someone with whom to deal?
   - Do you matter in my scheme of things?
   - Am I giving serious attention to your interests and views?
   - Do I recognize the potential long-term quality of this relationship?

Contracting Tends to Make Relationships Unresponsive

In transaction relationships, the offer to sell (or the request to buy) is explicit. Both parties know what is involved. The worker knows his or her job description. The supplier has specifications issued by purchasing. The customer can examine the product in the marketplace. Where everything is known, transactions lend themselves to legal contracts. Therefore, there is a tendency to equate contracts with communication and understanding without realizing that the purpose of a contract is to eliminate uncertainty or change and therefore to restrict the possibility of responsiveness. The purpose of a written contract is to identify both parties' expectations, put them in writing, and have each party sign off on the written document. Problems arise when people, looking for a responsive provider of benefits, use contracts designed to eliminate change. This occurs when one or both parties become frustrated by the inflexibilities of the agreement. They desire a provider who is responsive to changing needs, but each change requires a new contract. This becomes obvious once the principles of contracting are seen in context.

The principle of written contracts began in 1677, when the English Parliament prohibited bringing any fraud case to court over a year after the agreement was made unless the agreement was written.[12] Thus written contracts were a method of spelling out all conditions of long-term agreements as understood by both parties at consummation. This was done to prevent the courtroom confusion when the testimony of each party, polarized by the emotions of conflict and time, provided no objective method of determining intent at the time the agreement was made.

Written contracts now are required by law under the following conditions:

- The agreement cannot be fully carried out in less than one year.
- The agreement is made upon consideration of marriage.
- The agreement is for the sale of land.
- The agreement is to serve as an executor or administrator of an estate.
- The agreement is for suretyship to be responsible for the debt of another person.[13]

In practical terms, however, written contracts typically are used only where:

- The desired benefits are understood clearly by both parties to the extent that all details can be stated explicitly in advance. If the need is still so general that it can be stated only in abstract terms such as "responsive," "high quality," "satisfactory service," "fair prices," and "to be provided when needed," it is difficult to write a meaningful contract because these words are subject to interpretation.
- The agreement is for an extended time period, such as in a conditional sales contract or a lease.
- It is a large purchase where there may be extreme risk to either or both parties, as with the purchase of a home or business.
- Delivery is to occur in the future, as in the case of constructing a home or payment of insurance.

Attorneys who write contracts are trained to write comprehensive, consolidated contracts. Contracts are considered to be comprehensive when they cover all possible future eventualities. Contracts are considered to be consolidated when all possible aspects of the agreement are covered. A consolidated contract covers not only the price but also such items as payment method, conflict resolution, performance criteria, all possible conditions for nonperformance, and contract changes.

The purpose of contracts is to create legal certainty and stability, not flexibility and responsiveness. Contracts are to be explicit (i.e., all relevant duties and conditions totally defined) and written to cover a stated period of time. This provides certainty and stability for both sides for the life of the contract. The objective of responsiveness, on the other hand, is to increase cost-effective delivery under changing conditions. When people or firms want solutions instead of predefined things or procedures, they want a relationship where the other party is responsive to their evolving needs, is sensitive to any special requirements that might evolve, and is more interested in solving evolving problems than being constricted by past agreements. Contracts, whether labor contracts or future performance contracts, tend to reduce flexibility and responsiveness.

Building Relationships

Relationships are developed, not negotiated. The motivation for a relationship is mutual benefit. Benefit is a measure of how well deliveries solve customer needs. The value of a relationship can be expressed as follows:

$$\text{Value of relationship} = \text{future value} \sum_{i=1}^{M} (\text{expected benefits}_i - \text{cost of obtaining benefits}_i)$$

where

Cost of obtaining benefits = economic cost + hassle + risk

Expected benefits = solution value = (customer value × fit).

Economic cost is typically the price of the delivery. Hassle includes all noneconomic costs, such as the effort required to place orders and locate potential providers. Risk includes all of the uncertainties about the delivery and the cost of protecting against risk, such as insurance, inspections, and contracting. When relationships exist for extended periods of time, they improve need diagnosis and delivery effectiveness as well as establish procedures that minimize the hassle of communicating needs and responses. When relationships are cooperative, they reduce the need to take protective measures. When relationships are responsive, they reduce the need for standby capacity and capability to handle special needs.

Consider a recent Saturday afternoon in the life of Rudy Gassner, vice president for capital goods at AMP, a manufacturer of electrical and electronic connectors. As Gassner was savoring a day off at home in Lemoyne, Pennsylvania, catching up on his reading, the phone rang. It was Silicon Graphics executive Greg Podshadley. Gassner's eyebrows shot up. Sure, Silicon Graphics was a big, valued customer in a close partnership with AMP, but Podshadley had never butted into his weekend at home before.

What Podshadley had to say was equally unexpected. He was in trouble. An electrical connector going into a new workstation was proving to be so undependable that it threatened to cause major quality problems for the product. No, it wasn't one of AMPs connectors; it was made by a competitor. But could Gassner supply a substitute – and at once? The snafu had brought the whole project to its knees, shutting down the line.

Gassner called his sales manager and sent him and his colleagues to the distribution center to hunt down the needed parts. Combing the cavernous, deserted facility, they hit pay dirt – the right connectors, and enough of them to put Podshadley's line back in business. Trouble was, they needed to use a dauntingly complicated forklift to get the parts, and none of the managers could work it. So, lucky that no underling was around to watch the comedy, they taught themselves by trial and error, picked up the connectors, and drove them to the airport. Silicon Graphics assemblers were soldering them onto circuit boards in California the next day.

Gassner did all this with zero paperwork – and without hinting that that's what happens when you buy from an AMP competitor. Nor did he charge Silicon Graphics a premium for the service. "This is an IOU to collect sometime," he said. Not surprisingly, Podshadley says he owes Gassner a big one: A lot was at stake. You can point fingers, and relationships can deteriorate very quickly.[14]

Customers Concerns.   As organizations become more responsive, there is less reliance on standardized solutions. When products were standardized, customers could go to the marketplace to examine them or depend upon the selection of familiar brand names. As deliveries become more customized, there is less tangible evidence for predicting performance. When there is less tangible evidence, customers have concerns. These concerns include:

How do I find a competent provider with the capabilities required to meet my needs? There are many providers. Each provider has vastly different abilities to diagnose and develop responsive solutions. Some are effective and others are not. If the delivery is inconsequential, there is little risk, but when the need is for a consultant to develop a crucial business plan or information systems, a lawyer to develop a critical legal defense, or a health care provider to help deal with a particularly difficult illness, the risk is great. Unless the customer already has a relationship with a trusted provider, he or she seeks clues that indicate competence. Customers may seek providers that they have met in a social, civic, or community context and with whom they feel comfortable. Insurance agents and other service providers often take a major leadership role in community groups (e.g., PTA, Lions clubs), just as consultants play a major role in professional groups.

If the customer does not know a provider personally, he or she may seek for competency clues. A hospital may hold a doll clinic so that small children can bring their sick (i.e., ripped) dolls and have them sewn up. Although the seamstress used by the hospital may have little to do with medicine, he or she conveys a sense of caring and concern. An allergist may release daily pollution counts to the local news media, which faithfully report them each day. A hospital may regularly present television clips on new developments in medicine that explain in lay terms the problem and how the new procedures will solve it.

Another major source of information is word of mouth. Customers typically ask friends for recommendations and look for examples of customer satisfaction. They are looking for some indication of competency.

How do I make sure the provider understands my needs? Although the provider may be very competent, he or she must understand the customer's needs. One approach is to ask for proposals or estimates. Government and firms may ask consultants for proposals. The purpose of the proposal is to determine how the provider would approach the problem. The proposal is one indicator of how well the potential provider understands the need. Individuals often obtain detailed estimates. The estimate not only conveys anticipated cost but also specifies work that will be done. If there is a substantial difference between potential providers, the customer may become concerned about how well the provider understands the need.

Too often providers unilaterally diagnose the need and recommend solutions without involving the customer. The providers may feel that they are indicating their superior knowledge and capability, but it is easy for the customer to view this as a "Do I have a deal for you!" approach that includes little concern for the customer's needs and feelings. If the introductory and courtship periods of the relationship have not occurred before the proposal (i.e., estimate) stage, the trust level will not be high. One way of building this relationship is by the questions and answers provided during the proposal stage. Attorneys provide initial visits. Products are provided for free trials. However it is done, customers are looking for some indication of how well the provider understands their needs and what they can expect of the relationship. A proposal without customer input is simply the sale of a cookie-cutter solution, not a responsive solution to the customer's need. Even though the cookie-cutter solution may be appropriate, the customer may not perceive it to be, and the customer's perception is his or her reality.

How do I make sure the provider prescribes what I actually need? Unless there is a close relationship built on trust, the customer may be leery that the provider is more interested in increasing sales than in solving his or her needs. Do cabs take longer routes to run up the bill with riders who are unfamiliar with the area? Do auto repair centers make unnecessary repairs? Why does it seem that as soon as one thing is fixed something else needs to be worked on? Do physicians perform unnecessary surgeries or conduct unnecessary tests? Do chiropractors reschedule patients until their insurance benefits or ability to pay are exhausted? Do lawyers delay cases and create controversy to increase fees? Has an exterminator ever inspected a home and not found termites?

The customer is not always only concerned about overprescribing. Sometimes the customer wants greater benefits and the provider emphasizes cost. Fundamental to any relationship is the customer's perception that the provider understands his or her need and that the primary emphasis is on a delivery plan that is best for the customer. As long as that perception survives, the relationship survives. As soon as that perception is gone, the relationship is over.

What protective steps do I need to take to protect against possible risks? During delivery there are many concerns about issues other than the actual delivery itself. For example, "Can I leave my keys with the provider?" In many cases, the provider (e.g., an extermination service, an appliance repair service, an automobile repair shop, a parking attendant) needs access to a customer's home or car during delivery. The most convenient way to manage this is for the customer to give the provider a key to his or her home or car. Doing so, however, raises many kinds of security issues because the homeowner or car owner is in essence giving up the primary source of personal security in the home or car. (The provider's employee can make copies of the key and thus gain or give access to the home or car at will whether the owner is present or not.) The alternative is to supervise every action of the provider. This may require staying home from work, coordinating schedules, and spending the time it takes to watch all actions. Before the relationship develops, the customer may be concerned that delivery will not conform to the promise. That is one reason for elaborate tracking systems so that customer requests can be effectively answered. It is human nature for individuals to become anxious and seek reassurance when they have no tangible evidence of progress toward delivery. Part of trust is confidence that the provider will deliver as promised.

One action that may be the most destructive to a relationship is when the provider will not interact with the customer and recommend appropriate changes to a solution. One of the major concerns in government contracting is how to handle changes. In the majority of cases, government employees have not totally defined needs when they issue requests for proposals. In fact, the reason they request proposals is that they are looking for alternative approaches to solving a problem. Reviewers recognize that there are often many solutions for any given problem. A major concern is the relationship with the contractor once the contract is awarded. No one knows the future. Otherwise there would be no need for proposals; the customer would have known how the work should be done and would have had all the details defined. Therefore, the ability to work together and dynamically change the definition of the work to keep pace with the learning curve as work progresses is mandatory for success. Some contractors continually blame their unresponsiveness on the contract. Other contractors use the changes to justify negotiated charges. In fact, some firms will bid low on large projects to obtain the contract, knowing that they can profit from the change orders. It is the relationship that keeps changes and change orders balanced so that both groups win.

If the government procurement example seems too remote, think of returning to a garage to pick up your car and hearing a comment such as, "Your gas line is leaking but you didn't tell us to fix it. I wouldn't drive it if I were you." However it is manifested, customers want providers who will use their best judgment to benefit them (the customer). If additional information becomes available during delivery, the provider needs to communicate and act accordingly.

How can I know that delivery is effective? The more intangible the delivery, the more concern the customer has about its effectiveness. How does the customer know that the roof repair or termite treatment was effective? How does the customer know that the chemotherapy or the legal defense was most appropriate? How does the customer know that the automobile repair shop will fix the problem? How does the customer know that the title search was actually done? Sometimes it may take years to know the answers to such questions. By then the provider has the money and may be out of business. This is the reason for bonds, guarantees, and insurance. Otherwise, the customer only has faith in the relationship with the provider.

How do I get satisfaction in case the delivery does not solve my problem? If my need is not effectively solved, what recourse does the customer have? Will the provider deny responsibility, quibble over technicalities, blame it on someone else, or ignore the customer, or will the provider make sure my problem is solved? If the provider takes ownership of the customer's problem, the customer can relax. If not, the customer must take a variety of steps (e.g., incur Williamson's transaction costs) to protect himself or herself in case of service failure.

One method used to allay this fear is to offer guarantees. Some guarantees have extensive fine print, such as "we will match any price" (unless it is from a wholesale club or does not have our private brand on it) or "guaranteed for as long as you have a service contract." Others have guarantees such as Lands End's "Guaranteed. Period." and a track record that reinforces the words. Heskett suggests that guarantees should be meaningful to both the customer and provider, easy to define and invoke, credible, and able to define a standard of responsiveness.[15]

A second method for allaying this fear is to have well-developed recovery mechanisms backed by a recovery philosophy. This provides the front-line worker a guideline to follow for periodic failures and a philosophy to follow in case of a unique failure.

How long will I have to wait? Waiting brings uncertainty. Everyone knows that activities that require the interaction between two parties will involve a waiting period. One party will almost always be earlier than the other. The way that activities are scheduled indicates the perceived relationship between customer and provider. Activities are scheduled on a first-come, first-served basis when the provider's time is perceived as being more valuable than the customer's. The longer the wait, the greater the perception of difference in value. First-come, first-served queues are used to regulate flows, to maximize provider utilization, and to provide back-up demand to cover no-shows. All waiting is done by the customer. Thus there is a high cost to the user but little or no perceived cost to the provider – only to the relationship, if waiting periods are too long.

Activities can also be scheduled by fixed, chronological time. This method conveys an equality of time value but is expensive to both the customer and the provider. Both customer and provider need to allow "catch-up" time between appointment to allow for inevitable variation in the time required for prior activities. This also limits the ability of both the provider and customer to "work in" short-notice needs.

The term *waiting on* tables or *waiting on* customers alludes to this method. An alternative to having the provider wait for a single customer is to build an information system that can collect and organize requests for service and approximate contact time (between provider and customer) when the call is made. This method is used by radio-dispatched cabs. When the call is received, the customer is told that it will be approximately 20 minutes before the cab arrives. This method does not require "catch-up" time, but responsiveness will be dependent upon current capacity utilization. To maintain relationships with the customer, there should be some method of notifying customers as early as possible of any unforeseen time delays and of developing contingency plans for recovery.

Take, as an illustration, the case of Lee, a newly hired detail man for a pharmaceutical company. His boss explained the company's policy of calling on class A accounts every three weeks, class B accounts every five weeks, and class C accounts every ten weeks. Accounts were classified by sales volume. As a single parent with two young children in day care, Lee was concerned about the caregiver's reaching him in case his children had an emergency, so he obtained a beeper. Without thinking, Lee placed the beeper number on his calling cards. Lee soon began to receive calls from physicians and hospitals wanting information on drugs. He promised to always respond by the next day. Sales rapidly increased. So Lee obtained a cellular phone. Then he promised to return calls within five minutes. Sales again increased dramatically. His competitor, who had been serving the area from an office 180 miles distant, moved an additional salesperson into Lee's area just to counteract his impact. Sales increased so dramatically that Lee became one of the top salespersons in the company within a year's time and has remained at that level. The only problem was that Lee's company was concerned that Lee did not follow the company's plan of making regularly scheduled calls on customers. Lee explained, "I don't make sales calls, I just respond when they have questions."

However scheduling is done, the relationship is improved if the provider makes efforts to reduce the perception of wait times. There are various ways of doing this:

- Provide music, magazines, television, or other diversions to involve the customer during the wait because occupied time seems shorter than unoccupied time.
- Engage the customer in the service delivery as soon as possible because preprocess waiting periods feel longer than in-process waits.
- Take steps to let the customer know how long a wait to expect because uncertain waiting periods seem longer than known, finite waits.
- Explain the reasons for the waits because unexplained waiting periods seem longer than those that have been explained beforehand.
- Watch for individuals with special needs because anxiety makes waiting periods seem especially long.[16]

How will I interface with the provider? At the beginning of every relationship, both parties are uncertain how to interact. This interaction uncertainty takes two forms: locational uncertainty and functional uncertainty. How do I find the provider's facility? Where will I park? How do I get between different sites? These questions are especially important for providers such as hospitals, where patients may be routed to many different labs, clinics, and offices. Being able to follow colored lines, simple maps, or signs helps reassure and comfort the customer. Large stores, such as Home Depot, often present an imposing task for a customer searching for a particular small item. Clerks who nonjudgmentally offer guidance, alphabetic lists of items showing location, computerized self-help indexes, and other methods of reducing disorientation are most helpful. Even the organization of small items, such as fasteners and plumbing parts, to reduce "visual noise" can make a major difference to customers with visual problems such as presbyopia (which occurs suddenly for many people around age 45 and often necessitates bifocals) or a stigmatism.

Functional disorientation occurs when customers do not understand how an organization works. It results in people calling what the organization perceives to be the wrong department and being rerouted to several locations before having the problem solved. Customers may not understand the airline pricing system or all of the conditions for using tickets and frequent-flyer redemptions. They may not understand medical insurance and billing issues. They have difficulty understanding how to find their size when shopping at some clothing stores. One very enlightening exercise is to have a manager listen to CCPs and observe the percent of each CCP's time spent:

- Explaining to the customer how to use the firm's system.
- Rerouting the customer to the "proper" person to handle the problem.
- Disciplining the customer to follow the firm's procedures.

If a manager does this, he or she will be surprised to learn how often the CCP believes that the customer's approach for solving the problem is more logical than the organization's system. When this occurs, the CCP is often placed in the embarrassing position of admitting that the organization's system is illogical but that it was designed by management and that he or she, after all, is only an employee. Efforts made to provide a single contact person who is able to resolve all questions can substantially enhance relationships. Hospitals such as the Lakeland Regional Medical Center in Florida find that the use of cross-trained care teams reduces the number of staff members encountered by the patient during a four-day stay from 53 to 13.[17] It is comforting for the patient to know and understand who is responsible for solving his or her needs. Customers are comfortable contacting their travel agent, their doctor, their salesperson, their project monitor, their mechanic, their exterminator, their insurance agent, or their financial advisor with a need and feeling confident that all of the details required to solve the problem will be considered. In fact, when customers use the terms "*my* mechanic" or "*my* doctor," it is a good sign. This shows that the relationship has reached the point where the customer has begun to identify with the provider. Customers want the bonding. This bonding reduces customer stress because the CCP will take care of things and the customer will not have to learn the provider's system.

Thus, strong customer relationships develop where there is a corporate culture dedicated to solving the customer's problem and minimizing the hassle require for the customer to obtain a solution. For this to happen, the CCP must understand the customer's needs and management must provide the tools and facilities that enable the CCPs to respond and empower them to do so. For the relationship with customers to be strong, CCPs need to understand the value of the relationship and the importance of unconditionally constructive behavior. With time, trust develops. The greater the trust, the easier and more comfortable the relationship and the more cost-effective the delivery. Trust is not always giving in; it is often a faith that whatever happens, the parties will work together to resolve the problem. But how does an organization create relationships with employees so they accept their empowerment and focus on delivering value to customers?

Employee Concerns.   Responsive management, predicated on employees accepting empowerment, requires reversing the traditional management/ labor class system and hierarchical command structure. (For many years, the family-owned farm provided workers who understood empowerment, but with the decline in farms this supply of workers has diminished.) The traditional relationship between employer and employee has been based on several perceptions. These perceptions convey a set of beliefs:

- Management's role is to define and organize work, and the worker's role is to do as instructed.
- Management is responsible, so a worker cannot be fired who does

what he or she is told, but the employee who takes the initiative is not protected.

- Management is constantly trying to develop schemes to get workers to do more, lower wages, reduce job security, and avoid having to pay benefits. Management would like to hire less expensive young workers and lay off older workers before they are eligible to receive their retirement.
- "You get paid less than you're worth in the first half of your career and more than you're worth in the second half."[18]
- If a manager is a company person, the company will give him or her job security.

These perceptions did little to encourage workers to accept the ownership of customer problems and to develop innovative solutions. Workers did not perceive their responsibility for initiating work rule changes or process changes or for maintaining customer relationships. Management initiatives were often viewed with suspicion. ("Here is another management scheme to get more work out of us or to reduce our entitlements. Hang tight and this effort will pass also.")

Some employees feel obligated to serve the customer in spite of management restrictions. Take, for instance, a regional jewelry and merchandise outlet that has a large share of the local wristwatch market. For many years, the chain would replace batteries in customer's watches. Now company policy does not allow employees to replace batteries in digital watches. Two of the eleven employees in the jewelry section empathize with customers and explain that the problem is that some digital watches need to be reset after the battery is replaced and that most employees have not been trained how to do that. These two employees then tell the customer how to reset the watch. It takes approximately 20 seconds to make the explanation. If the customer is fortunate and talks with one of these two employees, the conversation goes like this: "The fellow in the blue shirt by the diamond case is the manager. If you come back while he is on break in about 45 minutes, I will put it in for you." When the customer returns while the manager is on break, the employee replaces the battery at no charge (except for the battery) and appears to be glad to help. The customer is delighted by the worker and a relationship begins to develop. The employee apologizes for having to have the customer come back but explains that he would be "written up" if the manager saw him replace the battery. The relationship bond with the store (and the manager) are not strengthened, however.

The task facing responsive management is to reverse the centuries-old culture. This culture has involved:

- Standardized processes and procedures,
- Training employees only for tasks they are required to perform,
- Restricting employees to performing only tasks they are trained and instructed to do,
- Careful supervision to make sure employees do as told.

Responsive management must change cultures so it is ok if employees want to serve customers, want to be part of the work team, and truly feel empowered to commit the company to serve the customer and to make suggestions for changing the delivery process. Workers sometimes understand the benefit of doing so, but the perceived need to protect themselves is very great. After all, management may give lip service to empowerment today but revert to traditional managerial styles tomorrow.

Change is often easier if it can be focused on solving a specific customer's needs or helping a specific employee improve. Workers can identify with individuals, whether they are customers or employees, but they have difficulty identifying with impersonal processes and procedures unless they were personally involved in developing them. Employees (both workers and managers) often view process and procedure changes handed down by higher management with suspicion.

Therefore, relationship building works best when it is focused, preferably on individuals who are convinced that their input is indeed wanted and used. Deming used the term "quality circle" to describe teams of 5 to 15 employees assigned to address quality problems.[19] He indicated that quality teams could be effective if they were composed of people from multiple disciplines that could "work without fear of taking a risk."[20] Workers understand participative, representative government, so when they are chosen to represent their discipline (e.g., their department or skill), their perception of their role changes, just as it does when they are appointed to the transit authority or to the school board. When they perceive that their role has changed, they act differently. If the organization is to build on this perceived role change, management must facilitate committee efforts to implement the recommended changes.

Unless management facilitates the implementation of the team's efforts, the entire process loses credibility. Deming expressed this well:

> In my experience people can face almost any problem except the problems of people. They can work long hours, face declining business, face loss of jobs, but not the problems of people. Faced with problems of people (management included), management, in my experience, go into a state of paralysis, taking refuge in formation of QC-Circles and groups for EI, EP, and QWL (Employee Involvement, Employee Participation, and Quality of Work Life). The groups predictably disintegrate within a few months from frustration, finding themselves unwilling parties to a cruel hoax, unable to accomplish anything for the simple reason that no one in management will take action on suggestions for improvement. These are devastatingly cruel devices to get rid of the problems of people. . . . The possibility of pride of workmanship means more to the production worker than gymnasiums, tennis courts, and recreation areas. Give the work force a chance to work with pride, and the 3 percent that apparently don't care will erode itself by peer pressure.[21]

The purpose of the concept room described in Chapter 13 is to help managers and worker teams as they visualize and reach consensus on needed improvements. For information systems, the visualization tools may include entity relationship diagrams and screen generators for various business events. Concept rooms are not just used for the development of information systems. They can be used anytime to get a group of knowledgeable people together to focus their attention on a specific area and to develop a consensus solution. The key elements of the concept room are:

- A facilitator who can keep the discussion moving and on track,
- Visualization tools that help the group focus on the issue at hand.
- Knowledgeable people who understand the need and can offer suggestions and arrive at a consensus,
- A recorder who is able to capture the essence of the discussion.

The same approach can be used to design animated movies, design information systems, review existing protocols, or even review diagnostic methods used to identify a customer's needs. In some cases, the "visualization" tools may be auditory. For example, a recording of a particularly bad 911 call can be played to the group to focus their attention on improving future responses.

Relationship management is an attitude between management and workers. This relationship can be the traditional autocratic "do as you are told" connection, or something more interactive. Hyrum Smith, developer of the Franklin Planner, describes the role of the servant-leader who motivates people to perform at a higher level. Workers observe management's interest in them, and this motivates workers to have the same interest in supporting the manager and the organization's goals.[22] When management is there to understand and facilitate workers, workers will in turn be there to understand and facilitate the solution of customer problems. This is another way of saying that when management removes the risk of employees taking pride in their work and accepting empowerment, employees respond. As long as management is concerned primarily about controlling performance, the risk to the employee is too high.

The Ritz-Carlton has done an outstanding job of empowering and enabling employees to respond to customers. This is especially significant because of the immense socio-economic differences between the guest and the workers. Many of the workers are young, often without extensive formal education, and not always from the same higher income groups they serve. Significantly, the president of Ritz-Carlton, Horst Schulze, began as did many of his employees – as a worker in one of the hotels. Each employee is given a card that he or she is expected to memorize and to carry at all times. The central message on the front of the card minimizes this difference in socio-economic status between worker and guest: "We are ladies and gentlemen serving ladies and gentlemen." The credo on the card defines the hotel's desired relationship with the customer.

> The Ritz-Carlton Hotel is a place where the genuine care and comfort of our guests is our highest mission.
>
> We pledge to provide the finest personal service and facilities for our guests who will always enjoy a warm, relaxed yet refined ambiance.
>
> The Ritz-Carlton experience enlivens the senses, instills well-being, and fulfills even the unexpressed wishes and needs of our guests.

Responsive Relationships

The three steps of service are designed to focus employee attention on the customer:

1. A warm and sincere greeting. Use the guest's name, if and when possible.
2. Anticipation and compliance with guest's needs.
3. Fond farewell. Give guests a warm good-bye and use their names, if and when possible.

Twenty basic principles are listed on the inside of the card. These basic principles emphasize the importance of various standards and procedures:

- Using teamwork;
- Training certification to build employees' knowledge base;
- Anticipating and knowing customer needs;
- Identifying facility or other defects throughout the hotel;
- Taking ownership of each customer's complaint, which means each employee who receives a complaint pacify the guest immediately and follow up in 20 minutes to verify customer satisfaction;
- Recording all guest complaints;
- Doing what it takes to solve problems;
- Maintaining cleanliness. Cleanliness everywhere is every employee's responsibility;
- Being "on stage" with smile, eye contact, and proper vocabulary (e.g., "Certainly," "I'll be happy to," "My pleasure");
- Escorting guests rather than pointing or directing guests, which applies to every employee;
- Being able to answer all guest questions;
- Using good telephone etiquette, including answering with a smile and minimizing transfers;
- Presenting a good appearance with uniforms, cleanliness, name tags, and grooming;
- Knowing contingency guidelines and roles in case of emergencies;
- Using backup (supervisors) to resolve issues such as safety hazards, injuries, or equipment problems the employee is unable to handle;
- Ensuring that every employee takes responsibility for protecting Ritz-Carlton assets.

Every supervisor is responsible for making sure that every input from every employee is handled with respect. The workers are the eyes and the ears. They do the work. Management must not only facilitate the workers in their role but make sure that they know they are important. They are indeed "ladies and gentlemen serving ladies and gentlemen," not servants.

Just as responsive relationships with customers are dependent upon empowered relationships with employees, they are also dependent upon effective relationships with suppliers.

Supplier Relationships. The relationship with a supplier is based upon the supplier providing solutions to problems, not just products or services. Like customers, a major relationship motivator is the expected value of the relationship. The major inhibitors are hassle and risk. Too often firms talk relationships but their actions and procedures speak so loudly that suppliers cannot understand their words.

Firms are just now beginning to develop an experience base for initiating partnerships. Typically, they begin by selecting a few primary suppliers that have a proven track record. (This simply means that they have worked together long enough to begin to develop a level of trust.)

The supplier becomes more solution oriented when the customer opens up previously confidential data (e.g., sales forecasts, production schedules, design requirement, and so forth) so that the supplier can apply its knowledge base to developing a solution. This has been done in many ways. The sales forecast and production schedules allow the supplier to produce according to customer forecast so that the supplier has the maximum possible lead time. The design requirements allow the supplier to suggest alternate designs that may be more cost effective. Wal-Mart did this with P&G, applying what Don Bechtel refers to as "inverting the traditional bow-tie communication pattern" shown in Figure 14.1. Traditionally firms routed all communication to the customer through the salesperson. Likewise, all communication from the customer was filtered through purchasing.

The Wal-Mart/P&G approach was to bring supplier personnel on-site to work with their counterparts. (See Figure 14.1.) This allowed P&G marketing personnel to work directly with Wal-Mart marketing personnel, P&G logisticians with Wal-Mart logisticians, and so forth. In essence, this eliminated the filter and time delay caused by the sales-

Responsive Relationships

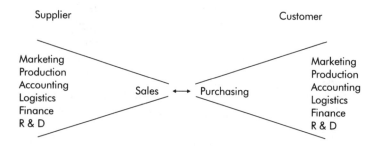

Supplier   Customer

Marketing   Marketing
Production   Production
Accounting   Sales ←→ Purchasing   Accounting
Logistics   Logistics
Finance   Finance
R & D   R & D

Figure 14.1. A traditional bow-tie relationship.

(Source: Presentation by Wal-Mart and P&G at the Council of Logistics Management Annual Meeting, October, 1992.)

purchasing interface. As a result of this organizational structure, each functional area created many different improvements that substantially reduced cost and increased effectiveness.

Partnerships also reduce transaction costs. Cooperative efforts allow the integration of information systems to lower the cost of processing transactions. Scan data can be relayed to suppliers to permit continuous replenishment. Insurance claims can be processed electronically, thus eliminating the cost and time required to process paper, write checks, send invoices, and so forth. Firms can track deliveries, place their own orders, check flight availability, reserve rooms, and even transfer cash electronically. As relationships develop, the boundaries between customer and supplier become more transparent, not only for personnel but also for information. As firms cooperate, they begin to understand each other's needs and find opportunities for reducing costs. Deming stressed the need for more reliable output to eliminate the need for inspections, scrap, and rework. But these are not the only risks that need to be addressed. Organizations have other risks. The purchaser has concerns:

- *The risk of nonavailability.* The purchaser may be concerned that the product or service will not be available when needed. The supplier may have operational complications such as labor, suppliers, fire, or other difficulties. On the other hand, the customer's needs may grow faster than the supplier is able to respond. This

Figure 14.2. Interactive, cross-functional teams.

(Source: Presentation by Wal-Mart and P&G at the Council of Logistics Management Annual Meeting, October, 1992.)

is one reason that traditional procurement methods included multiple suppliers.

- *The risk of nonadaptablility.* The purchaser may be concerned that the provider will not be able to adapt to meet changing customer needs. Even very respectable firms sometimes have difficulty adapting to change, as evidenced by the struggle by firms such as IBM, Wang, and DEC to adapt to new-era client servers using microcomputers.

The provider also has risks:

- *The risk of losing business.* Firms are quick to describe examples of small firms entering into partnership agreements with larger firms and being treated well for the first year but finding that by the second year the customer may begin to demand concessions. By the third year, the demand for concessions may become too great, and the supplier realizes that the customer views the supplier as expendable.
- *The risk of specialization.* The supplier, responding to the specialized needs of the partner, may make a large investment in specialized capacity or capability. When this is done, the supplier's investment is at risk unless the relationship will continue for the life of the assets.

Currently, firms are obtaining the advantages of cooperation but avoiding these risks by focusing on large providers of stable needs and developing long-term agreements. It has been difficult for many partnership managers to think of integrating activities across organizational boundaries. They have justified the required effort to integrate information systems, production schedules, and distribution channels by focusing on large relationships or by increasing the size of the relationships. The size of the relationships is increased by reducing the number of suppliers.

As firms learn to relate to suppliers on a cooperative basis, they will understand that they can also relate to customers on a cooperative basis. They will learn that they can develop information systems as described in Chapter 13 that allow them to have the same cooperative relationship with customers of various sizes. Management becomes customer responsive when it realizes that the benefits of cooperation can be obtained from virtually all relationships once they understand how to apply cooperative methods generally. Grocery chains are beginning to develop methods of identifying customers electronically and tracking their activity. Initially, these electronic marketing efforts are justified by showing the value of customer retention for the 10% of customers that make the most purchases.[6] (See Table 14.2.)

The proponents of electronic marketing advocate providing special treatment (e.g., pricing, credit) to these frequent buyers to increase customer loyalty. As supply-chain firms become comfortable with this approach, cooperative relationship-building efforts will expand and be extended to all customers, large and small. It will then become as illogical to use different systems for different customers as it is to limit the use of automatic tellers to large customers only or to only use airline or hotel reservation systems for frequent flyers. As firms become more comfortable with their prototypes, they will increasingly use the information on the customer's files to differentiate customer's needs so that various guidelines can be used to respond to customers individually. Then even supply-chain firms become customer-responsive service organizations.

---

6. For an excellent study of electronic marketing, see *Measured Marketing: A Tool to Shape Food Store Strategy*, Atlanta, Coca-Cola Retailing Research Council, 1994 (1-800-GET-COKE).

Table 14.2. Grocery Store Customer Activity by Decile[6]

Decile	Average annual purchase
10	3,674
9	1,830
8	1,148
7	733
6	480
5	313
4	205
3	129
2	74
1	29

Summary

Historically, a firm's business relationships – whether with customers, employees, or suppliers – have been predicated on the firm's knowing what it wanted. The firm unilaterally planned and produced a product and offered it to the customer. The firm unilaterally determined its labor needs, defined the job descriptions, and offered employment to potential workers. The firm unilaterally determined its need for raw materials and supplies and contacted suppliers with their specifications. All relationships were based on unilateral offers; the other party could accept the offer, make a counteroffer, or withdraw from the transaction. The common characteristic of all these relationships is that each party knew its needs and had an arm's-length relationship with the other party.

In the fourth era, each party recognizes that it does not have all the information it requires to totally define its needs. The parties seek solutions to their needs, not just products. They depend upon the knowledge base of the other party to help them fully diagnose the need and develop a plan for solving it. When the customer or firm was merely seeking a product, the product stood on its own merits. If the product met specifications, it did not matter who supplied it. When a customer goes to a firm for help in diagnosing and solving a need, it is a much different experience. It takes time and effort to interact with different providers to get their recommendations.[7] It is expensive for firms to diagnose complicated needs and develop plans for solutions.[8]

As needs become more complicated and as conditions become more dynamic, relationships shift from the impersonal, unilateral relationship in the marketplace to a much more interactive, collaborative, and personal relationship. These relationships are typically long-term relationships built not on long-term contracts but on a thorough understanding that the long-term value to both parties is too great to let any individual item disrupt the relationship. There are various reasons why these collaborative, long-term relationships not only increase the effectiveness of diagnosis and delivery but also reduce delivery cost. Relationships work when there is trust, shared values, and the ability to resolve differences. Characteristics of a good relationship, including the balancing of emotion and reason, understanding the other party, being reliable, and using persuasion rather than coercion. Relationships fail when we interpret relationships differences as failure, maintain partisan perceptions, or rely upon reciprocity. There are steps that can be taken to build a strong relationship. Contracts work well when all conditions of an agreement are understood in advance, but they are not effective in dynamic situations where conditions and needs are consistently changing.

In relationships, each party has concerns. Customers have concerns. Employees have concerns. Providers have concerns. For relationships to be effective, the concerns of each party need to be addressed because relationships work well when both parties feel comfortable working with each other.

---

7. Public agencies often issue requests for proposals (RFP). The purpose of the proposal is to have each provider describe its understanding of the problem and submit its recommendations for a delivery plan.

8. It is expensive for firms to write proposals to solicit government contracts. It is expensive for contractors to draw up plans and cost out construction projects. It is expensive for automobile repair shops to diagnose needs and give estimates on repairs. Often there is a substantial charge for the diagnosis and estimate. This charge may be refunded if the customer has this provider do the work.

References

[1] Lewis Stern at 1994 American Marketing Association Faculty Consortium, Stone Mountain Park, Georgia, June, 1994.

[2] Ronald Henkoff, "Service is Everybody's Business," *Fortune*, June 27, 1994, pp. 48–60, © 1994 Time Inc. All rights reserved.

[3] Adapted from GETTING TOGETHER. Copyright © 1988 Roger Fisher and Scott Brown. Reprinted by permission of Houghton Mifflin Co. All rights reserved. p. vii.

[4] Ibid., p. 7–8.

[5] Ibid., p. 10.

[6] Ibid., p. 11.

[7] Ibid., p. 11.

[8] Ibid., pp. 11, 12.

[9] Ibid., p. 31.

[10] Ibid., p. xiv.

[11] Ibid., p. 38–40.

[12] Reprinted from *The Law of Contracts*, John D. Calamari and Joseph M. Perillo, Second edition, 1977, with permission of the West Publishing Corporation. pp. 672–673.

[13] Ibid., pp. 672–673.

[14] Myron Magnet, "The New Golden Rule of Business," *Fortune*, February 21, 1994, p. 60. © 1994 Time Inc. All rights reserved.

[15] James L. Heskett, *Managing in the Service Economy*, Boston: Harvard Business School Press, 1986, p. 3.

[16] David H. Maister, "The Psychology of Waiting Lines," *The Service Encounter*, edited by John A. Czepiel, Michael R. Solomon and Carol F. Surprenant, Lexington, KY: Lexington Books, pp. 113–123.

[17] Len Berry, 1994 American Marketing Association Faculty Consortium, Stone Mountain Park, Georgia, June, 1994.

[18] James Medoff, cited in Brian O'Reilly, "The New Deal: What Companies and Employees Owe One Another," *Fortune*, June 13, 1994, p. 50. © 1994 Time Inc. All rights reserved.

[19] Reprinted from *Out of the Crisis* by W. Edwards Deming by permission of MIT and The W. Edwards Deming Institute. Published by MIT, Center for Advanced Engineering Study, Cambridge, MA 02139. Copyright 1982 by The W. Edwards Deming Institute.

[20] Ibid., p. 64.

[21] Ibid., p. 85.

[22] Hyrum W. Smith, *The 10 Natural Laws of Successful Time and Life Management*, New York: Warner Books, 1994, p. 204.

CHAPTER 15

THE EVOLVING BUSINESS FOCUS: PRODUCTION TO CUSTOMER RESPONSIVENESS

When a new era evolves, there are many events that contribute to its evolution. Many of these evolving concepts at first appear to be unrelated, but collectively they have enabled the new era to evolve. Customer responsiveness is no exception. Most of these events have their origins outside of business management, but each has had a strong impact on business process design. These events are not organized chronologically or in order of importance. In fact, if this era is in fact different, it is in the number and diversity of factors that are concurrently ushering in the customer responsive age. Some of the more obvious of these factors are:

1. The rethinking of the mass-production approach to productivity,
2. The rise and restructuring of the services economy,
3. The evolution of organizations,
4. The shifting view of capitalism from ownership to resource,
5. The evolution of the information age,
6. The information modeling approach to analysis,
7. The evolving restructuring of responsive organizations.

Rethinking the Mass-Production Approach to Productivity

Taaiichi Ohno has been quoted as saying that the impetus for the Toyota production system was cost reduction. The result, however, was a rethinking of the mass-production, scientific-management approach to organizing business processes. After 39 years, Ohno learned that to achieve true cost control, Toyota needed to "accept orders from each customer and make products that differ according to individual requirements" and to realize that "it is much more economical to make each item one at a time." He continued that "the Toyota production system, however, is not just a production system. I am confident it will reveal its

367

strength as a management system adapted to today's era of global markets and high-level computerized information systems."[1]

Toyota has achieved high visibility. The U.S. car industry was shocked into becoming open-minded by the loss of market share to Japan. Toyota was a prominent part of Japan's success. American automobile manufacturer managers listened to Ohno and others who helped identify those factors that inhibited responsiveness. The Toyota production process taught:

1. Even automobile manufacturing, the classic example of mass production, could allow customers to *special order* according to their individual needs and receive their request within a few days.

2. Instead of large-lot, mass production of automobiles, Toyota, for cost reasons, mingled products of different units on the same production line. Monden explains that at Toyota "the means for adapting production to variable demand is called *production smoothing.* Through production smoothing, a production line is no longer committed to the manufacture of a single type of product in vast lot sizes; instead, a single line must produce many varieties each day in response to variegated customer demand. Therefore, production is kept up-to-date and inventory is cut."[2]

3. Toyota *separated the scheduling of capacity to do work from the scheduling of the work itself.* Capacity is the ability to do work. When employees are *cross-trained,* they can do maintenance, cleaning, and other work besides assembling vehicles. When one worker needs relief, the connecting workers are able to cover in a manner similar to the use of the baton touch zone used in track and field relay races.[3] This allows work to be scheduled in the immediate run. The separation of capacity and work scheduling allowed a different relationship with the customer. The traditional approach had been either to stock large inventories so customer orders could be filled off the shelf or to require the customer to commit to long lead times so there would be adequate time to plan production schedules. Once commitments were made, they could not be changed. Instead Toyota used historical data and market forecasts to predict capacity needs.

Next, they encouraged dealers to order early. The early order (ten days) was not invariable but could be changed any time up to two days before production began. Just like hotel or airline reservations, these orders have not been seen as locked-in commitments but rather early manifestations of intent to assist Toyota in fine-tuning production forecasts (as described in Chapter 8). The Toyota production process allows the focus to be on eliminating the unexpected variation rather than on eliminating variation in demand.

4. Toyota demonstrated that it could be no more responsive to customers than its suppliers were to them. Thus they developed a *just-in-time* (JIT) supply of components whereby work was dispatched by tickets called "Kanbans." At first Japanese suppliers resisted. They wanted to retain long lead times and locked-in commitments.[4]

5. Production lines could be made more responsive even for the mass production of automobiles. Machine tool changeover could be done in seconds or minutes rather than days or weeks. Workers could be trained to do many tasks instead of specializing in only one. Production lines could be organized to intermix models. In fact, in one plant where Toyota had a contract to produce a car for a European manufacturer, the production line could intermix various Toyota models and the competitor's models.

6. Each unit had to be ready for delivery at the end of the production line when it is promised. There was no time to put it in inventory where it could be "fixed." Therefore, each step had to be right the first time. For this to happen, each employee had to be involved in self-inspection and carefully monitor his or her own work as well as all previous work. Ohno described this as analogous to the autonomic nervous system: "In the human body, the autonomic nerve causes us to salivate when we see tasty food. . . . These functions are performed unconsciously without any direction from the brain. . . . An autonomic nerve means making judgments autonomously at the lowest possible level . . . without having to consult the production control or engineering departments that correspond to the brain in the human body."[5]

If when the hand touched something hot it had to send a message to the brain and then the brain had to develop a plan and send the command back to the hand before something could be done, the hand would be badly burned before it received permission to move. So it is with inspection.[6]

Anyone finding a defect is empowered to shut down the production line until it is fixed. When the line is shut down, everyone in the plant focuses on the problem and the worker who discovered the abnormality is a hero, not a pariah. If an employee is having a problem, he or she is expected to turn on a light on the light board. A red light stops the line, a yellow light brings help to enable the worker to catch up.

This principle is reflected in an event that occurred at the Toyota plant in Georgetown, Kentucky. An employee noticed small flecks in the paint on several cars. The line was stopped and all attention focused on finding the problem. The problem was quickly traced to an employee who had changed his brand of underarm deodorant. How long would it take a research team to sample hundreds of defective cars pulled off after final inspection to determine the problem? By that time the employee may have switched back to the original brand of deodorant.

7. The Toyota production process focused attention on the process rather than on the plan. Staff members were brought out of the planning tower and placed at the production site, where they could support the production process. When the production line was stopped, they were expected to help resolve the problem. Quality circles were developed to address production problems and staff members were expected to support the production workers, not simply predefine what they were expected to do, often with little understanding or feedback of the actual production process.

These methods emphasize the need for continuous improvement (Kaizen) rather than waiting for the annual model changes. It also highlights the need for statistical process control (SPC) to identify problems and focus attention on the most effective solutions.

Ohno's Toyota production process got the attention of American industry. It forced the very industry that had epitomized the traditional approach to the mass-production process to question if mass-production assumptions upon which scientific management was built were scriptural or simply one way among many for producing things raising the possibility that some of the other methods might be more cost effective. At the same time that Ohno was challenging traditional production methods, another trend was challenging the belief that customers wanted products. This was the growth in service organizations.

The Rise and Restructuring of the Services Economy

Quesney thought that only agriculture and mining created wealth. For many years, agriculture was the primary livelihood for the majority of workers. The development of farm machinery revolutionized farming. One worker with a modern combine can harvest as much wheat as hundreds of individuals without equipment. Although we now produce far more that we ever have, agricultural employment is below 3 percent and many of those workers are in agricultural services such as custom combining, testing services, crop dusting, and applying fertilizer. Likewise, manufacturing as a percentage of the GNP has remained relatively constant, but the percentage of the labor force involved in manufacturing has declined rapidly. It is now in the 17 to 20 percent range (depending upon how various Census SIC (standard industrial classification) codes are grouped. Drucker predicts that it will be closer to 12 percent by 2010.[7] Quinn suggests that the majority of workers in manufacturing are actually service workers such as accountants, engineers, maintenance workers, office staff, and managers.[8]

It is not the exact number or percentage of workers in manufacturing and agriculture that is important. What is important is that by far the majority of people spend their working lives providing services, not making or moving products. Nine out of ten new jobs between 1955 and 1984 were in the service industries.[9] In a service, the products (i.e., the supplies) are merely a means to an end rather than an end in and of themselves. As the nation becomes increasingly service oriented, the emphasis will shift from product planning to defining the benefits that customers value.

Attention has not – and will not – dramatically turn from the production process to service delivery. This also is an evolutionary process, and the evolution has been much slower than may be realized.

Clark in 1940 stated that the economics of services remained to be written.[10] Fuchs in 1968 called services the "stepchild" of economic research[11], and Channon in 1978 described services as the "Cinderella industry of academics and politicians."[12] Even in 1984, when the Marketing Science Institute (MSI) asked its advisory board why there were not more journal articles written on services, they were told that there was not yet a sufficient database of validated service studies from which to draw manuscripts.[1] Consequently, MSI funded the development of a computerized bibliography of service marketing literature. Ray Fisk, director of the MSI project, found only 161 articles on service marketing written from 1964 to 1973, compared with 1,411 written during the following decade. By 1985 there was a total of 1,991 articles on service marketing. However, only 340 of these addressed conceptual issues relating to services in general; the rest were primarily industry specific or case studies.[13] The development of services courses has also been relatively recent. A 1984 *Wall Street Journal* guest editorial made this clear with the suggestion that MBA graduates must realize that their degree should read "manufacturing business administration" rather than "master of business administration."[14]

Attention to services was delayed because of the way services were provided. First, *professional services* typically were delivered by individual proprietorships. The individual, whether a physician, engineer, CPA, contractor, plumber, or dentist, operated as an independent proprietor with three accountabilities: to him- or herself (his or her own unique professional interest), to the client, and to the code of ethics promulgated by a professional board or organization. The law gave special recognition to the confidentiality of the client-professional relationship. The profession determined licensing procedures, malpractice enforcement, and until recently defined fees and promotional methods.

Second, *human services* were traditionally provided by the church or other nonprofit organizations. As early as 1602, the English Poor Law was passed, which allowed establishment of poor houses by churches to care for the large number of peasants made homeless by the enclosure movement.[2] Later, there was a strong movement to have government

---

1. Telephone conversation with Diane Smallansee, 1986.
2. The enclosure movement occurred when the landowners found it more

provide human services. This movement was so strong that political labels were assigned to proponents of each political philosophy: *liberals* thought that government should provide human services, whereas *conservatives* thought that this should continue to be the responsibility of nonprofit organizations. Even today, one does not have to look far for a state university or a church-sponsored college, a city or a nonprofit hospital, a public or a nonprofit adoption agency, publicly financed health insurance or nonprofit mutual insurance companies. Both types of groups also operate children's homes, pension programs, arbitration services, and many other benevolent human services.

Both the government and nonprofit groups operated according to the same principles. Neither was required to pay taxes. Neither was expected to be profitable. Because they provided unprofitable services, they did not expect competition. Rather than maximizing profit, each group had a mandate that they were expected to fulfill insofar as their budgets would allow. The voters or the legislature provided the mandate for public agencies, and the contributors or the parent nonprofit organization provided the mandate and budget for the nonprofit agency. Rather than operate according to the pressures of the marketplace, they operated under direct oversight of a policy-making board – the legislature in the case of government body or a board of directors in the case of a nonprofit organization.

After 1850, a third kind of service began to evolve: *public utilities* and *financial services*. These required large investments and were generally profitable. The public utilities included the railroads and other transportation services, telephone service, electric service, water and sewer services, and terminals such as airports. By 1887, legislation was passed to operate these services not by market forces but through oversight bodies, beginning with the Interstate Commerce Commission (ICC) and later including the Federal Communications Commission (FCC), Civil Aeronautics board (CAB), Federal Maritime Commission (FMC), state regulatory bodies, and local authorities. These regulatory bodies generally restricted competition and controlled both rate and service levels. Although banks and financial services date back to before the 13th century, their real growth occurred during the latter half of the

---

productive to raise sheep to provide wool for the new textile mills rather than for tenants to farm the land.

Industrial Revolution concurrent with the growth in mass production. Commercial banks have typically been controlled and regulated by the central banks, which are often nationalized or strongly influenced by the government. Financial intermediaries such as finance companies, savings banks, investment banks, trust companies, and home loan banks have also been highly regulated by state or federal oversight bodies.

A fourth type of service, the *labor of employees*, was typically obtained by contracts of employment. Prior to the Industrial Revolution, it was not uncommon for a business to depend upon a network of independent craftspersons to provide the support services needed. Individuals or companies needing special services would call upon the teamster, the blacksmith, the tinsmith, the cooper, the tanner, or the mason. With the Industrial Revolution came the large factory. When a company wanted services to support its production line (whether maintenance, engineering, bookkeeping, employee health care, or management services), it would hire the personnel needed. This is changing. A recent *Fortune* cover story predicted that jobs as we know them will rapidly disappear:

> [T]he job. That much sought after, much maligned social entry, a job, is vanishing like a species that has outlived its evolutionary time. . . . Most societies since the beginning of time have done just fine without jobs. The job is an idea that emerged early in the 19th century to package the work that needed doing in the growing factories and bureaucracies of the industrializing nations. Before people had jobs, they worked just as hard but on shifting clusters of tasks, in a variety of locations, on a schedule set by the sun and the weather and the needs of the day.[15]

The fifth type of service, *small independent proprietors*, operates small businesses such as barber shops, motels, local restaurants, repair services (e.g., garages, plumbing companies, and electrical firms), construction, and cleaning services used by both individuals and other businesses. Frequently, it makes little difference whether the individual provides services as an employee or as an individual contractor. In fact, an individual may be an employee providing plumbing support service as an employee during the day and moonlighting as an individual small business after work hours. Likewise, an organization may obtain support services either by contracting with a small business or by hiring a person on a long- or short-term basis. Temporary employment services and craft union halls are service organizations that facilitate temporary employment arrangements. Many of the services formerly provided by small independent proprietors are now being provided by chains. The home office develops the processes and support systems but establishes many small operating units close to the customers. Tax services, muffler shops, and home cleaning services are familiar examples.

Dramatic changes have occurred in the way services are delivered. These changes can be categorized as follows:

1. *The deregulation of public utilities.* This began when the telephone companies were ordered by the courts to allow outside suppliers to connect their equipment to the telephone system. Next there was the 1982 separation of the Baby Bells from Ma Bell to allow greater competition for pricing of long-distance services and equipment. Congress embarked on the massive deregulation of transportation from 1976 to 1982. Banks and financial institutions were deregulated from 1980 to 1982. More recently, cable television and Baby Bells have been deregulated to participate in two-way communication into homes.

2. *A decline in control by professional organizations.* Beginning in 1977, when the Supreme Court ruled that local bar associations could not restrict attorneys from advertising, control over professional practice has continued to diminish for virtually all professional groups.

3. *A blurring of the distinction between nonprofit and for profit.* Originally the churches handled virtually all family needs, including even domestic conflicts, which today are settled by domestic courts. As nonprofit organizations (especially the hospitals, insurance companies, and universities) have become larger, they have sought to broaden markets and now, at least from the customer's perspective, there is virtually no difference. The courts have recognized this and virtually eliminated the concept of charitable immunity from liability for nonprofit and public organizations.

4. *A decline in manufacturing and agricultural investment opportunities.* As these two sectors become a smaller part of the

economy, investors, even traditional manufacturing firms, are looking for investment opportunities in what they perceive to be the growing opportunity area (i.e., services). The dramatic growth of janitorial services, food services, cleaning services, pest control services, auto rental services, elder care services, and home health care are becoming very familiar.

5. *A shift from the liberal-conservative paradigm to privatization.* The 1980s can be marked as the decade when government began to shift its attention from having human and public services provided by the government or by nonprofit agencies to contracting out with the private sector to provide the services under bid to the government. It is fitting that James M. Buchanan won the Nobel Prize in economics. It was he who stressed the separation of the funding and delivery of public services. For example, the government did not have to construct a bridge itself to make sure that the community had the services of a bridge. It could fund the bridge and contract to have it built. Privatization facilitates downsizing in government.

6. *A change in the way we do business.* The post-World-War-II model promoted vertical integration: The firm owned all raw material sources, the manufacturing and distribution facilities, and, in many cases, the retail outlets. All workers and supporting personnel were company employees. This is changing in what Drucker calls "the growth of the organization." The growth in organizations is dramatically changing the way firms are organized. This change goes by many terms, including "industrial partnership," "outsourcing," "downsizing," "right sizing," and "networking."

7. *The recognition that every firm provides a service.* Whether it is labeled "creating customer value," "benefit delivery," or "customer-desired quality," the emphasis is on solving specific needs of customers and making the delivery happen.

Just as the Toyota production process forced managers to rethink their mass-production process, the growth in service organizations is shifting management's focus from products to benefits that provide value to the customer. Simultaneously, there is a trend away from the traditional method for operating businesses. Instead of the tightly controlled vertical organization, there is a rapid growth in organizations. Likewise, services – whether professional, nonprofit, governmental, or utility – are being treated as any other business.

The Evolution of Organizations

Drucker wrote that "no one in the United States – or anyplace else – talked of 'organizations' until after World War II. Once again the *Concise Oxford*, England's authoritative dictionary, did not list the term in its current meaning in its 1950 edition."[16] Business thought focused on producers (e.g., manufacturing and distributing companies) and consumers (i.e., customers). The law focused on owners and renters, employers (i.e., masters) and workers (i.e., servants), buyers and sellers, and contractors and contractees. Sociology, on the other hand, talked about groups (e.g., the family, community, society, class, clan, or tribe). Peter Drucker has pointed out that "an organization is a human group, composed of specialists working together on a common task."[17] As knowledge becomes more important in doing work, we shift from traditional-type groups to the organizational approach. In the organizational structure, there are groups of knowledgeable individuals organized to be able to perform some function or task very well. Drucker cited as an example that the best radiologists are not the ones who know general medicine best but the ones who specialize in ultrasound, magnetic resonance, X-ray, and various other body-scanning methods.

Knowledge by itself is ineffective. It is only when an organization has an effective process for integrating the activities of knowledge holders and has the ability to coordinate the assignment and tracking of work that organizations become effective. Thus an organization is a group of knowledgeable people with a core competency that they can focus on solving a problem. Organizations can legally be private, public, for profit, or nonprofit, but they always have specialized knowledge that can be used to address a specific task. Churches, the Boy Scouts, Bell Labs, NASA, the Chamber of Commerce, and labor unions are all organizations. Increasingly businesses are beginning to form organizations. Third-party contract logistics companies, walk-in medical centers, eye centers, and tax services are all organized collections of knowledge-based workers with complementary skill that can be brought to bear on a specific task. As business firms seek solutions, they turn to organization. In an era of change and downsizing, organizations are turning to consultants. As John Byrne has written, "Even as corporations continue to lay off thousands of employees, they're hiring consultants in unprecedented numbers, creating an all-time boom in the field. . . ." Change is driving the business. Companies are expanding, contracting, changing structures, and going global."[18]

People tend to innovate and improve business processes in which they are interested. If a medical practice hires several custodians to maintain its offices, it is highly unlikely that the physicians will become so interested in custodial practices that they will begin to attend trade shows; regularly read trade publications; and constantly experiment with new pieces of equipment, supplies, and methods to improve the custodial process. Instead, they will focus their interest and attention on improving the business process in which they have their specialty. Therefore, if they want effective custodial service that is continually being improved, they will contract with another organization that specializes in the delivery of custodial services. The organization that specializes in providing custodial service will be much more likely to develop new, innovative methods and continually improve the process. The custodial organization promotes individuals who innovate and find better ways of managing. The custodial organization has the only staff that has the interest and focus necessary to innovate, push change, and develop more cost-effective business processes. It is the only provider that has those with the knowledge base and with an interest in improving the delivery of custodial services. The physician, hospital administrator, and plant manager of a manufacturing firm will not receive a raise or promotion for developing an improved method for cleaning floors – but the manager of the local custodial service will.

Although vertically integrated firms may be managed by the traditional hierarchical-command model, organizations function differently. Organizations are made up of experts (i.e., workers with a core competency) and coordinators (i.e., managers). The managers establish and facilitate relationships with customers, obtain the resources needed to complement the core competency of the organization, and assign work to employees. The manager is the worker enabler or facilitator. The manager also organizes the work so that it can be assigned and coordinated.

Organizations are not all things to all people, but when they are networked (i.e., integrated) on a long-term, short-term, or intermittent basis, the integrated networks can become almost all things to all people. For example, an airline cannot compete in all markets, but a travel agency can meet virtually any travel need by networking with various airlines, hotels, and car rental firms. A computer manufacturer – even IBM – cannot be all things to all people, but even a small, well-networked, value-added retailer (VAR) organization can be almost anything to many key customers. It is the logistician (e.g., product manager, primary physician, or contractor) who develops the responsive business processes that coordinate and integrate activities among organizations. Networking allows solution or customer management, rather than product or procedure management. What is the role of organizational management? To quote again from the *Fortune* cover story mentioned earlier: "To oversimplify, there will be two main flavors of [new style] manager: process managers and employee coaches."[19] We are suggesting that the role of organizational management should be best-practice-guideline (i.e., business process) management, relationship management (i.e., serving as coaches for the front-line workers), and infrastructure (i.e., communications and information) building.

The Shifting View of Capitalism from Ownership to Resource

Not only are trends evolving that change how we produce (i.e., flexible manufacturing), how we deliver benefits (i.e., services), and how we structure work (i.e., organizations and ad hoc teams), but even ownership is changing.

"Ownership" and "capitalism" have traditionally been synonymous. The owner raised the money to start the business. Ownership brought with it the right to control. For years society was seen as belonging to two social camps: the capitalists, who owned and controlled the means of production, and the workers, who did as they were hired and instructed to do. This gave rise to the two political camps. One emphasized protecting the means of production and the other emphasized protecting the rights and needs of the workers. Political party membership was often organized according to these two positions. During the capitalist age, economists and nations organized around these polarized views (i.e., free enterprise versus socialism or communism). The capitalists argued that for the economy to survive, they needed to be free to allocate capital where it was most productive and that owners who had a vested interest in results would be most involved in keeping capital productive. Marxists, on the other hand, argued that "all capital is accumulated through expropriation of the wage earner."[20]

With the rise of the professional manager, "capitalism" and "ownership" were no longer synonymous. Professional managers with little or no ownership used capital, obtained by stock or loans, to control the means of production. "Professional management controlled without ownership stake." "Property" had become "investment," not ownership.[21] Managers began to see themselves as being responsible for maximizing the stockholders' return on their investments. This meshed nicely with the managerial accounting methods developed to manage vertically integrated firms (e.g., DuPont) and multidivisional firms (e.g., GM). It also placed firms in the position of being managed to maximize short-run profitability. Stock was not ownership but a speculative commodity. Now capital is concentrated in pension funds. Pension funds are actually employee earnings deferred until retirement. To quote Drucker:

> In the United States at the end of 1992, institutional investors held at least 50 percent of the share capital of large corporations. They also held an almost equal proportion of the fixed debt even of America's medium sized – let alone large – businesses, whether publicly or privately owned. And the one hundred largest pension funds held something like one third of all pension fund assets at the end of 1992. ... But neither the managers who run them nor their owners are "capitalists." Pension fund capitalism is capitalism sans the capitalists. ... Legally, pension funds are "owners;" but only legally.[22]

Pension funds are administered by professional managers.

Pension fund capitalism is also capitalism without "capital." In pension fund capitalism, the wage earners finance their own employment by deferring part of their wages. Wage earners are the main beneficiaries of the earnings of capital and of capital gains.[20]

Marx would be amazed to learn that workers now own organizations through their pension funds, and the traditional capitalist would be amazed to discover that when you own over 50 percent of a business it is difficult to continually shift funds to get a higher rate of return. How do you shift? Do you simply switch investments with other pension funds? When pension funds contain so much of the nations stock of capital, the emphasis turns to maximizing the long-term value of employees' pensions. This requires that pension fund managers establish a long-term relationship with the firms in which they have invested. This requires that managers not be given free rein as though they were owners but that managers be held to strict accountability for creating long-term pension fund value that becomes available to the workers when they retire.

This has introduced a new type of managerial accounting criterion described as economic value added (EVA). Traditional accounting methods were transaction based. Transactions included sales (i.e., revenue) and expenses (i.e., purchases and interest payments). Return (revenue minus expenses) provided the return on investment (ROI) measure used to determine profitability. When no payment is made to stockholders, there was no perceived cost to using equity capital. EVA includes both borrowed capital and stockholder capital (equity) as expense items. Borrowed capital still uses the interest payment as its cost. Because stocks have traditionally yielded an approximately 6 percent higher return than long-term government bonds, that is considered to be the cost of equity capital. If the firm uses a combination of borrowed and shareholder (i.e., equity) capital, the capital cost is a weighted average of the two. The EVA from operations then is calculated as revenue less expenses (i.e., purchases, capital, and taxes). In essence, because all costs are incurred in the calculation of EVA, EVA is a measure of value created from operations. EVA can be calculated for the firm or for any component of the firm. It makes it easier to determine if various subsidiaries are adding value to the enterprise.

EVA is a significant measure because it recognizes that capital, whether borrowed or equity, is simply another resource used in the organization. It begins to expand the definition of ownership. Ownership comes not only from the stockholders, who share the risk of the venture, but also the employees, whose motivation and involvement create EVA. As firms shift to EVA analysis, the next step is to see how increases in value should be distributed to the various owners. Logically, some of the excess value should go to the shareholder, but how about employees? After all, don't the employees play a large part in determining how much value the firm can create? Therefore, most EVA programs have some method for distributing bonuses and dividends to the workers. These bonuses and dividends are determined by EVA. Workers expect wages.

Stockholders expect a normal return on investment. The excess value is distributed by formula. Some firms even use the excess profits to buy stock for distribution to workers, and others pay out a portion of the EVA to workers as bonuses.[3]

When managers are forced to see capital (borrowed plus equity) as a resource, they develop strategies to accomplish several objectives:

- *Earn more profit without using more capital.* When the emphasis was on costs, cutting measurable costs was the favorite method. Because equity was not a measurable cost, there was a strong incentive to use increased investment to reduce costs. When equity has a cost, the firm may create more economic value by making employees more effective rather than increasing capital investment.
- *Use less capital.* Because EVA is addressing capital effectiveness, attention is focused on developing methods that deliver more value for less capital. The traditional assumption behind mass-production economics was economies of scale. More capital meant more efficient production. EVA forces managers to think of alternative methods. These may include building a network of relationships with providers, outsourcing, cross training employees, or developing tools and even compensation programs that motivate employees. The saved capital can also be returned to stockholders, put into stock buybacks, or put to alternative uses.
- *Invest capital in high-return projects.* When surplus capital is invested in high-return projects, it creates growth – growth for the economy, high-value benefits to customers, and value for employees. The key is to make sure the new projects create value (i.e., EVA) over and above the total cost of capital.

Owners increase wealth by increasing the yield on equity investment. Pension funds increase in value by receiving higher yields on their funds. The emphasis is on yield from the investment. Yield, as described in Chapter 11, is two-dimensional. First, there is the income received. Second, there is the amount of resources used to generate the income.

---

3. For an excellent discussion of EVA and the concepts presented in this section see: Shawn Tully, "The Real Key to Creating Wealth," *Fortune*, September 20, 1993, pp. 38–50.

EVA is a yield concept. Thus organizations move to yield (as opposed to transaction) management in two ways: yield from scheduled capacity and yield from investment.

Yield management is a more all-encompassing concept than transaction management. For example, transaction pricing was acceptable when firms produced a single product that could be inventoried. Value could be captured in the product and maintained in inventory until the product was sold. Standardized products could be costed. Profit was determined by price minus cost. After-tax profits became owner equity. It is no longer enough to increase stockholder equity. The emphasis is on increasing the efficiency with which stockholder equity is used. Likewise, service organizations cannot capture value in inventory. Capacity perishes with each tick of the clock. Therefore, unit profit has no meaning. Services must use yield management (i.e., revenue generated for the capacity scheduled). Hotels, airlines, and many other service organizations evaluate operations on yield.

Where deliveries are not standardized but rather customized, it is not logical to use standardized pricing. Each delivery has a different customer value. Yield pricing is a mechanism for capturing the customer value and using excess capacity to capture the customer deficit. In the world of mass customization, the words "cost," "revenue," and "profit" have no meaning by themselves. Cost of what? Revenue from whom, when, where, and for what? These terms only have meaning when placed in context with the event that caused them. They are attributes of specific activities in the organization. It is true that costs, revenue, and profit can be totaled. But they are just that – total costs, total revenue, and total profit. Separate from an event, these terms have no meaning.

This has led to the development of event-driven business systems. In event-driven business systems, the focus is on measuring the revenue, the cost, the contribution, and other factors influencing the delivery of each event (i.e., customer requests). Aggregate data for standardized product lines are not sufficient. Also, all information needed to price and coordinate individual deliveries is needed, not just financial measures.[4]

---

4. For an excellent discussion of these concepts, see Eric L. Denna, J. Owen Cherrington, David P. Andros, and Anita Sawyer Hollander, *Event-Driven Business Solutions*, Homewood, IL: Business One Irwin, 1993. Much of this section is taken from this work.

Central concepts include the following:

- Focus on individual business events (i.e., customer requests).
- Simplify business processes. This is the intent of reengineering efforts.
- Integrate data (from all areas of business). No longer is it sufficient to separate financial and performance data. All data relevant to each activity must be collected on a disaggregated basis.
- Integrate information processes and controls. Integrate data collection with the process itself. Capture data as they occur.
- Realign system component ownership. Integrate data needs by event process rather than function.[23]

There are four questions that need to be asked and captured for each event:

- *What* happened and *when*? ("What" identifies the event and "when" describes the beginning and ending times.)
- What *roles* were played and *who* or *what* performed the roles?
- What kinds of *resources* were involved and *how much* resources were used?
- Where did the event occur?

We are involved in developing accounting and information systems for event-driven business systems. Thus our orientation is the development of accounting systems using current technology based on entity relationships. Customer-responsive management builds on these concepts by integrating several additional functions, such as capturing preference data that facilitate relationship building with customers and resources, dynamic dispatching and tracking of work, and capturing the organization's guidelines (i.e., becoming a learning organization).

The Evolution of the Information Age

Not only are these trends occurring, but new tools are also becoming available to facilitate major changes in the way we do work. One tool is information-handling capability.

Traditional planning and control methods were very logical business processes when customers were willing to make do with standardized solutions, when the competition was also limited to standardized solutions, and when it was difficult to collect, store, and retrieve information. It is the information revolution that enables competition to be responsive and customers to begin to expect responsiveness. The information explosion is not attributable to a single cause but is the result of six major interlocking trends that have revolutionized the way we think about information.

First Trend – Miniaturization and Microcomputers

The first trend was miniaturization and the development of the microcomputer. In the middle 1970s, a few isolated entrepreneurs began connecting chips, developed for calculators and watches, into very sophisticated machines with on-line storage, monitors, keyboards, printers, and other peripherals. Perhaps the most famous of these entrepreneurs were Waznek and Jobs, who began the Apple computer company in their garage. Since then, computing power has been doubling every 18 months (Moore's Law).[5] Although capability and storage capacity have been growing exponentially, prices have continued to decline. These dual trends have provided dramatic performance-to-price ratios. Also, hardware investments can be made incrementally with many decisions no longer made in the boardroom but purchased with petty cash or unspent budget at the end of the year. The ability to network computers has allowed the low-cost personal computers (PCs) to become the corporate mainframe. It has been said that "the network is the computer."

Second Trend – Development of Interface Standards

The second trend occurred as computer entrepreneurs developed the microcomputer. Several major decisions evolved. These decisions evolved out of necessity rather than by consensus. Many of these entrepreneurs had small operations. They did not have the funds or time to develop proprietary operating systems, buses, and components. Thus standards developed out of necessity. These entrepreneurs built computers using standard components, and when they developed innovations, they designed the innovation to follow industry standards.

---

5. Moore's Law, as posited by Intel Corporation Chairman Gordon Moore is that "at any given price level, microchips will double in performance every 18 months." John W. Verity, "The Information Revolution," *Business Week*, Information Revolution 1994 issue, p. 18.

It was the standardized bus (S-100, Apple) that allowed every innovator's design to interface with other standardized components. (Just as the standard 110-volt alternating current [AC] electrical outlets allow any number of electrical appliances to be connected to the national AC bus, so the computer bus allowed any number of cards to be interconnected.) The bus is the common interface. But computers cannot operate without software. Gary Kidall wrote a standard operating system (CP/M) that could be customized for any machine by simply adding a few parameters to interface with the unique peripheral devices. Unlike a proprietary mainframe computer, the microcomputer has its roots in a standardized interface. When IBM entered the PC market in the early 1980s, it gave the microcomputer credibility and provided a fledgling company, Microsoft, which ported CP/M to Intel 8086/8088 machines, a market and the opportunity to become the new standard interface. Until that point, CP/M was the operating system standard.

These standards made it possible for even the smallest innovator to make a contribution. There were few barriers to entry, so entrepreneurs could respond to very small, niche markets. With standard operating systems, software developers were assured of large potential markets because their software would run on any standard machine.

Third Trend – Self-Identification

The third trend began at the same time that microcomputers were developing. The grocery industry was developing standardized bar-coding systems. Although the banks had used magnet encoding on checks for a decade, the grocery industry wanted a scannable code that could be printed on the box so that products would identify themselves. When the Apple II computer was still the current rage, Harry Dalton at Federal Express began development of the super tracker (the hand-held device still in use) and COSMOS 2B, the computer system that permitted the dynamic tracking of packages. These were two very visible success stories. UPS found it was no longer sufficient to consistently deliver packages across country in five working days. Customers wanted the reassurance of being able to call Federal Express and know the location of their package. Federal Express's market share soared. Customers visiting the grocery store several times a week became convinced of the viability of scanning as they watched their purchases being talleyed. Now virtually everything from football tickets, student identification cards, credit cards, supplies, and even automobiles at toll gates can be scanned and UPS is using bar codes to enable overnight packages to be rerouted right up to the time they are placed on the delivery truck.

Fourth Trend – The Mobile Connection

The fourth trend occurred with the development of cellular phones, satellite transmission, radio frequency transmission, and the Internet. These developments have liberated computers so they could become mobile. UPS now has computers in its trucks; pilots have computers in their planes. Both can be redirected in route. Stores can send scanned data from store to supplier each night for automatic stock replenishment. Wal-Mart implemented this technology and has become the nation's largest retailer. By using satellites to liberate it from its dependence on an undependable foreign phone system, Wal-Mart was able to enter the Mexican market using automatic replenishment methods.

Computers can be mounted on forklifts, installed in customer service vehicles, or placed in any other location. Whirlpool is dispatching customer service representatives from its Knoxville Customer Assistance Center. The computer in Benton Harbor contains information about the inventory quantities on each representative's truck and in each warehouse. The customer assistance center has a system that is able to diagnose the probable cause and expected part usage from the interaction with the customer. The service representative's schedule is based on customer availability, representative availability, and part availability. The customer assistance center can also transmit wiring diagrams, parts lists, and diagnostic charts to the repair representative's truck while he or she is at the customer's site. When the representative writes up the customer's ticket, the information is automatically captured and paperwork is automatically handled.

Fifth Trend – Systems Development Shifts toward Users

The fifth trend has occurred in the development of software. In the 1950s, the coding was done at machine level by direct wiring (electronic accounting machines) or in numbers (40 = card read). In the 1960s, programming languages such as assemblers, COBOL, FORTRAN, and LISP were developed. Graphical user interfaces, developed at Xerox's Palo Alto Research Center but implemented by Apple, allowed users to work with icons and menus rather than by typing in syntax-sensitive commands. Object-oriented databases and CASE application development tools began to come into their own during the 1990s.[6]

The impact of this trend is that software definition and development have been moving from the domain of the technical programmer to the domain of the manager and the user. During the technical era businesses were trained to rely on information systems departments to develop software. Computer usage surged when users and managers become involved. No information systems department could ever have the impact that is achieved by giving users with a job to do computers on their desks and easy-to-use software, such as electronic spreadsheets. When systems development software makes it as easy to develop systems as it is to use a spreadsheet, another surge will occur. In the meantime, the task is rapidly becoming easier, as was illustrated in Chapter 13, and innovation is growing rapidly. As Harmon and Hall have written:

The key programmers of the year 2000 will be the users of OO/KBS (object oriented/knowledge based systems) CASE tools, who will quickly create powerful, strategic systems that will gather data, reason about it, and make recommendations. These "programmers" will be specialists who have knowledge about how to make strategic corporate decisions. They won't know as much about programming, as such, since the tools will handle most of the actual coding tasks."[24]

As managers begin to integrate technology into business strategy, they will see technology not as a necessary business function but as an enabling tool that allows them to change the way they relate to customers, the resource network, and with employees. As this integration evolves, managers will see three basic types of applications. With time these three areas will become more integrated.

Information Retrieval Systems. Information retrieval systems are based around the public Internet, which allows anyone with a phone line and computer to access information virtually anywhere in the world, much as they could physically in a well-stocked library. The Internet allows virtually instant access to any server on the network and makes use of hypertext links so that by selecting

---

6. For a detailed discussion of the evolution of software, see: Paul Harmon and Curtis Hall, *Intelligent Software Systems Development: An IS Manager's Guide*, New York: John Wiley, 1993.

highlighted words, users can navigate to more or less detailed information. Users are also allowed to make structured responses. The biggest problem with the Internet currently is the lack of security and authentication procedures. For example, there is difficulty in ascertaining the true identity of the author. The security of credit card numbers is also an issue. A natural application would allow individuals to review college catalogs on-line, select departments, and navigate across detailed descriptions of courses, faculty, admission requirements, costs, and other appropriate information. The reader might also request additional information.

Groupware Systems. Groupware systems allow the networking of work between groups. Instead of a highly structured work flow with myriad clerks processing paper forms according to rigorously prescribed procedures, work can be organized and processed on a task-by-task basis. Groupware eliminates the space and time separation of individuals working on group projects. Groups can communicate over the Internet but this requires each individual to have the same software on each end to take care of security and authentication concerns. Groupware changes the way we coordinate activities.

John Seely Brown describes a very simple beginning for groupware at Xerox Palo Alto Research Center. He described how Xerox recognized that people learn by sharing "war stories." Just as the hunters gathered around the campfire and told of innovative ways they stalked game, modern workers also tell war stories. Field service repair persons, airline pilots, and physicians share particularly difficult experiences in the same way. These stories are internalized. The next time another person encounters a difficult problem, he or she will remember who it was that had the experience, try to remember the logic that person used to solve the problem, and call the storyteller for help if need be.

Based on this belief, Xerox began to experiment with two video cameras and two monitors. Each person had a monitor and a camera in front of him or her. Each individual could see and hear the other person as he or she spoke. If a person had something he wanted to show, he would simply put it on his lap and turn his back to the camera so that the camera would pick up the visual over that person's shoulder.

Now groupware allows capture of spreadsheets (i.e., budgets), pictures, audio clips, X-rays, and many other objects. If, for example, a physician encounters a particularly difficult problem, he or she can take a video shot of the specimen. The physician can then call four or five other colleagues who can be reached anywhere by cellular, satellite, or phone line and arrange a conference complete with voice and visuals on the screen. Any one of the participants can point to or modify the visual on the screen and the change is shown on all the other screens. This dramatically changes the need for travel and meetings. Frequently a short groupware conference can save days of travel and meetings. It also allows virtually unlimited knowledge resources to be made available on short notice to virtually any person. It is the essence of a flexible, responsive organization. 3M is using this approach to establish virtual customer service teams to provide customized responses to its customers.

Another advantage of groupware is that it allows flexible work-flow management. Traditional production process design had a standard way each task should be performed. Groupware allows implementation of responsive business processes. Salespeople, for example, can record customer requests as they occur and transmit them to the home office over the phone. Customer requests can range from data on availability, to shipment tracing, to request for test samples, to specifications, or to environmental hazard procedures for the company's various products.

Each request-product option can have a different response protocol. For example, if the request is for a sample of a specific product, the protocol may include a call from the chief chemist within ten days of delivery. Can you imagine the comfort that the customer's production chemist would receive knowing that the manufacturing chemist had just called and offered to provide any assistance needed to work out problems so the sample material could be integrated into the new production line? The results of the call would be automatically routed to the purchasing agent and salesperson so they could understand the support given and not feel shut out of the loop.

Groupware automates flexible work flows. The manufacturer's chemist does not have to track down calls that have been scheduled. When the computer is turned on, the list of calls is displayed on the screen. With the click of a mouse, a complete history of the relationship between the two companies is available. A screen is provided to record the results of the phone call by clicking the mouse again. The record of the phone call is immediately available to all parties involved in the relationship as soon as the chemist completes the record.

Structured Information Systems for Highly Routine Activities.

When information is highly structured, such as with order entry, highly efficient information systems can be developed using CASE tools and event-driven, object-oriented databases.

Collectively, these trends have enabled a sixth trend. Increasingly, information systems are being designed for ex ante organizing and assigning of work instead of ex post facto reporting of work. As this happens, the computer system truly becomes an enabling tool rather than an obligatory task that must be performed after the real work is done. The purpose of Chapter 13 was to show how to achieve greater worker involvement and ownership of the system's design process. That is necessary before workers feel totally empowered and adopt the system as their own.

Thus, information systems allow organizations the ability to be flexible, learning organizations that can integrate a large network of resources and coordinate delivery at a reasonable cost regardless of location or time considerations.

The Information Modeling Approach to Analysis [7]

Another important tool that is changing the way we work is the way we can dynamically analyze data and detect patterns of change.

One critical element of customer-responsive management is the ability to analyze data in a just-in-time (JIT) manner. Is the new protocol more or less effective? Has customer activity reached a turning point, and, if so, does this mean that he or she has lost confidence in the organization's ability to deliver? How do we detect these turning points? How accurate are the predictions for the time required to perform various activities? These are some fundamental questions confronting the practitioner.

---

7. The authors are indebted to two colleagues, Hamparsum Bozdogan and Greg Kellar, for their guidance on this chapter.

Data analysis in general is not a one-time activity but a dynamic process. When management developed standardized procedures, it may have been sufficient to perform a study, use the data to make a decision, and put a policy in place. However, that is not sufficient with responsive activities. Data must be tracked and monitored so that the system indicates when there are changes or when attention should be addressed to evolving areas. But this raises a question: How do we build statistical models to address questions we need to answer just in time?

Such analysis is presently constrained by the limitations of statistical methods. Statistics is so central to the process of nondescriptive research that mindsets have been established around some of the more common statistical methodologies. For instance, "research" often consists of posing a hypothesis and then testing to see if it is right or wrong. Most commonly, a researcher equates having a good hypothesis with having done "good research." A more natural way to do research, however, would be to ask questions, such as, "What factors are most important in correctly diagnosing a customer's need?" or "What factors make a protocol most cost-effective?" Traditional statistics procedures do not adequately address such questions. Traditional statistics suffers from these and other limitations. Researchers should be anxious to find a tool that will overcome some, if not all, of these difficulties.

Traditional statistical methods were developed prior to the wide-spread availability of computing power. Thus the methods were often developed to simplify the burden of making calculations. The advent of the tremendous calculating power of new computers has brought new statistical methodologies that have the ability to expand research to levels never before possible. Limitations associated with traditional statistics can be overcome, yielding quick and accurate solutions to questions such as "What is the best choice or decision of the many available?" This "best choice" can refer to almost anything, from best summary statistical description to the best fitting model, and is determined by the problem at hand. These new techniques are known as information theoretic statistics (ITS).

Traditional Statistics

To understand why the development of methods such as ITS has been so elusive, it is helpful to look at traditional statistical methods.

There are many tools available to the researcher who uses traditional statistical methods. One of these is descriptive statistics.

Descriptive Statistics.   Descriptive statistics are the well-used measures of means, medians, modes, ranges, variances, covariances, moments, and so forth. Descriptive statistics can be used to characteristize a phenomenon and are very useful in working with standardized activities such as average cost, average revenue, and average profit. There are many questions that are not answered by these measures, however. An example would be "Is Drug A an effective treatment of malady X?"

Regression Analysis or Model Fitting.   Another powerful and often-used tool in traditional statistics is regression analysis, or model fitting. Researchers often wish to mathematically model a phenomenon that has been (or can be) measured. This could be undertaken with the purpose of interpolation or extrapolation. Regression analysis allows the researcher to describe measured phenomena with mathematical functions. An example of this might be the development of a mathematical function to describe the number of train-track miles in use by year. Annual data for the last 50 years could be used to interpolate mileage at points during the course of the year or to extrapolate the mileage ten years in the future.

Such modeling efforts require expert input in model choice. Current methods do not allow the data to drive the model selection. The choice of variables to be included in a given model or choice of model to fit to a given data set is usually prescribed by the expert. For example, is year the best predictor of track mileage, or should the researcher choose instead (a) the number of miles of interstate highway completed, (b) the number of trucks purchased, or (c) some measure of manufacturing output. Perhaps the best predictors may be some of these values measured five years earlier.

Hypothesis Testing.   Traditionally, quantitative approaches have dominated research, and hypothesis testing has been used to provide needed answers. Hypothesis testing is probably the most used tool in research. As stated earlier, sometimes research and hypothesis testing are equated. It is not uncommon for a researcher to be asked, "What is your hypothesis?"

Hypothesis testing consists of proposing a solution to a problem or an answer to a question and then designing a study that is meant to show whether the solution or answer is valid or not. There are numerous techniques and methodologies that facilitate the use of hypothesis testing. In fact, hypothesis testing is basic to much of the field of statistics and has been thoroughly studied. The problem with hypothesis testing is that it presupposes that an expert can understand the environment sufficiently to make correct guesses on what influences the phenomenon being studied. The research is boiled down to "Yes, I guessed correctly" or "No, I was mistaken."

This leads to very binary types of thinking. Research becomes equated with finding pertinent questions that can be answered "yes" or "no." A more natural question might be "What is the most effective option or choice?" For example, if researchers want to fit a mathematical model to some collected data, hypothesis testing demands that they ask, "Is my proposed model valid?" A much more natural question is "What do the data show is the best-fitting model?" This allows the data to guide selection of the model rather than the prejudice of the researcher. Traditional statistical methods are unable to do this.

Another example would be research on cancer prevention via lifestyle changes. Hypothesis testing requires that each lifestyle be tested on an individual basis, that all other possible variables be controlled, and then that the results be compared with a second lifestyle, then a third, and a fourth, and so on. A more efficient and useful way to do research would be to test all of the variables at once to see which makes the most difference and to see how each lifestyle variable affects the incidence of cancer and how each lifestyle variable influences other lifestyle variables. Again, traditional statistics is unable to handle such a project.

Information Theoretic Statistics

In order to use automatically collected data to improve decision making, statistical analysis of the data is necessary. To be truly useful, this analysis must be dynamic and give results in real time. Traditional analytical methods are often cumbersome, sometimes confusing, and at best are time-consuming, making real-time data analyses difficult or even impossible. New statistical tools designed for dynamic data analyses are needed to replace existing methods. These new statistical tools must possess several attributes. Among other things, they must possess the ability to be embedded in automated decision support systems and must identify changing business patterns as they occur. Further, they must be easily understood so that they can be a tool in the hands of nonquantitative front-line personnel, and they must improve the accuracy of statistical model identification and forecasts made by currently available tools.

The recent introduction of neural networks directly addresses these issues. One of the most important neural network systems for dynamic data analysis was discovered in 1973 by Hirotugu Akaike and is called "information theoretic statistics" (ITS). (It is sometimes also referred to as "likelihood ratio method" or "probabilistic neural network.")[25] ITS, by its very theoretical framework, has the attributes that are needed for dynamic analysis tools. In fact, ITS can be automated to analyze automatically collected data in a wide variety of situations, yielding quicker and more accurate "results" than are possible with traditional methods.[8] For example, many dynamic forecasting systems currently implement some form of ITS.[9][26]

Part of the power of ITS comes from its ability to compare large numbers of competing statistical models simultaneously by assigning to each a comparable scalar value, where this scalar value is a ranking or score that is independent of units of measurement. In assigning these rankings, Akaike extended the theories of L. Boltzmann (Generalized Entropy, 1877)[27] and of S. Kullback and R. A. Liebler (Negentropy or Information Quantity, 1951)[28] to balance model complexity with "goodness-of-fit." This balancing – or the search for a simple model – is known as the "principle of parsimony."[29] These two characteristics – comparability and parsimony – are critical attributes not found in more traditional statistical methods.

The importance of the first attribute – that all models may be compared – overcomes a major shortcoming found in many multiple comparison procedures (MCPs) such as ANOVA or MANOVA – namely, the lack of transitivity. In particular, using traditional statistics, it is possible to compare three competing models, A, B, and C, and to find that model A should be preferred over model B, that model B should be preferred over model C, and that model C should be preferred over

---

8. The word "accurate" as used here means accurate statistical model identification or forecasting.

9. For example, see Gutwein, Barry Joe, *Analysis and Prediction of Regional Irrigation Water Demand (Evapotranspiration)*, Dissertation from Colorado State University, 1991, Volume 52 / 09-B of *Dissertation Abstracts International*, p. 4851.

model A. When this situation occurs, it is not clear which model should be preferred, A, B, or C.

ITS overcomes this shortcoming by assigning a scalar value or score to each model. These scores indicate a ranking among the competing models where the lower the score, the better the alternative. This allows an identification of the most appropriate model by an ordering of the ITS scores.[10] For instance, using the previous example of models A, B, and C, suppose that model A has an ITS score of 67, model B an ITS score of 77, and model C an ITS score of 87, as shown in Figure 15.1. It then becomes clear that model A is preferred to either model B or C, and that model B is preferred over model C.[29]

The importance of the second attribute – that model complexity is balanced with "goodness-of-fit" – is illustrated in the following example. Consider three competing linear regression models, model A based upon the variable X, model B based upon the variables X and Y, and model C based upon the variables X, Y, and Z. The issue is to select the most appropriate model from the three under consideration. A common method of selection compares an R^2 score for each model. The R^2 score will increase with complexity and will indicate the "full model" (i.e., the model that uses all variables).[11] On the other hand, ITS will find the

---

10. Many distinct ITS scoring criteria exist and some actually compete with each other. (For a comparison of several of these, see Bozdogan, Hamparsum, "On the Information-Based Measure of Covariance Complexity and Its Application to the Evaluation of Multivariate Linear Models," *Communications in Statistics, Part A: Theory and Methods*, Marcel Dekker, Inc. New York, A19 No. 1, 1990, pp. 221–278.) A common point of comparison for many of these papers is the original ITS scoring criterion, namely, Akaike's Information Criterion (AIC). Most other scoring methods, such as Hamparsum Bozdogan's ICOMP criterion, are improvements on Akaike's original. Nonetheless, the original AIC criterion yields results that far surpass traditional methods in correct model identification, and AIC yields virtually identical results with other ITS criteria when used with large sample sizes.

11. With respect to linear regression, AIC measures complexity as the number of parameters or exogenous variables. (See Bozdogan, Hamparsum, "On the Information-Based Measure of Covariance Complexity and Its Application to the Evaluation of Multivariate Linear Models," *Communications in Statistics, Theory and Methods*, A19 No. 1, 1990, p. 224.)

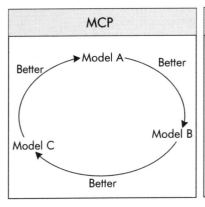

Figure 15.1. The lack of transitivity in traditional MCP versus complete comparability using ITS.

optimal model that balances the competing concepts of goodness-of-fit and lack of complexity or "parsimony."[30] In particular, suppose that A has an R^2 score of .999 and an ITS score of 67, B an R^2 score of .9999 and an ITS score of 77, and C an R^2 score of .99999 and an ITS score of 87. Clearly, the contribution of the variables Y and Z are negligible. However, the R^2 criterion is inadequate to determine this, whereas ITS properly identifies the most effective model.[12] The ITS advantage of balancing goodness-of-fit against model complexity extends beyond linear regression to virtually all traditional statistical methods.

Because ITS possesses these attributes, it has the ability to answer a different, and often more useful, set of questions than traditional statistical techniques. For example, traditional hypothesis testing answers the questions: "Is model A better than B?" "Is model A the same as model

---

12. For a discussion of R^2 in multiple regression models, see Myers, Raymond H., *Classical and Modern Regression with Applications,* Second Edition, PWS-Kent Publishing Company, Boston, 1990, pp. 95–96. For a discussion of ITS in multiple regression, see Hamparsum Bozdogan, "On the Information-Based Measure of Covariance Complexity and Its Application to the Evaluation of Multivariate Linear Models," *Communications in Statistics, Theory and Methods*, A19 No. 1, 1990, pp. 221–278.

B?" and "Is model A worse than model B?," whereas ITS answers a different question, that is, "Which model is best?"

This distinction puts ITS in a position to make a great contribution to dynamic decision-making because many research questions are most naturally posed as "Which of these many alternatives best meets certain criteria?" For example, if a TL carrier contemplates serving the Knoxville-to-Denver market and wishes to determine a model to describe the line haul time required to make this run, the model could include a wide variety of variables, including distance, the time of day the pickup would take place, the number of stops, whether or not the truck is routed through a major metropolitan area, the time of day the delivery would take place, and so on. In order to develop the best model, decisions must be made as to which variables are significant enough to include and which only add confusion or complexity. ITS is able to answer this question quickly, directly, and elegantly.

The application of ITS just mentioned is known as "optimal model selection." Another common application of ITS is multicluster analysis.[31] This was alluded to with the mention of MCPs such as ANOVA and MANOVA. Multicluster analysis allows data to be aggregated or disaggregated optimally. For example, ITS could address the question, "How should the time periods – 12am–8am, 8am–4pm, 4pm–12am – be grouped (clustered) together?" Table 15.1 shows all possible clusterings and illustrates how ITS identifies the best clustering or degree of disagreggation of data.

Table 15.1 indicates that all records with PU times from 8am to 12am should be aggregated together and that the records with PU times from 12am to 8am should be treated differently. Thus the data should be disaggregated by PU time with those records with PU times before 8am being treated differently than those with PU times after 8am.

By carefully taking advantage of the power of ITS, multisample cluster analysis can be combined with model selection criteria to find optimal models. This allows both the use of optimal models and the use of data that are aggregated or disaggregated optimally. The flowchart shown in Figure 15.2 shows how this is accomplished.

Another advantage of ITS is the ease with which it can be used to improve computer-based decision-support tools.[13] Using currently avail-

---

13. Many comparisons of the advantages of ITS over traditional statistical

Table 15.1. Multicluster Analysis

Model	ITS Score
(12am-8am), (8am-4pm), (4pm-12am)	123.2
(12am-8am, 8am-4pm), (4pm-12am)	138.5
(8am-4pm), (12am-8am, 4pm-12am)	102.4
(12am-8am), (8am-4pm, 4pm-12am)	95.1
(12am-8am, 8am-4pm, 4pm-12am)	143.2

able computer technologies, ITS analyses can be programmed to be repeated over and over again virtually instantaneously and without user interpretation or interaction as new data are collected. This allows a computer system to make optimal model selections automatically and in real time to aid in dynamic decision making.

To appreciate this advantage, consider the following example. Suppose that a TL firm wishes to measure the revenue-generating time associated with a transaction. Currently, the firm captures PU date and time and delivery date and time. Although it would seem that the revenue-generating time could be calculated as the time between the PU and delivery, complications preclude this. For instance, sometimes, for the convenience of the TL carrier, freight will be picked up on Monday that does not need to be delivered until Friday (even though the actual time needed for the loading, driving, and unloading might be only eleven hours). Furthermore, sometimes weekends will complicate the picture, as drivers will pick up freight on Friday and deliver it on Tuesday after a weekend of rest and relaxation. Finally, no historical data exists on new markets, preventing calculation of the time involved.

Management believes that a regression model could be used to measure the transaction time. This model could overcome all the difficulties mentioned above. In order to develop this model, independent variables that influence revenue-generating time are identified as the following: line haul distance (X1), number of stops (X2), whether the

---

methods with regards to accuracy (i.e., correct model identification) can be found in Bozdogan, Hamparsum, *STAT*-683, 1990.

ITS multicluster analysis

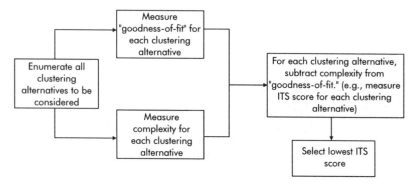

ITS model selection analysis

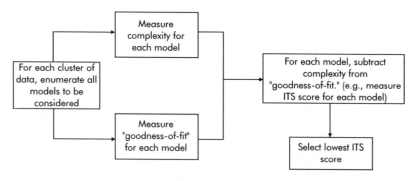

Figure 15.2. Multicluster analysis and model selection criteria.

pickup is in a major metropolitan area during rush hour (X3), whether delivery is in a major metropolitan area during rush hour (X4), and the number of resting periods required by law (X5).

Management is able to identify the records in which the line haul time reflected by the recorded data accurately represents the amount of time of equipment using and labor. Using these records that were identified as "good" and utilizing all the variables considered important by management, a series of linear regression models is developed, as illustrated in the left-hand column of Table 15.2. ITS analysis is then used to choose the best of these models.

Table 15.2. Linear regression results for competing models.

Model	ITS Score
$X_O{}^a$	131.7
$X_O X_1$	121.2
$X_O X_2$	111.1
$X_O X_3$	117.3
$X_O X_4$	109.4
$X_O X_5$	121.6

Thus, new information modeling techniques enable organizations to dynamically monitor customer data and methods that define patterns that require changes in organizational responses. These new statistical methods, combined with computers that have the ability to capture and process information, will provide new ways of measuring and monitoring performance.

Customer-Responsive Health Care Providers

There is another major development moving us toward customer-responsive management. Currently, the largest growing segment of the economy is being forced to shift from a procedure to a benefit orientation as a means of controlling costs. The sheer size of the health care sector is so great that this shift in orientation will have a substantial impact on the social culture of society.

Health care was traditionally provided by private family physicians and hospitals. The family physician knew and understood the family. The customer database was often maintained informally in the physician's memory. If the family physician found something that required different or greater skills, referrals were made to specialists or to the hospitals. These hospitals were frequently operated by religious or public institutions.

Later, physicians began to specialize. Specialists had greater earnings and frequently did not have to be on call constantly. As the number of specialists increased, they began to solicit new business and even advertise. A referral from a family physician no longer was necessary. As a consequence, the patient was confronted by a vast array of specialists listed in the yellow pages but a noticeable lack of family physicians who were seen as primarily concerned about the total health care of the individual.

Health care practitioners continued to support fee-for-service payment methods. Health care costs increased dramatically as more people had better insurance coverage and government developed health care programs for those without insurance coverage from their employers. But for many people, no one had responsibility for efficient and effective health care delivery. Providers would treat anyone who asked them. Bills were sent to the appropriate insurer. The insurer would simply pay what was billed and pass the cost on to the employer or government. The patient was simply glad to have access to care. In many cases, the patient was treated by many different health care specialists, but no one was responsible for oversight of the delivery plan. Patients often did not have the knowledge to know if they were receiving good care or not. Fee-for-service pricing created an incentive for providers to be more interested in providing procedures than in evaluating overall delivery effectiveness.

This resulted in the familiar health care crisis. Patients wanted benefits and providers wanted to sell capacity (i.e., procedures). Insurance paid whatever was billed and passed the changes on to policy holders (employees and government). The cost of health care became such a financial burden that it was making industries uncompetitive with foreign producers, creating strong financial drains on government, and individuals without some form of insurance coverage simply could not obtain health care.

This crisis created extensive debate, finger pointing, and many proposals and counterproposals. Through all of the rhetoric, one concept became clear. Health care delivery needed to be more cost-efficient and more delivery-effective. Patients want someone to take personal responsibility for the effectiveness of their health care delivery. Patients want to stay well, not to see how many days they can spend waiting in physicians' offices and hospitals. Employers want to cap health care costs. Many different programs are developing, but the central theme is that someone must take responsibility for meeting all of a customer's health care needs for a fixed price. The responsible group has two primary functions:

1. To interact with the individual customer, diagnose individual customer illness, and develop customized, long-term care pro-

grams. Often family physicians, nurse practitioners or other skill types perform this function.

2. To coordinate the delivery process. Delivery coordination consists of identifying resources (i.e., physicians, pharmacies, therapists, and so forth) who have proven track records, set up appointments, review results, develop long-term wellness plans, and evaluate the fees paid for the benefits delivered.

Success is measured by factors such as resources required to make the deliveries (e.g., hospital stay days and office visits), the patient's perception of care level, and the cost required.

Thus the evolving health care organizations are similar to those described as customer-responsive organizations. They are situated between the customer and the resources, and their role is to diagnose customer needs and coordinate delivery. The same type of organization is evolving in manufacturing. Here the organizations are called contract logistics firms.

Contract logistics is evolving as many business firms recognize that their specialty is in developing standardized, deterministic business processes. They do well by developing business processes based on mass production, scientific management, total quality management, or project-planning methodologies. They do not, however, have a core competency in building flexible customer-responsive business systems. Thus they contract with contract logistics firms to design and manage the responsive business processes. As more and more activities become customer responsive, contract logistics firms will undoubtedly become a greater presence between customers and resource organizations.

Computer firms are also using contract firms to coordinate customer-responsive activities such as repair service, software support, and help desks. As contract logistics and customer-support firms become positioned between customers and resource organizations, they become the eyes and ears for those organizations and will probably become a major supplier of market research data for the manufacturer and the guardian of the customer databases that capture information about individual customers and their individual requests.

Inc. magazine highlighted a similar type of organization but with a much different group of customers. This organization, Capital Concierge, sets up concierge services in local office buildings. The concierges provide services such as picking up dry cleaning, making lunch arrangements, locating tickets for sporting or cultural events, making travel arrangements, picking up cars from repair shops, researching hair transplant options, and locating canine vacation kennels.[33]

Each of these organizations follows the same design. That is, a customer contact person builds a relationship with customers, and an infrastructure and process facilitate the rapid development of customized delivery plans and the coordination of individual deliveries.

Summary

Several major trends are having a dramatic impact on current organizational practice. It is no longer sufficient to develop preplanned solutions to offer to customers; organizations must be responsive to individual customer needs. As Ronald Henkoff has described this situation:

> Service – bold, fast, unexpected, innovative, and customized – is the ultimate strategic imperative, a business challenge that has profound implications for the way we manage companies, hire employees, develop careers, and craft policies. . . . Says Eric Mittelstadt, 58, president and CEO of Fanuc Robotics North America: "Everyone has become better at developing products. . . . The one place you can differentiate yourself is in the service you provide." . . . The changing nature of customer relationships demands a new breed of service worker, folks who are empathetic, flexible, informed, articulate, inventive, and able to work with minimal levels of supervision. "Rather than the service world being derided as having the dead end jobs of our time, it will increasingly become an outlet for creativity, theatricality, and expressiveness," says Larry Keeley, president of Doblin Group, a Chicago management and design consulting firm.[32]

When the word "service" is used today, it is used to mean responsiveness. This has not always been the case. From Adam Smith to Karl Marx to spokespersons of the 1980s, many people thought of services as intangible products. Services were considered to be unproductive and of no value because they could not be inventoried, taxed, or used as collateral. Now we are switching to a second definition of "service" that considers a benefit to be a service if it is responsive to a customer's need. Electricity and water services are connected and ready at the flick of a switch or turn of a faucet. Now instead of thinking of services as a means of supporting the sale of products, we are beginning to think of solving customer needs with products (prepackaged services) as simply being one method of doing so. Service is now being seen as benefits that respond to individual customer needs how, when, and where the customer wants them. Services require mass customization of deliveries. Whether the need is met with a product or a service, the emphasis is now on providing the specific benefits desired by the customer. As competition forces organizations to be more responsive, firms are looking for ways they can have the flexibility to be responsive.

As firms seek to become more responsive, they will discover that a new way of organizing work is developing. Instead of the vertically integrated firm that DuPont prototyped in 1903 or the multidivisional organization developed at General Motors in the 1920s, there will be many smaller organizations, each organized around a core competency. For these organizations to function, there must be one organizational type whose core competency is the building and managing of flexible, responsive business processes. These organizations will be responsible for the integration of resource organizations and the coordination of deliveries. This organization will cultivate relationships with groups of customers and develop networks of providers that can be used to deliver benefits to this customer base. The organization, responsive to this customer base, will develop the processes and infrastructure that allow it to diagnose individual customer needs, develop customized solutions, assign the work to the resource network, and coordinate delivery. The organization will be responsive to this customer base for a variety of needs. Responsive firms will focus on meeting more of the needs of the key customers but by infrastructure and resource network creation will become more effective at meeting more needs for more people.

This change will not be dramatic as a new invention or new discovery may be dramatic. The change will be evolutionary, but the rate of change will be as overwhelming as the industrial revolution, capitalism, mass production, or total quality management ever were. To those who do not understand the direction of the changes and why it is occurring, these changes may be frightening and mystifying. To those who understand its natural evolution and the principle upon which it is based, the change will be exciting and filled with opportunity never before possible. The rate of change, however, is accelerating. The future belongs to those that understand:

1. The lifetime value of a customer,
2. How to build relationships with customers based on solving customer problems,
3. How to organize to facilitate flexibility so that front-line workers can interact with customers and develop customized solutions using networks of resource organizations,
4. The integration of resources using conditional and changeable best-practice guidelines,
5. The coordination allowed by responsive information systems and responsive business processes,
6. The importance of sharing ownership of the information system's design and definition by the workers themselves.

Is this a new concept? No, it has been steadily evolving and will continue to evolve. We hope this book will be helpful and help the readers experience the excitement that the future holds. If it does that, it will have been worth the effort required to write it. It will be up to the reader to write the next chapter in this exciting evolution. Please share this with us on our personal home pages, which you can locate at www.utk.edu.

References

[1] From *Toyota Production System: Beyond Large-Scale Production* by Taiichi Ohno. English translation copyright © 1988 by Productivity Press, Inc., PO Box 13390, Portland, OR 97213-0390. (800) 394-6868. pp. xiv–xv.

[2] Yasuhiro Monden, *Toyota Production System*. Reprinted with the permission of the Institute of Industrial Engineers, 25 Technology Park, Atlanta, GA 30092. (770) 449-0461. Copyright © 1983, p. 55.

[3] Ibid., pp. 72–73.

[4] Ibid., pp. 45–50

[5] Ohno, op. cit., p. 45.

[6] Monden, op. cit., pp. 137–142.

[7] Peter F. Drucker, Post-Capitalist Society, New York: HarperCollins, 1993, p. 69.

[8] James Brian Quinn, Jordan J. Baruch, and Penny C. Paquette, "Exploiting the Manufacturing-Services Interface," *Sloan Management Review*, Vol. 29, Issue 4, Summer 1988, pp. 50, 52.

[9] James L. Heskett, *Managing in the Service Economy*, Boston: Harvard Business School Press, 1986, p. 3.

[10] Colin Clark, *The Conditions of Economic Progress*, London: MacMillan & Co., 1940.

[11] Victor R. Fuchs, *The Service Economy*, New York: National Bureau of Economic Research, 1968.

[12] D. F. Channon, *The Service Industries*, London: MacMillan & Co., 1978.

[13] Raymond Fisk, Patriya Tansuhajand, James G. Hromas, "Assessing the Services Marketing Literature," *Creativity in Services Marketing: What's New, What Works and What's Developing*, ed. M. Venkatesan, Diane Schmalensee and Claudia Marshall, Chicago: American Marketing Association, pp. 173–175.

[14] Christopher Lovelock, "Biz Schools Owe Students Better Service," *Wall Street Journal* guest editorial, Feb. 10, 1984, p. 26.

[15] William Bridges, "The End of the Job," *Fortune*, September 19, 1994, pp. 62–64.

[16] Drucker, op. cit., p. 49.

[17] Drucker, op. cit., p. 48.

[18] John A. Byrne, "The Craze for Consultants," *Business Week*, July 25, 1994, p. 61.

[19] William Bridges, op. cit., p. 74.

[20] Drucker, op. cit., p. 78.

[21] Adolph A. Berle and Gardner Means, *The Modern Corporation and Private Property*, 1933.

[22] Drucker, op. cit., pp. 77–78.

[23] Denna et al., op. cit. pp. 47–50.

[24] Paul Harmon and Curtis Hall, *Intelligent Software Systems Development: An IS Manager's Guide*, New York: John Wiley, 1993, p. 26.

[25] H. Akaike, "Information theory and an extension of the maximum likelihood principle." In *Second International Symposium on Information Theory*. B. N. Petrove and F. Csaki (eds.), Akademiai Kiado, Budapest, 1973, pp. 267–281.

The Evolving Business Focus

[26] Hideo Nakamura, "Statistical Identification and Optimal Control of Thermal Power Plants," *Analysis of Statistical Information*, Symposium on the Analysis of Statistical Information, The Institute of Statistical Mathematics, Tokyo, December 5–8, 1989, Paper No. 21, pp. 337–362.

[27] L. Boltzmann, †ber die Beziehung zwischen dem zweitin Hauptsatze der mechanischen WŠrmetheorie und der Wahrscheinlichkeitsrechnung respective den SŠtzen †ber das WŠrmegleichgewicht, Wiener Berichte, 76, 1877, pp. 373–435.

[28] S. Kullback and R.A. Leibler, "On Information and Sufficiency," *Annals of Mathematical Statistics*, 22, 1951, pp. 79–86.

[29] Hamparsum Bozdogan, "Model Selection and Akaikes Information Criterion (AIC): The General Theory and Its Analytical Extensions," *Psychometrika*, Vol. 52, No. 3, 1987, Special Section (invited paper), 1987, pp. 345–370.

[29] Hamparsum Bozdogan, "Multi-Sample Cluster Analysis as an Alternative to Multiple Comparison Procedures," *Bulletin of Information and Cybernetics Research Association of Statistical Sciences*, Vol. 22, No. 1–2, 1986, pp. 100–101.

[30] Bozdogan, 1987, op. cit., pp. 345–370.

[31] Bozdogan, 1986, op. cit., pp. 95–129.

[32] Ronald Henkoff, "Service Is Everybody's Business," Fortune, June 27, 1994, p. 48–49, copyright © 1994, Time Inc. All rights reserved.

[33] Susan Greco, "The Road to One to One Marketing" *Inc.*, Oct. 1995, pp. 56–66.

INDEX

accounting
   cost accounting, 35–7
   cost of quality system of,
      40–1, 180
activities
   comparison of offering- and
      customer-response-based,
      66–9
   comparison of offering- and
      responsive-based, 82t
   components of customer-
      responsive, 72–8
   offering- and customer-
      response-based, 4–8
   steps in any, 63–4
actual yield, 201
Akaike, Hirotugu, 395
Albrecht, Karl, 222
ANOVA, 395, 398
assembly line, 34

benefit value determinants, 211–12
best-practice guidelines
   for dispatching, tracking, and
      delivery, 174–5
   in firm infrastructure, 276–7
   in interface management,
      187–8
   management, 169–72
   matched with customer
      request information, 299–301
   to meet defined need, 264
   in priority dispatch list, 163–4
   as protocol, 78–80
Boltzmann, L., 395
business-event diagrams, 316–19
business systems, event-driven,
   383–4
Byrne, John, 378

capability, customer-response
   delivery, 64
capacity
   cost of, 219–20
   scheduling in customer-
      responsive firms, 218
capacity acquisition costs, 219
capacity demand
   defined, 200–1
   as derived demand, 204–5
   determinants of, 211–12
capacity management
   defined, 218
   in service organization, 175–87
capacity utilization
   defined, 175
   as focus of responsive manage-
      ment, 229
   methods to increase, 230–6
   percent utilization, 185
car load (CL), 188
Carlzon, Jan, 95–6, 150, 153, 223–4
CCP. See customer contact person
   (CCP)
channel management, 188
Channon, D. F., 372
Chase, Richard B., 152
Clark, Colin, 372
concept room, 307–8
conquest marketing, 150n
consumer surplus
   defined, 242–3
   in product demand curve, 207
context diagrams, 308–13
contingency plan, 79
continuous improvement
   concept of, 10–12
   recommendations for, 13–14
cooperative networks, 183–7

Index

cooperative partnerships, supplier,
181–3
coordination
of activities, 82–9
in customer-response action, 65
of work by dispatch, 173–5
cost accounting, 35–7
cost allocation, yield management,
190–3
cost effectiveness
components of, 22–3
in response to customer, 9
cost of quality accounting system,
40–1
costs
of capacity, 219–20
direct and indirect, 190
fixed and variable, 224–36
fixed capacity and service
delivery, 184–5
scheduled capacity, 184, 219–20
Crosby, Philip B., 41, 180
cross training (of employees), 179
customer
defining response to, 69–82
diagnosis management, 153–60
diagnosis of needs, 99–100
establishing trust, 147–9
loyalty of, 56
managing interaction with,
149–53
organization objectives in relationship with, 8–9
relationship with, 97–9
customer-based-response approach,
66–9
customer concerns, 345–53
customer contact person (CCP)
coordination with delivery
units, 120–4
in definition of work task, 173
front-end diagnosis by, 141
function of, 93
Kanban system, 121–4
Pizza Hut example, 119–20

in question-based diagnosis,
156–8
relationship with specific
customer, 152
role in customer relationship,
99–103
role in customer-service
management, 160–7
in Subway example, 118–19
support for, 95–6
customer deficit, 243
customer delight, 202
customer information categories,
301–3
customer needs
current, 209–10
customer-response-based
approach to, 2–4
future, 210–11
offering-based approach to, 2–4
speculative needs, 211
customer-responsive model, 93–4
customer responsiveness
activities related to, 4–5
characteristics of activities
related to, 211–14
customer value with, 21–3
defined, 2
era of, 43–8
customer-responsive strategy,
97–103
customer retention
as predictor of profits, 143
rate of, 56–7
customer-service management,
160–7
customer value
concepts, 214–15
creating, 21–3
defined, 197
determinants of, 199–200,
209–14
expressed in equal and unequal capacity units,
198–201

as marginal revenue, 207–9
in mass production era, 39–40
See also customer deficit
data analysis
building statistical models, 392
using information theoretic
statistics, 394–404
data (customer information), 301–3
decision making
using costs in, 224
using ITS, 398–9
delivery
best-practice guidelines for,
169–73
effectiveness, 197
use of prioritized dispatch list
for, 173–5
delivery error, 165–6
delivery units
capability and capacity, 64–5
coordination with CCP, 120–4
See also Kanban system
demand
defined, 197
direct and indirect, 204–5
for provider capacity, 198
See also capacity demand
demand curves
product demand, 206–7
traditional production, 196–7
demand point, 199
demand schedule
customer value as, 199–200
defined, 200
Deming, W. Edwards, 41, 180–1
descriptive statistics, 393
deterministic systems
design and performance of,
16, 18
static process of, 20
diagnosis
display-based approach, 155–6
listening approach, 154–5
management of, 153–60, 167

prototype-based, 158–9
question-based approach, 156–8
screening-based approach,
159–60
using best-practice guidelines,
171–3
diagnosis error, 165–6
dispatchers, 115
dispatching
as alternative to scheduling, 84
back room delivery modules,
141
dispatch lists, prioritized, 120,
173–4
display-based approach to diagnosis,
155–6
distribution requirement's planning
(DRP), 39
Drucker, Peter F., 35, 371, 377

economic price, 45
economics, production
demand curve construction,
196–214
traditional, 195
economic value added (EVA), 381–3
effectiveness
cost effectiveness, 22–3
delivery, 200
in response to customer, 65
efficiency, 65
efficient consumer response (ECR),
43
employees
concerns of, 353–7
cross training in capacity
management, 179
focus on customer, 358
See also customer contact
person (CCP)
entity relationship diagrams
(ERDs), 312–16
errors
delivery, 165–6
diagnosis, 165–6

Index

event forecasting, 175–8
expectations, customer, 145, 153, 165

Falvey, Jack, 152
field use, 40
Fisk, Raymond, 372
fixed capacity costs (FCC), 184, 219
flexibility
  to achieve customer responsiveness, 23–4
  conditions with lack of, 236–8
  of customer-responsive organization, 46, 60–1, 162–3
  with dispatching, 84–5
  firm's response to individual customers, 88
flexible manufacturing, 60–1
Ford, Henry, 34
forecasting of capacity, 175–9
Franklin Planner, 122–3
Fuchs, Victor, 372
functional silos (mass production), 13–14

goodness of fit, 395–6
governance, 15, 187
guidelines. See best-practice guidelines

Hall, Curtis, 388
Harmon, Paul, 388
hassle
  components of, 145
  defined, 197
  hassle cost or price, 45
Hayes, Robert H., 152
health care providers, customer-responsive, 401–4
Heilbroner, Robert L., 28–31
Henkoff, Ronald, 329–30
Heskett, James, 202–3
Hout, Thomas, 268–9
hypothesis testing, 393–4

industrial revolution, 33–4
inflexibility, firm, 24
information
  about customer, 301–3
  infrastructure development, 278–9
  processing in networks, 20
information age, 384–91
information analysis, modeling approach, 391–404
information systems
  design criteria, 297–9
  impact on responsive management, 265–9
information theoretic statistics (ITS), 392–404
infrastructure
  components of, 276–9
  prioritized dispatch list in, 271
  requirements of customer-responsive, 301–7
  role and requirements of, 301–7
infrastructure development plan, 276–82
In Search of Excellence (Peters and Waterman), 149
intangibility, 5–6
interaction management, 149–53, 167
inventory
  customer-responsive businesses, 218
  in offering-based business, 217
  organizations without, 217–18
ITS. See information theoretic statistics (ITS)

Johnson, H. Thomas, 35–6
joint application development (JAD), 69
Juran, Joseph M., 180
just-in-time (JIT)
  data analysis in manner of, 391
  dispatching as, 84

Kanban system, 121–24
Kaplan, Robert S., 35–6
Kotler, Philip, 206
Kullback, S., 395

lead time, 84
less-than-truckload (LTL), 188, 192
Liebler, R. A., 395
likelihood ratio method, 395
listening approach in diagnosis, 154–5
logistics
    defined, 283
    mass market distribution, 39
    principles of, 285
    supply-chain and service-
        response, 283–4
loyalty, customer, 56
LTL. *See* less-than-truckload (LTL)

The Making of Economic Society
    (Heilbroner), 28–31
management
    best-practice guideline, 169–73
    capacity, 175–87
    of company network, 19–20
    diagnosis, 153–60
    of interaction with customer,
        149–53, 167
    methods to reduce transaction
        costs, 15–16
    offering-based, 47
    resource interface, 187–8
    scientific, 35
    supply-chain logistics, 39
    task, 173–5
    total quality, 4
management, customer-responsive,
    2, 21, 47–8, 330
    benefits of, 51–60
    of customer relationship, 143
    customer-service, 160–7
    dimensions of, 4–5
    information system design
        criteria, 297–9

prioritized dispatch list, 120–4
role of information systems in,
    265–9
management principles
    customer-responsive, 111–14
    traditional, 109–11
MANOVA, 395, 398
manufacturing, response-based,
    103–8
marginal revenue curve, 207–9
marketing
    concept of, 37–8
    conquest, 150n
    relationship-based, 150n, 151
markets
    market price concept, 207
    market research, 38
    market segmentation, 38
Marshall, Alfred, 33, 220–2
mass customization
    from mass production to,
        10–13
    requirements of, 14–15
mass marketing
    differences from customer-
        responsive activities, 8–9
    with mass production, 71–2
mass merchandising, 37
mass production
    approach to delivery, 22–3
    circumstances for, 12–13
    concept of, 9–10
    as continuous process, 72
    functional silos of, 13–14
    mass marketing with, 71–2
    rethinking, 367–71
    trends in responsiveness to
        customer, 9–10
master production schedule (MPS),
    83
material requirement's planning
    (MRP), 39, 83
model fitting, 393
model selection criteria, 398–401

Index

modularization concept, 10–11
moment of truth, 96, 150
Moore's Law, 385
multicluster analysis, 398–401
multifunction team concept, 13–15
multiple comparison procedures
(MCPs), 395, 398

network delivery system, 89–90
networks
    cooperative, 183–7
    design and performance of,
        16–20
    information processing in, 20
    in infrastructure, 277–82

offering-based approach
    comparison of activities with
        customer-response-based
        approach, 66–9
    to customer needs, 3–8
Ohno, Taiichi, 42, 58–60
organization, customer-responsive
    design of, 46–7
    distribution center example,
        124–6
    fixed and variable costs,
        227–36
    focus of, 45–6
    hospital example, 130–3
    infrastructure requirements,
        301–7
    management, 47–8
    military campaign example,
        126–30
    Pizza Hut example, 119–20
    process of, 299–301
    roadway logistics systems,
        136–40
    Subway model, 118–19
    Union Bank of Switzerland,
        133–6
organization, flexible
    with networking, 20
    responsive networks in, 16–20

in shift from mass production
    to continuous improve-
    ment, 10–13
organization, modular, 10–11

Pareto charts, 162–3
partnerships, cooperative, 182–3
Pascale, Richard Tanner, 27
perceived quality, 165
periodic forecasting, 176–9
Peters, Tom, 27, 149, 151, 152
Pine, B. Joseph, 12, 264
plan
    contingency, 78
    defined, 78
potential yield, 201
prices
    in customer-responsiveness
        era, 44–5
    economic price, 45
    hassle price, 45
    market price, 207
pricing
    customer value, 207–10
    firm-level by output, 189
    implementation, 258–61
    product, 241–4
    public good, 244–9
    responsive activity, 249–58
probabilistic neural network, 395
product design
    customer-responsive ap-
        proach, 53–6
    offering-based approach, 51–6
production
    flexibility with mass customi-
        zation, 11–12
    Toyota's production system,
        58–9
    See also continuous improve-
        ment; mass customization;
        mass production
products
    focus of production era, 44
    identification of intangible, 5–6

profits
  customer retention rate, 57
  factors in increased, 56–7
project management, 174
protocol, 78–9
prototype-based approach to diagnosis, 158–9
public good pricing model, 244–9

quality
  production era definition, 40
  quality of design and conformance, 40
Quesnay, François, 30–1
question-based approach to diagnosis, 156–8
Quinn, 371

rapid application development (RAD), 69
regression analysis, 393
Reichheid, Frederick F., 56
relationships
  characteristics of viable, 335–6
  cultivation of, 331–4
  defined, 330–1
  relationship management, 330
  relationship marketing, 150n, 151
research, 392
resource interface management, 187–9
resource organization, 179–80
resources
  network as part of infrastructure, 279–82
  networking of, 183–7
responsiveness
  in definition of services, 5–6
responsive-service pricing model, 250–2
return on investment (ROI), 381

Samuelson, Paul, 195, 220
Sasser, W. Earl, 56

scheduled capacity costs (SCC), 184, 219–20
scheduling
  advantages and disadvantages, 82–3
  defined, 82
scientific management, 35
screening-based approach to diagnosis, 159–60
service delivery costs, 184-5, 220
services, 5–6
Smith, Adam, 30–4
solution value
  defined, 197–8
  determinants of, 197–8
speculation, 211
Stalk, George, 268–9
standardized interchangeable parts, 34
statistical methods
  traditional, 392–4
statistical process control, 41
Stern, Lewis, 329
structure, organizational
  impact of activity coordination method on, 85–7
  for offering- and customer-response-based activity, 4–8
supplier
  cooperative partnerships with, 181–3
  cooperative strategies, 181–7
  relationship with, 359–62

target markets, 38
task management, 173–5
Taylor, Frederick Winslow, 35
total capacity costs, 220
total quality management movement, 39–43
total quality management (TQM)
  cost control methods, 180
  relationship between supplier and customer, 181–2

Index

transaction costs
 group interaction and risk, 15–16
 methods to reduce, 16–18
 at organization interface, 187–8
trust, 147–9
Tuguchi, Tenichi, 41–2

value
 customer, 21–3
 determination of customer,
  56–7
 See also benefit value determinants; customer
value; solution value
value added concept, 21–2
Vavra, Terry, 57, 145, 150n, 151
visualization tools, 307–19

Waterman, Robert, 149, 151, 152
The Wealth of Nations (Smith), 31–4
Whitney, Eli, 34
Williamson, Oliver, 15–16, 187
willingness to pay, customer's, 205
Waldrop, 144

yield
 as demand curve, 201
 factors influencing, 202–9
 from investment, 382–3
 potential and actual, 201
yield curve, 201
yield management, 190–3, 383

Zemke, Ron, 222